Women in Frankish Society

University of Pennsylvania Press
MIDDLE AGES SERIES
Edited by
Edward Peters
Henry Charles Lea Professor
of Medieval History
University of Pennsylvania

SUZANNE FONAY WEMPLE

Women in Frankish Society

Marriage and the Cloister
500 to 900

PENN

UNIVERSITY OF PENNSYLVANIA PRESS
Philadelphia

THIS BOOK WAS PUBLISHED WITH ASSISTANCE FROM THE PUBLICATIONS PROGRAM
OF THE NATIONAL ENDOWMENT FOR THE HUMANITIES.

Library of Congress Cataloging in Publication Data

Wemple, Suzanne Fonay.
  Women in Frankish society.

  (The Middle ages)
  Bibliography: p.
  Includes index.
  1. Women—History—Middle ages, 500–1500. 2. France
—History—To 987   3. France—History—Medieval
period, 987–1515.   4. Women and religion.   5. Women—
Legal status, laws, etc.   6. Merovingians—History.
7. Carlovingians—History.   I. Title.   II. Series:
Middle ages.
HQ1147.F7W45   305.4'09'02   80–54051
ISBN 0–8122–1209–6   AACR2

Printed in the United States of America

4th paperback printing 1996

To my mother, Magda Mihályfy Széchényi,
and to my daughter, Carolyn Wemple.

CONTENTS

vii

TABLES

GENEALOGICAL CHARTS

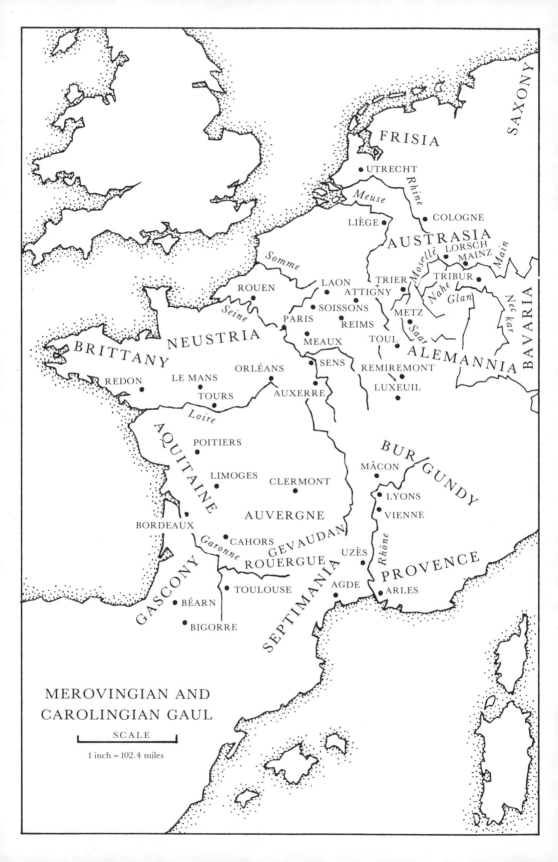

MEROVINGIAN AND
CAROLINGIAN GAUL

SCALE

1 inch = 102.4 miles

THE ANCESTORS OF CHARLEMAGNE

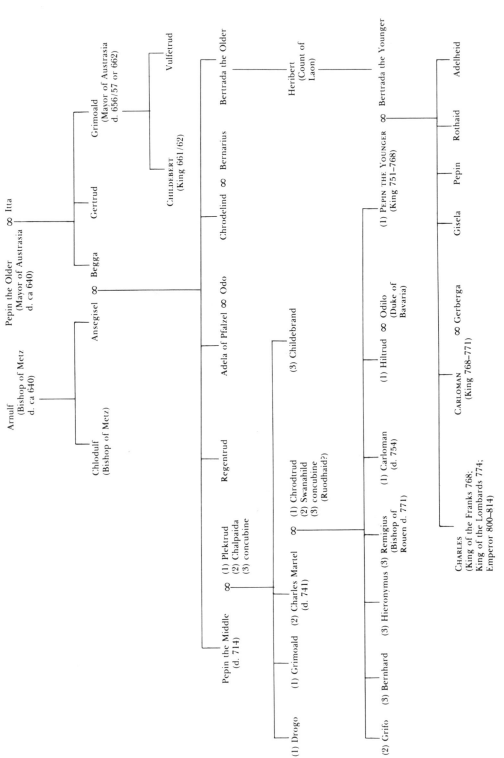

WIVES, CONCUBINES, AND CHILDREN
OF MEROVINGIAN KINGS

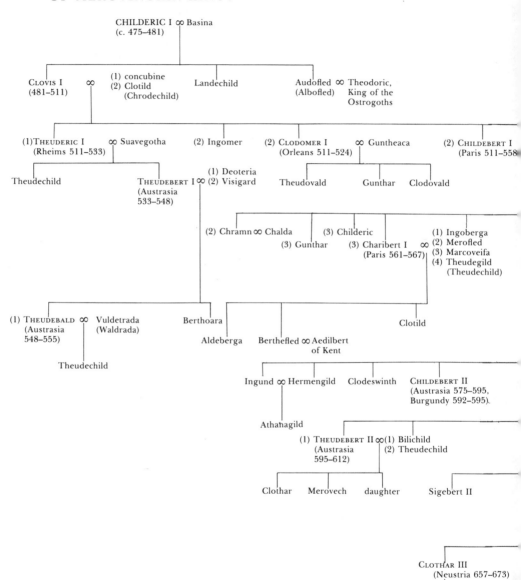

xii

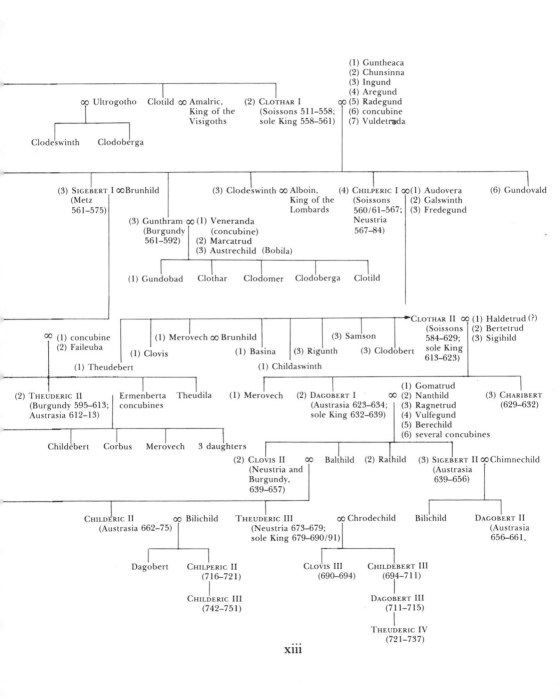

WIVES, CONCUBINES AND CHILDREN OF NINTH-CENTURY FRANKISH EMPERORS AND KINGS

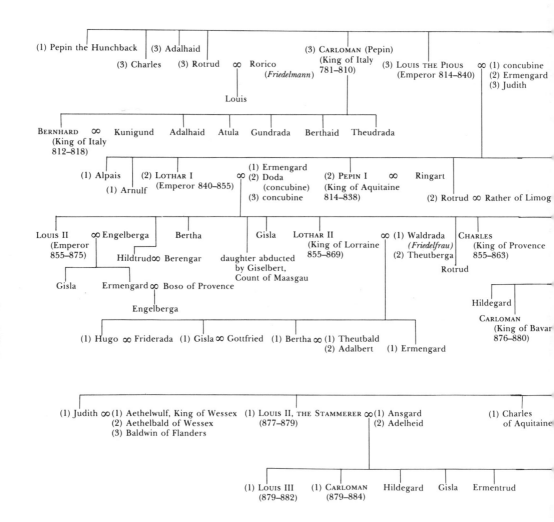

CHARLES
(King of the Franks 768;
King of the Lombards 774;
Emperor 800–814)

(1) Pepin the Hunchback   (3) Adalhaid

(3) Charles   (3) Rotrud ∞ Rorico
(*Friedelmann*)

(3) CARLOMAN (Pepin)
(King of Italy
781–810)

(3) LOUIS THE PIOUS ∞ (1) concubine
(Emperor 814–840)   (2) Ermengard
(3) Judith

Louis

BERNHARD ∞ Kunigund   Adalhaid   Atula   Gundrada   Berthaid   Theudrada
(King of Italy
812–818)

(1) Alpais   (2) LOTHAR I ∞ (1) Ermengard
(1) Arnulf   (Emperor 840–855) (2) Doda
(concubine)
(3) concubine

(2) PEPIN I ∞ Ringart
(King of Aquitaine
814–838)

(2) Rotrud ∞ Rather of Limog

LOUIS II ∞ Engelberga   Bertha   Gisla   LOTHAR II ∞ (1) Waldrada   CHARLES
(Emperor   (King of Lorraine   (*Friedelfrau*)   (King of Provence
855–875)   855–869)   (2) Theutberga   855–863)

Hildtrud∞ Berengar   daughter abducted   Rotrud
by Giselbert,
Count of Maasgau

Gisla   Ermengard ∞ Boso of Provence   Hildegard

Engelberga   CARLOMAN
(King of Bavar
876–880)

(1) Hugo ∞ Friderada (1) Gisla ∞ Gottfried (1) Bertha ∞ (1) Theutbald
(2) Adalbert   (1) Ermengard

(1) Judith ∞ (1) Aethelwulf, King of Wessex (1) LOUIS II, THE STAMMERER ∞ (1) Ansgard   (1) Charles
(2) Aethelbald of Wessex   (877–879)   (2) Adelheid   of Aquitaine
(3) Baldwin of Flanders

(1) LOUIS III   (1) CARLOMAN   Hildegard   Gisla   Ermentrud
(879–882)   (879–884)

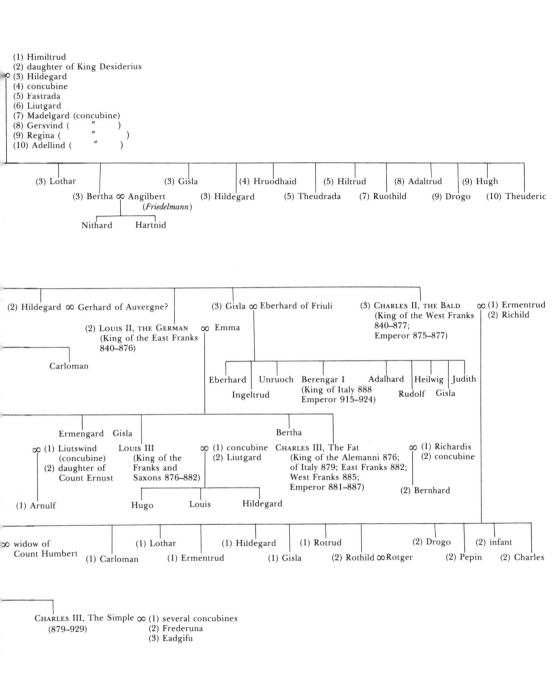

ACKNOWLEDGMENTS

One of the pleasures in publishing a book is acknowledging publicly the institutional and personal support one received while writing it.

First, I would like to express my gratitude to three of my colleagues in the Barnard History Department. Professor Annette K. Baxter, Professor Chilton Williamson, and Professor Emeritus Basil Rauch had sufficient confidence in my judgment that sources for the history of women in the Middle Ages existed, even though they have not been systematically explored, to encourage me to teach and write on the subject. Collaboration with Professor JoAnn McNamara, of Hunter College, on three articles proved to be most fruitful. Through long discussions we managed to formulate a conceptual framework for the history of women in the early Middle Ages.

A grant from the National Endowment for the Humanities for 1974–1975 made research in France possible. In Paris I had the gracious help of Professor Pierre Riché and the cooperation of the staff of the Institut de Recherche et d'Histoire des Textes. Invitations to lecture at the Medieval Club of New York, Haverford College, the Graduate Center of CUNY, the Women's Center at Barnard, and the Columbia Seminar on Legal History enabled me to test and refine my ideas.

My greatest intellectual debt is to Dr. Mary Martin McLaughlin. She called my attention to new publications, listened with sympathy to my problems, and gave me the inspiration to investigate women's contributions to the development of new forms of spirituality. From Professor John Mundy, Professor John Contreni, and Denise Kaiser I received constructive criticism. I also wish to thank Ann Fagan for her suggestions on organization and style, Catherine McGee for helping with the tabulation of the data from the Lorsch cartulary, and Mary Jane Chase, Denise Kaiser, and Wendy Wemple for typing parts of the manuscript.

The editors of this book, Gail Levin, Jane Barry, Lee Ann Draud, and Susan Oleksiw, saved me the embarrassment of inconsistency in the anglicizing of well-known Frankish names. They also encouraged me to include genealogical tables and maps. I had Jane Bishop's help in drawing these. None has independent value; each is merely intended to serve as a guide to complex family relationships or political subdivisions of the *Regnum Francorum.*

Most importantly I should like to acknowledge a special debt to my husband, George B. Wemple. He not only read the manuscript and helped me to improve it but also took charge of our children and household while I was away doing research and busy writing the book.

Barnard College
October 1980

INTRODUCTION

The legacy of women in the Middle Ages is riddled with contradictions. Women in Latin Christendom were far more visible than in pagan societies: throughout the Middle Ages women exercised power and applied their talents outside the domestic sphere, whereas women in antiquity seldom transcended sex roles and became visible only through scandalous behavior. But by no means did women reach legal and social equality with men during the thousand years known as the Middle Ages. In fact, in the later Middle Ages their rights in some areas were more circumscribed than in the early Middle Ages. In trying to understand the forces at work in expanding and limiting women's sphere of activity and scope of influence, I focused initially on the legal and economic position of women in the Carolingian Empire. Medieval attitudes concerning the place and role of women in the social and economic structure were already discernible in ninth-century Carolingian Frankland, but to explain the ambiguities underlying these attitudes I had to reach farther back to the foundation of the Frankish Kingdom.

From the late fifth century, when Clovis carved out a kingdom in the disintegrating Western Roman Empire, until the late ninth century, when the semblance of unity of Charlemagne's empire gave way to feudal decentralization, the Franks were catalysts of Western culture. In the territories under their control, new beliefs, attitudes, and institutions, reflecting three distinct cultural influences, German, Roman, and Christian, came into being. The study of women in the Frankish Kingdom yields not only an insight into the nature of these three legacies but also a comprehension of the new forces at work.

Clovis and his successors, called the Merovingians after their legendary ancestor Merovech, did not impose a uniform system of law upon the areas they occupied. Instead of territoriality of law, they followed the principle of personality of law, which meant that each individual had to live under the law of his or her father, or, in the case of a married woman, under the law of her husband.[1] In areas south of the Loire, where there was a population of Gallo-Roman descent, Roman law continued to be observed in a simplified form; elsewhere Germanic customs prevailed. As people intermarried and moved from their places

1

of birth, the intermingling of customs gradually brought about new assumptions in matrimonial arrangements and property claims. Incorporated later into feudal customs, these assumptions defined the rights of women as daughters, wives, and widows for centuries to come.

In family law, Christianity began to exercise an influence only in the mid-eighth century, after Pepin had dethroned the last Merovingian king in 751. To legitimize his own rule, Pepin presented himself as a minister of God responsible for restructuring society according to Christian ideals. Foremost in his program was translating Christian teachings on marriage into secular legislation. The work begun by Pepin was completed by Charlemagne and Louis the Pious, who endeavored to devise an imperial system that would give an earthly expression to Augustine's *City of God.* The new laws, after meeting a dramatic test under Louis the Pious' sons and grandsons, were upheld by late ninth-century popes and a series of local synods, the last of which met at Tribur in 895.

The transformation of Frankish society under the Merovingians from a relatively primitive tribal structure to a more complex hierarchical organization, along with the shift under the Carolingians from the extended family to the conjugal unit as the reproductive and economic center of society, provides a sufficient variety of situations to test the validity of two important hypotheses formulated by today's feminist historians about forces determining the position of women in past societies. It is possible to examine whether or not the development of an administrative structure and social stratification within the framework of Merovingian society adversely affected women and intensified inequalities along sex lines. Another key issue is whether the emergence of the nuclear family and the enforcement of monogamy in Carolingian times enhanced or eroded the power and influence of women.

The history of the period raises other questions, which, although more specialized in nature, hold equal significance for scholars committed to exploring the experiences of women in past societies. Clovis built his kingdom on three pillars: the Catholic hierarchy, a Gallo-Roman administration, and a Frankish military retinue. Women had no place in these institutions and groups. But as wives and mothers they did contribute to the amalgamation of the Gallo-Roman senatorial aristocracy with the leading Frankish families. It remains to be seen how women used their key position as a bridge between two influential kin groups. Were they mere passive instruments in the hands of their male relatives, or did they play an active part in promoting the social and political advancement of members of their natal family? It is also important to investigate the extent to which women were able to use circumstances to improve their own status and to contribute to vertical mobility in society.

Another important subject is the position and influence of women in the Frankish church. Like women in the early centuries of Christianity, women in Merovingian Gaul were the staunchest supporters of the new religion, converting their husbands, baptizing their children, building churches, and nourishing the faith with monastic foundations. Their role in the Frankish church, however, was not extensive; indeed, it became progressively more limited. Does this constitute the same pattern that historians have observed in other revolutionary movements, which welcomed women for their dedication but, at the moment of victory, forced them to return to traditional domestic activities?

The life of ordinary women must be studied as well. Was there any discrimination against women in the dependent classes, or were men and women equally subject to a lord, at least economically if not personally? Closely related to this inquiry is the nature of the work Merovingian and Carolingian women performed. Did they share with men the cultivation of the land, and, if so, were they recognized as equals of men of their own class?

In recent years American scholars have pioneered in using the records of early medieval manors to study various aspects of peasant family life: marriage patterns, infanticide, and household composition. This book will not attempt to pursue this quantitative inquiry; rather, it will touch upon peasant women only within the context of the two main areas of investigation: the status and activities of women in the family and in the church. Because of the dearth of evidence on the life of lower class women in sources other than manorial records, the emphasis will be on upper class women in both sections.

Records for the history of women in secular and religious life are more limited for the Merovingian than for the Carolingian period, when writing came into more general use. For the earlier centuries, I have relied extensively on legal sources, both secular and ecclesiastical. To judge the extent to which the laws were obeyed, I have supplemented an analysis of the laws with information derived from records of property transfers, collections of *formulae,* narrative sources, letters, and poems. The more numerous legal sources for the Carolingian period cover a broader range: royal capitularies and court cases as well as conciliar legislation and *formulae.* Similarly, the Carolingian period offers a richer variety of literary sources, including treatises on the virtues and vices of different classes of people. In addition, some monastic and ecclesiastical cartularies contain a sufficient number of documents from the eighth and ninth centuries to permit at least a rudimentary form of statistical approach.

The institution of marriage and women's property rights have been extensively studied by historians of private law, a field that is indebted to nineteenth-century German scholarship. Apart from the surveys of Germanic law, beginning with the pioneering study of Jacob Grimm and continuing down to the fourth edition of Karl von Amira's work, revised by Karl August Eckhardt,[2] more specialized subjects have been treated in detailed studies, including R. Schröder's work on Germanic marriage settlements, Julius Ficker's volume on German inheritance rights, and Heinrich Brunner's essays on Germanic family and property laws.[3] These older works are still useful because of their careful scholarship. Histories of Germanic law written under the National Socialist regime must be used with caution, for they tend to glorify the position of Germanic women.[4]

Among French legal scholars, Brissaud and Chénon have dealt briefly with the position of women in Frankish society, and Lemaire and Cornuey have studied dowry settlements in the Merovingian and Carolingian periods.[5] More recently, the Belgian historian François Ganshof has provided a comprehensive analysis of the status of women living under Germanic law. For the position of Merovingian women living under Roman law, Conrat's survey of Roman law in the Frankish Kingdom, published in 1903 and reprinted in 1963, remains an essential source.[6] These works have been supplemented by studies on various aspects of matrimony in early medieval society presented at the *Settimana di Studio* in 1976.[7]

In contrast to the extensive work being done on early medieval family and private law, the history of women in the early medieval church is a neglected field. Lina Eckenstein's monograph, published in 1896, was based on narrative sources.[8] Although more scholarly in its approach, K. H. Schäfer's history of canonesses, published in 1907, is marred by the author's insistence that institutes of canonesses were among the earliest monastic foundations.[9] More recently, the learned Benedictine Dom Philibert Schmitz studied nunneries in the seventh volume of his history of the order. To Carolingian developments, however, he gave only a summary treatment, possibly because he had analyzed these in the context of male communities in his first volume.[10] The latest study by Friedrich Prinz has brought the history of Frankish monasticism to the end of the eighth century, but it does not pay particular attention to nunneries.[11]

Information on early medieval nunneries is also provided by histories of double monasteries. The most dispassionate account of the early development of double monasteries, published by Mary Bateson in 1899, needs revision in the light of modern scholarship.[12] Ferdinand Hilpisch's work, although it contains reliable data, suffers from the author's belief that nuns tended to live as parasites upon monks.[13] More helpful are the investigations of the history of specific institutions, such as Hlawitschka's work on Remiremont and Hocbanx's on Nivelles.[14] Finally, Bernhard Bischoff's research on early medieval manuscripts provides information on the activities of early medieval nuns and canonesses as scribes and book collectors.[15] Roger Gryson's recent monographs give a thorough survey of the policies affecting priests' wives and deaconesses in the Eastern and Western churches, but do not go beyond an institutional analysis.[16] There is a growing body of literature on these issues,[17] including Haye van der Meer's important theological-historical investigation of the church's opposition to the ordination of women and Martin Boelens's study of clerical marriage.[18]

Women occupy a more prominent place in modern social histories than in ecclesiastical histories. Pierre Riché, in his study of Carolingian life, paid careful attention to the experiences of women in that society. The two articles he wrote for the *Histoire mondiale de la femme* give an excellent summary of women's activities in the early Middle Ages.[19] Genealogical research on the early medieval aristocracy, stimulated and encouraged by Gerd Tellenbach and currently pursued by such leading scholars as Eduard Hlawitschka, Karl Schmid, and Karl Ferdinand Werner, has contributed a great deal to our understanding of the role of women in the upper echelons of Merovingian and Carolingian society.[20] Eugen Ewig's study of Merovingian royalty—the age at marriage of princes and princesses, the social origin of royal consorts, and the fate of repudiated or widowed queens—provides a systematic analysis of the experiences of women in the highest echelon of early Frankish society.[21] Following the same line of inquiry but focusing on two queens, Brunhild and Balthild, Janet Nelson has examined the opportunities for Merovingian queens to play political roles, as well as the limitations of their power.[22]

Among American scholars, David Herlihy has applied demographic data to the history of early medieval women, and Emily Coleman has followed in this area with research on the Carolingian peasantry.[23] Archibald Lewis has provided many examples of the economic power of women in southern France from the late ninth century.[24] Diana Owen Hughes has studied the substitution of dowry for brideprice in Mediterranean Europe.[25]

Early medieval attitudes toward women have also been studied.

Marie-Louise Portmann has analyzed these attitudes in the chronicles, and Maria Stoeckle has investigated the ideal of womanhood in Saxon hagiography.[26] Patristic views of women have been synthesized in two recent publications: Mary Daly's *The Church and the Second Sex* offers a scathing criticism, while George Tavard's *Woman in Christian Tradition* tries to give a less partisan presentation of the contradictions inherent in Christian doctrine and practice. The articles on which I have collaborated with JoAnn McNamara sketch the Christian ideals and secular laws governing women's lives in the early Middle Ages.[27]

The purpose of this book is to explain the gap between the ideals and laws on the one hand and the social reality on the other. It will attempt to settle the question of the meaning of *Friedelehe*. Was this an ancient form of Germanic marriage, or a form of concubinage? Recent discussion has centered on the economic power of women. Historians have observed that women controlled more land in areas where Roman law prevailed. Does this mean that in these areas women were more independent and self-assertive than in areas where Germanic law prevailed? Of greater interest outside scholarly circles is the debate concerning women's position in the early church. Are there any historical precedents for the role of spiritual and pastoral leadership that contemporary women are claiming in the Catholic church and have recently gained in other Christian churches? In searching for answers to these and other questions in primary sources, I have sought not merely to settle controversies but also to gain an understanding of the relationship between men and women and to provide insights into women's experiences in this formative period of European history.

PART ONE
Women in Secular Life

"We see women of noble birth and richly endowed becoming indigent because of a lack of self-restraint, ending their lives as beggars. We also hear of many being killed because of fornication. On the other hand, we see others of less noble birth rising from poverty to wealth because of their intelligence and self-restraint."

Christian of Corbie (*PL* 106, 1414)

1

The Triple Heritage of Merovingian Women

The Merovingian era was a period of rapid social change. The structure of society in the Frankish Kingdom, established by Clovis in the last decades of the fifth century, differed from that of both the moribund Roman Empire and the old Germanic tribes. Clovis had recognized the value of the Roman social and economic system at the same time that he had accepted his wife's suggestion to convert to Catholic Christianity, and hence, in governing his kingdom, he could rely on support from both the Gallo-Roman senatorial aristocracy and the Catholic church. Frankish customs, however, were so different from Roman and Christian ones that, despite Clovis's intention to conform to the Roman way of life, radical transformations took place in all aspects of life. Under Clovis's successors the Roman institutions were gradually obliterated while the assimilation of Roman and Germanic peoples and customs continued. By 751, when the Merovingian era came to an end with the removal of the last member of Clovis's dynasty, a new society with its own distinct legal conventions and economic systems had evolved.

Women played an important role in the creation of this new society although they seldom had access to the sources of public power. By marrying across ethnic lines and converting their husbands to Christianity, then bearing children and transmitting to them a mixed cultural heritage, they were instrumental in bringing about the demographic and cultural amalgamation of the people living in the Merovingian kingdom.

Intermarriage took place first between the leading families of the Gallo-Romans, residing mainly south of the Loire, and of the Franks, settled by Clovis in the depopulated areas of Gaul north of the Loire or living in the Rhineland around Cologne and spreading as far north of the Rhine as the river Somme. Eventually all the subject people intermarried, including the Visigoths, who remained in Aquitaine, the Burgundians, who were conquered and annexed in 534, and the Alemans, Thuringians, and Bavarians, who retained a semblance of autonomy while subject to Frankish domination during the sixth century.

   The status of Merovingian women in their families of birth and in
their husbands' families was thus governed by a complex set of customs
originating in the markedly different Germanic and Roman social systems. Even if a woman married within the same ethnic group, her relationship to her husband was influenced by practices followed in other
parts of the Frankish Kingdom. This chapter will analyze the conflicting
legal, social, and religious traditions shaping the lives of Merovingian
women and defining the spheres of their action and the extent of their
influence. It will examine the situation of women first in the Germanic
tribes and then in the late Roman Empire. Finally, it will outline the
most essential aspects of Christian teachings on the role of women and
the relationship between the sexes.

GERMANIC TRIBES

   They are almost unique among barbarians in being satisfied with
   one wife each. The exceptions, which are exceedingly rare, are of
   men who receive offers of many wives because of their rank. . . . The
   dowry is brought by husband to wife, not by wife to husband.
   Parents and kinsmen attend and approve of the gifts, gifts not
   chosen to please a woman's whim or gaily deck a young bride, but
   oxen, horse with reins, shield, spear and sword. For such gifts a man
   gets his wife, and she in turn brings some present of arms to her
   husband. . . . She is coming to share a man's toils and danger.[1]

These observations by Tacitus provide the earliest glimpse of the relationship between the sexes in the warring Germanic tribes. Because the
social structure of the Germanic people before their appearance in the
Roman Empire is hidden in the darkness of their own illiteracy, the
historian must rely on the chance testimony of Roman authors to supplement the mute archaeological evidence.
   Both Caesar and Tacitus testified that the most cohesive bond of
the Germanic tribes was kinship. The clans or kindred composing the
tribes provided the basic security for their members; revenge for an
injury and retribution for a crime were considered the responsibility of
the entire kin. "The larger a man's kin and the greater number of his
relations by marriage," Tacitus noted in *Germania*, "the stronger is his
influence when he is old." The close ties between a mother's son and
a mother's brother, which according to Tacitus were regarded by some
as sacred, suggest that at one time Germanic clans may have been
matrilineal.[2] By the end of the first century, however, the Germanic
kindred included both the agnates of male descent and the cognates of

female descent, and the rules of inheritance favored the males among the agnates. If a man had no children, first in the line of succession came his brothers and then his uncles, first on his father's and then on his mother's side.[3]

Women were valued in this society because they not only provided a network of kinship ties as wives and mothers but also gave inspirational support and were nurturers and providers. Tacitus praised the wives of the barbarians for accompanying their husbands to the battlefield, tending to the wounds of their men, and bringing food and encouragement to them.[4] Two and a half centuries later, Ammianus Marcellinus maintained that Germanic wives took an active part in the fighting itself.[5] Tacitus also testified that the Germans "believe that there resides in women an element of holiness and prophecy, and so they do not scorn to ask their advice or lightly disregard their replies."[6] This special regard, however, must have been limited to a few prophetesses, for women were excluded from the assemblies.

More essential was the contribution of women to the care of hearth, fields, and children. Disdained by able-bodied men, the heavy work was relegated to women, according to Tacitus. Only old men and weaklings assisted in cultivating the fields.[7] Citing archaeological evidence on the introduction of the horse-drawn plow, E. A. Thompson has argued that the responsibility for tillage was transferred to men by the end of the first century.[8] Even if Tacitus exaggerated the contempt Germanic men had for laboring in the fields, his comments suggest that women continued to be responsible for agricultural production. The slaves the Germans had by this time may have assisted women in the fields.[9] On the other hand, German women were not relieved of household chores by slaves. Tacitus stressed that the wives of barbarians had no servants or wet nurses: they did their own housework and nursed their children at the breast.[10]

Tacitus, seeking to rebuke the Romans for their immorality, glorified the purity and stability of German family life. Caesar also noted the honor accorded chastity by the Germans.[11] Both authors undoubtedly painted a misleading idealistic picture of German matrimonial arrangements. Tacitus clearly indicated that chastity was required only from women. In addition to his observation that there was polygyny among those of high rank, Tacitus enumerated humiliating penalties for adultery, which applied only to wives. The female corpse found by archaeologists in the peat bog at Windeby in Domland, buried naked with a blindfold over her eyes, a hide collar on her neck, and her hair shaven, lends credence to Tacitus' description of how a cuckold husband punished his wife. "He shaves off his wife's hair," Tacitus wrote, "strips her in the presence of kinsmen, thrusts her from his house and flogs her through the whole village."[12] Cruel punishment was also inflicted upon the wife's partner in crime.[13]

Tacitus' remark that the dowry was brought by husbands to wives rather than by wives to husbands, as was the custom in Rome, has not escaped the attention of historians. Some have interpreted it as a misunderstanding or idealization of the nature and disposition of the Germanic brideprice, a settlement the groom had to pay to the bride's kinsmen.[14] Others have accepted Tacitus' comment as it stands. For example, Diana Hughes has argued that Tacitus' remark referred to the *morgengabe,* a gift the groom gave to the bride on the consummation of the marriage. Tacitus' failure to mention the brideprice, according to Hughes, "may indicate that by the end of the first century the brideprice had been replaced by the husband's gift to the bride among those tribes that lived on the fringes of the Empire."[15] An equally valid conclusion is that the brideprice had already been transformed into a *dos* among these tribes. Pledged or given by the groom before the marriage, the *dos* rather than the *morgengabe* was upheld in the Germanic codes as the legal form of marriage settlement. In some of the early codes the *dos* appeared in a transitional stage between the brideprice and the bridegift with only a part of the settlement being turned over to the bride and the rest being retained by her kin.

The matrimonial arrangements of the early Germans remain controversial because of insufficient documentation, and various scholars have proposed different theories. By comparing the laws of all Germanic people, including the Danes, Norwegians, and Swedes, and drawing evidence from their sagas, nineteenth-century German scholars distinguished three patterns of wedlock among the early Germans. Through marriage by capture *(Raubehe)* and marriage by purchase *(Kaufehe),* a woman became the chattel of her husband; in a marriage by mutual consent *(Friedelehe),* she remained, together with her children, under the power of her own kin. As her husband's *fridila,* friend or beloved, she received from him a gift *(morgengabe)* after the consummation of their union. The concept of *Friedelehe* as a romantic match was reaffirmed in German scholarly circles by Heinrich Meyer's study published in 1927.[16]

Historians writing under the National Socialist regime tried to deny that their ancestors had ever been so barbarous as to sell women. Without adducing new evidence, they maintained that the only form of Germanic marriage was *Friedelehe,* a union among equals inspired by love and concluded through mutual consent. In this arrangement the woman retained her free status and became the mistress of her husband's household.[17] In a carefully researched study published in 1946, Noel Senn refuted this thesis, isolating remnants of the old purchase price in the Germanic codes.[18] The romantic aspects of *Friedelehe* were minimized by K. A. Eckhardt in 1967 when he described *Friedelehe* as an endogamous marriage, as opposed to *Kaufehe* and *Raubehe,* which were exogamous unions.[19] More recently, in 1970, the very concept of *Friedelehe* as a separate form of marriage was questioned by S. Kalifa's thesis that it constituted a marriage by capture, accomplished through the cooperation of the woman.[20]

It may help our understanding of Germanic marriages if, instead of concentrating on the different forms of marriage, a habit historians have acquired by comparing Germanic and Roman marriages, we examine the function of women in Germanic societies and the choices available to the familial group in determining the type of marriage for a daughter. Among the early Germans, marriage was not, as it is today, a legal relationship created by the fulfillment of prescribed procedures. Rather, it was an arrangement, accepted as a social fact, whereby a man cohabited with a woman for the purposes of copulation, procreation, and the division of labor.

In the Germanic tribes, although social gradations were not absent by the end of the first century, the division of labor was determined not by class but by sex. Men served their society as warriors; women bore and raised children, worked in the fields, and looked after the home. Apparently, by the time of Tacitus, marriages were normally patrilocal, which meant that the suitor brought a bride to his own house. Hence the marriage of a daughter was both a gain and a loss, creating a new network of kinship but also depleting the number of workers in the familial group. Although daughters could be replaced by daughters-in-law, families did not have equal numbers of marriageable daughters and sons. Valuable livestock, probably the kind Tacitus said the groom gave the bride, was used to recompense the Germanic family for the loss of a daughter's labor.

On the other hand, if a bridegroom was a well placed man, a king or a chieftain, he probably did not have to present either a brideprice or a bridegift.[21] Tacitus mentioned that wives were offered to men of high rank without any compensation, the kinship ties resulting from such a union apparently outweighing all other considerations. It is also possible to surmise from Tacitus' remark about the occasional "sacred ties" between nephews and uncles on the mother's side that, in exceptional cases, marriages were matrilocal. A king or a chieftain might reward one of his military companions with the hand of his daughter. In this case, although he might give the woman presents, the suitor would not provide either a brideprice or a bridegift, the couple would live with the wife's family, and the woman and her children would remain under the protection of her own kin.[22]

The common characteristic of these two arrangements, both of which may be called *Friedelehe* because the bride was neither sold to her husband nor captured by him, was that they involved a man and a woman of unequal rank. Whether or not these marriages came into being through mutual consent may never be established in the absence of written testimony. A powerful chieftain might have allowed his daughters to choose their own husbands from among his military followers, but it is equally possible that he used his daughters to reward the bravery of his warriors. Similarly, there is no evidence to support the hypothesis that a girl who was offered to a chieftain in *Friedelehe* or the daughter of a chieftain who was given as a reward to one of her father's armed companions had a better chance to express her wishes than a girl who was sold. As Julius Ficker pointed out, for a *Friedelschaft* to be legal, the girl's guardian had to give his approval.[23] On the other hand, even in the case of marriage by capture, a woman might cooperate with her abductor, or, in the case of a marriage by purchase, she might encourage the man to bid for her hand.

Tacitus' remarks indicate that women entered into unions without being captured or sold. The term *Friedelehe* may serve to designate these unions as long as we do not attach to it a romantic connotation of equality. It is highly questionable that a woman who had entered a *Friedelehe* was in control of her fate, although, if she was her partner's social superior, she may have been treated with more respect than a woman who was sold or captured. The nature of the *Friedelehe* union in this early period must remain indefinite because of the lack of evidence.

We must conclude that, in the Germanic tribes, a bride's will was at best auxiliary; it was never fully coordinate, and certainly not decisive. As long as women were expected to perform most of the heavy labor, and the protection of lives and property rested with male heads of the kin group and not the state, marriageable women could not be free agents. This does not contradict Tacitus' observation that the Germans placed a high value on their women. In early Germanic societies, as in all societies where the socio-economic system is based on a simple division of labor—the men functioning as hunters and warriors and the women producing vegetable foods and tending to domestic details— women's contributions to the well-being of their society were fully appreciated. But, while Germanic women shared the life of their husbands, even to the extent of accompanying them to battle and giving advice, they were dominated by, and dependent upon, men's superior physical strength. Two directly conflicting notions about women governed the relationship between the sexes among the Germanic tribes: the wife was regarded as the helpmate of her husband, while the daughter was treated as a chattel, whose fate depended upon her nearest male relatives.

THE ROMAN EMPIRE

The relationship between the sexes and the position of women are much better documented in the Roman Empire than among the Germanic tribes. Although there are laws defining her rights, poems celebrating her beauty, and letters, plays, and histories describing her activities, the identity of the Roman matron remains elusive. According to one modern historian, she was frustrated and silent; according to another, she was emancipated and self-assertive. Whether women gained access to money and power under the Roman Empire, or were confined to the domestic sphere as the emperors were strengthening the nuclear family, is a subject of scholarly debate.[24] There is, however, general agreement that the legal position of women improved under the empire.

When the state undertook to weaken the position of the paterfamilias, it correspondingly strengthened the private rights of women, children, and slaves. Although women continued to be barred from public office and from taking legal action on their own behalf,[25] they gained considerable independence from male authority in their private lives. Under the republic, when the head of the family had extensive power on every level, women lived in complete subjection to his power, being classed as perpetual minors (*alieni iuris*). If their fathers died, they were placed under the control of guardians. If they married, they were transferred to the control of their husbands.[26] The underlying assumption of these regulations was "the weakness and light-mindedness of the female sex."[27]

To encourage the growth of the population, Augustus offered a reward for childbearing (*jus liberorum*). A free woman who had borne three children was exempted from male guardianship; a freedwoman had to bear four children to achieve this coveted status. The growing custom of *sine manu* marriages, in which power over the woman was not automatically transferred to her husband's hands (*manus*), also represented a step toward female emancipation "without the tedious preliminary of bearing three children," as Sarah Pomeroy has aptly phrased it.[28] After the conclusion of this kind of matrimony, a woman had only to return for three days every year to her father's house to remain under the power of her own family rather than being transferred to her husband's. She then had the right to own jointly with her father property over which her husband had no control.[29] After her father's death, she could chose her own tutor, whose authority was so weakened under the empire that he became a mere figurehead.[30]

Enterprising Roman matrons, thus freed from the control of their husbands, could exercise considerable economic power. Under Roman law, daughters inherited equally with their brothers when their parents died intestate.[31] Women could exploit this right once the laws provided them with the means for emancipating themselves from male domination.

Roman women could also make their wills prevail, at least according to the law, in the selection of their husbands. The validity of Roman marriage depended on mutual consent.[32] Normally, of course, girls were married very early—twelve was the minimum age set by Augustus.[33] It is unlikely that a girl of twelve would oppose her parents' wishes, and therefore a bride's right of consent was probably more meaningful in the case of a second or third marriage at a more mature age. Nevertheless, her relatives could pressure her if she tried to marry below her class, arguing that in so doing she dishonored herself and her family.[34]

If a woman of the lower classes attracted her master or patron, she had little choice but to become his concubine. Children issued from these unions were considered illegitimate even if their parents subsequently married. Although a man could free his slave concubine, he could not marry her if he was a member of the senatorial class. The laws also encouraged lesser men to keep freedwomen as their concubines. "It is more proper that a patron should make a freedwoman his concubine than wife and mistress of this household," the *Digest* declared. The inscriptions indicate that the men who freed and married slave girls were "generally freedmen or demobilized soldiers."[35]

Divorce and remarriage among the Romans were quite common. Despite some efforts by the emperors to promote connubial stability, divorce by mutual consent was easily obtained, especially if the man found a richer, better connected, and more desirable woman. As Tacitus noted, a Roman bride had to bring a dowry to her marriage. In the case of divorce by mutual consent, the wife could reclaim her dowry. Only if she had been convicted of some public crime could her husband retain her dowry or a portion of it. Adultery was one of these crimes. If it became publicly known that she had committed adultery, her husband had to divorce her, she was exiled, and half of her dowry was turned over to her husband. The adultery of the husband, on the other hand, was not considered a public crime. A wife had to tolerate her husband's infidelities with lower class women and prostitutes. Only if he had sexual relations with a married woman of his own class could she obtain a divorce, but even then he was not subject to criminal prosecution.[36]

Double standards of sexual behavior imposed on women of the upper classes, as well as the sexual exploitation of women of the lower classes by men of the upper classes, reinforced two contradictory and confining female stereotypes: woman as a sexual object and woman as a dutiful wife and mother. Slaves and freedwomen had little choice but to conform to the former model, while women of the upper classes were expected to live up to the latter ideal.

Historians who apply the methods of psycho-history and sociology to the study of Roman society have found that behavioral programming according to the two stereotypes was not altogether effective. Women brought up as slaves were not more promiscuous once they were freed than their more privileged sisters. Moreover, the exploitation of slaves and freedwomen, namely, that they had to make themselves available to their masters and patrons, did not prevent these women from forming permanent unions with men of their own or of a lower rank, unions based on true affection rather than on social necessity.[37] Many married women of the upper classes also defied the sexual double standards and took lovers, thereby risking divorce, exile, and occasionally even death. Because unmarried women of the upper classes could also be denounced for fornication *(stuprum)* and punished as adulteresses, some talented ladies had themselves declared prostitutes. Although they were then deprived of their right of inheritance, they accumulated considerable fortunes through the lavish gifts of their lovers.[38]

The insatiable greed and sexual appetites of empresses, as well as the daughters and wives of illustrious families, have been widely publicized down the centuries by Roman authors. The bias of Tacitus and other Roman moralists, springing from a nostalgia for a simpler past along with an inclination to blame women for the moral degeneration of their society, has not failed to escape the attention of feminist historians.[39] It cannot be disputed that Roman matrons, relieved by slaves from domestic duties and the task of raising and educating children, searched for personal fulfillment in such diverse activities as sex, entertainment, the acquisition of wealth, and behind-the-scenes politics. More intellectual women pursued learning, turning into bluestockings, according to Juvenal.[40] Although this may have been an exaggeration, Roman women did have access to education, through either private tutors or an elementary school in the Forum.[41] It is quite probable, however, that the majority of Roman ladies were able to internalize the sexual asymmetry of their society at least to the extent of seeking sexual satisfaction within the normal bonds of marriage. While the Augustan legislation encouraged women to remain at home and to bear children, it did not confine them to unhappy unions. Although a second or a third attempt at matrimony did not necessarily ensure connubial bliss, a divorcée or a widow might choose a more compatible partner than the one whom her parents had selected for her first wedlock.

The adoption of Christianity in the fourth century as the favored religion of the empire did not significantly alter the position of women. Sexual double standards remained enshrined in Roman laws. Although husbands were no longer compelled to divorce their adulterous wives, they could bring unilateral actions of divorce against them on the grounds of adultery, sorcery, or procurement. Should a husband succeed in proving his wife guilty of one or more of these crimes, he could retain her property. A wife could bring a similar action against her husband only for homicide, sorcery, and tomb robbery. If a wife did not prove her charges, she was deported, but, in the reverse situation, the husband had only to restore the dowry to his wife and was not allowed to remarry.

In addition, the emperors Honorius and Theodosius allowed unilateral divorce on moral grounds, such as theft or drunkenness, lesser offenses not punished with loss of property and not identified with specific female or male transgression. But the same emperors also ordered that a woman who had succeeded in obtaining a divorce could remarry only after five years and could not remarry at all if she had left her husband for a moral defect. The husband could remarry immediately if he had his wife convicted of a serious crime and after two years if he had divorced her for a defect of character. Only if he had repudiated her for a trivial disagreement was he required to live in perpetual celibacy.[42] Even though Constantine forbade married men to keep concubines, laws prohibiting marriages across class lines remained in effect and concubinage went on unabated.[43]

The one area in the relationship between the sexes on which Christianity did have an impact was celibacy and the legitimacy of marriage. Fourth-century emperors rescinded the financial penalties that Augustus had levied upon the unmarried. In addition, these emperors made it easier for both men and women to embrace celibate life by defining with greater precision what constituted a legitimate marriage, as opposed to an unbinding sexual relationship. Although clandestine marriages were not considered, by definition, unlawful unions, an increased emphasis was placed on the public celebration of nuptials, the exchange of gifts before the wedding, and parental consent, particularly in the case of minors.[44]

These laws strengthened the power of parents over their daughters. Diocletian's emancipation of women from guardianship at the end of the third century was rendered virtually meaningless by the fourth-century emperors' insistence that women under twenty-five, even if they were divorced or widowed, were minors who needed parental consent to marry.[45] In a society where women married and died very early—the first matrimony of a girl took place usually between the ages of twelve and fifteen and the median age of women at death was between twenty-eight and thirty-four—women could exercise full control over their own destiny and property only for a relatively short period during their lives.[46]

The status of women in the late Roman Empire, before the Germanic invasions, was therefore riddled with contradictions. Entitled to inherit equally with their brothers and to express consent to their marriages, women were nevertheless subject to male authority until the age of twenty-five. When they attained majority, they could control their own property and marry whomever they wished, but their freedom of action continued to be restricted by double standards governing divorce and sexual behavior as well as by the rigid social stratification of their society.

EARLY CHRISTIANITY

Although Christianity did not obviate sexual discrimination in the late Roman Empire, it did offer women the opportunity to regard themselves as independent personalities rather than as someone else's daughter, wife, or mother. It enabled women to develop self-esteem as spiritual beings who possessed the same potential for moral perfection as men. Christianity upheld, moreover, the sanctity of monogamous marriage.[47]

Christ himself had laid the foundation for this psychological revolution. Discountenancing contemporary social and sexual taboos and double standards, he responded with unreserved warmth to women's demands for religious instruction. He preached to the Samaritan woman, defended Mary of Bethany's preference for religious edification over housework, and accepted the ministrations of the repentant prostitute, repeatedly demonstrating his belief that women had the same mental and spiritual capacity as men. His ready forgiveness of the woman taken in adultery contrasted dramatically with his condemnation of her would-be executioners. In a society where a man could obtain a divorce on the basis of a trivial complaint, Christ preached in favor of lifelong monogamy. He thus enhanced the dignity of women as wives, though he would allow a man to divorce an adulterous wife, according to Matthew (19:3–10).

The women whom he honored proved to be faithful followers. Although the twelve apostles were all men, several women were among Christ's disciples. The women who had come with Christ from Galilee accompanied him to Calvary, bewailing and lamenting his suffering and death. They also received and announced the news of his resurrection. As prophetesses and missionaries, some women assumed a public role in the dissemination of the faith. Others, while remaining in the background, played an equally useful role by converting members of their families and households and opening their homes and giving financial support to fellow Christians.[48]

The apostles did not fail to recognize and appreciate the services of their sister Christians, but they were not as free of prejudices as Christ had been. Thomas and Philip were ready to acknowledge the full equality of women and to grant them leading positions in the new religion, but their views were condemned as heretical and their writings were suppressed.[49] Paul, the most dominant figure in Christianity after Christ, also defended the notion that women had as much claim to salvation as men. "There is no such thing as Jew or Greek, slave or freeman, male or female; for you are all one person in Christ Jesus," he proclaimed (Gal. 3:28). Yet a scrutiny of Paul's writings shows that he was ambivalent about the place of women in society in general and in the church in particular. His ambivalence stemmed, not from his ascetic temperament, as some historians have claimed, but from his social conditioning, which predisposed him to a respect for male authority.

Within the bonds of marriage, Paul supported partnership, rejecting the double standards inherent in Judaic law. Matrimony, he explained in the seventh chapter of First Corinthians, was a limited good created for the containment of lust. Married couples, therefore, should transform their marriages into spiritual bonds by eschewing sexual relations. The obligations of marriage, however, could not be unilaterally shirked by either partner. "For the wife does not rule over her own body, but the husband does; likewise the husband does not rule over his own body, but the wife does," Paul stated. "Do not refuse one another, except perhaps by agreement for a season" (1 Cor. 7:4–5). The mutual bond of marriage, moreover, was to last for life. "Not I, but the Lord commands that a wife is not to depart from her husband, and if she departs, that she is to remain unmarried or be reconciled to her husband," he preached. "And let not a husband put away his wife" (1 Cor. 7:10–11).

Paul's opposition to double standards in marriage did not extend to all forms of sexual discrimination. He could not altogether accept the equality of the sexes, either in theory or in practice. In a later chapter of First Corinthians, where he returned to the relationship between the sexes, he reaffirmed the old notion of woman's subordination. Referring to the creation of Eve from Adam's rib (Gen. 2:18–25) rather than to the simultaneous creation of man and woman (Gen. 1:27 and 3:16), Paul declared that "man is not from woman but woman from man. For man was not created for woman but woman for man." From this premise he concluded that woman was under the authority of man, for "the husband is the head of the wife, as Christ is the head of the husband who walks in righteousness." Hence, as a sign of her subjection, a woman either "praying or prophesying" was to cover her head (1 Cor. 11:3–10).

Interpolations and subsequent additions to the Pauline letters reveal a growing resentment toward the prominent role women played in the gnostic sects. In an attempt to disqualify women from preaching, the legal subjection of women is cited: "It is not permitted unto them to speak; but let them be in subjection as also saith the law. And if they would learn anything, let them ask their husbands at home; for it is shameful for a woman to speak in church" (1 Cor. 14:34). The author of the First Epistle to Timothy found in Genesis even more compelling arguments for excluding women from positions of religious leadership. "I permit not a woman to teach or to have dominion over a man but to be in quietness," he wrote. "For Adam was first formed, then Eve; and Adam was not beguiled, but the woman being beguiled hath fallen into transgression" (1 Tim. 2:8–14).[50]

Though barred from preaching, early Christian women were not denied the opportunity to act as equal partners with Christian men in the arenas before the lions and executioners. They were also allowed to embrace ascetic life and organize monastic communities when the church was legalized in the fourth century. The renunciation of worldly life appealed more to women than to men, particularly in Rome, as the number of women in Jerome's circle attested.[51] Men apparently found a more congenial outlet for their energies in the emerging clerical hierarchy. The only clerical office open to women, the feminine diaconate, was an auxiliary order limited to giving instruction to female catechumens and helping bishops and deacons in the baptism of women.[52]

The movement in favor of virginity and sexual abstinence, which also grew among non-Christians in the third century, was not altogether detrimental to women. By not marrying, some women could free themselves from subordination as wives. Celibacy of the clergy, however, tended to create unnaturally tense relationships between the sexes, reinforcing prejudices about women in the church. Ancient taboos associated with women reemerged as soon as the Western church began to advocate the celibacy of the higher clergy in the fourth century. Although the Apostolic Constitutions lifted the Old Testament ban on women participating in the divine services for seven days after the onset of their menses,[53] Jerome proclaimed that "there was nothing dirtier than a menstruating woman: everything that she touched became polluted."[54] Menstruating women, according to Jerome, were to abstain from sexual intercourse if they did not wish to bring forth children deformed with leprosy or elephantiasis.[55] They also had to refrain from taking communion, at least until the end of the sixth century, when in the West Pope Gregory I put an end to this discrimination. "Since menses were the result of original sin," wrote Gregory, "if women, after due consideration, did not presume to approach the sacrament of the Body and Blood of the Lord during their menses, they were to be commended, but they should not be disqualified from communion."[56]

The fathers tended to think and speak about woman as a creature of extremes: as the daughter of Eve, a vain and deceitful temptress, or as a chaste and dutiful virgin and mother imitating Mary.[57] In so doing they were undoubtedly influenced by the polarized Roman feminine stereotypes: woman as a sex object or as an obedient daughter, wife, or mother. Even in exhorting women to virtue, the patristic writings emphasized meekness, modesty, humility, and obedience, character traits that the ancient world had traditionally praised in the female sex. Women in every state of life were frequently counseled in the spirit of the Apostolic Constitutions to be

> meek, quiet, gentle, sincere, free from anger, not talkative, not clamorous, not hasty of speech, not given to evil speaking, not captious, not double-tongued, not a busybody. If she see or hear anything that is not right, let her be as one that does not hear . . . and when she is asked anything by anyone, let her not easily answer . . . remitting those that desire to be instructed in the doctrines of godliness . . . to the governors.[58]

Misogynistic tirades in the church began with Tertullian. Wielding a powerful influence over the Latin fathers despite his later Montanism, Tertullian regarded women as the embodiment of evil. He added a nasty twist to the argument that Eve was to be blamed for the fall of Adam, and hence for the "ignominy of the original sin," by proclaiming that woman was also responsible for the fall of the angels.[59] More sympathetic to women, Ambrose insisted that, although sin had entered the world through Eve, she also carried the principle of redemption:

> As sin began with women, so the good also begins with women, so that women too, leaving aside female doings, abandon their weakness, and the soul, which has no sex, like Mary who makes no mistake, devotes itself to the religious care of chastity.[60]

Not as open-minded as Ambrose, but more moderate in tone than Tertullian, Augustine accepted not only the tarnished image of Eve but also the ancient notion that a woman's mental powers were inferior to a man's. Woman's subordination to man was a natural condition, according to Augustine, "for it is only just that the one whose understanding is feebler should serve the one whose understanding is stronger."[61] Ambrosiaster, in a work attributed to Augustine, went further, questioning the belief that woman was made in the image of man:

> How can one say about the woman that she is in the image of God when she is subject to the domination of her husband and is not allowed to have any authority. She cannot teach, testify, act as a surety, or serve as a judge; hence, she surely cannot rule.[62]

Theories about the inferior condition of woman, whether culled from Genesis or found in the Roman tradition, enabled the Latin fathers to accept the legal subordination of women and to justify sexual dimorphism in social and religious tasks. On the issue of sexual double standards, however, the fathers remained faithful to the teachings of the apostles, insisting that, because both sexes were called to eternal life, what was forbidden to woman was also forbidden to man. Social conventions tolerating and even justifying promiscuity and adultery in men were rejected. Sexual intercourse, moreover, was to be confined to marriage, an indissoluble, lifelong union. With the exception of Ambrosiaster, who allowed husbands to divorce their adulterous wives, the Latin fathers did not waver in preaching the same precepts to both men and women. They would not sanction divorce, recommending instead forgiveness or abstinence and making no distinction based on the sex of the partner who had committed adultery.[63] Patristic views, however, did not always triumph over deeply ingrained social customs. Although fourth-century Western councils were generally firm in prohibiting divorce in cases of adultery, fifth-century Gallican prelates were more cognizant of social realities and made an exception in the case of cuckolded husbands.[64]

The injustices inherent in the sexual double standards of Gallo-Roman society were denounced by one of the leading churchmen. Around the time Clovis was setting up his kingdom in northern Gaul, Caesarius of Arles spoke up in defense of women. In several of his sermons he unmasked the hypocrisy of men who wanted to marry virgins, expected fidelity from their wives, and loved chastity in them and required it from their daughters while they sought sexual exploits and even boasted about them to their friends. To excommunicate all those who found concubines among their own slaves and maidservants and among the servants of their neighbors was not feasible, Caesarius sadly admitted—too many married and unmarried men behaved in this way.[65]

Even this sympathetic observer of women's plight failed to perceive that men might have been more responsible for abortions and infanticides than women in a society where double sexual standards prevailed. Calling upon fathers to instruct their daughters "not to take potions so as to bring about abortion or to kill their children after conception or birth," Caesarius also proclaimed that "a woman either was to nurse the children she had conceived or she was to entrust them to others to be nursed." To those who did not want to have children, the only counsel Caesarius could offer was abstinence. Married women, Caesarius wrote, "were to enter into a pious pact with their husbands, because chastity is the only legitimate cause for the sterility of Christian wives."[66]

The paradox of the church's teachings on the role of women is more apparent in Caesarius' sermons than in the writings of churchmen who were less sensitive to women's spiritual aspirations and less willing to acknowledge women's moral fortitude. Stressing that childbearing was the duty of married women and calling upon fathers to instill this duty into their daughters,[67] Caesarius gave moral sanction to the social control men exercised over women in both Gallo-Roman and Germanic societies. While denouncing the double standards by which most men lived, Caesarius confirmed the claim of men to act as arbiters of female morality. But he also enhanced the dignity of women by attaching a moral value to women's function of nurturing. In proclaiming that obedient wives and dutiful mothers served as moral guides to their menfolk, Caesarius paid a tribute to women. He comprehended, moreover, the nature of the feminine experience in marriage. Acknowledging that the burdens of wives and mothers were heavy, he encouraged women to eschew marriage altogether, or to persuade their husbands to transcend sexuality by practicing abstinence. Drawing a sharp distinction between the role of married women and the role of nuns, Caesarius exalted feminine monastic vocation as a call to corporal and spiritual freedom. At the same time, he also issued a challenge to married women to use their ingenuity and influence to transform society according to Christian ideals.

Caesarius' works, widely read in Frankish monasteries, served to counterbalance the misogynous sentiments found in some patristic writings. Although Caesarius failed to resolve the problem of double standards in sexual morality and acknowledged the subjection of women to men in secular life, he lavished praise on women's virtue as opposed to men's laxity and upheld the life of self-abnegation as a form of female perfection.

2

Merovingian Women in Law and the Economy

The Franks, like all Germanic people who had come into contact with the Romans, developed a more complex political, social, and economic organization than the primitive tribal society that Tacitus had described in his *Germania*. Assisted by military followers of Frankish origin, as well as royal officials and Catholic bishops descended from the late Gallo-Roman senatorial aristocracy, Clovis and his immediate successors undermined the power of the Germanic kindreds. Although kinship remained a potent force of social control, the king assumed the function of providing protection and acting as arbiter of disputes, which, in the new kingdom, were to be settled by compensations instead of blood feuds. At the same time, the power of the Roman paterfamilias, attenuated by the emperors, was further undermined by Germanic custom. The rights and obligations of women, as of all members of Merovingian society, were defined by codifications of Germanic and Roman law. An unmarried woman was protected by the laws of her father and a married woman by the laws of her husband.[1]

The purpose of this chapter is to investigate the legal and economic rights of women in Merovingian society. A brief analysis of sexual stereotyping will be followed by an examination of how Germanic and Roman marital customs, sexual practices, and economic arrangements affected the lives of Merovingian women. The opportunities women had for self-assertion and acquisition of power will be examined in this context. Much of the evidence will be drawn from the laws, both Germanic and Roman.

Primitive Germanic customs were reflected in the Salic *Pactus,* issued by Clovis between 507 and 511 and reissued with additions between 511 and 513 and between 567 and 596, the Ripuarian Code compiled in the seventh century, and the laws of the Saxons, Frisians, and Thuringians compiled in the ninth century. Roman influences appeared in the laws of the Burgundians and Visigoths, tribes which had been in contact with the Romans for centuries, and to a lesser extent in the laws of the Bavarians and Alemans, which were compiled in the eighth century on the model of the Burgundian and Visigothic codifications. Roman laws, virtually unaffected by Germanic customs, were contained in the *Breviary* of Alaric, an early sixth-century Visigothic compilation that was used by the Franks for their Roman subjects. Germanic customs were superimposed on the *Lex Romana Burgundionum,* probably issued by Gundobad (474–516), for Burgundians of Roman descent.[2]

To judge the extent to which the laws were obeyed, I have supplemented the legal analysis with information derived from deeds, testaments,[3] collections of documentary forms *(formulae),*[4] narrative sources, and archaeological evidence.[5] In addition, conciliar legislation is examined for principles supporting or contradicting secular laws.[6]

WOMEN IN A MAN'S WORLD

All sources, whether legal, narrative, or archaeological, convey the impression that the settlement of the Germanic tribes was paralleled by the domestication of their wives. Certainly, by the sixth century, Germanic women no longer exhibited the martial spirit Tacitus had ascribed to them. There were exceptions, like Fredegund, who, as regent for her son, gathered an army, camouflaged her retainers as trees, and led them in a surprise attack against the Austrasians and Burgundians. "Then she returned home with much booty and many spoils," her chronicler tells us.[7] Others, in the absence of male relatives, defended their own or their daughters' honor with arms.[8] But fighting ceased to be a function of Frankish women long before their settlement in Gaul. Modern scholars have identified the small, spear-shaped blades, found in Frankish female graves of the fourth and fifth century, not as weapons but as knives used in eating.[9] For example, the two sixth-century tombs discovered in 1959 under the choir of the Cathedral of Cologne confirm this identification. The smaller one, the grave of a six-year-old prince, yielded a shield, a sword, two spears, a battle-ax, a bow and arrow, and only one piece of jewelry, a gold ring. The other tomb, that of a princess, contained a rich array of gold and silver personal ornaments embellished with garnets, but held only one sharp instrument, a gold-handled knife, which hung from her belt, together with a crystal ball and a small silver container for carrying either an amulet or perfume. Archaeological and narrative evidence attest that it was not unusual for a woman to be buried with jewelry, her status symbol,[10] and the Aleman Code understandably prescribed a double fine for the robbery of a woman's grave.[11]

Although a woman was not expected to defend herself, and was in fact discouraged from doing so, she was not valued less than a man. On the contrary, the Aleman and Bavarian Codes set her *wergeld,* the compensation her family would receive if she were killed, at a sum twice that for a man of the same status. Moreover, for any bodily injury inflicted upon her, a woman was entitled to twice the compensation allowed for a man. The Bavarian Code justified this custom on the ground that a woman could not protect herself with arms.[12] Indeed, should a woman choose to fight like a man, she forfeited this special right.[13] The Burgundian law, which had been codified much earlier, did not yet assume that women were defenseless. On the contrary, it tried to prevent feminine belligerence by denying any compensation to a woman who had gone forth from her courtyard to fight.[14]

The Salic laws were more forthright in indicating why women were valued so highly: they tripled the value of a woman of childbearing age. The same *wergeld,* 200 *solidi,* had to be paid for killing either a Frankish man or woman. But if the murdered woman was of childbearing age—over age twelve and not past her prime, which was usually considered age forty—her family was entitled to a compensation of 600 *solidi.* Equal value was attached only to the lives of counts, royal "antrustiones" (military followers), priests, and boys under twelve years of age. The political and social implications of these laws are clear. For the proper functioning of their society, the Franks thought it necessary to create special safeguards to protect the life of royal officials, churchmen, future warriors, and childbearing women. Sixth-century additions to the Salic Code reinforced this view by increasing compensations for assaults on pregnant women—Frankish, Roman, free, and slave—especially if these resulted in their aborting a female fetus.[15]

The high value placed on the life of women by the Germanic codes has been interpreted as evidence of the significant appreciation of women during the early Middle Ages.[16] But it would appear that women's ability to bear children, rather than their worth as helpmates or prophetesses, was prized. The emphasis in the codes on women's reproductive function and defenselessness fostered acceptance of the concept of feminine passivity and dependence, particularly in the upper classes, where women were not expected to perform physical labor. Discouraged from bearing arms and defending themselves, women of the Merovingian aristocracy were isolated in more narrowly defined sex roles than their Germanic ancestors. The prevailing stereotype of women as helpless creatures provided, moreover, justification for sexual double standards and the subjection of women to the authority of their husbands, principles that were incorporated in the Germanic codes.

Roman legal tradition reinforced the notion that women, being inferior to men, had to be ruled by their husbands. Under the empire, the assumed levity of the feminine mind apparently explained women's incapacity to act in court and to hold public office.[17] Although women were not barred from pleading and testifying in court in the *Regnum Francorum*, the codifications of Roman law increased the control of husbands over their wives.

Patristic statements about the moral deficiency of women also served as arguments for the legal subjection of married women. One of the leading Gallo-Roman prelates, Avitus of Vienne, set to verse the story of Eve's punishment. For acting as a temptress, he wrote, woman was to serve and fear the man who had been her companion before the Fall.[18] Although patristic authors held the opinion that men were more prone to sexual activity than women,[19] Merovingian churchmen upheld the position that men were more rational than women; hence, they claimed, men were better able to control their passions than women. Even such a staunch opponent of sexual double standards as Saint Caesarius of Arles did not hesitate to declare that the rational sense in humans was to be understood as the male and the flesh as female.[20] A seventh-century monk known as the Defensor Grammaticus argued that:

> A woman's reputation of modesty is so fragile that it quickly languishes at the slightest suggestion, as if it were a flower that would wither at the lightest breeze, especially when her age inclines her to vice and she is not ruled by a husband.[21]

In the Merovingian period, Christianity contributed only indirectly to the improvement of women's status. Even on the question of the spiritual equality of women, sixth-century prelates harbored doubt. In 586 the Council of Mâcon settled in favor of women the dispute over whether the designation homo in the Bible included both males and females, an important point in the dispute over whether or not God intended to save women. The solution the council provided was a semantic one. Because in the beginning God had created male and female and called them Adam, and because Christ, the Son of the Virgin, was called the Son of Man, homo referred to all human beings, irrespective of gender.[22]

By converting their husbands and children, endowing churches, founding monasteries, and dispensing charity, Merovingian women called attention to their own individual spiritual worth. But feminine contributions to the bonds of faith and the ecclesiastical network, even though essential, failed to earn for women the recognition that they

possessed a potential for social productivity comparable to men. Even
the accomplishments of Saint Balthild, the wife of Clovis II (639–657)
and an exceptionally active woman as both regent for her son and
patroness of the church, were characterized by her biographer in terms
of obedience to her husband and nurturing others, behavior patterns
Merovingian men encouraged in women:

> She obeyed her husband as her ruler, was like a mother towards her
> stepchildren, a daughter towards priests, and a pious nurse towards
> infants and adolescents. Being amicable with all, she loved priests
> as fathers, monks as brothers, the poor as members of her house-
> hold, and the pilgrims as her sons.[23]

Locked into stereotypes, subjected to the authority of their husbands, Merovingian women were nevertheless not altogether deprived
of legal and economic rights. Although by modern standards these
rights appear insignificant, they did allow women to assert their wills
and exercise influence.

BETROTHAL AND MARRIAGE

Perhaps in no other area was the assimilation of Germanic and Roman
customs as rapid as in marriage law. As a result, the authority of the
husband over a woman living under Roman law was strengthened. The
Roman marriage of *sine manu,* which enabled a woman to remain under
the power of her family, was not recognized by the Visigothic and
Burgundian codifications of Roman law. A woman, whether of Germanic or Roman descent, came under the power of her husband if
she went to live with him out of her own volition.[24] This meant that he
could represent her in court and manage her property, even though
he could not alienate it without her consent. The power gained by her
husband was not as unlimited as that of the patria potestas, the almost
unlimited sovereignty a Roman father exercised over his minor daughters and sons, and their property.

In the Merovingian kingdom a widow was able to assume all her
husband's rights. Whether she lived under Roman or Germanic law, she
became the head of the household, gaining control of property and the
guardianship of minors. She had to relinquish these rights only when
she remarried. Thus, a woman was not a perpetual minor as she had
been in the Roman Empire: as a widow she did not need a man to act
on her behalf in court and financial transactions.

An unmarried woman, on the other hand, remained under the

power of her family until she reached the age of majority. The father retained the right of making matrimonial arrangements for his minor children, both male and female, a right that passed to his widow or, if she died or remarried, to the child's brother or paternal uncle. Mutual consent, the legal criterion for a valid union under Roman law,[25] did not provide a more effective guarantee that parents would consult their children's wishes than it had in the Roman Empire. A young woman's right to arrange her own marriage was particularly circumscribed. She could dispense with parental approval only when she came of age, that is, when she reached twenty-five under Roman law issued for the Burgundians and twenty in the Visigothic Kingdom.[26] But the union of a Merovingian woman was usually concluded much earlier. Daughters of the aristocracy were betrothed around twelve and, as in pagan Rome, were given away in marriage by the time they reached fifteen.[27] Men also married young, in their mid-teens; but they also reached *legitima aetas* sooner, at age fifteen under Salic and twelve under Ripuarian law.[28] The Visigoths upheld twenty as *perfecta aetas* also for men, but allowed males over fourteen to marry as they chose when both parents were dead. The exemption was not granted to females. Visigothic girls were subject to legal punishment if they married without parental consent; boys were not, probably because few were foolish enough to take this step without property to live on and pledge as a bridegift. On the other hand, there is no evidence to suggest that parents were less likely to consult their daughters than their sons when they arranged their marriages. As P. D. King has observed, "mutual agreement" between parents and children "was no doubt the rule rather than the exception."[29]

When a young woman married, her father or guardian conveyed his right of protection (*mundium*) over her to her husband. The husband then could claim compensation for any injury she or their future children might suffer. To gain this right, he had to present a marriage settlement, which, as we will see later in this chapter, was either in part or entirely turned over to his betrothed as her bridegift.[30] Like the Roman institution of the *donatio ante nuptias,* a marriage settlement presented by the groom to the bride,[31] the Germanic bridegift (*dos*) provided compensation, indeed economic security, to a woman in case she was repudiated. The more powerful a family, the more lavish a bridegift the suitor had to supply or pledge.[32]

The arrangements made for the marriage of a daughter were similar in both Germanic and Roman families. Normally three steps were involved: the suit (*petitio*), the betrothal (*desponsatio*), and the wedding (*nuptiae*). The suitor usually sealed his agreement with the parents by giving a pledge (*arrha*). If the parents accepted it, they then entered into a legally-binding contract, confirming it by a written or oral covenant and an exchange of rings before witnesses at the formal betrothal. At some later date the girl was delivered to the groom's house.[33]

Once the parents accepted the pledge, the engagement could not be unilaterally broken. Even if the girl was a mere child, not older than four or five years of age when she had been engaged, and even if she opposed her engagement, her parents had to go through with the matrimony once they had promised her. Gregory of Tours tells us of a father who nearly lost all of his possessions because he refused to recognize his daughter's betrothal, which his wife had arranged in his absence. In this unusual case, his adversary was an extortionist who demanded 16,000 *solidi* in compensation.[34] Under Burgundian law, a rejected bridegroom could demand only 300 *solidi*. If a betrothed woman married another, she could be executed as an adulteress.[35] Roman law treated women more humanely. If the girl or her parents broke the engagement, the groom was entitled to demand only fourfold the *arrha* he had paid; if, for any reason, two years had elapsed since the engagement, the woman was free to marry another man.[36]

The Germanic codes upheld double standards with respect to breach of contracts. Betrothals arranged by parents for their minor children bound young women very strictly. Young men, on the other hand, could escape with relative ease from unwanted engagements. Should a man choose to terminate the contract, he only had to pay the bridegift. Under Bavarian and Aleman laws, he also had to swear before witnesses that he was doing so, not because he found any fault in the girl or in her parents, but because he had fallen in love with another woman.[37] The chronicles refer to young men who simply chose to ignore the pledge given on their behalf and concluded a union according to their own heart. For example, Theudebert I honored his engagement to a Lombard princess, Visigard, only after seven years. His reluctance to fulfill the contract, according to Gregory of Tours, created such a scandal among the Franks that finally Theudebert found it politically expedient to repudiate Deoteria, the woman whom he had married for love in the meantime. The stories Gregory tells us of Theudebert's and Deoteria's stormy marriage shed, however, a different light on the situation, suggesting that Theudebert had tired of Deoteria and used political pressure as an excuse to abandon her and marry Visigard, who had continued to honor the betrothal.[38]

Although in the Merovingian kingdom a woman was not sold, she could still be captured. Saint Caesarius of Arles found this custom offensive. "How is it that sometimes a very brave man goes forth to battle," he inquired, "[and] then as a result of his victory he takes a young girl as booty." But Caesarius was an exception. No one was surprised when the Franks captured Radegund, the daughter of the vanquished Thuringian king, and the sons of Clovis contested her hand in a judicial battle.[39]

Only within the kingdom was the capture of a woman resisted and penalized. Gregory of Tours tells us of a mother who repelled the abductor of her daughter with her slaves, "killing many of his men," so that "he did not come off without disgrace."[40] Even abortive abductions, when for one reason or another the woman was returned, were punished by law, especially if the woman was engaged or married. If the abductor retained her, the consequences of his acts were more serious. For example, the Salic *Pactus* levied the same compensation, 200 *solidi*, for killing a man and for stealing his wife. If the woman was unmarried, her abductor had to pay only her bridegift, 52½ *solidi*, and an additional fine of 15 *solidi* if she was engaged. Apparently this was not a sufficient deterrent, for toward the end of the sixth century Childebert II decreed that whoever abducted a woman against her will would be killed or exiled. In issuing this decree, he was probably influenced by Roman law, which punished rape with death. The admission that the abductor of a reluctant woman committed a more serious offense than one who had her cooperation represented an important step toward the legal recognition of the bride's consent as an essential element in the wedlock.[41]

Indeed, the Bavarian Code, issued two centuries after the Salic Pact, acknowledged that a woman had the right to arrange her own union. But in such a quasi marriage (*quasi conjugium*) she did not have the same economic protection as in a formal matrimony contracted by her parents. If the man changed his mind, she was entitled to claim only 12 *solidi*, half the compensation she would have received had she been lawfully engaged by her parents.[42] The same indemnity of 12 *solidi* was available also to the girl whose lover refused to marry her.[43] Although the law in question has been cited by the proponents of *Friedelehe* as proof for its existence, it actually provides a corrective to the romantic picture German historians usually present of *Friedelehe*. A freewoman who entered into a *quasi conjugium* was distinguished from a slave concubine who had no legal right to claim anything from her partner, but the law granted the jilted *Friedelfrau* only a slight compensation, the same indemnity that it allotted to a promiscuous freewoman.[44]

The Bavarian Code was exceptionally liberal with unmarried women who had the courage to risk either living with a man or having sexual intercourse with him without a formal contract of betrothal. Other codes defined a voluntary sexual union as adultery, which was to be punished, usually at the expense of the woman. Neither the Visigothic Code nor the Burgundian Code, both of which had influenced the Bavarian Code, made provisions for the protection of a woman whose union was not arranged by her parents. According to the Visigothic Code, if her partner was willing to pay her *dos,* her parents had to acquiesce, but they could punish her for her dishonorable behavior by denying her an inheritance.[45] The Burgundian Code warned that a woman had no claim upon a man with whom she had sexual relations. She could not bring against him charges of moral corruption, nor was he under any obligation to marry her if he paid 15 *solidi.* Should she go to live with him, he could return her to her parents with the payment of her *dos;* if she was a widow, he did not have to pay anything.[46]

The legal consequences of a union concluded without the approval of the bride's family were severe. If her parents chose to press charges, the man was penalized with heavy fines. Moreover, the woman had little or no protection against her partner's change of heart. The form of union that the codes sought to encourage was clearly not *Raubehe,* marriage by abduction, or *Friedelehe,* quasi marriage with a freewoman, but a more formal arrangement whereby the husband obtained from his bride's family the right of protection over her and their future children.

The Frankish church lent support to these laws. Although the Roman legal principle that the validity of a marriage depended upon mutual consent had been upheld by the Christian fathers, it did not appear in Merovingian conciliar legislation.[47] On the other hand, the necessity of paternal consent did. Even if the couple took refuge in church and the girl cooperated with her abductor, she was to be returned to her father, according to the first Frankish council which met at Orléans in 511. Later councils prescribed excommunication for a man who "impiously" married a girl against her parents' wishes, even if he had obtained royal permission to do so.[48] The implication of these pronouncements is not that the Merovingian bishops rejected the legal significance of mutual consent, but rather they did not accept it as sufficient for a valid marriage.

Despite legal strictures and ecclesiastical bans, marriage in the Merovingian kingdom remained a social fact. The approval of the bride's parents was not an essential condition for the validity of marriage. As long as the woman was not engaged or married to someone else, and her relatives did not object, it was sufficient for a couple to live together publicly to be considered husband and wife. The critical elements in a valid marriage were the the partners' acknowledgment and the community's recognition that they were married. Bishop Bertram of

Bordeaux tried in vain to argue that his sister's union was invalid because it was not sanctioned by her relatives. Others, including Gregory
of Tours, thought otherwise. In their opinion, the fact that Bertegund
had lived with the man for thirty years made her, without question, his
wife.[49]

The blood feuds, recorded by the chroniclers, also prove that naked
force was the only recourse for a family whose daughter married against
their wishes. Saint Rictrud's brothers killed her husband several years
after her abduction, even though the union had produced by that time
several children.[50] Other men were able to avert vendettas by making
amends. In a *formula* drawn up in the seventh century by Marculf, the
husband acknowledged that he had endangered his life by uniting himself with his wife by means of rape against the wishes of her parents and
that he was saved only through the intervention of priests and good
men.[51]

Even the payment of the *dos* was not essential for the validity of a
union or the legitimacy of children. The code issued for the Burgundians
of Roman descent added to the standard Roman criterion of mutual
consent for a valid union the restriction that, without the public transfer
or promise of the *donatio nuptialis* (a gift from the bridegroom to the
bride), children born from the union could not inherit their father's
property.[52] Other codes did not distinguish between legitimate and
illegitimate children.[53]

Only unions between free and unfree were condemned both by
Germanic and Roman laws as illegitimate *contubernia,* as opposed to
nuptiae, matrimonia, conjugia, or *quasi conjugia.* If the free partner was a
woman, she stood to lose her life, or freedom and property, and her
children were reduced to servitude and could not inherit. A man was
also punished with enslavement if he contracted a union with someone
else's slave, although he could claim that the relation was a casual one
and avoid punishment by compensating her master. No laws prevented
him from having sexual relations with his own slave girl; if he wished,
he could recognize her children as his heirs and free her as well.[54] These
laws were observed only on the higher levels of Merovingian society.
Among the peasantry, as we will see in the next chapter, free and slave
intermarried with the blessing of their lords.

Marriages between close blood relations and in-laws were also dissolved. Children issuing from these unions were marked with infamy
and excluded from inheritance. In the beginning of the sixth century,
kings were able to disregard incest laws with impunity, but by the end
of the century they could no longer do so: the church took a firm stand

on this issue. Theudebert of Austrasia, for example, had to perform penance for having married his brother's widow.[55] The scope of the net cast by the incest laws, however, was not so wide as to prevent double alliances between lineages. The marriage of a brother or sister with one of her in-laws, a subject to be treated in the next chapter, strengthened the power of the woman as a wife. The prohibition of incest, moreover, worked in favor of women of the lower classes. It prevented the creation of a closed aristocracy and encouraged exogamous unions, thus facilitating the social ascent through marriage of women of humble birth.

Merovingian women had a broad range of options to choose from when attempting to contract advantageous unions. Both the Germanic and the Roman laws protected them against being forced into marriages by their abductors. Although their parents or the king might impose undesirable husbands on them, such matches were not likely to be contrary to their economic or social interests. The authority of the parents, on the other hand, was not absolute: it could not invalidate marriages contracted without their consent. Determined women might present their families with a *fait accompli.* Emancipated from the authority of their fathers, widows and divorcées were free to make their own arrangements, except under the Saxon law.[56] Most important for the dignity and social advancement of women was the recognition that they could transform casual sexual relations into quasi marriages by living publicly with the man, and the children issuing from these unions were legitimate.

Whenever it was feasible, women tried to obtain the protection of a formal contract of betrothal. For example, when Clovis decided to marry Clotild, the orphaned niece of the Burgundian king, he sent her a ring. She accepted it with the proviso that, "if he wishes to marry me, forthwith he should request me through an envoy from my uncle." Heeding her advice, Clovis sent envoys to Gundobad. They gained his consent to the marriage, paid him a *solidus* and a *denarius,* which were customary among the Franks, according to Fredegar, and took Clotild to Clovis.[57] Such formalities were not observed when Theudebert I married Deoteria. They met when he captured Béziers in 532 or 533. She had lost her husband in the battle and encouraged his sexual advances. Summoned from her side, he did not forget her. Even though he was engaged to a Visigothic princess, when he became king in 534 he sent for and married Deoteria.[58] The marriage of Fredegund and Chilperic I was even more informal. After he had his Visigothic wife Galswinth strangled, Chilperic simply declared that his former companion, Fredegund, was his new queen.[59]

POLYGYNY AND DIVORCE

However her union was contracted, a married woman was subject to the authority of her husband. She had to obey his command and act according to his pleasure rather than her own. Above all, she had to guard her chastity if she did not wish to be repudiated or killed. Her husband, on the other hand, did not owe her fidelity.

Double standards in Merovingian marriages were even more pronounced in some respects than in the late empire or in the Germanic tribes. A Roman matron was expected to remain faithful to her husband, but she did not have to share her position with other wives. In Germanic tribal society a wife did not have to compete with concubines for her husband's attention. The combination of the Germanic polygyny and the Roman institution of concubinage gave almost complete license to men to be promiscuous, furthered male dominance, and accentuated sexual double standards in Merovingian society.

As long as there were no strict requirements for the legalization of unions and the legitimization of children, polygyny continued unabated in the royal family. Four Merovingian kings, Clothar I, Charibert I, Chilperic I, and Dagobert I, are known to have indulged in this. At least two of Clothar's wives, Ingund and Aregund, and possibly also Chunsinna and Radegund, were married to him at the same time. Gregory of Tours's account leaves no doubt that Clothar practiced polygyny. It specifies that he loved his second wife, Ingund, with "unico amore" until she asked him to find a suitable husband for her younger sister Aregund:

> On hearing this, the king, who was most amorous by temperament, began to desire Aregund, and betaking himself to the domain where she lived, he married her. When she was his, he returned to Ingund and spoke as follows: "I have done my best to procure for thee the reward thy sweetness asked of me. I sought a man wealthy and of good wit, whom I might give in marriage to thy sister, but I found none better than myself. Know therefore that I have taken her to wife, which I believe will not displease thee." She answered: "Let my lord do that which seemeth good in his sight; only let his handmaid live in the enjoyment of his favor."[60]

The dates given by Eugen Ewig for Clothar's subsequent unions with Radegund and Chunsinna are so close in time that they suggest polygyny rather than serial monogamy. The marriage to Aregund took place around 537 and soon produced a son, Chilperic. Three years later, around 540, Clothar had a son, Chramn, by another wife, Chunsinna.

By 540, he probably had also consummated his union with Radegund, a Thuringian princess. Captured in 531 and won by Clothar in a judicial battle, Radegund was educated at Athies as Clothar's future wife. Since none of the sources describes her as an "infans" at the time of her capture, we can assume that she was at least six years old in 531 and of marriageable age by 540. It is possible that by 540 Clothar had abandoned the two sisters, but Gregory of Tours makes no remark about their repudiation. Ecclesiastical censure of incestuous unions began only toward the end of Clothar's reign in 566, when the bishops asked Clothar to relinquish the last of his wives, Vuldetrada, the widow of one of his nephews.[61]

Clothar's example was emulated by two of his sons. Charibert I, Ingund's son, divided his attention between two sisters, Merofled and Marcoveifa, and an additional wife, Theudegild. Gregory of Tours reports that Charibert became angry with his first wife, Ingoberga, left her, and married Merofled. But Gregory did not mention that Charibert abandoned Merofled for the sake of Theudegild, or that he replaced Theudegild with Marcoveifa.[62] Chilperic, Aregund's son, also practiced polygyny before he married Galswinth. When Chilperic I contracted a union with the Visigothic princess, he left "Fredegund and others whom he had as his wives," according to Fredegar.[63] The Frankish chroniclers were careful to distinguish between wives and concubines, referring to freewomen as wives and reserving the term concubine for their slave companions.[64]

Attachment to one consort also remained unusual in the next generation of kings. Clothar II, Chilperic's son, was singled out by a chronicler for having loved his second wife, Bertetrud, with "unico amore."[65] Their son, Dagobert I, made up for his father's uxoriousness. After he had repudiated the wife whom his father had chosen for him, he married the beautiful Nanthild and two other women. During one of his campaigns, he also had an affair with an Austrasian woman who bore him a son without earning the position of a wife. In addition, Dagobert had so many concubines that Fredegar declined to name them for fear of making his volume too bulky.[66] The sexual exploits of Dagobert's son, Clovis II, remembered by a chronicler as a "fornicator and exploiter of women," were even more extensive, but, unlike his father, he did not have several simultaneous wives.[67]

Polygyny was forbidden only by the Visigothic Code, and keeping a concubine while a man was married was prohibited only by the Roman code issued for the Visigoths.[68] The Visigoths did not treat these laws lightly. There is reason to believe that Galswinth was given in marriage to Chilperic I on the condition that he repudiate his earlier wives. We know that Chilperic had to take a solemn oath (sacramentum) that he would not degrade her from her position as queen. Galswinth interpreted this to mean not only that he would not repudiate her but also that she would have exclusive rights to her title. When Fredegund, Chilperic's former companion, reappeared in court, Galswinth complained. Reluctant to let her return to Spain with her treasures, Chilperic had her strangled, and, after making a semblance of mourning for a few days, he declared Fredegund his new queen.[69]

Not only queens but occasionally wives of magnates also had to share their position with co-wives. The Carolingians, when mayors of the palace, practiced polygyny. Chalpaida, the mother of Charles Martel, was Pepin's second wife. When Pepin married her, he did not repudiate his first wife, Plektrud. She remained at his side and continued to sign documents as his wife until his death. Politically less prominent, Chalpaida enjoyed all the rights of a legal wife. Her son, Charles Martel, recognized in all respects as equal to the sons of Plektrud, became Pepin's sole successor after the death of his half-brothers. On the other hand, Pepin never recognized Childebrand, another son by a nameless concubine, as his heir.[70]

The position of second and third wives—whether simultaneous or successive—and their children was protected by the Bavarian Code. If a man had several wives, and each had free status, his sons were to share the inheritance equally, according to the code. Sons by slave companions, however, were to receive only what the legitimate sons, borne by free mothers, were willing to grant them.[71]

Polygyny was probably less frequent in the upper classes than in the royal family. The chroniclers recorded mainly unsuccessful attempts—cases where the girl resisted, her family objected, or the king intervened. Duke Amalo probably intended polygyny when he sent his wife to another estate and pursued a certain freeborn girl. Although she refused him, he brought her to his house by force. Though beaten and handcuffed, she managed to slay him, escape from his men, and obtain royal protection against the vengeance of his kinsmen.[72]

Concubinage, on the other hand, was a common occurrence on the upper levels of Merovingian society. Gregory of Tours's history, composed toward the end of the sixth century, is replete with stories of counts taking maidservants as their concubines. For example, the son of Duke Beppolen "had abandoned two wives, both still living. . . . He had forsaken his first wife for the commerce of serving maids. . . . He had used his second wife in the same way . . . and now did the same with this, his third wife."[73] The church apparently was powerless to stop this behavior. Indeed, by the eighth century, its own ranks were infiltrated by sexually promiscuous clerks. At least according to the Anglo-Saxon missionary Saint Boniface, members of the Frankish clergy did not shy from having four or five concubines in their beds each night.[74]

Whether married or single, lay or clerk, a man could follow his inclinations with relative abandon in the Merovingian kingdom. Secular laws punished him only when he infringed upon the rights of other men.[75] Even the penitentials penalized him less severely for illicit sexual relations that did not involve a scandal. For example, the Penitential of Saint Hubert, an eighth-century Frankish compilation, prescribed seven years of penance for an adulterer, defining indiscriminately as an adulterer one who raped or had intercourse with a married or betrothed woman. For raping a noncommitted virgin or widow, the penalty was only three years, the same penance as that for frequenting whores.[76]

Though their husbands might be licentious, Merovingian women had to guard their reputations. The contrast between a married woman and a whore—the former engaging in sex for procreation and the latter for pleasure—a legacy of the ancient world and the Christian church, was reinforced by the protection that the Germanic codes extended to respectable women. To call a woman a whore was as serious a slander as the accusation that she was a witch.[77] Even for minor sexual affronts, women could bring suits. Under Aleman law, if a man lifted a woman's skirt and exposed her knees, or took off her headdress, she was entitled to collect 6 *solidi* from him. If he lifted her skirt to reveal her genitals and buttocks, he had to pay a compensation of 12 *solidi.* Raping a woman and chopping off someone's nose were considered comparable offenses, punishable with 40 *solidi.* Salic law imposed higher fines for sexual molestation: for touching a woman's fingers, 15 *solidi,* or her arms, 30 *solidi;* for holding her by her elbow, 35 *solidi;* for touching her breast, 45 *solidi;* for raping her, 52½ *solidi,* which was the equivalent of her legal bridegift.[78]

The traditional interpretation of these laws is that they aimed at the protection of women.[79] In an age of violence, they certainly provided some safeguards against sexual assaults. It must be noted, however, that they were as concerned with the honor of a woman as with her safety. These laws reinforced the false sense of modesty that was instilled in Merovingian women at an early age. A sexual assault had such a devastating psychological effect on the victim's self-esteem that normally she preferred to conceal her shame rather than take her case into court. Those unfortunate enough to be raped blamed their assaults on demons, and it was not unusual for women who had been defiled to kill themselves. We know that some accused of adultery committed suicide rather than stand trial.[80]

Divorce laws also enshrined double standards. It was not more difficult, at least for a man, to break his marriage than to break his engagement. Divorce was a simple affair in the Frankish Kingdom. In addition to the dissolution of a marriage by mutual consent, allowed by both Roman and Germanic law,[81] the Germanic laws made it easy for a man to repudiate his wife. Under Roman law a husband could escape from an unwanted union only if his wife gave her consent to the dissolution of the marriage, or if she had committed adultery, sorcery, or acted as a procuress. If he divorced her for any other reason, she had the right to reclaim her dowry and nuptial gift, and her husband could not remarry. Should he remarry, she could claim his whole property.[82]

Under Germanic law, a man could repudiate a woman for her inability to bear children, as well as for any serious crime. If she was beyond reproach, he could unilaterally divorce her as long as he was willing to relinquish control over her property and to pay her a compensation equal to her bridegift. If he were not prepared to make such a sacrifice, he could try to drive her into a relationship with another man. Once she committed adultery, he had no further obligations to her. Indeed, if he caught her in the act, he had the right to kill both her and her lover.[83]

A wife, however, did not have these options. She had to remain faithful and obedient to her husband, and, even if he were a drunkard or a gambler, or mistreated or neglected her, she could not initiate separation. Nor could she sue him on the ground of adultery. The Burgundian Code went as far as to declare that a woman was smothered in mire if she tried unilaterally to divorce her husband.[84] Even women living under Roman law were not in a much better legal position. The Visigothic and Burgundian codifications allowed a woman to divorce her husband only in the extreme event that she could prove him guilty of homicide, violation of graves, or necromancy.[85] Under Visigothic law, a woman could divorce her husband only if he were found guilty of pederasty or of having forced her to fornicate with another man.[86]

Occasionally, when a woman had an extremely powerful protector, she could flout these laws. We know from Gregory of Tours that Clovis, the founder of the Merovingian dynasty, owed his existence to the brashness of his mother Basina, who had left the king of Thuringia and offered herself to Clovis's father, Childeric.[87] Another way for a woman to escape from an unhappy union was to have her husband murdered. This was the solution adopted by Queen Fredegund when her husband Chilperic I began to suspect her of adultery.[88]

In a case of particular brutality in high rank, Gregory of Tours relates that Eulalius, Count of Auvergne, neglected his wife Tetradia for harlots, beat her, and squandered her jewelry and gold. A nephew of Eulalius took pity on Tetradia and, with the assistance of Duke Desiderius, arranged her escape. The young man's intention, according to Gregory, was to marry Tetradia. At least this is what Eulalius alleged when, finding his wife gone, he slew his nephew in a fit of rage. He could not deal with Tetradia in a similar manner. Duke Desiderius gave her refuge and married her upon the death of his own wife. Subjected to ridicule when he charged Tetradia with adultery in King Gunthram's court, Eulalius dropped the case and remarried. But he did not mend his ways and the taunts of his concubines drove his second wife crazy. Neither did he abandon his desire for revenge. When Desiderius died, leaving part of his vast fortune to Tetradia, Eulalius reopened the case, suing her for having absconded with his property. A synod of bishops, assembled from the counties of Auvergne, Gevaudan, and Rouergue, not only adjudicated the property dispute but also inquired into the validity of Tetradia's second union. Despite his notoriety for wife abuse and fornication, Eulalius won the case. Tetradia's children by Desiderius were declared illegitimate, and she was ordered to compensate Eulalius fourfold for the value of whatever he claimed she had taken from his house. The one mitigating aspect of the sentence rendered against Tetradia was that she was told she could return to Auvergne, where she had inherited property from her father, without fear of further revenge. This suggests that she was granted a divorce from Eulalius.[89]

The settlement of this dispute by a synod of bishops (attended also by some lay magnates) was in keeping with the declaration of the Council of Agde held in 506 under the leadership of Caesarius of Arles. According to that council, men could not repudiate their wives without presenting their charges to an ecclesiastical court. Ecclesiastical courts may have provided a modicum of protection to married women against arbitrary treatment by their husbands, but, judging by the sentence rendered against Tetradia, bishops accepted the double standards found in the secular codes. The Merovingian church made no effort to introduce more equitable divorce laws. Only the Council of Orléans, held in 533, took up the question of divorce, forbidding it on the grounds of illness. There is no evidence of further attempts by the Frankish church to legislate on divorce until the latter half of the eighth century, when the Carolingians introduced into both canon and secular law the principle that marriages were binding for life.[90]

MARRIAGE SETTLEMENTS AND INHERITANCE RIGHTS

The most important development in the history of Merovingian women was the gradual improvement of their economic rights under Germanic law. This improvement can be traced through the evolution of the brideprice into a bridegift and the granting of power to women to hold and inherit landed property.

Some historians have detected in the evolution of the Germanic *dos* the influence of the Roman *donatio ante nuptias,* a settlement presented by the groom to the bride.[91] According to this thesis, the recognition in late Roman law of the husband's countergift led to provisions in the Germanic codes allowing a married woman to claim a part or the whole of her brideprice (*wittemon, nuptiale pretium, uxoris pretium*) as her bridegift (*dos*).[92] A more plausible explanation is that these regulations reflected both the barbarians' desire to imitate Roman customs and their leaders' intent to weaken the power of the kin by taking over the protection of the weak and injured members of society—in this case, women who had been repudiated or who had lost their husbands. Unlike their sisters living under Roman law, Germanic women did not have equal rights of inheritance, and received not a dowry but only personal and household goods from their family at the time of their weddings. Thus, by granting them the right to receive a bridegift, the codes brought the economic position of Germanic women into line with the more favorable situation of women of Roman descent.

The Burgundian Code, issued in the early sixth century, constitutes a transitional stage in this development. The bride was to receive a third of her *wittemon* and her family the rest. The *wittemon* for a widow went to her deceased husband's relatives but, if a woman was married for a third time, she was entitled to retain the entire settlement. Other codes were more generous to women.[93] Under Visigothic law, the parents had the right to manage their daughter's *dos,* but upon their death it passed into her own hands.[94] Salic law allowed a girl's relatives to claim only a token payment of one *solidus* and a *denarius* from her suitor. The marriage settlement belonged to the bride, although she could not alienate it if she had children. If she had lost her husband and wished to remarry, she had to pay about one-tenth of the *dos* as release money (*achasium*) to her dead husband's relatives.[95]

By the seventh and eighth centuries when the Ripuarian, Aleman, and Bavarian Codes were promulgated, the bride's family had lost all control over her marriage settlement. Upon her husband's death she had the right to claim the amount specified in the codes as her legal *dos* and could do with it whatever she wished, as long as she had no children. If she had children, she was entitled only to its usufruct. By transforming the brideprice into a bridegift, the codes assured the economic security of women deprived of their husband's support.[96] Only the Saxons, who remained outside the Frankish sphere of influence and codified their customs under Charlemagne, failed to make similar provisions; they continued to award a substantial sum of 300 *solidi* to the bride's father.[97]

The financial settlement that women received upon their marriage was described by the seventh-century Spanish bishop Saint Leander in unflattering terms. "It is customary for men when they marry to bestow upon their wives a *dos*," he wrote. "In exchange for the loss of their modesty, as a reward, they turn over to them a part of their patrimony so that it appears that they had purchased their wives rather than that they had married them."[98] Saint Leander might have confused the *dos* with the *morgengabe,* the morning gift or *pretium pulchritudinis, pretium virginitatis,* which a bride received after the consummation of her marriage. But the codes and documents of practice made a clear distinction between the *morgengabe* and the *dos.* The *morgengabe* was usually a more modest settlement than the *dos.* For example, under Aleman law, a widow had the right to demand twelve *solidi* as her *morgengabe* and forty *solidi* as her *dos.*[99] According to the proponents of the *Friedelehe,* it was the payment of the *morgengabe* that distinguished these unions from casual relationships.

While the codes expressed the amount of bridegift and morning gift in money, the deeds and *formulas* of the seventh century show that often the usufruct of land or even the unrestricted ownership of real property was increasingly turned over to women.[100] Only the Saxon Code limited the husband's right to give gifts of movables to his bride.[101] For example, when Chilperic I married Galswinth, he gave her the cities of Limoges, Bordeaux, Cahors, Bearn, and Bigorre as *dos* and *morgengabe.* After her death, the property went to her sister, Brunhild, and did not revert to her husband.[102]

Direct ownership of land received as *dos* and *morgengabe* represented an important step toward the economic independence of women. Although a husband had the right to manage his wife's property, he could not alienate it without her consent. If the alliance was dissolved or the husband died, the woman assumed full ownership. Even though she could not freely dispose of her property if she had children, she could exercise economic power. This was an important development that undermined the old Germanic prejudice against women holding and inheriting real property.

Under the influence of Roman law, which recognized the right of women to hold land and allowed daughters to claim an equal share with their brothers in the paternal inheritance,[103] Germanic inheritance laws gradually became less restrictive. But the old prejudices were never completely eliminated, and marriage remained the principal means by which women came to possess land and the concomitant economic power.

The earliest Visigothic compilation discriminated against unmarried daughters and grandchildren *ex filia,* and only Chindasvind (642–650/53) attempted to bring Visigothic customs into line with Roman law by ruling that children, regardless of their sex, inherited equally in the case of intestates.[104] At the opposite end of the spectrum were the laws of the Germanic tribes living on the fringes of or outside the Frankish Kingdom; these remained largely unaffected by the new attitude toward women's property rights. Under Thuringian law, a woman could inherit land only in the unlikely event that she had no male relatives within five degrees.[105] The Saxon Code was less intransigent in this respect: it entrusted a woman with the task of transmitting the family's patrimony if she had no brothers or nephews on her brothers' side.[106] The most ancient redaction of the Salic Code, issued by Clovis, excluded women altogether from the inheritance of land. In the first half of the sixth century, this discrimination was somewhat mitigated when women were permitted to inherit land other than Salic land, that is, property that came to their parents as part of their patrimony, as distinguished from land that had been purchased. Chilperic I (560/61–584) further eased the restrictions, admitting daughters to the inheritance of Salic land in the absence of sons.[107] The Burgundian, Ripuarian, Aleman, and Bavarian Codes arrived at the same compromise.[108] The new attitude tolerating the transmission of land into the hands of females also left its mark on the laws regulating a mother's right to inherit landed property from her sons. Whereas an earlier article of the Burgundian Code accorded a mother only the usufruct of her dead son's property, a later decision admitted her to the ownership of half of the land, giving the rest to the son's paternal kin.[109]

More equitable were the Germanic laws regulating succession of movables, although they did not compensate women for being preempted by men in the inheritance of land. Indeed, as women gained the right to own land under Salic law, they lost their previous advantage in the inheritance of liquid assets. The earliest version of the Salic Code had provided for the passage of movable property through the female line in the absence of children. It stipulated that, in these cases, the mother had a preferential successorial right; next in the line of succession were sisters and brothers, who were to have equal shares; then came the mother's sister, with the father's sister following her. As the incapacity of women to hold landed property was relaxed, this law of succession for movables came to apply also to landed property in subsequent versions of the code. At that point, however, the father gained preference over the mother, and the father's sister over the mother's sister.[110] The Burgundian Code gave women preferential successorial right only in regard to their mothers' and sisters' clothing and ornaments.[111]

In addition to inheriting the personal belongings of her female relatives, the daughter of a Germanic family was entitled to receive a trousseau. It was the custom to send a bride to the home of her husband with household and personal goods. The former consisted of furnishings, such as bedding, linens, a bed, covered benches, and stools; the latter included dresses and jewelry, called *malahereda* or matronly ornaments. Archaeological findings demonstrate that Merovingian women of the upper classes wore expensive jewelry—earrings, pins, necklaces, rings, amulets, bracelets, belts, and clasps. Their attire was also lavish, including several elaborate layers of shifts, tunics, girdles, gowns, and capes, embroidered and trimmed in gold.[112] The trousseau of an aristocratic woman represented a considerable fortune. The jewelry that the Visigothic princess Galswinth brought to her marriage was so splendid that her husband Chilperic is said to have murdered her rather than let her reclaim it after their divorce.[113]

Without this paraphernalia, even a royal princess could not expect to get a husband. When Clovis married Clotild, he requested treasures from her uncle.[114] Plundered of her belongings when she was on her way to marry a Visigothic prince, Chilperic's daughter Rigunth had no other choice than to return home.[115] On the lower levels of society, the household goods that a bride brought into marriage were essential items and were considered valuable assets. For example, the Salic Pact specified that, if a widow wished to remarry, she not only had to pay release money to her dead husband's relatives but also had to leave behind some of her furniture.[116]

A bride's trousseau has been characterized by some historians as the daughter's share of her family's patrimony. The Salic Pact described it as comparable to the gifts that a son received upon his initiation into manhood.[117] Since none of the codes specified what portion of a family's patrimony had to be set aside for a daughter's trousseau, we can assume that these gifts varied with the inclination of the parents. The rights of daughters who did not marry but vowed themselves to the service of God were better protected. Under Burgundian law they were entitled to the usufruct of a third of their fathers' patrimony, on the condition that after their death the property reverted to the nearest male relative.[118]

The codes also provided special protection for the economic well-being of women bereft of husbands. In particular, they looked after the interest of widows. A childless widow and, as we have already seen, a woman divorced through no fault of her own could assume full control of her *dos* and *morgengabe*.[119] As long as she did not remarry, a widow could also claim as her dower the lifelong enjoyment of a portion, usually one-third, of her husband's land.[120] As women gained the right to hold and inherit land, the claim of a dower came to be restricted to those who had not obtained land from either their parents or their husbands.[121] Even then, a widow was entitled to a share of a joint conjugal property, estates that her husband acquired by means other than inheritance during their marriage. For example, Fredegar informed us that the dowager Queen Nanthild requested a third of all property that Dagobert had conquered while they were married.[122] Invoking the same law, widows of churchmen retained, as their rightful share of common assets, donations given to the church by their husbands' parishioners.[123]

The laws regulated only intestate succession. By testamentary bequest a man could settle property on his female relatives, even when the laws did not grant them rights as residual heirs. There are not enough deeds extant from either the sixth or seventh century to attempt a statistical calculation of how many men bypassed the laws through wills and bequests. But it is evident that some did. For example, Burgundofara, who lived under Frankish law and had a brother, disposed of land she had inherited from her father in a testament dated 632.[124] Marculf included a will in his compilation in which a father protested against the unjust and inappropriate discrimination of inheritance laws:

> For a long time an ungodly custom has been observed among us that forbids sisters to share with their brothers the paternal land. I reject this impious law: God gave all of you to me as my children and I have loved you all equally, therefore you will all equally rejoice in my goods after my death. Against the exclusive claim of your brothers, my own sons, with this letter I make you, my beloved daughter, an equal and legitimate heir in all my patrimony . . . so that you will not receive in anything a lesser portion than they.[125]

The *formulae* also attest that husbands provided generously for their wives.[126]

Through the bridegift, morning gift, dower, trousseau, inheritance, wills, and bequests, a woman could accumulate much land and treasure.

As a widow, particularly if she had no living sons, she could exercise considerable power in transmitting and alienating praedial and other kinds of property. For example, after the death of her husband and son, Ermentrud, a Frankish noble woman (*illustris matrona*), held an immense fortune in both movable and immovable goods. Her property included landed estates with dependent peasants, carriages drawn by oxen, horses, furniture, jewelry, and clothing. Around 700, in a will, she bequeathed most of her possessions to her grandson, and divided the rest among her granddaughter, daughter-in-law, and various monasteries and churches in the neighborhood of Paris, where she lived and her properties were located.[127]

Women of lesser status, as other wills and deeds demonstrate, were equally determined to dispose of their property according to their own wishes and preferences.[128] Records of litigations, moreover, show that some widows were resolute even in asserting property rights at the expense of their own children. For example, Gregory of Tours reported that after the death of Bertram, Bishop of Bordeaux, a dispute arose between his mother and sister. Bertram's mother claimed that she was her son's legal heir; Bertram's sister demanded a share on the ground that the property originally belonged to their father. A court decision allotted Bertram's sister a quarter portion, awarding the rest to his mother and the son of his brother who had predeceased him.[129]

A widow's freedom to exercise economic power in the male-dominated Merovingian society was surprisingly extensive, precluding simplistic conclusions about the position of women in that society. Although the laws treated women as less autonomous creatures than men, they defended women's interests.

Attempting to weaken the power of the kin, Merovingian kings granted Germanic women private rights comparable to those enjoyed by the more emancipated Gallo-Roman women. An improvement in the status of women was also reflected in codifications of Roman law. Liberated from the complex tutorial system, women of Gallo-Roman descent gained recognition as independent persons after the deaths of their husbands. In the relationship between the sexes, Germanic and Roman double standards served to reinforce one another. Whether a Merovingian woman was of Roman or Germanic descent, her sexual freedom, as well as her right to choose her own mate and divorce her husband, were severely curtailed. On the other hand, Germanic laws ceased to treat women as mere objects of sale and capture, eased the incapacity of women to own and inherit land, and ensured the economic independence of women bereft of husbands. Under Roman law, women continued to enjoy equal inheritance rights with their brothers, although they could no longer contract a *sine manu* marriage, which would have enabled them to exclude their husbands from the management of their property.

An important element in the improvement of women's status was the flexible nature of Merovingian matrimony. Marriage brought women the chance not only to escape from parental control but also to improve their own social status. Lower class women, former slaves and concubines, could now marry members of the ruling elite. Upper class women, on the other hand, could derive power from alliances with influential families.

The opportunities for Merovingian women to overcome social barriers through marriage and exercise economic independence as widows were unprecedented in antiquity. Those who made the most of these opportunities had greater power than women in either the early Germanic tribes or the late Roman Empire.

3

Wives and Mothers in Merovingian Society

Social mobility was much greater in the Frankish Kingdom than it had been under the late Roman Empire.[1] By rewarding his Frankish subjects with land, Clovis created a new Frankish aristocracy that soon adopted the life style of the Gallo-Roman provincial landowners. Other Germanic tribes conquered by the Franks followed the same pattern, developing social distinctions and dividing labor more along class lines than according to sex. Merovingian society came to resemble the late Gallo-Roman one in many ways, but it remained more open and flexible. Though hierarchically organized, the new society was not rigidly stratified: the Franks did not practice either social or racial discrimination. It was possible to rise in the social hierarchy through royal or ecclesiastical service, or through marriage across ethnic and class lines.

The contribution of Merovingian women to the transformation of their society, their role in horizontal and vertical social dynamics, and their influence in families through social bonding and other means is the subject of this chapter. Marriage patterns in the propertied families, beginning with the royalty and the aristocracy, families whose members were known as *optimates* and *primi,* and including also less exalted people referred to as *mediani,* will first be reviewed.[2] How wives in the landowning aristocracy created interfamilial alliances, how they advanced the status of their own kin, and how they developed relationships with their children will also be explored. An analysis of the marriages and work roles of women married to slaves and to semifree, freed, and free peasants concludes the chapter.

MARRIAGE PATTERNS

The composition of the Merovingian aristocracy has engaged scholarly attention since the 1940s. Approaching the subject from a male perspective, historians did not investigate how women operated within the aristocracy. In the controversy that arose over the question of nobility of race versus nobility of service *(Uradel* versus *Dienstadel),* which has been summarized by Leopold Génicot,[3] marriage patterns were neglected.

Although the debate has not altogether subsided, the prevailing view today is that, in the sixth century, the Gallo-Roman aristocracy retained control over the royal and ecclesiastical administration. It was replaced toward the end of the century by a Franco-Roman court nobility, which in turn was supplanted, beginning in the mid-seventh century, by provincial aristocracies centering around ducal families. One hundred years later, the Pepinids, whose holdings were in the northeast, around the city of Metz, defeated the other territorial princes and overthrew the Merovingian dynasty.[4] In recent years, systematic studies on land ownership, together with painstaking research in prosopography, genealogy, and place names, have yielded dramatic evidence that bilateral kin relations constituted the very core of the Merovingian power structure and that the eclipse of one dominant group by another was accomplished mainly through marriage alliances.[5]

The role of women in marriage alliances is one of the most intractable of historical topics. Merovingian sources rarely identify by name the wives and daughters of great men. A further obstacle is the lack of information about the relative dates of marriages of daughters and sons in a family. Hence, there is no way of knowing whether a woman's prestigious marriage paved the way for the advantageous union of her brother, or her matrimony was facilitated by the position of her brother's wife. Enough is known, nevertheless, to indicate that brothers and sisters tended to marry into the same circle. Moreover, women were not mere pawns in these interfamilial alliances, but played an active part in promoting the interests of their own kin, instilling in their children loyalty to the maternal side.

As is suggested by archaeological evidence, Germanic men were eager to marry Gallo-Roman women, who converted their husbands to Christianity and thus came to dominate the newcomers, according to Edouard Salin.[6] Other historians have remarked that judicious intermarriages with influential Gallo-Romans secured for the Frankish nobility ascendance in the royal administration and the church in the late sixth century.[7] For example, the sister of Bodegisil, a royal official in Germany, married Mummolinus, Count of Soissons. She named their son not after her husband, as was customary, but after her brother. Bodegisil married a Roman woman, Palatina, the daughter of Gallimacus, the referendary of King Childebert I (511–558). Through his sister and wife Bodegisil gained sufficient influence to be appointed governor of Marseilles.[8]

The power and preeminence of Neustria in the seventh century was the result of a network of alliances that the Frankish nobility in that region concluded with the leading families of Burgundy and the descendants of the late Roman senatorial order in Aquitaine. The basis for these alliances, as Rudolf Sprandel has demonstrated, was marriage. Straddling two powerful kin groups, women could exercise influence in a number of informal ways. They could mobilize their own blood relations on behalf of their husbands' and sons' political ambitions and use their husbands' influence to promote the interest of their own kin. Proud of its mixed lineage, the new aristocracy did not fail to appreciate the bonding role of its women. For example, Bertram, bishop of Le Mans between 586 and 626, an influential man in the Neustrian court, identified his mother as Aquitanian and his father as Frankish in his testament. He mentioned that one of his close female relatives (*parens proxima*) married Avitus, a member of the powerful Gallo-Roman aristocracy of Le Mans. Another member of Bertram's kin, Warnachar, also maintained close ties with the Gallo-Roman aristocracy. Appointed mayor of the palace in Burgundy in 613, Warnachar married a Burgundian woman called Bertha. By another woman he had a son to whom he gave the Roman name Godinus.[9]

Royal connections on the female side explain the family's success in obtaining prominent offices and concluding advantageous unions. Eugen Ewig has identified Bertram of Le Mans as the deacon Waldo-Bertram, whose maternal relatives—his uncle Bishop Bertram of Bordeaux, mother Bertegund, and grandmother Ingitrud—are well known from Gregory of Tours. King Gunthram, according to Gregory, acknowledged Bertegund as "parens nostra" and referred to Bertram of Bordeaux as "parens . . . ex matre nostra."[10] Gunthram's mother, Ingund, as Ewig has so convincingly argued, was Bertegund's and Bertram of Bordeaux's maternal aunt, the sister of their mother Ingitrud.[11]

Another influential family of the late sixth century with Frankish and Gallo-Roman connections was that of Desiderius. Treasurer of Neustria, Desiderius was of Gallo-Roman lineage on his father's side and Frankish on his mother's side. One of his paternal ancestors, Syagrius, had led the Roman resistance against the Franks in 486. A century later, in 585, Desiderius' brother, Count Syagrius, was sent by King Gunthram on a diplomatic mission to Constantinople and served as a judge under Clothar II. Syagrius' marriage to Bertilia (Bertolena), a lady of Germanic descent, suggests that his mother may have been instrumental in selecting his wife.[12] The family's landed wealth, accumulated and retained through carefully planned marriages, was so enormous that in 739, one of the descendants, the lady Syagria, was able to give to the monks of Novalesca "lands scattered from the region of Mâcon to that of the Gap."[13]

An aristocratic group could maintain political leadership only as

long as it had a number of compliant daughters and sons of marriageable age. During the second half of the seventh century, women in
Neustrian-Burgundian families concentrated on the creation of a network of monasteries rather than on the conclusion of politically advantageous unions, while families whose holdings were in the northeastern
parts of the kingdom, centering around the city of Metz, were more
concerned with the acquisition of power through carefully arranged
marriages.

When Begga, the daughter of the Austrasian mayor Pepin the
Elder (d. 640), married Ansegisel, the son of Arnulf of Metz, the ascendancy of the northeastern region over other parts of the kingdom was
assured. This matrimonial alliance prepared the way for the replace-
ment of the Merovingian ruling house by the Carolingian dynasty. The
circumstances leading to this alliance are well known to historians.
Almost as important was the union of Begga's and Ansegisel's son,
Pepin the Middle (d. 714), and Plektrud, which has been analyzed by
E. Hlawitschka.[14] With the politically powerful seneschal Hugobert as
her father and the heiress Irmina as her mother, Plektrud was a coveted
bride. Because she had only sisters and no brothers, she inherited vast
domains in the country between the Rhine, the Moselle, and the Meuse,
and these became the basis for her husband's political maneuvers. Her
two sons further enhanced Pepin's power by marrying women with
political connections in the north and northwest. Drogo took as his wife
Anstrud, the widow of the Neustrian mayor of the palace; Grimoald
married Theudesind, the daughter of the Frisian chieftain. It was
through the help of Drogo's mother-in-law Ansfled (Anseflidis) that
Pepin was able to secure his hold over Neustria.[15]

The fragmentary evidence in narrative and documentary sources
indicates that, in the upper echelons of society, women were active in
arranging matrimonial alliances. The personal feeling of a woman was
of little consequence, and she was expected to subordinate it to her
family's interest. A good illustration is the second union of Anstrud, the
daughter of Waratto and Ansfled. When her first husband, the Neustrian Mayor Berthar (Bercharius) was murdered after a defeat by Pepin,
she married Pepin's son, Drogo.

The more highly placed her family, the more attention a marriageable daughter commanded. The church might have lost a saint, and the
Carolingians might have gained political ascendancy sooner, had Pepin
the Elder lived long enough to prevail upon his second daughter, Gertrud, to marry the son of an Austrasian duke. After Pepin's unexpected
death, his widow, Itta, acceded to Gertrud's wishes and built for her the
abbey of Nivelles.[16] Gregory of Tours reports that when Clovis I's niece,

an Ostrogothic princess, eloped with one of her slaves, her mother sent
an army to chastise her and restore the family honor. Such scandalous
conduct was usually punished with the loss of the woman's life or of her
freedom and property. In this case, only the slave was killed. A princess
was so valuable a commodity on the marriage market that, her escapade
notwithstanding, Clovis's niece was later married to a suitable
husband.[17]

Merovingian princesses normally married the sons of kings. The
aim of these dynastic alliances was to secure good relations with the
neighboring kingdoms. Clovis I had set the example by marrying his
sister Audofled to Theodoric, king of the Ostrogoths, in 494 and his
daughter Clotild to Amalric of Spain in 526. Although marriages with
the Visigothic royal house were most frequent, Merovingian princesses
were given in marriage also to Lombard, Anglo-Saxon, and Waringian
kings.[18]

Daughters of influential families, even if they were not of royal
blood, expected to marry men of equal status, but there were always
men who tried to improve their own station by marrying women of
higher nobility and wealth. Marriages between partners of unequal status were frowned upon at best in Gallo-Roman circles. Caesarius of
Arles denounced the upward marriages of men as particularly odious
and opportunistic.[19] The Franks did not make a moral issue of marriages across class lines, but normally it was the wife, not the husband,
who was of a lower rank. Gregory of Tours found the reverse situation
sufficiently unusual to remark that Tetradia's father was of low descent
and her mother of noble blood.[20] The severe legal penalties imposed
upon abductors or the fears of vengeance by the girl's family must have
deterred many ambitious men from forcing their way into the aristocracy through marriage.[21] On the other hand, Merovingian kings were
quite ready to grant their favorite servants permission to abduct girls
from wealthy families. Resistance to these unions led Merovingian kings
to promise repeatedly that they would not continue to sanction this
practice. Ecclesiastical legislation encouraged a woman who feared abduction by a man of inferior status to take refuge in a church until either
her relatives through princely intervention or priests through ecclesiastical intercession freed, defended, and married her to a suitable
husband.[22]

Not all of the great families were involved in the ruthless pursuit
of marriage strategies. Some parents were so worried about the celibacy
or dissolute life of their sons that they were happy to see them settle with
a bride of modest background. Saint Patroclus' widowed mother merely
stipulated that she wanted him to marry a beautiful girl of free status.[23]

Lifting earlier restrictions when he codified Roman law, Alaric permitted a man of senatorial rank to marry below his station, as long as the woman was respectable and had reputable parents.[24] We also know from Gregory of Tours that Tetradia's lack of illustrious descent on her father's side did not prevent her from marrying first a count and then a duke.[25]

A union in which the woman was of a lower birth than the man was normally concluded as a *quasi conjugium (Friedelehe)* and often represented the man's second or third attempt at marriage. By marrying downward, a man assured his dominance over the woman and escaped the obligation for her bridegift, which could be a substantial piece of property. Balthild's biographer may have invented the episode of her hiding under foul rags in a dark corner in order to escape the attention of her master, Erchinoald, as a chastity motif obligatory in the life of a female saint. But if marriages between older, established men of the aristocracy and younger women of lower birth had been as unusual as some modern historians contend, the biographer would have attributed dishonorable intentions to Erchinoald instead of stating that the mayor of the palace had proposed not concubinage but marriage to the saint.[26]

It is well known that the practice of marrying women of humble background became prevalent in the royal family in the middle of the sixth century.[27] Clovis I and his sons had concluded matrimony only with the daughters and widows of princes and magnates, and the first to make a woman of low birth his queen was Charibert I of Paris (561–567). Enamored of two sisters, Merofled and Marcoveifa (maidservants of Queen Ingoberga), Charibert was not receptive to Ingoberga's insistence that the girls did not merit his attention because they were the daughters of a weaver. Leaving Ingoberga, the king married Merofled. Not satisfied with only one wife, he also married Theudegild, the daughter of a shepherd, and finally married Marcoveifa as well.[28] Charibert's younger brother, Gunthram (561–592), king of Burgundy, also became disillusioned with his high-born wife. Jealous of Gunthram's son by a concubine, Marcatrud had the child poisoned. The queen's role in this sordid affair did not escape Gunthram's attention. When Marcatrud's own son died, Gunthram repudiated her and married his slave concubine, Austrechild, in 566.[29] A third brother, Chilperic I, ruler of Neustria (560/61–584), may also have raised a former slave to the throne when, following his unsuccessful marital venture with Galswinth, he married Fredegund in 567. The *Liber historiae francorum,* an eighth-century chronicle, traced Fredegund's origin to the "familia infima" of Chilperic's first queen, Audovera. That this was not a later invention is attested by the remark Gregory of Tours attributed to Fredegund's daughter. During a violent mother-daughter argument, Rigunth blurted out that Fredegund's proper place was among the servants of her children.[30]

In the seventh century, at least four queens are known to have begun their careers as slaves. Bilichild and Theudechild, wives of Theudebert II of Austrasia (595–612), ascended the throne from the position of royal concubines. Nanthild, a striking beauty, appears to have risen directly from her lowly origin of royal slave to the exalted status of Dagobert I's (623–639) queen. Her daughter-in-law, Balthild, wife of Clovis II (639–657), characterized by her biographer as "beautiful, clever and of strong character," was so attractive that suitors overlooked her servile origin. As queen, Balthild did not forget her own humble background and took an active interest in improving the condition of slaves. She prohibited the sale of Christian slaves and personally purchased the freedom of many slaves.[31]

As long as marriages could be easily dissolved and no legal barriers stood in the way of lower-class women marrying upper-class men, women could use their beauty, seductiveness, and social and political skills to improve their own status and that of their kin. The marriage of lower-class women to upper-class men broadened the base of the Merovingian aristocracy. As we will see later in this chapter, not only the woman but also her relatives gained prominence through such a union. But this system had disadvantages; it encouraged male arrogance, reinforced double standards in marriage, and led to rivalry among women. Competition for the favor of a king was particularly fierce. The intrigues spun and the murders committed by women striving for a king's attention are perhaps best illustrated by the story of Deoteria, the wife of Theudebert I. Afraid that the king would fall in love with her daughter from a previous marriage, Deoteria sent her daughter headlong over a bridge in a litter harnessed with wild oxen.[32]

Replacing aging wives by younger, more attractive women was by no means a universal rule. Narrative sources, donations, and wills attest to the existence of conjugal love in Merovingian times.[33] It was not unusual for a husband and wife to be buried together.[34] Even when this was not the case, tombstone inscriptions afford an insight into the close personal ties that existed between husband and wife. For example, the seventh-century tombstone of a noble Frankish lady, which was found in Kempten (near Bingen), identified her not only as the daughter of the "illustrious patron Mactichild," beloved by the people for her beneficence, but also as the wife of Ebregisil.[35]

WOMEN IN THE ARISTOCRACY

A wife could balance her dependence on her husband's favor by maintaining close relations with her own kin and children and building alliances with churchmen. Regardless of whether or not a woman married
a man whose status was equal to or higher than her own, she did not
forget her own relatives. By the end of the sixth century, the church had
managed to enforce its incest legislation, which prohibited the marriage
of one man to two sisters. Even though a queen could no longer follow
the example of Ingund (the wife of Clothar I), who selflessly accepted
her sister as a co-wife, she had other means to ensure the social ascent
of a sister. For example, Sigihild, the third wife of Clothar II (584–629),
arranged the marriage of her sister Gomatrud with a stepson, the future
Dagobert I. She also obtained influential posts for her brother Brunulf
and charged him with the education of her own son.[36] Brothers were
also apt to take wives from the circle into which their sisters had married.
When the daughter of the duke of Bavaria, Theudolinda, married a
Lombard prince, her brother Gundobald followed her to Italy. After
marrying a Lombard lady, he was entrusted with the Duchy of Asti.[37]

It was in the interest of a married woman to secure power for her
own kin. By improving the status of her brothers and sisters and further-
ing their careers, she not only strenghtened bonds of natural affection
but also enhanced her own position. The more influential a woman's
relatives were, the more effective was their assistance when she asked
for their help. Related to the Frankish royal house through her maternal
grandfather, the Lombard queen Gundoberga was freed from imprison-
ment through the intervention of her Frankish cousins.[38] Bertegund
turned to her brother Bertram, Bishop of Bordeaux, when her efforts
to join her mother's religious community at Tours were thwarted by her
husband.[39] Economic conflicts, often pitting brother against brother in
this violent age, did not shatter the sense of family on the female side;
a man usually maintained good relations with his sister. For example,
Clovis I was so deeply affected by the death of his sister Audofled that
Remy, Bishop of Reims, had to remind him that it was not proper for
a king to show intense grief in public.[40]

The sense of kinship was very strong among cognates; it was a
question of honor to defend the interest of one's female relatives. King
Childebert I (511–558) felt obliged to rescue his sister Clotild from her
Visigoth husband, Amalric, who "beat her so cruelly that she sent her
brother a kerchief soaked with her own blood."[41] Such incidents could
lead to wars between kingdoms and to vendettas between noble families. Gregory of Tours reports that a Frank of Tournai rebuked his

sister's husband for abusing her and neglecting her for other women. When the brother-in-law failed to mend his ways, the angry young man killed him.[42] The tender concern that Brunhild and Childebert II (575–595) showed for Athanagild, the orphaned son of Ingund (Brunhild's daughter and Childebert's sister), suggests that families felt responsible not only for the well-being and honor of daughters and sisters but also for their children.[43]

In her husband's family a woman could gain security and exercise a modicum of power through her children, but a barren wife had little chance of retaining her position. Gomatrud's repudiation by Dagobert I (623–639) was justified on the ground of sterility by an eighth-century chronicler.[44] Because the rate of infant mortality was high, a woman had to bear several children for some to survive into adulthood. The loss of children had a profound effect on the mother, as the story of Queen Fredegund burning the tax books when her infant sons were dying from an epidemic attests.[45] It was not unusual for a man to blame the death of a child on his wife and make a fresh start with another woman. Queen Marctrud's repudiation after the death of her son has already been mentioned.[46] Saint Monegund's husband raised no objection when she decided to become a recluse after the death of their two daughters.[47]

A great deal has been written in recent years about infanticide and child abuse in antiquity and the Middle Ages.[48] Indeed, even the sale of children was not uncommon in the Merovingian kingdom. In aristocratic families, however, only children born with birth defects were treated in this manner, and there is some evidence to indicate that even in these cases a mother tended to protect her offspring. Gregory of Tours relates the story of a woman who gave birth to a deformed child, a misfortune she attributed to the fact that she had conceived the child on a Sunday when married couples were expected to observe continence, according to Christian teaching. To erase the memory of her sin, she sold the infant, although less scrupulous parents might have killed the child.[49] The father of Saint Odilia interpreted her blindness as a punishment for his own sins and ordered her to be killed. She was saved, however, by her mother, who had placed her in the care of a trusted maidservant.[50]

The moral and religious upbringing of children was considered the province of mothers. Although it was not unusual for sons to be taken at an early age from their mother's side and used as hostages, or to be entrusted to a great man's care,[51] mothers and even grandmothers appear to have played an important role during the impressionable, formative years of Merovingian males.[52] In a poem, Auspicius described the father of Count Arbogast as a just, virtuous, and sober man, and

then showered lavish praises on his beloved mother for developing
Arbogast's character and instilling in him noble virtues.[53] Loyalty to the
uterine line was inculcated in aristocratic males in their early childhood,
and hence we should not be surprised to learn that Clotild asked her
sons, not her husband, to avenge the murder of her parents.[54]

Even after their sons were fully grown, mothers did not cease to
advise them, exhort them to virtue, and worry about their physical and
spiritual welfare. In the large, broadly based households of their married sons, widowed mothers were welcome and held an honored position. Widows often maintained particularly close relations with sons
who had entered the clergy, living with them and running their
households.[55] The strong bond of affection between a Merovingian
mother and her son is illustrated by the touching letter written by
Leodegar from prison. Tortured, mutilated, and expecting to be executed at any minute, he told his mother that he found comfort in the
knowledge that she was safe at Saint Mary of Soissons and was praying
for him. He urged her to regard the monastic community as her extended family and to regard the abbess as her mother, sister, and daughter.[56] The pathetic letter that Herchenfreda wrote to her son Desiderius
after the murder of her other son Rusticus demonstrates the importance
of sons in a mother's life:

> What shall I, an unfortunate mother, do now that I have lost your
> brothers? If you were also to die, I would have no children left! But
> you, my most pious son, my sweetest, you must constantly guard
> yourself against murder, for now that I have lost your brothers, I
> cannot lose you too![57]

While mothers in the aristocracy depended on their sons for emotional support and physical protection,[58] they tended to dominate their
daughters. The duty of a mother was to safeguard her daughter's sexual
purity and secure her future. Social conventions required mothers to
raise daughters to be obedient and disciplined, in full control of their
passions. Because tenderness and compassion were not compatible with
this training, vigilance and worry were the normal manifestations of
maternal feelings. For example, the biographer of Saint Gertrud mentions that, after the death of Pepin the Elder in 640, his widow Itta
pondered daily on what was to become of her and her daughter. Upon
the advice of Saint Amand, she complied with her daughter's request
and ordered the construction of a monastery where she and Gertrud
would retire. While Nivelles was being built, Itta tonsured Gertrud so
that "the violators of souls should not drag her daughter by force into

illicit pleasures of the world."[59] In 665, when Saint Balthild was forced to retire to Chelles, she took along with her a goddaughter, but even the protection provided by the convent did not relieve her anxiety about the fate of the child. When the little girl died unexpectedly, Balthild was overjoyed and thanked the Lord for not letting the child survive her.[60]

A mother's importance was acknowledged in law insofar as she had the right to assume the guardianship for her fatherless children. In the propertied classes, this meant that a widow could exercise considerable power by managing the estates of her minor children and arranging for their marriages. Queens seized the opportunity to act as regents, wielding political power in the name of their sons. On the lower levels of society, on the other hand, some widows relinquished the right to act as guardians and remarried, leaving their children with their dead husband's relatives.[61]

Ties with influential churchmen also had political benefits for Merovingian women. The very nature of a wifely role in an aristocratic family, with its attendant domestic and nurturing activities, gave a woman access to movable wealth—jewels, foodstuffs, articles of clothing, and medicaments—which could be used to cement alliances with bishops and monks. By distributing alms, building oratories, extending hospitality, and entrusting the education of her children to churchmen, a Merovingian woman gained not only assurance of supernatural help in her daily activities but also practical assistance if she were later divorced or widowed. Although her friends in the church could not ensure the happiness or permanence of her marriage, they could shield her from the brutality of her husband and ease her transition to widowhood or divorced status. The roles played by Saint Medard and Saint Germain in persuading Clothar I (511–561) to release Saint Radegund from her marital obligations are well known. But equally important was the generous settlement Clothar granted her, probably also at the behest of her influential friends. After Saint Medard had consecrated her a deaconess, Radegund lived in a villa near Poitiers, which Clothar had given her. Somewhat later, when Saint Germain persuaded Clothar not to reclaim her as his wife, Clothar ordered the construction of a monastery at Poitiers, where Radegund established a female community.[62] Undoubtedly, Saint Monegund also had excellent ecclesiastical connections. She retained, at the time of her divorce, her residence at Chartres, where, as a recluse, she lived for a while in the manner of an aristocratic woman. Attended only by a few maidservants, she cultivated her garden, raising medicinal herbs, and took care of the poor.[63] Noble widows also often transformed their dead husbands' property into a monastic community, gaining not only security for their old age but also the opportunity to provide patronage for their own kin, build a cemetery for relatives, and establish a family cult center. With the prayers of her congregation and the relics of her church, the foundress secured supernatural help for members of her family and gained the respect and cooperation of bishops and royal officials.

The careers of Ingitrud and Bertegund, the mother and sister, respectively, of Bertram of Bordeaux, were described by Gregory of Tours in sufficient detail to indicate the sources and limitations of a woman's power in Merovingian society.[64] Ingitrud was already a widow when she caught Gregory's attention. Her religious habit, service in the *atrium* of Saint Martin's basilica, wealth, and royal connections apparently were not sufficient to enable her to establish a convent at Tours: she had to befriend the local priests and bishop by offering them wine under the guise of performing a miracle. When we next hear of her, she has invited her daughter, Bertegund, to take charge of the female community that she had founded near the basilica. Determined to establish an institution that would enhance her family's influence, Ingitrud was unconcerned that Bertegund was a married woman with young children.

Ingitrud extended her invitation around 575 or 576. By this time, Bertegund was in her late thirties or early forties. Disillusioned with her husband, whom she had married without her parents' consent, she was ready to abandon him and her children. Only when her husband appealed to Gregory of Tours did Bertegund relent. Afraid to risk excommunication, she returned home with her husband, but neither mother nor daughter forgot the plan. Three or four years later, around 578 or 579, Ingitrud again sent for her daughter. This time, Bertegund arrived with numerous treasures, including her husband's valuables, and one of their sons. But Ingitrud's plan for a family monastery again collapsed. Fearing that she would be accused of being an accessory to theft if Bertegund remained at Tours, Ingitrud sent her on to Bordeaux, where Bertram served as bishop.

Bertram proved to be a formidable protector of his sister. Time and time again he refused to return her to her husband. When King Gunthram at last intervened and ordered Bertram to restore her to her legal husband, Bertram sent Bertegund to Tours, where she pretended to do penance at Saint Martin's in the habit of a nun. The ruse worked. After a last solemn encounter with Bertegund in the church, her husband accepted her wish to dissolve the union and disappeared from her life.

Had Bertram not died unexpectedly, Bertegund probably would have eventually joined her mother and taken over the convent's administration. Bertram's death, however, left Bertegund a rich woman. By testamentary bequest, Bertram turned over to her all his property.

Rather than sharing this wealth with her mother and putting it at the disposal of the monastery, Bertegund quarreled with Ingitrud. Blaming Ingitrud for the loss of her husband and children, Bertegund left Tours and moved to Poitiers. Ingitrud did not fail to retaliate. She had Bertram's testament stolen and took Bertegund to court, claiming a part of Bertram's property as her widow's dower. The mutual recrimination of mother and daughter, their battles in court, Ingitrud's determination to disinherit her daughter, Bertegund's contempt for legal judgments, and her final triumph when, after her mother's death, she stripped the convent of its furniture and emptied its storehouses were faithfully reported by Gregory of Tours. Of greater interest to us than the sordid end of the affair are the means the two women used to achieve their different ends. Ingitrud had a political vision. In order to establish a family cult center, she was determined to use her wealth, children, and influence, and was careful to retain amicable relations with churchmen. More selfish and materialistic, Bertegund sought only personal freedom and wealth. The help of her kin and the protection of the church enabled her to leave her husband, but when she gained economic independence, she had no further need for her kin and was ready to defy the church as well.

The power of queens, while far more extensive, was also contingent on the careful exploitation of personal ties. Whatever their origin, highborn or slave, women who married kings gained access to the male world of politics and power. They had their own residences and retainers.[65] With their husbands, they could participate in assemblies and issue donations and privileges. As royal consorts, they received secular and ecclesiastical officials; they could also influence episcopal elections and draw upon the treasury to build a network of personal loyalties.[66] Not every queen made use of these opportunities to wield political power. Those who did managed to retain their positions and to secure the throne for their sons or the regency for themselves if they were widows with minor sons. The sources of power exercised by queens have been studied by Janet Nelson through the careers of Brunhild and Balthild.[67] Both were ambitious and intelligent, but neither was a typical queen. Each exploited to the fullest the powers inherent in her position, though Brunhild concentrated on exercising influence through her sons and grandsons and Balthild, on ecclesiastical patronage. Other queens also made use of their prerogatives, but, unlike Brunhild and Balthild, they failed to develop new policies and institutions for the exercise of royal power.

The accomplishments of Brunhild and Balthild may best be understood through a comparison of their policies with those of Fredegund and Nanthild, also women of courage and acumen, who served as regents during the minority of their sons. Fredegund and Brunhild are well known through their intense rivalry, which dominated Merovingian politics in the second half of the sixth century. Married to half brothers, Fredegund to Chilperic I of Soissons (560/61–584) and Brunhild to Sigebert of Metz (560/61–575), the two women became irreconcilable enemies when Chilperic had his earlier wife Galswinth (Brunhild's sister) murdered in order to marry Fredegund.[68] Less notorious, the careers of Nanthild, the wife of Dagobert I (623–639), and of her daughter-in-law Balthild, the wife of Clovis II (639–657), provide perhaps even better insight into the nature and extent of female power in Merovingian times.

Even Fredegund, the most ruthless and manipulative of the four, could not rely entirely on sexual and other forms of seduction, but had to resort to ecclesiastical protection and kinship ties when Chilperic I died in 584, leaving her a widow with an infant son barely four months old. Fredegund's hold over Chilperic I, evident in Gregory of Tours's description of the king's order for the murder of Galswinth and his rejection of his sons from an earlier marriage to Audovera, should not be attributed solely to her ability to satisfy his sexual drives. From 566, when she first appeared in Chilperic's court, until his death in 584, she rendered him many political services. Her willingness to make arrangements through her own servants for assassinations, for example, for that of Sigebert, and for handling bribes, such as one that Gregory of Tours refused to accept, made her a political asset to the king.[69]

Equally daring, although politically less astute, was her later liaison with Landeric, the mayor of the palace in her husband's kingdom. If we are to believe the *Liber historiae francorum,* when Chilperic became suspicious, Fredegund had him murdered.[70] Although Gregory did not link her directly with this crime, he did mention that Sigebert's son attributed the murder to her. Gregory, moreover, took pains to describe Fredegund's actions following the murder of Chilperic; she took refuge in the Cathedral of Paris under the protection of Bishop Raynemod and sought the assistance of her brother-in-law, Gunthram. Her possession of a substantial part of the treasury, "which had been safely deposited for her within the city walls," undoubtedly helped her cause with the bishop, but it did not prevent Gunthram from entrusting the government of her infant son's kingdom to a group of Frankish nobles and sending her to the estate of Reuil, in the diocese of Rouen, where she was to reside as a dowager queen. Not one to be satisfied with the loss of her power, Fredegund repeatedly postponed the baptism of Clothar, which would have formalized the guardianship of Gunthram as Clothar's godfather. Gregory noted that Gunthram, disturbed by the delays, began to question if Clothar was his brother's child. To clear her own name and her son's title, Fredegund assembled three bishops and three hundred laymen of the highest birth; all took a solemn oath with her that the boy was lawfully begotten by Chilperic.[71] The overwhelming number of laymen at the *compurgatio* suggests that Landeric played a role in mobilizing the Frankish nobility.

With the treasure in her hand and the bishop of Paris and the nobility of the kingdom supporting her, Fredegund assumed the regency of her son. When Landeric fell in battle, she took command of the army, following the tradition of earlier barbarian queens. Carrying Clothar in her arms, she led the Neustrians to victory.[72] Even though she did not hesitate to seize an ax to kill troublemakers in the kingdom and personally administer poison to those who dared to criticize her, she preferred to delegate the murder of troublesome ecclesiastics to others. When it came to eliminating Praetextatus, a bishop who was Gunthram's protégé, she hired assassins and offered the help of her own physician to the dying bishop.[73] She finally came to terms with Gunthram in 591, accepting him as Clothar's godfather and protector.[74] Had she lived longer, Fredegund might have turned to charitable works, such as founding and endowing churches, but she died in 597, when she was probably not more than fifty years old, and was buried with great pomp at the basilica of Saint Vincent in Paris. She did not live long enough to have the satisfaction of witnessing the execution of Brunhild.[75]

Endowed with an equally indomitable will and qualities of intelligence and statesmanship as well, Brunhild ruled on and off for more than thirty years over Austrasia and Burgundy through her son, Childebert II (575–595), and grandsons, Theudebert II of Austrasia (595–612) and Theuderic II of Burgundy (595–613). As a young widow in her early twenties at the time of Sigebert's death, deprived of her treasures and banished to Rouen by Chilperic, Brunhild was quick to accept the marriage proposal of Merovech, Chilperic's son. Merovech's motive in marrying her and Brunhild's realization that she could more easily exercise power as regent for her son if Merovech were confined to a monastery have been analyzed in detail by Janet Nelson. Kurth's romantic picture of Brunhild as a woman deprived of her husband's companionship and leading a life of humiliation at the hands of the Austrasian nobility until 585 when her son Childebert attained majority is no longer tenable. It is evident that, by opening relations with Spain, Brunhild was already emerging as a key figure in Austrasian politics during her son's minority.[76]

The foreign relations Brunhild developed with Spain and Byzantium were, in fact, as Janet Nelson aptly characterized them, "extensions of family relations," cemented through the marriage of her daughter Ingund with the Visigothic prince Hermengild, and through Brunhild's concern for the fate of Ingund's son Athanagild, who was placed in the hands of Byzantine imperial agents after the death of Hermengild and Ingund.[77] Brunhild's friendship with Pope Gregory I may also be regarded as an extension of the ties she cultivated with influential Frankish and Burgundian churchmen.[78] Nor did Brunhild neglect to build alliances with her in-laws. The Treaty of Andelot, concluded with Gunthram in 587, procured for Childebert the kingdom of Burgundy.[79]

Brunhild understood only too well that she could shape royal policy only as long as she retained a dominant position in the royal court. Rather than yield her position to a younger woman, she broke the engagement of her son Childebert II to the Bavarian princess Theudolinda and intrigued to terminate the matrimony of her grandson Theuderic II of Burgundy to the Visigothic princess Ermenberta.[80] But she accepted, perhaps even arranged, Childebert's marriage to his ex-mistress Faileuba, a self-effacing woman. The only action of Queen Faileuba that Gregory of Tours recorded (her discovery of a plot to replace her with another wife and drive her mother-in-law, the dowager queen Brunhild, from the court) suggests that she was Brunhild's protégé.[81]

The insults Brunhild received from Bilichild, her former slave whom her grandson Theudebert II of Austrasia married after the division of Childebert's kingdom and the expulsion of Brunhild from Austrasia in 599,[82] only strengthened the dowager queen's resolve to prevent the marriage of her other grandson, Theuderic II. Her fixation on this issue and her attempts to revenge the humiliation she had suffered in Theudebert's kingdom led to her eventual downfall. With the help of Protadius, her purported lover, whom she had managed to have nominated mayor of Burgundy in 606, Brunhild almost succeeded in carrying out her plans, but the mayor was assassinated by a faction of the nobility opposed to the war against Austrasia. Although Brunhild prevailed and punished the conspirators, her subsequent role in the Ermenberta affair and her banishment of Desiderius, the bishop of Vienne, who dared to criticize her policy of surrounding the young king with concubines, did not enhance her popularity. Fredegar blamed her and Aridius of Lyons for the stoning of Desiderius.[83] Whatever Brunhild's role in that tragic affair may have been, her subsequent quarrel with Saint Columban reinforced her reputation as a vengeful and troublesome woman. When he revisited the court in 611, Columban refused to bless Theuderic's children on the ground that they were the offspring of prostitutes. Outraged, Brunhild chased the saint from the court and the kingdom.[84] After the sudden death of Theuderic in 613, Brunhild found herself without a friend and supporter. Betrayed by the mayor of the palace, Warnachar, Brunhild had no alternative but to come to terms with Clothar II of Neustria in another attempt to secure the regency for herself during the minority of her great-grandsons. But Fredegund's son was not inclined to mercy. He subjected the old queen to a cruel and humiliating death. Tortured and paraded before the army as an abject criminal, then tied to the feet of horses, Brunhild's body was torn limb from limb and, in a final act of contempt, thrown into the fire.[85]

By the seventh century, when Nanthild and Balthild assumed the regency for their sons, the mayors of the palace, the court nobility, and the territorial aristocracy had gained ascendancy over the kings. For a queen to exercise power, therefore, it was even more essential than earlier to have the support of influential friends and relatives. Nanthild was married to Dagobert I (623–639), who had managed to reunite all of Frankland under his personal rule. The second of his four wives, Nanthild had the advantage of being Dagobert's only queen to bear him a son, Clovis. (Dagobert had another son, Sigebert, by a concubine.) Politically astute, Nanthild managed to retain her title, founding Hasnon jointly with Dagobert in 633. On his deathbed, in 639, Dagobert placed her under the protection of Aega, mayor of the palace.[86]

Complying with Aega's wishes, Nanthild kept only one-third of the royal treasury for herself and divided the rest between her son Clovis II, who was to rule Neustria, and Sigebert II, who succeeded his father in Austrasia. When Aega died in 641, Nanthild appointed Erchinoald, a relative of Dagobert's mother, as his successor. The following year, she arranged the marriage of her own niece, Ragnoberta, with the mayor of the palace in Burgundy, Flachoald, thereby gaining the allegiance of Burgundy for Clovis II and weakening the influence of Sigebert in that region. Nanthild's political career, based on her ability to create a network of family alliances, came to an abrupt end with her untimely death in 642.[87]

Balthild, the wife of Clovis II (639–657), commanded the allegiance not only of secular officials but also of bishops and abbots. Perhaps to compensate for his own debauchery, which included, according to a chronicler, fornication, violation of women, drunkenness, and gluttony, Clovis II assigned Genesius as almoner to his wife. The saintly abbot served not only as Balthild's spiritual adviser but also as her political mentor, developing alliances for her within the circle of the court nobility and the Frankish bishops. When Clovis died in 657, she had two of the most influential churchmen in Neustria, Chrodobert of Paris and Audoen of Rouen, supporting her regency for her eldest son, Clothar III (657–683).[88] When Erchinoald, her former master and mayor of the palace, died in the following year, Balthild replaced him with Ebroin, a *miles palatinus*, a young man trained in the court.[89]

Balthild's role in the marriage of her younger son, Childeric, to Bilichild, the heiress of Austrasia, in 662, as well as her contribution to the unification of Neustria and Burgundy, are subjects of historical controversy.[90] There can be no doubt, however, that her friendship with Waldebert of Luxeuil, a member of the Austrasian nobility who headed the famous monastery in Burgundy, paved the way for the election of Childeric II (662–675) to the throne of Austrasia. Moreover, her ties with Theudefrid of Corbie and Filibert of Jumièges, abbots with important connections in Burgundy, must have helped her to arrange the concord of peace that was observed among the three kingdoms during her regency.[91]

Balthild gained the friendship of influential churchmen through her activities as a reformer. She worked for the abolition of simony, the adoption of rules in monasteries, the redemption of slaves, the prohibition of the enslavement of Christians, and the punishment of infanticide. She founded Chelles and Corbie and generously endowed other monasteries and basilicas.[92] Eugen Ewig has assessed these activities as creating cult centers for the Merovingian dynasty and a new economic basis for the monarchy by redistributing resources between the bishoprics and monasteries.[93]

The emphasis on Balthild's political skills has resulted in difficulties for historians seeking to interpret her downfall in 664 or 665. The events leading to her forced retirement to Chelles are better understood if we remember that she was not only a queen but also a saint, unwilling to compromise her principles for the sake of political expediency. Her *Vita*, written by a member of Chelles shortly after her death, attributed her downfall to her opposition to the murder of Sigobrand, bishop of Paris. Because the exemptions Balthild granted to monasteries and basilicas deprived bishops of administrative and economic power, historians have suggested that the hagiographer's reference to Sigobrand's "superbia" meant that the bishop had attacked Balthild's *Klosterpolitik*. But why, then, would Balthild try to protect Sigobrand?[94]

If one takes seriously the hagiographer's emphasis on Balthild's dedication to the enforcement of peace, the whole affair appears in a different light. As regent, Balthild ordered executions, but only after due process of law. She would not condone arbitrary killings, especially not after Aunemodus of Lyons, whose safety she had guaranteed to Waldebert of Luxeuil, had met martyrdom while on his way to stand trial in her court. In 664 she was determined to prevent a similar incident. Perhaps she was emboldened by the fact that Clothar III was soon to reach majority, when he could dispense with the magnates' tutelage. But Balthild underestimated the magnates' strength. A powerful faction of the court nobility not only deprived her of the regency, but also prevented her from goading the king to bring charges against the assassins by "permitting" her withdrawal to Chelles.

Although the personalities and aims of Fredegund, Brunhild, Nanthild, and Balthild differed, their power as regents rested on their ability to develop and exploit ties of affection and association. The control they exercised over the royal household and treasury as well as the key position they occupied in the royal family gave them more than ample opportunity to develop a network of patronage and to shape events in their kingdoms. Their influence, however, was only an extension of the influence they exerted as queens. As long as regency and the position of queen were not institutionalized, women of talent and vision, like Brunhild and Balthild, could take the initiative to develop new policies and instruments of government. But because they were women, their power, even as regents, depended on their success at manipulating others and reaching compromises.

Neither secular nor ecclesiastical laws defined or delimited the powers of kings, queens, regents, or royal officials. But it was understood that kings, counts, and dukes would resort to military action to make their will prevail, while queens, even as regents, normally would not. Ursio, one of the leaders of the Austrasian magnates under Brunhild's regency for Childebert, suffered no harm when he rebuked Brunhild for her attempt to stop his army from marching against Lupus, the duke of Champagne, his private enemy. When Brunhild threw herself before his soldiers, Ursio said:

> Stand back from us, O woman: let it suffice thee to have borne sway under thy consort. But now thy kingdom is thy son's and it is upheld not by thy protection but by ours. Stand therefore back from us, lest our horses' hoofs trample thee.[95]

Although her position was precarious, Brunhild disputed with Ursio for some time, finally persuading him to desist from open war with Lupus.

Brunhild's ability to cement international alliances and Balthild's establishment of royal monasteries could not alter the fact that the regency was not a right but a temporary privilege, conferred at the magnates' pleasure, to be shared with royal relatives and royal officials. Concentrating her energies on the prevention of the marriage of her grandson, the aging Brunhild made the fatal mistake of not maintaining at least the pretense of trying to accommodate churchmen. Thus, when Theudebert II died, she did not command sufficient loyalty either to assume the regency for her great-grandsons or to protect herself against the fury of Fredegund's son. Similarly, when Balthild overstepped the traditional female role of accommodation, the magnates turned against her and ensured that she would not exert influence over her son.

WOMEN IN THE PEASANTRY

Greater equality between the sexes prevailed in the lower echelons of society. Sex roles were less clearly defined, and women, regarded as helpmates rather than dependants, probably enjoyed greater freedom in the choice of a husband. On the other hand, economic considerations undoubtedly limited their choices. Whether married or not, peasant women made important contributions to the economy by spinning, dyeing, weaving, tending the garden, raising livestock, and even cultivating land. Members of a peasant family—men, women, and children —had to work as a team to provide the bare necessities of life and to meet the obligations to their lord. The early medieval manor was a communal agricultural regime where work was shared by men and women. David Herlihy has demonstrated that the labor of women was highly valued both by the lord, in whose household slave women were the favorite domestic servants, and by the peasants themselves, who made every effort to prevent married daughters from leaving the village.[96] Merovingian women of the lower classes apparently were not only good workers but also enterprising in supporting themselves and lending support to their families. Certainly the poor widow who, according to the biographer of Saint Amantius, sold wine near the church at Tours was not an exception in supplementing her meager income through commerce.[97]

Whatever their status, women commanded a *wergeld* twice that for men of the same social class. Only the life of a female slave was not valued higher than that of a male slave, and this rule might have been restricted to the Alemans.[98] As in the case of noble women, the chastity of lesser women was protected by means of fines against violation, albeit not against the attentions of their masters. The least value was attached to the life and virtue of the ordinary *ancilla*, followed by the semifree *lita*, then the freed *liberta*; at the very top were the church and crown slaves.[99] A further distinction was made between skilled and unskilled women. Those who served as domestics or artisans in a *gynaeceum* had a higher *wergeld* than ordinary female slaves.[100] The fines for the murder or rape of dependent women were collected by their masters, but women received the compensation in the case of a minor injury. For example, under Burgundian law, if a freewoman had her hair cut off, she could collect twelve *solidi,* a freedwoman could claim six *solidi,* and a maidservant was entitled to a compensation of three *solidi.*[101]

Lower class women had greater freedom to marry a man of their own choice than upper class women. Those who were not free had to obtain the permission of their master, who did not care whom they married as long as they remained on his land and produced children. In the case of the dependent classes, the Council of Orléans held in 541 equated the lord's permission to marry with the arrangements that parents made for the marriage of a daughter.[102] The church could not serve as a sanctuary to slaves and the semifree marrying without their lord's consent any more than it could serve as one to the free who were entering into a union without their parents' sanction.

The power a master could exercise over his dependants sometimes had tragic consequences. Gregory of Tours reports that Chilperic I ordered many from the royal estates to accompany his daughter Rigunth to Spain, thus breaking up families so that "father was torn from son, daughter from mother."[103] This seems to have been, however, an exceptional case. We have other evidence to suggest that lords, usually pursuing an enlightened policy of benevolence with regard to their dependants' family ties, were quite willing even to go against the laws in sanctioning unions between free and unfree peasants.

Marriages between persons from the different categories of dependants, slaves, semifree, freed, and free were discouraged by law. For example, the Ripuarian Code enshrined the principle that children from these unions followed the status of the more lowly parent. This ran counter to Roman law, under which the status of the mother determined the status of the children. Under Germanic law, if a semifree *lita,* a freedwoman, an *ancilla regis,* an *ancilla ecclesiae,* or a freewoman married below her status, her children were denied the higher rank that she had enjoyed.[104]

The question of social status among women of the lower classes was apparently not significant. By the late sixth century we have evidence of freewomen marrying slaves, despite the laws. The lords encouraged these unions by issuing deeds acknowledging the wife's free status and guaranteeing that any children she might have would also be free. In a deed issued in 573, Abbot Aredius of Attigny and his mother, Pelagia, gave a slave, Valentianus, to the monks of Saint Martin of Tours with

the stipulation that the monks recognize the freedom of Valentianus'
wife, Subfronia, and the freedom of any children the couple might
have.[105] That this arrangement was not exceptional is indicated by the
form drawn up by Marculf, in which the lord acknowledged that his slave
had married a freewoman without her parents' consent, but that he, the
lord, sanctioned the union. In addition, he guaranteed that both he and
his heirs would recognize not only the woman's freedom but also that
of her children, specifying that the woman's children would have to turn
over the "dues on the land annually, as is the custom of freemen."[106]
In bypassing the laws that punished women who married below their
status, landowners were undoubtedly prompted by the desire to attract
to their property a fresh supply of labor. They may have also been
worried about the low ratio of women to men. As David Herlihy has
shown, in Carolingian times, among the dependent peasants of the
Church of Saint Victor of Marseilles, marriageable men outnumbered
marriageable women at the ratio of 106 to 100. In the same epoch, on
the lands of the monastery of Farfa in central Italy, the sex ratio was even
more unbalanced: there were 155 men for every 100 women.[107] The
preponderance of marriageable men was even more pronounced
among the populations of Saint-Germain-des-Près, where the number
of men fluctuated between 115.7 and 156.2 per 100 women, according
to Emily Coleman.[108] Although comparable data do not exist for Merovingian times, there is archaeological evidence that women lived shorter
lives than men.[109]

Emily Coleman has pointed out that, in a society where men outnumbered women and the labor of women was appreciated, "one would
have expected the women to make excellent marriages in terms of both
economics and status." Coleman's explanation for the frequent downward marriages on the lands of Saint-Germain-des-Près was that a girl
who had brothers could not offer an "economic incentive toward marriage to a man of her own status."[110] Hence she had to settle for a
husband of lower status, who was attracted by her legal freedom and
higher social position. But evidence from the Merovingian period allows
us to interpret downward marriages in a more positive light. In marrying
a slave or a man of lower status than her own, a woman was influenced
not only by the economic security that her husband's tenure provided
but also by the additional land tenure that some lords conceded to
freewomen who were willing to marry their slaves. In one of the early
formulae, a lord granted to a freewoman who married a slave one-third
of the yield from the land that she was able to cultivate.[111]

We do not know whether or not the peasant women who married

downward retained ties with their natal families. Marriages in the dependent classes were probably more stable than those in the upper classes, and therefore married women may not have had to rely on their own kin's protection. It is clear that, under the more distant authority of a landlord, women had greater opportunity to be independent and self-reliant than in the upper classes.

This survey of marriage customs in the higher and lower levels of Merovingian society reveals that women on the highest echelons had less freedom to marry according to their own inclination. In the propertied classes daughters had to assist in their family's bid for power. Women of high birth normally expected to marry men of equal or higher social status. In so doing, they created economic and social alliances, increasing the power and influence of their own blood relatives; in return they could count on loyalty and protection from their kin. As catalysts for horizontal social mobility, Merovingian women of the upper classes helped to bring about the fusion of the late Roman and Frankish aristocracies. As wives they compensated for the sexual double standards and the insecurity that governed their lives by earning the affection of their husbands, developing significant emotional ties with their children, and looking after the interests of their blood relations. In their role as widows, they did not shirk from exercising economic power and, whenever possible, political authority.

On the lower levels of society, a woman's parents were less involved in the choice of her mate. A woman of less illustrious birth could more easily make arrangements for her own marriage and enter into a union of *quasi conjugium,* which was not preceded by an engagement and did not offer the woman the economic security of a more formal arrangement. Women of beauty and character used their quasi marriages to improve their own status and that of their relatives. Because marriage and concubinage were not clearly defined, some women could even rise from the lowly status of a slave concubine to that of a legitimate wife. Even more remarkable was the accomplishment of ordinary peasant women. These women participated in economic production as equal partners with their husbands while they continued to bear children through their reproductive years. Economically self-sustaining and productive, they could marry men below their own status, yet retain the privileges of their own status for themselves and their children. By entering into unions with unfree men, freewomen contributed to the peasantry's emancipation from conditions of slavery in the Merovingian kingdom. Whether they married upward or downward, Merovingian women of the lower classes gained for themselves economic security and eased the rigid stratification that had characterized late Roman society.

On a variety of levels, the energy and resourcefulness of Merovingian women are impressive. They made the most of the opportunities that marriage or concubinage offered them not only to improve their own status, but also to contribute to the social and economic advancement of their families. In both the upper and lower classes, they played an essential role in the creation of a new society that was neither Germanic nor Roman but medieval.

4

The Ascent of Monogamy

The rise of the Carolingian dynasty during the second half of the eighth century opened a new chapter in the history of marriage in the Latin West. Marriages in the Merovingian period had remained remarkably free from the influence of Christianity. They were arrangements made for the maintenance and enlargement of kin or the working force through the procreation of children.[1] By tolerating polygyny and concubinage, as well as sanctioning divorce, practices which assured that the male genetic power of the great aristocratic families was widely disseminated, secular laws came into conflict with the Christian ideal of lifelong monogamy. The laws in effect in the Merovingian kingdom coincided with Christian principles only in their condemnation of abortion, abduction, and female unchastity. The aim of these laws was not to translate Christian teachings into practice, but to ensure the growth of population and to eliminate vendettas resulting from rivalry over women and disputes over paternity.

Christianity did not require chastity from women alone, nor did it restrict the definition of adultery to the sexual promiscuity of women.[2] As Georges Duby has observed, the Christian concept of marriage was built on two contradictory exigencies: "to fill . . . heaven with new denizens . . . [and] curb the carnal impulses of human nature."[3] The gap between these two exigencies was bridged by the ideal of monogamy, but the Merovingian church made little attempt to enforce this ideal. The only council to consider the question of divorce prohibited it when the wife was ill,[4] but permitted it if she had committed adultery. During the sixth, seventh, and early eighth centuries, the silence of the Frankish church on sexual relations and matrimonial disputes was broken only by conciliar legislation against incest and abduction and by occasional warnings against concubinage from individual reformers.[5]

In Carolingian times, the indissolubility of marriage became a central issue. Debated by popes and bishops, reaffirmed by the Frankish councils, it was finally incorporated into the royal capitularies. By insisting upon the binding nature of matrimony, the Carolingians brought about not only a moral, but also a social revolution, which had a significant impact on the status of women. The purpose of this chapter is to analyze the most essential aspects of this revolution and assess the reaction and adjustment to it on the highest levels of society, among the royal family and territorial aristocracy. Legislation, both secular and ecclesiastical, court cases, and genealogical data have been consulted.

CAROLINGIAN LEGISLATION

The early Carolingians' attempt to regulate relations between the sexes was prompted not by personal convictions, but by political considerations. Because the new dynasty had usurped the throne, it needed ecclesiastical sanction for its position and a legal justification for extending control over the nobility. In 747, when one of the mayors of the palace, Carloman, withdrew from political life to a monastery, the other mayor, Pepin the Younger, found in Saint Boniface a valuable ally in his effort to transfer the crown. The English missionary's ideas about the reform of sexual relations, moreover, provided Pepin with an effective weapon against the widespread network of alliances among the great families, which was formed mainly through marriages.

The marital customs he observed among the Germanic tribes in general and among the Franks in particular troubled Boniface deeply. He sought advice from popes on the definition of adultery and incest. Gregory II answered him with a series of prescriptions on incest, and Pope Zachary sent Pepin excerpts from the *Dionysiana* on impediments to marriage.[6] The church's concept of incest was so broad, extending the prohibitions to the seventh degree of consanguinity, as well as to relationships by affinity and spiritual kinship, that it considerably restricted the capacity of aristocratic families to form extended alliances through marriage. Introduced into the Frankish councils by Boniface, the prescriptions were included by Pepin the Younger in the capitularies.[7] As a further measure for exercising control over marriages, the national synod of Verneuil, over which Pepin presided, declared that "all men of the laity, whether noble or not, must marry publicly."[8]

In an effort to eradicate all forms of incest, Boniface also concerned himself with extramarital fornication between relatives. Sexual intercourse before or after marriage with a relative of the spouse was held to constitute a bond of affinity similar to that arising from betrothal, marriage, baptism, or confirmation. Disregard for these bonds of affinity or for consanguinity, even in the case of casual intercourse, was considered a serious offense and disqualified the transgressors from marriage for the rest of their lives. Their punishment was lifelong penance,[9] to which Charlemagne added confiscation of their property.[10]

Pepin proceeded more cautiously on the question of the indissolubility of marriage, a more explosive but politically less useful issue. He may originally have balked at this prescription, remembering his own attempt to repudiate Bertrada in order to marry another woman, an attempt that he abandoned only because of papal intervention.[11] On the other hand, unlike his grandfather Pepin the Middle, who had two wives simultaneously, Pepin the Younger did not intend to practice polygyny.[12] Nor does he seem to have followed the example of his father, Charles Martel, of keeping a concubine.[13]

Boniface, on the other hand, viewed the indissolubility of marriage, rather than polygyny and concubinage, as the foremost concern. When the English missionary queried the popes about "adulterous relations," he had in mind marriages contracted after a divorce. One of the earliest councils held under his direction, at Soissons in 742, revived the prohibitions of fourth- and fifth-century Gallican councils against second or third unions contracted while a previous partner was still alive, making allowance only for the man who had repudiated his wife for adultery.[14] Although Pepin enforced the Soissons decree, councils held later in his reign considerably mitigated Boniface's earlier stand on divorce. In 757 the Council of Compiègne, stressing that both men and women were subject to the same laws and that neither could deny the conjugal rights of the other, allowed both husband and wife to remarry if one of the partners was reduced to servitude, if one of the partners entered a monastery with the consent of the other, if one had contracted leprosy, or if the marriage had been forced upon the woman by her stepfather or upon the man by his seignior.[15] The Council of Verberie, meeting around the same time (758–768), justified divorce and remarriage in the case of a man whose wife had tried to kill him or refused to follow him. It also provided some protection to wives by prohibiting the remarriage of a man who had forced his wife to take the veil. Moreover, it permitted both husband and wife to remarry if the marriage had not been consummated.[16]

The rules issued by these two councils represented a reasonable compromise between the position of the Western fathers and the deeply ingrained customs of the people living under Frankish rule. The *formulae* of the period give ample evidence that divorce by mutual consent remained popular.[17] The penitentials compiled around this time made allowance for circumstances that justified divorce either by husband or wife, thus recognizing the right of women to seek a divorce. For example, according to Pseudo-Egbert, a man could remarry immediately if he had repudiated his wife for adultery. Otherwise, he had to wait for five years and could then contract a new union only with the consent of his bishop. A woman could remarry if her husband entered a monastery or was impotent; she had to wait for a year if he was taken into captivity and two years if he was reduced to servitude for theft or fornication.[18] Even the papacy was moving toward parity of men and women in matters of divorce. The Roman synod convoked by Pope Eugenius in 826 allowed the innocent party—husband or wife—to divorce and remarry in cases of adultery.[19]

This broad-minded attitude, however, was not in keeping with the image of a Christian emperor held by Charlemagne's advisers. They believed that the ruler of a state modeled upon Augustine's *City of God* and vying with the Eastern Empire in enforcing Christian morality should uphold only the most rigorous standards in matters relating to marriage. It is significant that Charles' first legislation on this subject was issued in 789, when plans for the transfer of the empire to the Franks were already germinating. In his *Admonitio generalis,* Charlemagne cited the ninth synod of Carthage, which prohibited the remarriage of any divorced man or woman.[20] This instruction appears to have been directed against the prevailing custom of remarriage after a union had been dissolved for reasons other than adultery. But Charles did not stop at this point. In 796, with the bishops he had gathered at Friuli, he unequivocally decreed that adultery could not dissolve the marriage bond. Even though a husband could separate from an adulterous wife, and even though she might be subject to severe punishment and penitence, he could not remarry while she lived.[21] In 802, two years after his coronation as emperor, Charlemagne incorporated this legislation into his *Capitulary to the Missi,* extending it to the entire Frankish Empire.[22]

The marriage practices of Charles and his family exemplify the difficulties, complexities, and contradictions that resulted from the new legislation. When he succeeded to the throne in 768, Charles was living with Himiltrud, the mother of Pepin the Hunchback.[23] When he ended that relationship upon his mother's request and contracted a politically more favorable union with a daughter of Desiderius, the Lombard king, Pope Stephen reproached him severely.[24] A year later, when he divorced the Lombard princess, he was rebuked by his own cousin, Adalard.[25] These events predated Charles' legislation on the indissolubility of marriage. After his second divorce, he never reverted to his youthful behavior, and with his next three wives—Hildegard, Fastrada, and Liutgard—he became a model husband, living steadfastly with each until her death. On the other hand, Charles did not believe that sexual pleasures had to be confined to the bonds of matrimony. Einhard stresses his attachment to Hildegard, but, according to the latest genealogical research, Charles consoled himself after her death with a concubine. After the death of his fifth wife, Liutgard, in 800, he never married again. But he did ease the burdens of the imperial office and old age by enjoying the companionship of four concubines, Madelgard, Gersvind, Regina, and Adellind, each of whom bore him at least one child.[26]

Blessed with eighteen children, Charles was an indulgent father, particularly in regard to his daughters. He did not impose on them sexual double standards. Rather than marrying them to suitable husbands or pledging them to a life of virginity, he kept them at his side and accepted their love affairs. Much has been made of Charles' attitude. Einhard thought he loved his daughters too much to part with them. A twentieth-century historian, Fichtenau, has suggested that his behavior as a father was that of a barbarian chieftain.[27] Indeed, the most appropriate term for the princesses' alliances is *Friedelehe* or *quasi conjugium,* the ancient form of Germanic union concluded between a man and a woman with the tacit acquiescence of her relatives. The earlier instances of this type of union cited by historians involved polygynous marriages, such as the one Pepin the Middle concluded with Chalpaida, in which the woman was of lower social standing than her husband. In the princesses' liaisons, the social position of the parties was reversed.

Though indulgent, Charles would not have tolerated his daughters' unions if he had thought them to be demeaning. Notwithstanding Pepin the Younger's declaration that marriages were to be publicly celebrated, no stigma was yet attached to this type of informal union. Not until the next generation, under Louis the Pious, were quasi marriages censured, but, even so, this view was not widely accepted. In Charlemagne's eyes, his daughters' matches probably represented convenient alternatives to more formal arrangements that his own legislation made binding for life. The union Charles planned for Rotrud with the Byzantine Emperor Constantine VI would have been a wedlock indeed. Only when plans for that alliance fell through was she allowed to console herself with Count Rorico, who became the father of her son. Rotrud's younger sister, Bertha, also had a *Friedelmann,* the poet Angilbert, who gave her two sons. Three additional consorts of Charlemagne's daughters have been found by the German historian Karl Ferdinand Werner, although the princesses to whom these men were attached remain to be identified.[28]

Louis the Pious, Charlemagne's only surviving son, was a man of a different, more puritanical temperament. He took to heart the Christian injunction that one should marry in order to restrain lust. Although in his teens he had at least one concubine, who bore him two children, Alpais and Arnulf,[29] Louis contracted marriage with Ermengard when he turned sixteen. He was motivated, according to one of his biographers, by the fear "that otherwise, overcome by the innate heat of his body, he would be forced against his will to seek multifarious sexual pleasures."[30] The informal unions of his sisters were so distasteful to him that, immediately upon succeeding to the throne in 814, he excluded the entire female company from the palace.[31] Three years later, in his *Ordinatio imperii*, he preempted bastards from succession to the throne, tying legitimacy to the validity of the parents' marriage.[32]

Although the imposition of monogamy entailed a distinction between bastards and legitimate children also on lower levels of society, there was considerable hesitation over whether bastards were excluded from inheritance when there were no legitimate children. A further confusion arose from the lack of clear definition as to what constituted a legitimate marriage. A ninth century *formula* inspired by Roman law merely stated that bastards could not inherit if their father had a legitimate child. Louis the Pious's friend and adviser, Jonas of Orléans, urged priestly blessing of unions as a safeguard for the children's right of inheritance.[33] Men of Germanic descent living in quasi marriages, as the *formulae* attest, apparently felt that their children's inheritance rights were threatened and hence transformed their unions into formal marriages by giving bridegifts to their wives.[34]

By an ironic twist of fate, even worse accusations of moral depravity and licentiousness than those Louis had made against his sisters living in quasi marriages were levied against Louis's second queen, Judith of Bavaria. Urged by his councilors to remarry after the death of Ermengard, Louis, at age forty, chose a young woman under twenty. Beautiful and cultivated, according to all accounts, Judith was hated by many for her efforts to secure a portion of the empire for her own son Charles. A powerful coalition of nobles, led by Ermengard's sons, tried to alienate the aging emperor from Judith by defaming her. Characterized as a Jezebel and a Justina, Judith was accused by one of her enemies, Paschasius Radbertus, of engaging in debauchery and witchcraft with her purported lover, Count Bernard of Septimania, Louis's chamberlain and trusted adviser. In a more realistic vein but in equally scathing terms, Agobard of Lyons described her activities as a consequence of the emperor's advanced years. When the emperor failed to discharge his marital obligation, Judith sought illicit pleasures "first secretly, and later impudently," according to Agobard.

Despite the charges, Louis clung to his attractive wife. Finally, her enemies resorted to force. Twice they forcibly placed her in a convent, but in each instance Louis managed to rescue her. In 830 he was compelled to judge her guilty of adultery and to promise, according to one source, that he also would embrace monastic life. But as soon as Louis was able to rally his own supporters, he allowed her to purge herself with an oath and reclaimed her as his empress.[35]

Judith's story demonstrates clearly that, by this time, the principle of marital indissolubility was generally accepted. As much as her enemies wished to remove her from the emperor's presence, they could not demand Judith's repudiation. In 829, only a year before accusations against Judith were openly aired, four reforming councils held in different parts of the Frankish Kingdom had forbidden repudiation and urged reconciliation in cases of adultery; the councils upheld the principle that adultery did not dissolve the marriage bond. A man could not repudiate his guilty wife, and, further, he became guilty of adultery if he nevertheless contracted another union. During the same year, Louis had subjected men who had repudiated or killed their wives to public penance.[36] The only recourse available to Judith's enemies, therefore, was to prove her guilty of adultery and to subject her to penance in a convent. To prevent her reconciliation with Louis after a suitable period of punishment, he was forced to enter a monastery.[37] An alternative solution would have been to convict her of incest, and the fact that Bernard was Louis's godson was apparently not overlooked by Judith's enemies.[38]

Some of the more astute and sensitive churchmen in Louis the Pious's entourage recognized that the emperor's legislation against divorce did not bring an end to sexual double standards and the incest laws even enabled some to have their marriages annulled. In his *De institutione laicali,* a work often cited by historians analyzing the ideals of Christian marriage, Jonas of Orléans complained that male sexual activity was not confined to marriage and that men dissipated themselves with lust before marriage and gave free rein to sexual pleasures within and outside of marriage.[39] Writing in stricter legal terms, Hrabanus Maurus (784–856) held that the broad definition of incest was excessive and that the practice of annulling marriages on the grounds of distant relationships, whether by consanguinity, affinity, or ritual kinship, weakened the church's teaching against divorce. To Hrabanus, the overwhelming need was to change sexual habits by applying strict punishments for fornication and adultery.[40]

These pleas for a more fundamental reform of sexual morality were generally unheeded. Louis the Pious tried to rid the imperial palace and royal residences of women of questionable conduct (*meretrices*) by ordering that they be brought to justice and flogged in the marketplace. He also barred men living in concubinage, their whores, and bastards from testifying in court. After the death of the emperor, two councils addressed the problem of sexual promiscuity. In 846 and 847, the bishops assembled at Meaux and Paris issued a plea to men and, in particular, to women of the ruling classes to guard against adultery, concubinage, and incest in their homes. Six years later, the Council of Metz warned married men that they would be deprived of communion if they kept concubines. The same council also acknowledged that unmarried men were not subject to punishment.[41]

During the second half of the ninth century, when the imperial authority was disintegrating and the empire was being subdivided into kingdoms, the successors of Louis the Pious had other concerns than upholding Christian teachings on sexual behavior. Without the active support of the secular power, the ecclesiastical hierarchy could not promote additional reforms. The councils that were held, the papal decretals that were issued, and the collections of canons and capitularies that were compiled with forged insertions sought mainly to refine the matrimonial regulations of the early Carolingians. With the exception of incest and divorce, the church accommodated secular customs in the second half of the ninth century.

The Frankish church mitigated its earlier intransigence on rape and abduction. In an effort to approximate the principles promulgated by Louis the Pious in 819, the Council of Meaux-Paris (845–846) departed from the earlier councils' narrow position that unions resulting from abduction had to be dissolved. As long as no other impediment stood in the way of the marriage, the couple could be reunited after the man had performed suitable penance for his action. If the woman had been engaged, her injured *sponsus* had to be suitably compensated. Even an adulterous wife might marry her lover after her husband's death, as long as the couple performed a public penance and neither was suspected of having murdered the deceased man. If they were accused of murder, but neither could be convicted with suitably tested witnesses, they could purge themselves legally of the defamation and then marry.[42] The abduction of a married woman, on the other hand, was punished with increased severity when the Council of Mainz in 852 added penance and perpetual celibacy to the sentence of exile imposed on a certain Albigis, who had publicly abducted the wife of Patricius.[43]

On the question of concubinage, as noted above, the Council of Mainz came to terms with secular practice. It reiterated the decision issued by the Council of Toledo in 400 that a man who kēpt a concubine was not to be deprived of communion as long as he limited himself to one woman. A concubine, the council declared, was a woman who had no formal contract of betrothal and could be summarily abandoned.[44] This definition differed from the traditional Roman and Germanic one, according to which a concubine was an unfree companion, and reinforced the view held in Louis the Pious's entourage that a woman in a quasi marriage was a mere concubine.

The prelates assembled at Mainz made no attempt to protect these women by urging the conversion of a *quasi conjugium* into a binding marriage. If a man gave up one concubine, he was free to take another or to marry. By not insisting that male sexual activity be confined to indissoluble unions, the bishops encouraged the survival of double standards in sexual behavior, losing sight of the early church's teaching that the containment of lust was one of the goals of Christian marriage. They also left men the opportunity to dismiss their wives on the ground that they were not united to them with due formality. For example, after Fulrich, a vassal of Emperor Lothar, had been excommunicated for his divorce and remarriage, he managed to free himself of the sentence in 853 by appealing to the decision of the Council of Mainz.[45]

In attempting to define a lawful marriage, the Frankish church moved closer to the secular model during the second half of the ninth century. Although the bishops tried to gain a hold over the marriage ceremony by calling for the benediction of marriages by priests, they were ready to accept worldly criteria in judging the validity of marriages. The indelible nature of matrimony was not necessarily tied to ecclesiastical ritual. Some marriages were celebrated with great solemnity in the presence of priests and bishops; others were not. Notwithstanding Jonas of Orléans's insistence on religious ceremony, the traditional Germanic procedures of parental consent and property settlement continued to be recognized as necessary steps for the legitimization of unions. Betrothal, bridegift, and handing over the bride *(desponsatio, dotatio, traditio)*, together with priestly blessing, were enumerated as essential elements for the validity of a marriage in the compilation of Pseudo-Isidore. In a similar vein, Benedictus Levita advised his readers that

> a marriage is lawful . . . if the wife was requested from those who appear to have power over her and guard her. If she was betrothed by her nearest relatives and in accordance with the laws she was provided with a *dos,* and when the time came, as it is proper, she was given a sacerdotal benediction with prayers and oblations by a priest, and, as custom teaches, she was guarded, attended, and requested at the appropriate time by bridal attendants, and she was given by her nearest kin according to the laws and was solemnly received . . . then their children will not be spurious but legitimate and will be eligible to be their heirs.[46]

To these definitions Archbishop Hincmar of Reims, the leading Frankish churchman of the time, added a further stipulation that a marriage was not complete until it was consummated.[47] Later, in the mid-twelfth century, when Peter Lombard introduced this notion into the definition of a valid marriage, he freed women from the necessity of obtaining parental consent to their marriages.[48] This was not what Hincmar had been advocating in the ninth century; he merely wanted to add an additional requisite for the validity of a marriage. While he argued against the binding nature of unconsummated unions, he also insisted that without parental consent, economic settlement, and public nuptials, a marriage was not valid, and that children from these unions were not legitimate and could not claim a share in their father's patrimony.

When Charles the Bald's daughter, Judith, eloped with Baldwin of Flanders, Hincmar supported Charles' demand to have his daughter returned under the abduction laws. After Pope Nicholas I (858–867) interceded on the couple's behalf and obtained the king's acquiescence to the union, Hincmar tried to uphold the pronouncements of an ecclesiastical and a secular court, both of which had pronounced the marriage invalid. Hincmar's demand that the king respect the judgments was of no avail. Even the penance prescribed by the laws as punishment for abduction was simply waived.[49] Lack of sanction by the groom's parents was also interpreted by Hincmar as an obstacle to a valid marriage.[50] In 862, the same year Judith eloped with Baldwin, two of Charles the Bald's sons took wives without their father's knowledge. The marriage of Charles of Aquitaine, an adolescent not yet fifteen, to the mature widow of Count Humbert was declared invalid the following year.[51] Louis the Stammerer kept his wife Ansgard at least until 864, when she gave birth to their second son, but he abandoned her at a later date on the ground that their union had been concluded without Charles the Bald's knowledge and consent. Hincmar raised no objection in either case, but Pope John VIII (872–882) did. The Pope, refusing to acknowledge the relevance of secular custom, would not crown the Stammerer's second wife, Adelheid.[52]

Earlier, the rift between Nicholas I and Hincmar on the question of procedures and conditions necessary for a legally valid union had not prevented the pope and the archbishop from taking a united stand on indissolubility. Their unanimous opposition to Lothar II's attempts to divorce his queen thwarted an effort to return to the secular model of marriage, which had successfully accommodated the economic and political strategies of the ruling class. This imbroglio began when Lothar II (855–869), king of Lotharingia, undertook proceedings in 858 to dissolve his marriage to Theutberga. A politically valuable asset, whom Lothar had been compelled to marry, Theutberga did not physically attract him. Failing to impregnate her after two years of marriage, he returned to the mistress of his youth, Waldrada, who had rewarded his devotion with a son. But Lothar faced a serious dilemma. To ensure the succession of his son, he had to divorce Theutberga and marry Waldrada.[53]

Lothar undoubtedly knew that his father, Emperor Lothar I, had incorporated into a capitulary Pope Eugenius's decision that the innocent party in cases of adultery may remarry.[54] But the younger Lothar was also aware that his two uncles, Charles the Bald and Louis II, the German, eager to partition Lotharingia, would invoke the well-known strictures of Charlemagne and Louis the Pious against divorce. He therefore decided to base his suit for dissolution on the safer claim of incest, which was simultaneously more difficult to disprove and more likely to gain for him strong ecclesiastical support.

Lothar was underestimating the strength of Theutberga's character and overestimating the naiveté and credulity of the churchmen. Accused of having had sexual relations with her brother before her marriage, Theutberga successfully purged herself in 858 of the taint of incest by ordeal. Lothar then imprisoned her until she declared her desire to exchange the married state for the life of the convent.[55] This request was submitted to the Lotharingian bishops at a synod of Aix in January 860, together with the transcript of the queen's private confession to the king's chaplain, Günther, the archbishop of Cologne. But when the queen refused to confess her guilt publicly, the bishops were not willing to proceed beyond a suspension of marital relations between the couple. The assembly was dissolved and the queen was probably threatened with torture, while a new assembly augmented by lay magnates and non-Lotharingian bishops was gathered. There, on February 15, 860, the queen confessed not merely to incest but to incest by unnatural femoral intercourse, which resulted in the conception of a child that she had aborted. Despite the biological improbability of her story, the queen was sentenced to public penance. The king's request for remarriage, however, was postponed until more experts in canon law could be consulted.[56]

One of these experts, Hincmar, responded in a long treatise. He raised several objections against the validity of the bishops' sentence and concluded that the queen's guilt had not been manifestly established according to legal procedures prescribed by the canons. Hincmar also took the occasion to stress that a legally constituted marriage, with the exception of incest, was indissoluble. Separation was permissible only if one or both parties wished to enter a monastery, or if fornication had been proved, but in neither case could the husband or wife remarry.[57]

While Hincmar was writing his treatise, Theutberga appealed to the pope; Lothar requested a papal review as well.[58] By the time Nicholas replied and sent two legates, a third assembly had been convened at Aix in June 862. With the aid of his two archbishops, Günther of Cologne and Theutgaud of Trier, Lothar induced the synod to annul his marriage on the ground of the queen's incest; he then proceeded to marry and crown Waldrada.[59] The pope's fury at these developments was further exacerbated when, with the help of two papal legates who were said to have been bribed, the Synod of Metz in 863 upheld the annulment. This decision was based on a new argument alleging that Lothar's youthful alliance with Waldrada had been a lawful marriage, which therefore invalidated his subsequent union with Theutberga. Pope Nicholas responded by calling his own synod to the Lateran, where he annulled the proceedings of Metz, deposed Günther, Theutgaud, and the two legates, denounced Lothar's treatment of Theutberga, and ordered Lothar to restore her to his bed.[60] In 865, under pressure from his uncles, Lothar complied.

The following year, Lothar once again attempted to seek dissolution by coercing Theutberga to request from the pope a separation on the ground that she was barren and wished to enter a monastery. Nicholas answered that childlessness was not a cause for separation and that Lothar could not remarry if Theutberga took the veil.[61] The infamous case was closed only after Waldrada had entered Remiremont and obtained absolution from Nicholas's successor, Hadrian II. In 869, when Lothar appeared as a penitent in Rome, Hadrian II absolved him also. Lothar's death on the way from Rome was regarded by contemporary chroniclers as a providential end to a sordid affair.[62]

The conflict between lay and ecclesiastical models of marriage was resolved in Lothar's case in favor of the latter. Lothar's arguments for divorcing his wife, though devious, were sufficiently varied to necessitate the definition of indissolubility in all sorts of cases: adultery, barrenness, and entrance into a monastery by one of the partners. Although the battle was fought on the pinnacle of society, its outcome affected the fate of less exalted people. It enabled the church to reassert the principle of indissolubility and to apply it to all cases coming to its attention.

Under the grandsons of Charlemagne, in the Carolingian successor states, the earlier imperial strictures against divorce were not rigorously enforced. For example, in 851 Count Eberhard of Alsace was reported to have repudiated his wife Addalinda and married a nun whom he had abducted from the Convent of Erstein.[63] There is no record of a protest either by church or state officials. Eberhard's transgression appears to have occurred before the church altered its policy of accommodating secular practices. The affair of Engeltrud (Ingiltrud) illustrates the change. Married to Boso, a powerful count in Italy under Emperor Lothar, she ran away in 856 with one of her husband's vassals. Although in 859 the irate Boso secured from Pope Nicholas I the excommunication of his faithless wife, Boso's attempts to bring her back brought no results for several years. Sympathizing with Engeltrud's plea that her marriage to Boso had been most unhappy, Lothar II gave her refuge. The fact that Boso happened to be Theutberga's brother undoubtedly helped Engeltrud's case in Lotharingia. No lesser personage than the royal chaplain, Günther, interceded on her behalf with Lotharingian and Frankish bishops. But Hincmar remained adamant, as did Pope Nicholas I. In 863, at the Roman Council during which Nicholas dealt with Lothar's case, he renewed Engeltrud's excommunication. Two years later he sent a legate to Lotharingia to bring the lady to Rome. Although Engeltrud escaped, Nicholas refused to accede to Boso's request that he be allowed to remarry.[64]

The principle of indissolubility was once again taken up by the Rhenish reforming councils, meeting under the leadership of Arnulf in the late 880s. This time annulments of marriages on the ground of procedural irregularities were scrutinized. In 895 the Council of Tribur rejected the plea of a man of Frankish descent that his marriage to a Saxon woman was invalid because it had been concluded according to Saxon and not Frankish legal procedures. Further, the council declared that the unfree origin of the wife could not serve as an excuse for the dissolution of a union. If she had been freed, given her legitimate bridegift, and honored in a public nuptial, she could not be dismissed.[65] Impediment of kinship remained the only ground for annulment recognized by the bishops.[66]

In the course of one hundred and fifty years, the church had accomplished a great deal. At the beginning of the Carolingian era, Frankish society was openly polygynous, at least on the highest levels, and divorce and remarriage were common occurrences on all levels. By the end of the Carolingian era, the Christian ideal of marriage, a union binding for life, was enshrined in secular and ecclesiastical legislation, albeit, beneath the formalism of this legislation, earlier customs remained. The new marital regulations, as the complaints of the Synod of Douzy held in 874 indicate, were not universally observed. Desertions and abductions[67] even on the highest levels of society went on unabated. Injunctions against endogamous unions were also defied, as the attempts of late ninth-century councils to dissolve these unions demonstrate.[68] But on the question of divorce the church had won at least a temporary victory. Those who did not want to contain their sexual impulses within lifelong matrimony had to find loopholes in the new laws or resort to concubinage. Although the Carolingian church came to terms with concubinage, it remained adamant on the question of divorce. Despite periodic setbacks, occasional vacillations, and disputes over definitions, the late ninth-century church attacked one by one all possible excuses for divorce, allowing annulments only on the grounds of consanguinity, affinity, or ritual kinship.

The introduction of monogamy changed the structure of the family and the descent of property, at least on the highest levels of society. The conjugal family, consisting of husband, wife, and children, emerged as the dominant economic unit. Concubines did not have economic rights, and children born out of wedlock were barred from inheritance where there were legitimate offspring.

NEW MARRIAGE STRATEGIES

Gluttonous, quarrelsome, or sickly, a wife must be kept until the day of her death, except if by mutual agreement both partners withdraw from the world. Therefore, before he accepts a wife, a man must get to know her well, both with regard to her character and health. He should not do anything rash that may cause him sorrow for a long time. If all decisions are to be made with advice, this one even more so; in matrimony a man surrenders himself. Most men, when they choose a wife, look for seven [*sic*] qualities: nobility, wealth, looks, health, intelligence, and character. Two of these, intelligence and character, are more important than the rest. If these two are missing, the others might be lost.[69]

These observations of a ninth-century monk, Christian of Corbie, summarized the church's advice to men when choosing their brides.

Variations on this theme, inspired by Isidore of Seville's description of the woes of husbands married to undesirable wives, appeared in most ninth-century admonitions addressed to laymen. "Whether she be a drunkard, irritable, immoral, luxurious, and gluttonous, a vagabond, cursing and swearing . . . whether you like it or not," wrote Hincmar of Reims, "you must keep her."[70] In a treatise dedicated to Lothar II, Sedulius Scottus advised the prince to choose a wife of noble lineage who was beautiful, rich, modest, and virtuous as well, while warning that the wrong wife could cause the downfall of the dynasty. She had to be intelligent to keep peace among the children and servants, willing to sacrifice her life for the king, and capable of serving as her husband's counselor and chief support. Above all she had to be pious and concerned with his salvation. In all her qualities, Sedulius concluded, she had to measure up to Placilla, the wife of Emperor Theodosius I.[71]

Secular magnates and kings shared the church's concern, although they tended to limit the criteria to nobility and wealth in selecting their sons' wives.

The legislation against endogamous unions and divorce forced the aristocracy to develop new marriage patterns. Incest laws made the concentration of aristocratic fortunes and power in the hands of a few families increasingly difficult. The simultaneous prohibition of divorce made it increasingly imperative for sons of great families to marry wisely. To ensure that their sons made no mistakes, upper class parents endeavored to control the marriages of their sons as closely as they had previously controlled those of their daughters. The marriages of young women continued to be arranged by their parents, but now young men were also compelled to further the economic and political interests of their lineage when selecting their brides. Undoubtedly, unions in the upper ranks of Merovingian society also had the intent of sealing political and economic alliances. But only the Pepinids, the ancestors of the Carolingians, pursued a carefully planned marriage policy, which did not extend, however, to the choice of their second wife. Marriage in Carolingian times became a serious affair. The new legislation prompted the great families to close their ranks and devise an exclusive marriage strategy. This meant that lower class women could no longer easily marry into the aristocracy.

Under the new laws royal marriages became a matter of public concern. Kings had to seek advice about their marriages from the great men of their realms. Especially after the subdivision of the empire, princes had to subordinate their personal preferences to territorial interests.[72] A comparison between the marriages and sexual unions of Charlemagne and those of his descendants indicates that political considerations increasingly determined the choice of a spouse in the royal houses of the ninth century. Charlemagne represented an earlier tradition. Although he was not oblivious to the political advantages of sexual unions, he was so powerful that he faced fewer constraints on his personal inclinations than his successors. Upon dismissing the companion of his youth, Himiltrud, he married a Lombard princess at the request of his mother. His third wife, Hildegard, strengthened his ties with the Frankish nobility through her father, Count Gerolt, and with the Aleman aristocracy through her mother, Imma, the daughter of Duke Hnabi. After Hildegard's death, Charles married Fastrada, the daughter of an East Frankish count, thereby reconciling the Aleman nobility. In his last marital venture, he reverted to the Merovingian kings' practice of marrying a woman of humble background. The family of Liutgard was so insignificant that none of the chroniclers bothered to record her parents' names. This union was a love match; Charlemagne, devoted to Liutgard, raised her from the position of concubine to that of queen. On the other hand, though still powerful, he did not marry any of the four concubines he had after Liutgard's death.[73]

Although free to follow their own inclinations when selecting their concubines, the descendants of Charlemagne felt greater pressure to contract politically desirable unions. The mother of Louis the Pious's illegitimate children apparently did not meet the standards for a royal bride. With his father's advice and consent, Louis abandoned her to marry Ermengard, the daughter of the powerful Count Ingram.[74] Louis's second wife, Judith, came from an equally influential family. Louis might have been imitating the practice of his Eastern counterparts when he chose her "after inspecting noble maidens who were brought to his court from all districts." In the Byzantine Empire all eligible women were allowed to compete; in the Frankish Empire the search was limited to ladies of the nobility.[75]

Arrangements for the marriages of Louis the Pious's sons followed a more traditional pattern; the emperor chose for each a bride with connections in the area that he was to govern. Lothar married Ermengard, daughter of Hugo of Tours, the head of the Eticho clan of Alsace.[76] Pepin's wife, Ringart, was the daughter of Theotbert, Count of Madrie, an area south of Chartres in the valley of the Eure.[77] Louis the German's union with Emma, Judith's sister, may have been planned to secure his loyalty to his stepmother; it also gave him a foothold in Eastern Austrasia, where the Welf properties were located.[78]

When the empire was divided after the death of Louis the Pious, territorial considerations became even more important in royal marriages. As the criteria for the selection of future queens narrowed, competition for marrying a daughter or a sister into the royal family increased among the aristocracy. Young women of the best families were offered as concubines to princes in the hope that this informal arrangement—a sort of trial marriage that German historians insist on describing as *Friedelehe*—would eventually be transformed into a legitimate union.

Waldrada, Lothar II's concubine, undoubtedly nourished similar hopes. As recent research has shown, Waldrada came from a noble family, though it did not rank among the highest aristocracy. But unlike Theutberga, to whom she had to cede her place, Waldrada did not have a brother who could guarantee the defense of the Alpine passes for Lotharingia.[79] The youthful alliances of Charles the Bald's sons were concluded when the princes were stationed in the provinces. Although both ladies were members of the local nobility, neither met Charles's expectations for daughters-in-law, and, therefore, they were ultimately abandoned.[80] Young women sufficiently realistic and independent to be wary of trial marriages were so few in number that a monk of Saint Gall, toward the end of the century, took the trouble of recording the scornful words uttered by the daughter of Salamon of Constance when she refused to prostitute herself with Arnulf, one of the last descendants of the Carolingians.[81]

Even such a powerful man as Adalard, Louis the Pious's seneschal, did not hesitate to offer his daughter as a concubine to one of Louis the German's sons.[82] In so doing, Adalard probably remembered his earlier success of having secured—by undue pressure, according to one contemporary source—no less a husband for his niece Ermentrud than Charles the Bald.[83] But that occurred in 842, and by 865 Charles the Bald was soured by the intrigues of his former adviser and marriage broker. Although the young prince, Louis, was infatuated with the girl and betrothed her against his father's wishes, he gave up the young lady upon the intercession of his uncle, Charles the Bald. We do not know what happened to her after she had been abandoned by her royal fiancé.

Another royal matchmaker, Boso of Vienne, had better luck when he gambled with the fate of his sister, Richild. The newly widowed, forty-six-year-old Charles the Bald was charmed by the young lady, more than twenty years his junior. He married her and crowned her queen three months after he had taken her as his concubine.[84] Handsomely rewarded for his services, Boso, now duke of Lyons and Charles the Bald's brother-in-law, was ready to marry into the royal family. His own father, Count Biwin, an Austrasian noble, had also married upward when he had taken Queen Theutberga's sister Richild as his wife. Proud of his wife's royal connections, Biwin named their daughter after Richild and Boso after Richild's and Theutberga's brother. An aunt and a sister as queens might have been sufficient credentials for Boso to ask the widowed empress, Engelberga, for the hand of her daughter Ermengard, but Boso took no chances. According to Hincmar, he relied on dishonorable means to persuade the princess to become his wife. Through Ermengard, Boso then claimed the kingdom of Provence after the death of Louis the Stammerer in 879.[85]

Other young aristocrats, although not always as successful as Boso in marrying into the Carolingian dynasty, were equally ruthless in improving their own positions and family fortunes through the choice of their brides.[86] For example, Bernard of Plantevelue, by contracting a union with the daughter of Count Bernard of Auvergne, secured for himself that county and built a territorial principality. His son, William, duke of Aquitaine, received recognition for all the *honores* that the Plantevelue had assembled by marrying the daughter of his formidable neighbor Boso.[87]

The sophisticated marriage strategies whereby the great families consolidated their power in the ninth century and the lesser nobility sought to penetrate the ranks of the imperial aristocracy have been studied by modern German historians. Gerd Tellenbach, pioneering in the research of the genealogy of the Frankish aristocracy, has noted that of 42 Carolingian families that can be ranked as high nobility, 19 were related to the ruling dynasty. Usually not one but two or more members of the same 19 families (52 persons altogether; an average of 2.7 per family) succeeded in marrying into the royal house.[88] Boso, therefore, was not alone in seeking to increase his power by arranging the union of his sister with Charles the Bald and then his own marriage with Charles' grandniece.

The painstaking research of a younger generation of German historians—many of them Tellenbach's students—has revealed a similar pattern of multiple matrimonial alliances among the leading houses of the Carolingian aristocracy. The mark of a noble family in the ninth century was twofold: blood ties with the ruling dynasty and other aristocratic lineages. By following a more ruthless strategy of exclusivity in their matrimonial pacts, Carolingian aristocratic families acquired more political influence and achieved greater concentrations of economic power than their Merovingian ancestors had.[89] No one would dispute that this insistence on bringing together equal lineages tended to end social mobility and made all aristocratic marriages something of a matter of convenience. But scholars have not pointed out that the success of this matrimonial policy depended upon making the best possible use of the exchange value of daughters and was often achieved at the risk of ruining the lives of young women by marrying them to older men or offering them in a trial marriage to men of higher rank.[90]

Daughters of powerful families did not encounter difficulties in finding suitable husbands. For example, the head of the Eticho clan, Count Hugo of Tours, arranged brilliant matches for all three of his daughters. Around 819, the eldest, Bertha, married Gerhard, count of Paris and then duke of Lyons and Vienne, and finally, under Charles the Bald, governor of the kingdom of Provence; Adelais married Empress Judith's brother Konrad and, after Konrad's death, Robert the Strong, thus becoming the ancestress of the Capetian kings of France; Ermengard married the future emperor, Lothar I.[91]

Women related to the royal house were besieged with marriage proposals. Because Saint Opportuna was the daughter of noble parents and had royal blood in her veins, the most powerful men of the realm were among her suitors. According to her biographer, she received offers of gold and silver, exquisite female ornaments inlaid with gems and pearls, serfs and maidservants, and manors.[92] Widows, if they came from and had married into noble families, could also easily find a husband. A good case in point is Boso's widowed mother, Richild, who married Count Eckhard of Autun, a widower.[93] But not all upper-class women fared as well. Many were compelled, because of age or the ambitions of their relatives, to enter into less formal arrangements, often in the nature of a trial marriage or concubinage.

The supply of potential brides apparently was large enough to allow men to be selective. To enable Saint Maura to find a noble husband, her brother left her his whole patrimony when he entered a monastery.[94] But an engagement might be broken if the man found a richer bride. Earlier, this breach of contract had been considered such a serious offense that it was punished with almost as heavy a fine as the unilateral termination of a marriage. During the second half of the ninth century, Hincmar of Reims reported that he received complaints from women who had been rejected and subjected to ridicule by their younger fiancés. In these cases, a promise of wedlock may have been used as a means of seduction by the younger men.[95]

It was normal for both princes and sons of the aristocracy to form sexual alliances that were not legitimized later because of parental opposition or the young man's change of heart. Premarital sex apparently was sufficiently prevalent for the Council of Aix to declare in 862 that it was rare, if not impossible, to find a man who would enter matrimony as a virgin.[96] Some thirty years earlier, Jonas of Orléans had warned men not to corrupt themselves before marriage either clandestinely with whores or publicly with maidservants. The various motives of young men seeking sexual experiences before marriage did not escape Jonas's attention. He noted that some did this impulsively because they were overcome by lust; others, led by the desire for territorial honors, postponed matrimony but not sexual experience.[97] Jonas indicated that the sons of the nobility turned to peasant women or prostitutes to be initiated into sexual pleasures. He failed to note that they could find willing partners also among women of their own class.

An outstanding example was the case of Count Stephen, who was charged in an ecclesiastical court by his father-in-law, Count Raymond of Toulouse, with having failed to consummate his marriage. Stephen defended himself on the ground that he had had previous sexual relations with a relative of his wife. Acknowledging the validity of Stephen's scruples that carnal intercourse with his wife would have constituted an act of incest, the court annulled the marriage without making even the slightest attempt to reprimand the young man for his adventure or to suggest that he might marry the lady in question.[98]

Since the name of Stephen's mistress is not known, it is not possible to trace her subsequent fate. Nevertheless, if we consider the cases of other women who found themselves in a similar predicament, we may assume that she was either pledged to a life of chaste perfection in a convent or married to a man of lesser rank willing to take her despite her sullied reputation. For instance, even the notorious mistress of Lothar II, Waldrada, was received with great honor at Remiremont, one of the most respected convents in Frankland.[99] On the other hand, her future daughter-in-law, the even more infamous Friderada, was not confined to a monastery when she gave birth to an illegitimate child. Rather, she was given in marriage to Bernhard (Bernarius), a vassal of Waldrada's illegitimate son Hugo. Motivated, though, by higher ambitions, Friderada managed to persuade Hugo to murder Bernhard, thus freeing her for a more suitable second wedlock with Hugo.[100]

The victims of abortive trial marriages were always the women and never the men. These relationships, usually approved by the woman's relatives, represented an essential aspect of the marriage strategy of the late ninth-century Frankish aristocracy. If the informal union were not transformed into a lifelong alliance, the family could develop new plans, but the woman in question had lost her reputation. In addition, she was subject to accusations of black magic if the subsequent marriage of her former partner failed to produce children or proved in any way unhappy. Hincmar of Reims was explicit on this point, warning men that their mistresses might bewitch them. They might concoct love potions, mixing human bones with ashes and coals, masculine and feminine hair, pubic hair, herbs, parts of serpents and snails, or they might resort to incantations and magical spells. "Dressed and covered with enchanted clothing, demented by the food and drink of the sorceresses, and spellbound by the songs of witches," Hincmar declared, men were made impotent. As a remedy, he recommended exorcism, which, he claimed, had worked in the case of a young couple whose marriage had remained unconsummated for several years but was then blessed with many children.[101]

The law codes and penitentials referred to both men and women as perpetrators of witchcraft and magic. The tendency to associate women primarily with mixing magical potions appeared first in the *Formulae Senonenses,* compiled between 768 and 775.[102] During the ninth century, instead of regulating extramarital sexuality, the church used the threat of impotence to deter men from extramarital sex, fixing the blame on women who were foolish enough to yield to men outside the bonds of marriage. This rather limited notion of bewitchment by concubines was soon expanded to include any woman who was thought to be exercising a socially or politically harmful influence.

Empress Judith, according to Paschasius Radbertus, filled the palace with "soothsayers . . . seers and mutes, as well as dream interpreters and those who consult entrails, indeed all those skilled in malign crafts." Her purpose in so doing was to bewitch the emperor.[103] The nun Gerberga, the sister of Judith's purported lover, Bernard of Septimania, was actually executed as a witch. It is not clear whether the unfortunate woman was held responsible for having placed her brother Bernard under a spell, or having bewitched the empress, or the emperor himself. The charges against Gerberga were voiced by the same group of men who had been unsuccessful in keeping the empress imprisoned. Gerberga appears to have been an innocent victim, a scapegoat upon whom Judith's enemies vented their frustration and hatred.[104] This is the first known instance in the Latin West of witchcraft being used as a legal ground for the execution of a woman.

The triumph of the Christian model of lifelong marriage not only increased the competition for husbands, rendering more difficult the upward mobility of women through marriage, but also widened the gap between wives and concubines. The ever more exclusive matrimonial strategies of the aristocracy forced many a woman into the role of concubine. The church tried to discourage these trial marriages by directing society's opprobrium against the women, depicting them as temptresses and sorceresses, but little effort was made to deter men directly from entering this type of union.

In the open and fluid society of the Merovingian period more women had access to wealth and status through marriage than in the ninth century. Earlier, when the distinction between marriage and concubinage had been less strict and marriages could be dissolved with relative ease, either unilaterally or by mutual consent, more women had the opportunity to penetrate the upper ranks of society through sexual unions, both formally and informally concluded. This system allowed men to replace their wives with more attractive, younger women, but not without compensating them with a substantial settlement. Although the laws provided more economic protection to a woman whose engagement was arranged by her parents, a woman's status in a *quasi conjugium* was that of a wife. Neither social nor legal discrimination was applied against her or her children, and the union, moreover, was as likely to endure as a more formal arrangement.

In the ninth century, in contrast, the continuance of aristocratic lineages could no longer be entrusted to a succession of wives or to simultaneous wives. Marriage became exclusively a social institution "by which families of the same standing among the aristocracy perpetuated themselves."[105] Thus, fewer women, only those whose unions were approved by their parents and in-laws and sealed with a *dos* provided by their husbands or husbands' kin, qualified to occupy the lofty position of wife. Women who had entered trial marriages—whether compelled by their families or of their own volition—were considered mere concubines. Even if they were of noble lineage, they ran the risk of being abandoned with a broken heart, an impaired reputation, and illegitimate children.[106]

5

The Consequences of Monogamy

Carolingian legislation on the indissolubility of marriage and the exclusion of illegitimate children from inheritance brought about a new concept of the family in the ninth century. Although the kin as a social and political force remained as influential as in Merovingian times, the conjugal unit came to be recognized as the fundamental unit of society. Acknowledged as an essential member of this unit, a wife had many responsibilities, which were carefully delineated, at least on the highest level of society. Her legal position was secure. Unlike her female ancestors, she could not be repudiated, although she could still be neglected or mistreated.

The purpose of this chapter is to examine whether or not this new concept of the family was paralleled by increased female influence within and outside the family. Of equal interest is the fate of women in the new monogamous structure if they did not marry, or if their husbands abandoned them or died. Because the economic activities of women provide a fairly reliable index of female influence and status, I have sought answers to these questions not only in legal and narrative sources but also in donations preserved in ecclesiastical cartularies.

WIVES AND WIDOWS IN THE ARISTOCRACY

The introduction of the Christian model of marriage did not alter the role of the wife, even though it increased her responsibilities. Bearing children, which might have been done by a succession of wives or simultaneous wives in an earlier period, and supervising domestic activities, which had been previously shared by all female members of the family, were now the exclusive duty of one wife. Further, a married woman in the ninth century had greater responsibility for land management than her Merovingian ancestors. She was thus expected not only to produce children but also to administer a complex family economy.

On the highest level of society, the position of the queen as her husband's partner, *augusta* or *consors regis,* was formalized in the middle of the ninth century by instituting the ceremony of anointment and

97

coronation and incorporating the queen's name in the *laudes,* litanies sung in praise of kings.[1] Charlemagne set the precedent for the official recognition of the queen's position. Although his own family remained extended and multigenerational, including bastards, concubines, his daughters' lovers, grandchildren, and his own mother,[2] Charlemagne made possible the concentration of power in the conjugal unit by delegating to his last queen, Liutgard, a line of command second only to his own. In the *Capitulare de villis,* Charlemagne declared that "anything ordered by us or by the queen to one of our judges, or anything ordered to the ministers, seneschals, and cupbearers, must be carried out to the last word."[3]

Charlemagne's purpose was to ensure that his queen's commands concerning the administration of the palace and royal estates would be carried out promptly by royal officials. In an age when no distinction was made between a ruler's private property and public domains, these were great powers indeed. Two generations later, when Hincmar of Reims described the administration of the palace, he explained that the queen, with the assistance of the chamberlain, was in charge of the royal treasury. She was entrusted with these powers because the king was occupied with the ordering of the whole kingdom and could not be concerned with domestic trifles.[4]

Merovingian queens also had access to the treasury but they were not entrusted with formal administrative functions. Whereas Merovingian queens acquired visibility in the economic sphere primarily through force of character, Carolingian empresses and queens were expected to serve as economic assistants to their husbands as a matter of course. Instead of being cloistered in the protective setting of their own residences, they were constantly on the move, accompanying their husbands on visits to different parts of the realm. For a queen or empress to remain at home was unusual enough for the chroniclers to take notice of it. Traveling with her husband, the queen participated in assemblies and issued donations jointly with the king. She also managed crown lands.[5] Only illness exempted her from her duties. Ermengard, Louis the Pious's first wife, died en route to Tours with the imperial court. Taken ill at Angers, she stayed behind in a monastery, the emperor returning to her side only shortly before her death six weeks later.[6]

In the ranks of the aristocracy, royal service and warfare absorbed the energies of the men, often leaving the supervision of the family estates in the hands of women. For example, the domains of Bernard of Septimania, imperial chamberlain and the most influential member of Louis the Pious's court, were run by his wife. Loyal and competent,

Dhuoda accepted her husband's command to remain at home at Uzès. With perspicacity and skill, she kept his patrimony intact, despite his persistent demands for cash. Although she was conscience-stricken for having to borrow constantly from Jews and other moneylenders, she succeeded in covering Bernard's staggering expenses and continued to finance his royal way of life. As she explained with pathetic candor in her *Manual,* an educational guide addressed to her oldest son, William, she did all this to prevent the lord Bernard, her seignior, from abandoning her and William.

It is hard to imagine that rumors of Bernard's alleged love affair with the empress did not reach Dhuoda's ears, but she received Bernard with wifely affection in 840, when, after the death of Louis the Pious, her husband returned home. He remained with her long enough to impregnate her for the second time, and then left to participate in the war of succession. In her lonely existence, Dhuoda could not even find solace in the companionship of her children. Bernard took William, their first-born, to be educated at the court. She also had to relinquish her second son while he was still an infant. To secure peace with an enemy, Bernard used this child as a hostage.[7]

The life of Dhuoda may have been exceptional in its tragic solitude, but other aristocratic women had to carry equally heavy administrative burdens. A capitulary of Charlemagne made it clear that, when a count was summoned to participate in a campaign, he was to leave behind only four of his men, two to protect his wife, and two to carry on the local administration.[8] Handling the myriad details of land management alone, countesses acquired enough expertise to continue as the head steward even after their husbands returned. Gisla, daughter of the Saxon Count Hessi and widow of Unwan, traveled constantly to oversee the cultivation of her own and her son's estates. She chose as her assistant, not her son, but a young woman of lesser stature, Liutberga, whom she removed from a convent and trained specifically for this task.[9] Even if the husband chose to exercise his prerogatives as a landowner, the wife remained in charge of the inner economy of the household.

The expression "he married her to rule his home," used by the biographer of Saint Glodesinda in 882, was not mere hyperbole.[10] It accurately described the function of a wife in the great families. Once married, even though she was normally only a teenager who had barely reached the age of menarche,[11] a young wife became responsible not only for the material comfort of her husband but also for the organization of his extensive household. She had to ensure that the storehouse was well stocked, the staff at the workshop was kept busy, and the kitchen was well run. Training for her executive tasks involved practical work experience from which even princesses were not exempt. Einhard made it clear that Charlemagne "made his daughters learn to spin and weave wool, use the distaff and spindle, and acquire every womanly accomplishment, rather than fritter away their time in idleness."[12]

Skill in household management and handicrafts were so much appreciated that a new type of female saint made her appearance in the ninth century, the professional housekeeper and teacher of domestic "science." Saint Liutberga, Countess Gisla's assistant, earned her sainthood by supervising her patron's household and estates during the day and devoting her nights to prayer. When, in her old age, Liutberga was finally allowed to retire to the convent of Wendhausen, she was visited there by the great men and women of the area, who sought her counsel and brought their daughters to learn from her the secrets of wool dyeing and similar arts.[13]

Childbearing kept women of the aristocracy busy as well. In the upper classes, where the procreation of many children was the purpose of marriage, women probably did not practice contraception,[14] but the absence of husbands for various reasons undoubtedly held down the birthrate. To relieve the burdens of lactation, women employed wet nurses. Hildegard, one of Charlemagne's queens, probably did not breast-feed her babies. She gave birth to nine children, including a set of twins, before she died at twenty-five. We know that one of the twins, the future emperor Louis, was suckled by a nurse.[15] Hildegard's successors were less fertile. Fastrada had only two children and Liutgard none. The list of Charlemagne's descendants compiled by K. F. Werner indicates that Hildegard's record was matched only by her granddaughter Gisla.[16]

The supervision of a child's upbringing was also the responsibility of wives. Children had to be placed in the care of governors and governesses and given a proper education. To keep peace between the children and servants was, according to Sedulius Scottus, also one of the duties of royal wives.[17] Moreover, solicitude for the religious training of children fell within the province of women.[18] The ninth-century biographer of Saint Salaberga, after transforming the saint into a married woman with five children, praised her for converting her husband and children to monasticism. The biographer of Saint Waldtrud mentioned as a matter of course that the saint postponed her vocation until her children had grown up, although the father of the children had felt free to join a monastery much earlier.[19] Nunneries and monasteries usually would not take children below the age of six or seven, although exceptions were made for children whose mothers had joined the institution.[20]

Recent studies on the history of childhood have shown that in the Middle Ages adult responsibilities were entrusted to children earlier than they are today. Certainly, in the ninth century boys and girls of fourteen were treated as adults before the law. According to the Council of Mainz, held in 888, they could take an oath and act as witnesses by this age.[21] The formal education of children began around age seven and concentrated on vocational training, which could be completed in a few years. For this purpose, boys were taken from their mother's care and sent to the court of a great lord or to a monastery.[22] Those who were destined for secular life were taken to public assemblies at age twelve.[23] Girls remained under their mother's supervision until they were married. This occurred in some exceptional cases at age twelve, but normally between thirteen and fifteen.[24] Thus, women spent fewer years rearing a child than they do today, but they married earlier and bore more children.

Carolingian women also lived shorter lives. On the basis of the life spans of four generations of Charlemagne's descendants, the only family group in the ninth century for which rudimentary biographical information is available, we can conclude that the average age of women at death was about thirty-six. In five generations of the Carolingian dynasty beginning with Charlemagne, K. F. Werner lists 176 people, including wives, husbands, concubines, and lovers. Of these, sufficient information exists for calculating the approximate age at death of 53 males and 47 females.[25]

The early childhood mortality rate was higher for males than for females; six boys and two girls died before age five. The ratio was reversed in the early teens, with one boy and four girls dying between the ages of ten and fourteen. A higher mortality rate also prevailed for women between the ages of fifteen and thirty-nine, with 31 percent of the men as opposed to 48 percent of the women dying. Only 39 percent of the women lived to age forty and beyond, compared to 57 percent of the men. The highest proportion of male mortality occurred between the ages of forty and fifty-four, and of female mortality between the ages of twenty-five and thirty-nine. Clearly the disparity between the two mortality rates had some connection with women's biological function. (See table 1.)

The shorter life span of a woman was by no means a general rule in the early medieval royalty and aristocracy. K. J. Leyser's study of the survival rate for the Saxon nobility and royalty has shown that men died earlier than women in the tenth and eleventh centuries. With their husbands and brothers perishing in wars and feuds, there was an abundance of elderly widows and spinster heiresses exercising influence,

TABLE 1   *Age at death of Carolingians*

Ages	Men	%	Women	%
1–4	6	11	2	4
5–9	–	–	–	–
10–14	1	2	4	9
15–19	4	8	1	2
20–24	3	6	2	4
25–29	1	2	5	11
30–34	5	9	6	12
35–39	3	6	9	19
40–44	7	13	4	9
45–49	6	11	3	6
50–54	7	13	2	4
55–59	1	2	4	9
60–64	4	8	5	11
65–69	1	2	–	–
70 +	4	8	–	–
Total	53		47	

prestige, and even authority in Ottonian Saxony. Although Carolingian princes also plunged into wars and feuds, they were more fortunate in escaping violent death than the Saxon nobility.[26]

A lower average age of mortality for women was also the pattern in families of lesser stature. David Herlihy's study of the life expectancy of peasant women in the ninth century reveals that men lived longer than women also on the lowest level of Carolingian society.[27] It is not altogether possible to draw a direct correlation between the mortality rate of women and their childbearing function. No royal descendant, wife, or concubine is known to have died during childbirth. It would be equally wrong to assume that a woman who bore many children would die sooner than one who had none. In contrast to Hildegard's death at twenty-five, her granddaughter, the equally fertile Gisla, lived to a ripe age of fifty-two to fifty-five. Fastrada, the mother of two, died at twenty-five or twenty-seven, while the childless Liutgard died at twenty or twenty-two. Since women, at least in the royal family, were not more prone than men to be victims of violence, their relatively low survival rate must be attributed to the combined effect of inadequate health care and an iron deficiency in the Carolingian diet, aggravated by menstruation, gynecological problems, and childbearing.[28]

As the responsibilities of a married woman increased, her contributions to the well-being of the conjugal unit gained recognition. Virginity as a more perfect state than marriage, a theme of patristic and Merovingian writings, received less emphasis in the ninth century.[29] Indeed, Haimo of Auxerre declared that a married woman pleased God as much as one who espoused chastity. By bearing children and giving them a religious education, a married woman carried out the work of God, according to Haimo.[30] The first poem celebrating women in every role was composed at this time. Virgins, married women bearing sons to please God, widows loyal to the memory of their husbands who encouraged their sons to serve God, and even reformed courtesans were, according to the court poet Notker, capable of defeating Satan and ascending to heaven on the ladder that the love of Christ made especially accessible to women.[31]

Another aspect of the celebration of women as wives and mothers was the veneration of Mary, which gained prominence in the ninth century. Ilene Forsyth has assembled evidence showing that manuscripts, ivories, and reliefs representing Mary in majesty with the child Jesus on her lap were produced in Carolingian ateliers. Hincmar had at Reims a gold altar portraying Mary as the mother of Jesus, a gold relief of Mary served as an altar frontal in the cathedral of Metz, and the monks of Luxeuil prized a silver retable of Mary.[32] Even earlier, on a reliquary given by Charlemagne to Witikind in 785, the matronly figure of the Virgin holding the Child appeared between the apostles Peter and Paul.[33] A homily on the assumption of Mary, composed by Paschasius Radbertus, enjoyed such popularity that Hincmar had it transcribed, and extracts from it were sung as antiphons at matins on the Feast of the Assumption. Mary's nativity and purification were also commemorated from the time of Charlemagne. Her merits were sung, moreover, not only by Paschasius Radbertus but also by Alcuin, Hrabanus Maurus, Walafrid of Strabo, Sedulius of Liège, and Hincmar of Reims.[34]

Ninth-century writers venerated Mary and praised women's accomplishments as mothers and wives but did not think of husbands and wives as equals. The subjection of wives to their husbands continued to be justified on the basis of the Pauline passages and the third chapter of Genesis.[35] Even the champion of women, Hincmar of Reims, while stressing equality of men and women before the law, referred to women as the weaker vessel and upheld the notion that a husband was the ruler of his wife.[36]

Complaints registered by wives against their husbands were handled with great caution by the Carolingian courts. A well-known case is that of Northilda, who brought charges against her husband to an assembly of lay nobles and bishops in 822. She accused him of forcing her to have sex with him in a shameful manner. Although unnatural intercourse was considered a grave sin, the lady's scruples did not move the judges. They refused to suspend marital relations between the couple, referring Northilda to a secular court, which, in their opinion, was more qualified to handle the case.[37]

Only when a woman was threatened with divorce or physical danger were the courts quick to intervene. Hincmar's bloodcurdling account of the atrocities committed by husbands suggests that the bonds of permanent marriage proved to be too much for some men to bear. When a wife was a burden or a nuisance, there were ways other than divorce to get rid of her. Hincmar pointed out that men, accusing their wives of adultery,

> lead them to the slaughterhouse to be butchered, and they bid the cooks to kill them with swords as it is the practice with sheep and pigs, or they personally murder them with the edge of their own swords, cutting them to pieces.[38]

To defend women in fear of their lives, the Council of Tribur in 895 authorized bishops to make churches available as sanctuaries.[39]

A woman could also seek shelter in a monastery if she were mistreated by her husband. Theutberga finally withdrew to Avenay.[40] Another barren royal wife, the Empress Richardis, entered Andelau after she had successfully defended herself against the accusation of her husband, Charles III, the Fat, that she had committed adultery with Bishop Liudward of Vercelli.[41] As earlier, wives were shielded also by their own kin. In a case of extreme brutality brought before the courts, a priest who had sought to reunite a woman with her husband suffered the greatest injury. The woman in question sought refuge with her brother, who became so enraged by the priest's entreaties that he had him castrated.[42]

If a woman were lucky enough to survive her husband, she did not fare much better than her predecessors in the Merovingian era. Even though the Carolingians placed them under special royal protection, widows still might be robbed of their property. To guard the interests of women bereft of husbands, the capitularies entitled them to seek the services of royal officials as their "defenders."[43] The sad story of the noble widow, recorded by Paschasius Radbertus, indicates, however, that the officials often extorted enormous fees from the women they were supposed to protect. The lady in question had been dispossessed of all her lands by a justiciar she had chosen as her "defender." When she complained to the emperor, he entrusted the case to his judges, who did not sympathize with the widow's plight. Her testimony that she had adequately compensated her "defender" by turning over to him half her possessions was discounted, and the case was adjudicated in favor of the justiciar.[44]

To be protected by the church, a widow had to join a convent. Earlier, she could take a vow of chastity and remain in the world as a *Deo devota*. Reforming synods, beginning in the late eighth century, required women to enter nunneries if they wished to devote themselves to the service of God.[45] Allegations that widows took fraudulent vows in order to remain free to lead a life of sexual abandon leave no doubt that the cloistering of widows represented an integral part of the church's effort to enforce monogamy. As this program met with success and the conjugal family emerged as the basic unit of society, the function of sheltering unmarried ladies, formerly assumed by extended families, was taken over by the convents. As in other spheres of life, here too the royal family led the way. Louis the Pious not only sent his notorious sisters to nunneries but also installed his widowed mother-in-law as abbess at Chelles.[46]

In earlier times, when the extended family was the dominant form of social organization, a woman could make herself useful in a variety of ways even if she were unmarried, divorced, or widowed. She could help her relatives with domestic activities and engage in religious pursuits. This wide range of options was not available to unmarried upper-class women in the ninth century. Those who were unwilling to or could not marry were confined to nunneries. No longer fulfilling a useful function, they were considered a threat to the stability of the conjugal unit or at best an anomaly in a society in which the center of economic activity was shifting from the extended family to the more restricted conjugal ménage.

The formalization of wifely duties in the ninth century, while enhancing the wife's influence in aristocratic families, strengthened male dominance in all other spheres and reinforced sexual stereotypes. The wife was occupied in a broad variety of domestic and nurturing roles and remained in the shadow of her husband. Should she try to exercise power in her own right, she met with criticism and was accused of unfeminine behavior. Women who were bold enough to petition assemblies were sternly rebuked by the Synod of Nantes in 895:

> It is astonishing that certain women, against both divine and human law, with barefaced impudence, plead in general assemblies and

with abandon exhibit a burning passion for public meetings, and they disrupt, rather than assist, the business of the kingdom and the good of the commonweal. It is indecent and even reprehensible, even among barbarians, for women to discuss the cases of men. Those who should be discussing their woolen work and weaving with the residents of women's quarters should not usurp the authority of senators in public meetings just as if they were palace officials.[47]

The few known cases in which women, other than queens, appeared in public assemblies suggest that they were defending their honor or property rather than meddling in the affairs of men.[48] Even queens, despite their public roles, merely acted as agents of their husbands, relieving them of the burdens of household and land management. The Carolingians acknowledged the importance of a wife, but they also perpetuated the notion that a woman's role was different from and auxiliary to that of a man. Women were to bear children and look after the spiritual and material welfare of their husbands and children, but their sphere of influence was to be restricted to family affairs. A woman could exercise public power only as an extension of her role as wife, mother, and property owner.

CAROLINGIAN WOMEN AS LANDOWNERS

David Herlihy's pioneering study of the economic situation of women in the Middle Ages suggests that female ownership of land declined in the ninth century. In an effort to arrive at an objective estimate of the control that women exercised over landed property, Professor Herlihy has searched through all published donations, sales, exchanges, leases, and other forms of contracts from southern and northern France, Germany, Italy, and Spain, beginning with the eighth century, when these documents first appear in significant numbers, to the end of the twelfth century. Of the three indices he has constructed, the first counts matronymics, the second refers to contiguous ownership of land by women, and the third indicates the frequency with which women appear as alienators of property. The last one is the most relevant for the Carolingian realm, and contains ample data for the eighth and ninth centuries from the northern, eastern, and southern parts of the Frankish Kingdom.[49]

The index includes 11 documents from the eighth century concerning land transactions in southern France, a number too small for statistical analysis. Of the 124 documents from northern France and the Low

Countries, 18 are feminine donations, which means that women appear as alienators of land in 14.5 percent of these documents. From Germany, Austria, German Switzerland, Alsace, and Luxembourg, Herlihy has located a more substantial number of charters; after analyzing 4,265 transactions, he found that 554, or 13 percent, were drawn up at the request of women (see table 2).

The percentage of women actors declines in the ninth century. Of the 455 documents that have survived from southern France in the ninth century, women appear as actors in 44, or only 9.7 percent of the total.[50] In the same century, the percentage of women exercising power over landed property in northern France appears to be much lower, only 7.2 percent (29 of a total of 403 transactions), whereas the alienation of land by women in the Teutonic regions (10.1 percent, or 236 charters of a total of 2,332) roughly equals the proportion in southern France (9.7 percent).

Of special interest to us is the decline in the alienation of land by women in the ninth century. There is the possibility of a correlation between Charlemagne's legislation against divorce and the frequency of women as principal actors in land transactions. Statistics show women in that role in only 9.7 percent of the total number of surviving ninth-century documents, as opposed to 13.0 percent for the previous century. A close scrutiny of Herlihy's figures indicates that the decrease in

T A B L E 2   *Women in land transactions**

	Southern France	Northern France and Low Countries	Germany
8th Century			
Female	1	18	554
Total	11	124	4,265
Percentage	–	14.5	13.0*
9th Century			
Female	44	29	236
Total	455	403	2,332
Percentage	9.7*	7.2	10.1

*The data are restated from table 4 in Herlihy, "Land, Family and Women," pp. 116–18, and show the percentage of female actors among total actors in land transactions in the eighth and ninth centuries. Two figures in Herlihy's table 3 (ibid., p. 108), which is based on the data of table 4, are corrected here: 13.0% rather than 15.0%; 9.7% rather than 8%.

the number of women as donors and sellers occurred in the second half of the ninth century, at the same time that both the western Frankish church under the leadership of Hincmar of Reims and the papacy took upon themselves the task of enforcing the principle of marital indissolubility. A reasonable inference is that these concerted actions resulted in fewer second or third marriages, which, in turn, meant that fewer women were able to marry into the landed aristocracy and acquire landed property through marriage settlements. Moreover, when divorce by mutual consent was no longer permitted, a woman, once she married, could not gain control over her own property before the death of her husband.

Herlihy's data, however, do not allow us to draw a definite conclusion. The first to admit the crudeness of his estimate of the importance of women as property owners was Professor Herlihy. These statistics, he remarked, may indicate the generosity of women toward churches in the eighth century rather than their importance as landowners, and more women may simply have held on to their land in the ninth century than in previous periods. Herlihy's tabulation has other limitations as well. It reflects the pattern of land control in the upper echelons of Carolingian society, a group for which we do not have sex ratios. Moreover, it has been assembled from a great variety of cartularies that individually pose different problems. Even if we accept that many of these cartularies were published in the nineteenth century and include loosely dated or even spurious charters, the remaining documents nevertheless reflect a wide range of local customs, diversely influenced by royal and imperial ordinances. It is quite possible that, in some areas, the fluctuations in women's economic activities as reflected in the cartularies resulted from particular local conditions rather than from the enforcement of Carolingian marriage regulations.[51]

The impact of Carolingian marriage legislation may be more accurately measured by documents recording land transfers in a specific region. The Lorsch cartulary, which contains over 3,500 deeds dating from the mid-eighth to the end of the ninth century, lends itself to this type of analysis. The cartulary has been carefully edited, according to standards of modern scholarship. The monastery itself was located in the eastern part of the Carolingian heartland, the home of Charlemagne's biographer Einhard. Its properties extended from the valley of the Nahe and the Glan rivers on the left bank of the Rhine to Frankfurt along the valley of the Main, and southward into the valley of the Neckar along the west bank of the Saar. With a landowning aristocracy mainly of East Frankish descent, the social and economic organization of the area may be regarded as typical of the Frankish Kingdom.[52]

The activities of women in the documents preserved in the cartulary were analyzed according to two major categories. The first includes
women acting independently of men, transmitting property alone or
acting jointly with other women in donating, selling, exchanging, or
pledging property. The second comprises women appearing as coactors
with their husbands, sons, brothers, or fathers, either as the equals of
males in the transaction or in a secondary role by approving with their
signatures the alienation of property by male relatives. Within each
category the status of the actor or the relationship of the coactors and
cosigners was also examined (see table 3).

The tabulation of these documents reveals a close connection between women's economic activity and the history of the family in the
region. The independent activity of women diminished between 814
and 840, during the reign of Louis the Pious, twenty-five years earlier
than this decline appears in Herlihy's tables. Beginning with Louis's
reign, women appear as sole actors or as coactors with other women in
only 10.4 percent of the Lorsch documents (see table 3). The level of
women's activity as sole donors or joint donors with other women
remains at the same level (10 percent) for the rest of the century. In
contrast, the earlier Lorsch documents indicate a higher incidence of
women's donations: 10.8 percent during Pepin's reign, 12.5 percent
during Charlemagne's reign as king, with an increase to 14.4 percent
during the years following his coronation as emperor.

The changes in the proportion of women acting alone or jointly
with other women do not permit us to draw meaningful conclusions, but
figures on women acting jointly with men clearly indicate that women
were less prominent as donors of land after the reign of Louis the Pious
than in the previous decades. Prior to the death of Louis the Pious, the
incidence of joint donations by women and men is fairly steady, fluctuat-
ing between 16 and 17 percent in the reigns of Pepin, Charlemagne, and
Louis. After 840, the incidence drops to 9.6 percent (see table 3). These
joint donations were issued mainly by married couples; the proportion
of women appearing in the Lorsch documents as coactors with sons,
fathers, or brothers was negligible, not exceeding more than 1 percent
in any given period. If we combine the transactions in which women
figure as donors and codonors, we find a significant drop in the visibility
of women controlling land after 840. The fluctuations in the reigns of
Pepin, Charlemagne, and Louis are between 26.8 percent and 30.3
percent, dropping to 19.6 percent after 840 (see table 3).

The drop in the proportion of women disposing of property with
their husbands or alone after 840 cannot be attributed to changes in the
form of landholding, because, with few exceptions, the transactions

TABLE 3 *Women in the Lorsch cartulary*

	Pepin (755–68)	Charles as King (October 768–99)	Charles as Emperor (800–January 814)	Louis the Pious (February 814–40)	(841–94)
Total Transactions	362	2,314	389	241	260
Women Alienating Land					
Alone	36	278	54	24	26
With other women	3	11	2	1	0
Total	39 (10.8%)	289 (12.5%)	56 (14.4%)	25 (10.4%)	26 (10.0%)
Women Alienating Land with Men					
Jointly	56	366	61	41	25
As signers	2	4	1	0	0
Total	58 (16.0%)	370 (16.0%)	62 (15.9%)	41 (17.0%)	25 (9.6%)

Identity of Female Actors

Deo sacrata	33
Widow	4
Mother/Daughter	6
Sister/Sister	6
Unspecified	386
Total	435

Relationship of Coactors

Wife/Husband	401
Wife/Husband/Child	9
Mother/Son	42
Sister/Brother	3
Mother/Daughter/Son	1
Aunt/Nephew	1
Wife/Husband/Father-in-law	2
Unspecified	97
Total	556

involved allodial land. Nor is it enough to say that the higher proportion of donations in which women participated as donors and codonors before 840 reflected a desire by men to provide for the welfare of their souls before going off to war.[53] The greatest military expansion of the Carolingian empire occurred under Charlemagne as king, when the proportion of donations in which women participated did not significantly increase (see table 3). Moreover, these donations had as their purpose the salvation of the soul of parents and children and most frequently of the donors themselves, but not of a husband, brother, or son alone. Finally, because the laws of inheritance remained unchanged, we cannot assume that less land passed into the hands of women by means of inheritance after 840.

A more satisfactory explanation of the lesser prominence of women in the transactions after 840 is that the marriage regulations of Louis, albeit unintentionally, resulted in fewer marriages among the upper echelons of Frankish society. The strict punishment of divorce upheld by the Council of Mainz, one of the four great reforming councils held in 829, had important consequences for the control of land in the Lorsch region.[54] Secular legislation against divorce began in 789, culminating in 802 with the instructions Charlemagne included in his *Capitulary to the Missi*. Cases reaching the courts after 802 were to be adjudicated according to the new laws.[55] Ancient customs, however, could not be changed suddenly. Renewed legislation against divorce by Louis the Pious suggests the widespread failure of Charlemagne's efforts. Finally, in 829, the four reforming councils, one of which met at Mainz in the vicinity of Lorsch, subjected husbands who had divorced their wives to public penance, the same punishment given a man who had killed his wife.[56]

With the promulgation of this decree, Louis the Pious opened a new chapter not only in the history of marital relations but also in the history of the ownership of land by women. The threat of public penance was sufficient to discourage divorces. As escape from inconvenient unions became more difficult, if not impossible, and as the definition of a legitimate marriage became more precise, men of the nobility began to exercise greater caution in choosing a wife. The casual arrangements, the *Friedelehe* or quasi marriages of earlier times, went on unabated. But in the ninth century, as we have seen in the previous chapter, they came to be regarded as trial marriages that denied the woman any legal claim as a wife. Although these relationships were occasionally transformed into legitimate unions, normally they served only as a means for men to enjoy more than casual sexual relationships before settling down to marriage. With men of the aristocracy marrying somewhat later, marrying women who came from the same social class, and remarrying only after their wives died, fewer women had the opportunity to gain control of property through marriage. A mistress, even if she was of high birth with powerful connections and treasures at her disposal, did not qualify as a coactor in land transactions.

The Lorsch documents indicate only occasionally the provenance of the property that was being turned over to the monastery. Hence, it is not possible to estimate what proportion of transactions in which women acted as donors or codonors represented property to which they had direct claim as part of their inheritance, bridegift, morgengabe, or dower. But the charters that mention the provenance of the property suggest that wives appeared as coactors not only in transactions involving land to which they had direct claim, but also in alienations of land that constituted part of their husbands' patrimony. In a few cases, in which the donation is known to involve the husband's patrimony, the wife only agreed to the transaction with her signature. In many of these transactions she appeared as a coactor and joint donor, suggesting that conjugal goods, regardless of their provenance, were considered by some couples as jointly owned. For example, in a donation jointly issued with his wife Willerat, a certain Hucbert specified that they were giving to the monastery "whatever I have inherited from my father." Other deeds, like the one drawn up by Gerald and Ruttrud in 776, failed to make even this fine distinction, describing the husband's land as "coming from our father." The donations of Gerolt and Imma, issued in 779 and 784, merely referred to the properties as jointly owned.[57]

It is important to note that some of the transactions in which the wife appeared as a codonor of her husband's patrimony predate Charlemagne's legislation on the indissolubility of marriage. These deeds thus confirm the evidence provided by law codes and narrative sources that a wife had considerable economic rights under the pre-Carolingian marital system, even though in other respects the system favored men. The Carolingian legislation made the position of wives more secure, but did not augment female economic rights. The emphasis on the indissolubility of marriage increased the effective association of conjugal goods, but it did not improve the opportunities for women to acquire control over landed property through marriage. On the contrary, the elimination of divorce prevented the dispersal of a man's patrimony among a succession of wives. A woman in the Carolingian era could gain full legal control over her own property and a part of her husband's patrimony only if she became a widow. Indeed, under the new monogamous structure, the bridegift was gradually transformed into a widow's dower. Instead of giving the wife full ownership of a part of her husband's patrimony, a growing number of marriage contracts guaranteed her only the right of usufruct, usually over a third of all his property.[58]

These observations are valid only for those areas where Frankish customs prevailed. From the south, where vestiges of Roman law favored the participation of women in the ownership of land, and from areas little affected by Frankish administrative edicts, such as Brittany, we do not have sufficient documentation to warrant a collective study. The cartularies of these regions, moreover, are less reliable in terms of dating and authentication, having been published for the most part in the nineteenth century. Hence, they can serve as the basis only for a very rough estimate of women's economic power.

The only two areas in the south for which there are more than a handful of charters are Auvergne and the Mâconnais. From Auvergne, two cartularies of Saint Julien of Brioude have been reconstructed with 89 private transactions. For the Mâconnais the cartularies of Cluny and Saint Vincent of Mâcon provide 130 charters. Auvergne, a part of Aquitaine, had a mixed Gallo-Roman and Frankish population; the Mâconnais, in addition to these two ethnic groups, had Burgundian inhabitants.[59] In close geographic proximity, these two areas shared a common political history during the last two decades of the ninth century. Under the Carolingians, the Mâconnais was administered either as a separate county or as a part of the Duchy of Lyons or of Burgundy. In 880, however, it was attached to Auvergne, which was then controlled by the powerful Bernard of Plantevelue. After Bernard's death, his son William the Pious lost most of his father's *honores* in the Midi, but managed to keep the county of Mâcon together with Auvergne, the Lyonnais, Autun, and Gevaudan.[60]

There is no way of judging whether the Carolingian legislation had any effect upon the economic power of women and the ownership of land in Auvergne and the Mâconnais. The dearth of documents from the first half of the century makes meaningful comparisons impossible. The documents reveal, however, a better balance between the economic power of men and women than in East Francia. This must be attributed to the particularly favorable legal provisions for women's rights of inheritance. The Roman laws promulgated by the Germanic kings accorded to daughters and sons equal inheritance rights. While not all women living in these areas enjoyed these privileges because the population was of mixed descent, a sufficient number of women did live under Roman law to increase substantially the proportion of women owning land. It is surprising, therefore, that, despite their greater economic power, fewer women appeared as independent actors than in East Francia.

Among the 89 transactions preserved in the Brioude cartularies, only 5 were drawn up by women alone. The low proportion of women actors, 4 out of 64 transactions, obtains in the cartulary of Saint Vincent of Mâcon, rising to 7 in 66 documents in the Cluny cartulary. On the other hand, women as coactors appear in 36 of the Brioude, 24 of the Saint Vincent of Mâcon, and 30 of the Cluny charters. If we add the transactions in which women appear as cosigners, we find 39 documents recorded in the Brioude cartularies, 25 in those of Saint Vincent of Mâcon, and 34 in the Cluny cartulary. (See table 4.) Although the figures are crude, the rather wide discrepancy between the proportion of women donating land jointly with their husbands and women acting alone suggests a pattern.

TABLE 4   *Women in the Cluny, St. Vincent of Mâcon,*
                  and Brioude cartularies

	Cluny (813–899)	St. Vincent of Mâcon (825–892)	Brioude (817–900)
Total Transactions	66	64	89
Women Alienating Land			
Alone	7	4	5
With other women	0	0	0
Total	7 (10.6%)	4 (6.2%)	5 (5.6%)
Women Alienating Land with Men			
Jointly	30	24	36
As signers	4	1	3
Total	34 (51.5%)	25 (39.1%)	39 (43.8%)
Relationship of Coactors:			
Wife/Husband	17	21	30
Wife/Husband/Child	9	3	0
Mother/Son	3	0	1
Sister/Brother	1	0	5
Total	30	24	36

Further scrutiny of these documents leads to the conclusion that many of the female actors were widows. If we exclude those whose deeds were purported to be approved by their young children, we are left with only one or two independent female actors in each area. Heiresses apparently had many suitors and married quite early; once married, they had less freedom to dispose of their property at will. They did retain control over their own property as coactors with their husbands and children, and they could exercise independent power if they were widowed and their children were small. The negligible number of women appearing as sole donors in the documents suggests that wealthy widows probably did not remain single very long and those who did were induced by sound economic judgment and concern for the family to retain their property.

Women who did not marry were careful to guard their prerogatives by seeking a male protector. A good case in point is Countess Ava, a woman with no sons to protect her. Although she did not lack a sense of independence and enterprise, she was eager to gain the good will of the local prince, William the Pious, who was probably her half-brother. She turned over to him a piece of property on which he was later to build Cluny, and received lifelong usufruct in exchange. She retained other parts of her extensive estates in her own possession, or distributed them among her vassals.[61]

Married women in Auvergne and the Mâconnais retained close ties with their own blood relatives, as is illustrated by the instances of women donating property to their brothers and giving alms for the salvation of their parents' and brothers' souls. This bond of affection seems to have been mutual, for we also find cases of brothers making a donation for the souls of their sisters.[62] The lack of similar cases in East Francia seems to suggest that economic and emotional ties between brothers and sisters in that area were not as important as those between husband and wife and between ascendants and descendants.

In Auvergne and the Mâconnais, where a greater number of daughters inherited property, the loyalty of married women to their families of birth appears to have ensured the stability of the landowning aristocracy. The relatively high proportion of deeds issued jointly by brothers and sisters in Auvergne, five as opposed to thirty issued by husbands and wives, seems to indicate that, in that area, families were making some attempt to keep their patrimony intact through joint ownership by brothers and sisters. These arrangements were ad hoc partnerships based on mutual affection. Close ties between blood relations in the Mâconnais, moreover, may explain why some women of the area, such as Benedicta, are listed in the *Liber memorialis* of Remiremont among their kinsmen, without any reference to their husbands.[63]

If we accept the transactions preserved in the cartularies as reflecting rough patterns of land ownership, we can conclude that women held a much greater proportion of landed wealth in areas in which Roman law survived. It is not possible, however, to draw a correlation between the more equitable inheritance rights women enjoyed under Roman law and the independent ownership of land by women. In East Francia, an area outside the influence of Roman law, the proportion of women actors was slightly higher than in Auvergne and the Mâconnais. Professor Herlihy's observation that in the Midi women administered their own property must be modified. The documents for Auvergne and the Mâconnais indicate that women shared this responsibility with their husbands, sons, and brothers. Social pressures and cognate relations, rather than the laws, explain the dearth of economically independent women in these areas.

The richest published cartulary for Brittany is that of Redon. It contains over three hundred documents for the ninth century, each sufficiently detailed to illustrate the peculiarities of the social and economic structure of an area that managed to free itself from Frankish tutelage in 841, after a brief period of domination by Charlemagne and Louis the Pious.[64] The marital legislation of Charlemagne and Louis the Pious had little effect in Brittany, if we are to believe one of the court poets in Louis the Pious's entourage. The poet accused the Bretons of being Christians in name only, of practicing incest—brothers sleep with sisters and rape their sisters-in-law.[65] These were ancient customs that Carolingian legislation may have been less successful in eradicating in Brittany than in other parts of Gaul. Frankish influence, however, was not completely absent in Brittany; even after 841 it was exercised in areas where families of Frankish descent had settled, that is, in the dioceses of Rennes and Nantes.

Women appear to have controlled much less land in Brittany than in East Francia. Women are found as independent actors in 5 of the 94 Redon documents issued before 840 and in 14 of the 228 drawn up after that date. In the Lorsch cartulary, even at the lowest ebb of feminine activity, women alienated land independently of men in 10 percent of the documents. Further evidence for the disproportionate male domination of Brittany's economic structure is provided by the low incidence of the appearance of women as coactors with men in the Redon cartulary. Of 322 charters, only 16 include wives, mothers, and sisters as coactors. If we add to this figure the wives who expressed their consent to the transaction by adding their signatures, we arrive at 18, which roughly equals the number of women appearing as independent actors

TABLE 5   *Women in the Redon cartulary*

	Before 841	841–900
Total Transactions	94	228
Women Alienating Land		
Alone	5	14
With other women	0	0
Total	5 (5.3%)	14 (6.1%)
Women Alienating Land with Men		
Jointly	3	13
As signers	1	1
Total	4 (4.3%)	14 (6.1%)

Relationship of Coactors:	
Wife/Husband	8
Wife/Husband/Son	2
Mother/Son	3
Mother/Son/Daughter	1
Unspecified Kin	4
Total	18

(see table 5). In the Lorsch documents the participation of women coactors in the alienation of land never fell below 9.6 percent.

A closer scrutiny of the status of the women appearing as coactors in the Redon cartulary indicates that half were wives and half were mothers and sisters. The relatively higher visibility of women in the latter roles, as compared to the Lorsch documents, reflects the survival in Brittany of an ancient form of communal landholding by extended families. A person's patrimony, unless otherwise disposed of by testamentary bequest, donation, or sale, collectively devolved on all of his or her descendants.[66] Many of the charters refer to cases in which sisters shared the corporate ownership of land with their brothers. When a sister married and became a mother, her children would have a claim to her portion. Although this system of inheritance was fair to women, it was tied to the system of communal landholding, which, by the ninth century, was being replaced by individual, conjugal, or institutional ownership of land. By the ninth century, collectively-held land was no longer treated as an economically indivisible unit and was passing into the hands of a few powerful men, husbands and wives, and the church. Once these patrimonies were broken up, they were no longer subject to the laws governing equal rights of inheritance and could be handed down exclusively through the male line. In accordance with the new system of inheritance, the genealogies traced in the documents show a shift from a bilateral reckoning of kinship to an emphasis on the patrilineal kin.[67]

Women in Brittany were apparently so unaccustomed to looking after their own property that as widows they were quite willing to exchange the control of their holdings for protection. Undoubtedly, invasions by the Franks, raids by the Norsemen, and bitter rivalry among local princes as well as a lack of experience in land management under the communal regime prompted their actions. The normal way to obtain protection was by marriage or, if a woman was beyond the age of marriage, by adoption. For example, the wealthy widow Roiantdreh, after the death of her only son in 861, attached herself to the most powerful family of Brittany by adopting Prince Salomon as her son. She turned over to him her vast possessions, stipulating only that he was to guard and defend her as long as she lived. In so doing, Roiantdreh disinherited her daughters.[68]

Married women were quite willing to relinquish their own shares in communal tenures. There are sale transactions that seem to imply that married women, eager to please their husbands, sold their shares in collectively-held land, thereby facilitating the breakup of communal tenures by kin groups. Although husbands and wives normally gave their consent only by appearing as witnesses to the sale of their partner's land, one of the charters indicates that it was possible for a husband to claim some of the proceeds. A part of the purchase price for Cleroc's share in property she held jointly with her brother and nephew was paid to her husband, Anauuanoc. He received five shillings and an ox worth three shillings, a good settlement considering that the whole property, including the brother's and nephew's share, was sold for fifty-two shillings and eight deniers.[69]

An analysis of the sales recorded in the cartulary indicates that landed wealth was gradually slipping from the hands of women. Records of sixty sales survive from our period; in two the vendors are family groups, in four, married couples, and in ten, women.[70] Among buyers, women acting alone appear only in six cases and with their husbands in eleven cases. These figures, albeit limited, suggest that communal ownership of land by kin groups was being replaced by conjugal ownership. Women, by selling their part in a collective patrimony and using the proceeds to purchase land jointly with their husbands, were instrumental in bringing about this realignment in the control of land. The signatures of sons in the resale of land point to the possibility that sons were being favored in the inheritance of this land.[71] The signature of a daughter appears only in one instance, a donation issued by Lanthild, a woman of Frankish origin.[72]

Although marriage could serve as a means for women to enrich themselves through land, financial gain more often came in the form of movable property. But there were exceptions. The Redon cartulary includes donations of land as rewards by husbands to their wives;[73] it also contains a reference to the practice of giving brides a *morgengabe*. The case of Roiantken, wife of Count Deuerhoiarn, illustrates how a willful woman married to a powerful man could amass considerable property. Her father-in-law, Count Rivult, was so wealthy that the compensation he had to pay for a murder committed by Deuerhoiarn did not impair the family's fortune. The property he gave to his daughter-in-law as her *morgengabe* was substantial enough to earn her the honor of being buried with her husband in the vestibule of the Cathedral of Saint Maxentius. She also held more modest property that she inherited from her own family and purchased. In 821, when she was very young, she had bought her brother Catuuten's share in their family's patrimony at Riantkar. When Catuuten tried to rescind the sale, she took him to court and won. Some forty years later, she purchased another piece of property, which she later turned over to the monastery. This donation was signed by her husband and son; she in turn signed a donation that they issued.[74]

The source of Roiantken's property was inheritance, *morgengabe*, and purchase. In contrast to cartularies surviving from areas dominated by Germanic laws, no transaction recorded in the Redon cartulary implies that it was customary for a married woman in Brittany to receive landed property as her *dos*.[75] This perhaps explains the lesser visibility of women as coactors and actors in property transfers in Brittany as compared with East Francia. In areas where the majority of the population lived under Germanic laws, the discrimination against women in the inheritance laws was partially offset by the practice of giving the young bride a piece of land as her *dos*. In Brittany these settlements appear to have been made in the form of movable property.

Squeezed out of the ownership of communally held land through economic, political, and psychological pressures, women ultimately owned less land in Brittany than in East Francia, where a great deal of land passed into female hands through marriage settlements. Neither the Frankish custom of turning over to women a piece of property as their *dos* nor the Carolingian regulations of marriage seem to have influenced the economic situation of women in Brittany.

On the basis of the evidence provided by the cartularies, we can conclude that the most important factors determining the economic power of women were the laws of inheritance and marriage settlements. The economic situation of women was least favorable in Brittany, an area unaffected by Roman law, where Germanic customs prevailed only in isolated Frankish settlements. Women appear as actors, coactors, and cosigners in only 11 percent of the Redon documents, as opposed to 27 percent, the overall average, in the Lorsch documents. The Brioude cartulary yields 49 percent. The corresponding percentage in the Mâconnais if we combine the documents from Cluny and Saint Vincent of Mâcon is 54 percent.

Although the legal influences were important, other sets of circumstances such as family structures and political, social, and economic pressures must also be taken into account in explaining these differences. Political upheavals and changes in the form of landownership prompted widows in Brittany to exchange their economic independence for male protection. Loyalty to their families of birth and the esteem heiresses commanded from their husbands explain the low incidence of women acting as independent agents in land transactions in Auvergne and the Mâconnais. The relatively high ratio of women controlling their own estates in East Francia suggests that women valued their economic independence in that region. On the other hand, full control of property meant less to women in Auvergne and the Mâconnais, where, as landowners through inheritance, they exercised considerable authority and power even when they married.

The economic power women held as heiresses in areas where vestiges of Roman law prevailed enabled them to cope better with the conflicting roles they were expected to play in Carolingian society. As helpmates of their husbands and as widows, women were esteemed for their energy and competence, while as daughters and wives they were supposed to accept their inexorable subordination to male interests and values. Passivity and submission, the behavior traits forced upon women as daughters and wives, were diametrically opposed to the self-assertion and resourcefulness women were expected to display as heads of the household and managers of property both during their husbands' lives and after their deaths. Contradictory sex roles, according to modern psychologists, result in personality conflicts and often lead to a lack of self-esteem. Women enjoying equal inheritance rights with their brothers undoubtedly had greater self-assurance in entering marriage and were thus better equipped to internalize these conflicts. On the other hand, women in the north were more prone to rebel against marriage, seeking spiritual freedom and perfection in monasteries. They were also more generous than women in the south in contributing their own property to churches.

The cartularies reflect patterns of landholding in the ranks of the aristocracy. Whether or not a woman of the dependent classes lived in an area of the *Regnum Francorum,* where Roman rather than Germanic law predominated, was of little consequence to her. Whether she gained control of her father's or husband's tenure as a single child or widow depended on manorial customs formulated by the lord. We do know that demographic and economic factors worked in favor of Carolingian women in this respect. The records of Saint-Germain-des-Près testify not only to periodic shortages of marriageable women on lands belonging to the abbey but also to single women acting as heads of households and manors.[76] These cases, however, were exceptional. As a recent study on the economic regime of the abbey of Prüm has revealed, tenants were normally men. Marriages were patrilocal, and patrilineal descent of property prevailed in peasant families. A widow shared her position as head of a manor with her oldest son and had to relinquish this position when the son married. Widowers, on the other hand, retained tenure even if they had grown and married sons living with them. Heavy labor in the fields and forest was performed by men. The women raised livestock, made beer, baked bread, worked in the vineyard, and were responsible for reaping and shocking at harvest time.[77] On the royal domains, as indicated by one of Charlemagne's capitularies, the primary functions of peasant women were manufacturing wool and linen textiles and producing articles of clothing.[78]

Carolingian legislation probably had very little effect on the marriage customs of peasants. The economic interdependence of a peasant couple made divorce unlikely, even in the Merovingian period. There is no doubt that, as the permanence of marriage and ecclesiastical distinctions between legitimate and illegitimate unions gained acceptance, women of low birth could no longer marry into the aristocracy. Only in the lower echelons of society did enterprising women continue to contribute to social mobility, bringing about the fusion of free and unfree elements. Not only individual lords but Charlemagne himself encouraged marriages between royal serfs and free women on the one hand and royal *fiscalines* and freemen on the other. By declaring that the free partner was to retain all the rights attendant to a person of free status, Charlemagne gave official blessing to a centuries-old practice that went against the letter of the law.[79]

By the ninth century, legal principles and social customs that were to define women's role in the highest and lowest echelons of European society were clearly enunciated. Among peasants, comprising about four-fifths of the population, women worked hard and lived in poverty, but had the freedom to choose their husbands. Although they could no longer aspire to marry into the governing classes, they could marry peasants of a diversity of conditions and statuses, ranging from small proprietors through free, semifree and slave tenants and day laborers.[80] As a member of the labor force, a woman could marry below her status, and her status was not determined by that of her husband. If she was a slave or semifree, she could marry a freeman and give birth to children of intermediate status.

A woman of the aristocracy did not have these choices. In the ninth century, as the great families closed ranks against the dilution of their bloodlines by lower-class wives, they came to attach an even greater importance to the biological function of their daughters. Regarded as political and economic assets, women of the upper classes were carefully guarded in childhood and were married at a tender age. The high value assigned to aristocratic women's reproductive and domestic duties led to definitions that limited their role to the fulfillment of those duties.

The translation into secular legislation of the ecclesiastical ideal of lifelong monogamy made the position of aristocratic wives more secure, but it did not enhance their economic power. Laws of inheritance remained unaffected and marriage settlements began to take the form of dower contracts. Where women had equal inheritance rights under Roman law, they appeared as donors and codonors of land in roughly fifty percent of the charters. Elsewhere, the economic position of women was less favorable. Where Germanic law predominated, women gained access to landed wealth primarily through marriage, and their control over donations of land did not exceed 30 percent and usually remained well below that level. Under both Roman and Germanic law, married women shared this control with their husbands; when they could exercise independent economic power as widows, family and social pressures combined to restrict their activities to the asexual milieu of the monastery.

The benefits of the Carolingians' efforts to impose lifelong monogamy on their subjects were reaped by women in the tenth and eleventh centuries. In the age of violence and political anarchy that followed the collapse of the Carolingian Empire, the family emerged as the most stable and efficient instrument of government. The effective association of conjugal goods under the monogamous structure enabled women to share sovereign rights with their husbands as political power came to be tied to the possession of land. Secure in their position as wives, women were equipped to act with authority as helpmates and *dominae* in both economic and political affairs. Profiting from the consolidation of landed wealth by their fathers and husbands, a growing number of women appeared in this first feudal age as chatelaines, mistresses of land, and proprietesses of monasteries, exercising attendant rights of justice, military command, minting, and taxation.

The astonishing prestige of noble women in Saxony during the tenth and early eleventh centuries has been recently attributed to the itinerant careers and early deaths of noble men. The fear of being dispossessed of the landed wealth that passed into their hands at the death of their brothers and husbands prompted a large number of Saxon ladies to found religious houses. Reserving the control of the advocacy and the right to elect the abbess, the foundresses of these houses wielded considerable political power. They also immortalized their own names by creating centers of culture where the arts and literature flourished.[81] The massive evidence from southern France on the public authority commanded by noble ladies has also been studied recently. To gain security against the hereditary claims of their male kin, wealthy widows did not have to establish monasteries in these regions. Their position as heiresses was protected by the laws even if they had brothers. Throughout southern Europe during this period, women participated with their husbands in the exercise of sovereign powers. On the other hand, they did not achieve fame as spiritual and cultural leaders.[82]

In the more structured Carolingian Empire, women could not exert extensive influence. By enforcing the principle of marital indissolubility, the Carolingians strengthened the position of women in the family, but they also confined women's activities to the private sphere of home and cloister.

PART TWO
Women in Religious Life

"I permit not a woman to teach" (1 Timothy 2:8). In her own home, a woman is allowed to teach members of her own sex, and boys as well, but in the church she is forbidden. Why this prohibition? Because she must be subject to the man for she is made of his body. Moreover, she is not allowed to teach because her sex is weaker than that of the man; hence it must be feared that, as Eve, seduced by the snake, brought death into this world, she too, lapsing so easily into sin, should lead others into the same sin.

Haimo of Auxerre, *In Epist. 1 ad Tim.* (PL 117, 790D–791A).

6

The Waning Influence of Women in the
Frankish Church

Religion in the Frankish Kingdom, as in the late Roman Empire, offered women an opportunity to transcend biological and sexual roles and to seek spiritual fulfillment. Women were involved in a broader range of religious functions under Christianity than paganism. Except for a few vestal virgins, women in the pagan Roman Empire were only passive participants in the state religion or the mystery cults. Whereas some of the mystery cults excluded women altogether from membership, Christianity welcomed both men and women to its worship and ritual. Although women were barred from the Christian priesthood, they could share in pastoral care as priests' wives, deaconesses, or virgins and widows dedicated to the service of God. They could also pursue the contemplative life, devoting themselves to prayer and meditation as professed virgins and widows, members of a religious community, or recluses.

Women's activities as wives of priests and deaconesses, however, were progressively limited in the Frankish Kingdom. Merovingian bishops, supported by their rulers, engaged in vigorous conciliar activity in the sixth century. They strengthened male domination of the hierarchy by abolishing the office of feminine diaconate, defining the order of widows as a religious state devoid of clerical status, and barring priests' wives from pastoral service. The purpose of this chapter is to describe this restrictive legislation and investigate the reasons for its adoption. Was the Frankish church more tightly organized than the late Gallo-Roman one and therefore placed in a better position to enforce earlier canons? Or was the limitation of women's activities in the church a reflection of new social-psychological attitudes toward women? Answers to these questions may be of interest not only to historians but to anyone concerned with the present status of women in Christian churches.

Clerical celibacy and the ministry of women have traditionally been studied as two unrelated developments. The prevailing view in the vast literature on clerical celibacy holds that its imposition in the West represented an attempt to create an ascetic image of ecclesiastical leadership. The other line of argument emphasizes ritual purity as the fundamental rationale for clerical celibacy.[1] Preoccupied either with defending or condemning clerical celibacy, historians have examined the struggle from a sectarian point of view, forgetting that the targets of attack were not only married clerks but also their wives. The only exception is Samuel Laeuchli, who remarked that the repressed sexuality of Western clerics gave rise to a "constant desire to punish women with whom they came into contact."[2] Even if the restrictive legislation merely gave rise to fears of being polluted by the touch of women, one ought to inquire whether or not it reinforced ancient misogynistic notions about the impurity of women. It also remains to be seen if there was any connection between the demand for clerical celibacy and the abolition of the feminine clerical office in the Frankish church.

The rich array of scholarly literature on the ministry of women acknowledges that women occupied an ecclesiastical position in the early church. But there are considerable differences of opinion about where and when women acted as ministers, whether or not they belonged to the clerical order, and why their office was finally abolished. Interpretations concerning the origins and the disappearance of the diaconate of women have been closely linked with the problem of the status and function of widows in the early church. Until 1873, it was assumed that there was only one ecclesiastical office for women in the early church, the holders of which were referred to as both widows and deaconesses by the sources. In that year, however, Theodor Zahn pointed out that, in the entourage of Saint Ignatius, elderly widows and younger deaconesses performed entirely different functions.[3] While the recognition of only one group continues to find supporters, modern historians tend to distinguish between deaconesses and widows, even though they may disagree about whether widows held an ecclesiastical office, or merely rendered auxiliary pastoral services proper to their religious status.[4]

Another subject of dispute is whether the ministry of women was abolished or came to be exercised by canonesses, whose institutes were among the earliest feminine religious communities.[5] Explanations of the causes leading to the abolition of the only clerical office women ever held in the Roman Catholic church range, moreover, from changes in baptismal customs and rites, rendering the function of deaconesses superfluous, to the prominent roles women played in the Gnostic sects, which created a prejudice against the ministry of women among the defenders of orthodoxy.[6]

Most recently the Belgian canonist Roger Gryson, in his *Le ministère des femmes dans l'Église ancienne,* advanced the thesis that in the Latin West, where the fear of heresy was strong, the feminine diaconate was never recognized as an ecclesiastical office, but remained a simple dignity or, rather, an honorific title. In presenting his thesis, Gryson did not attempt to ascertain the functions of deaconesses. Nor did he perceive that the fear of heresy served as an excuse for reviving in Christian guise ancient taboos about the cultic impurity of women. In a broader context, Haye van der Meer, in his *Women Priests in the Catholic Church?*, provided a more penetrating treatment of the attitudes prompting the exclusion of women from the holy orders. In addition to the opposition to Jewish tradition, the misreading of Paul, and false biological and psychological concepts, the learned Jesuit also singled out irrational fears. He noted that "it seems to be very common to see danger to celibacy in a female priesthood."[7]

One of the problems to be addressed in the following analysis concerns the activities of deaconesses in the Frankish Kingdom. Although a detailed examination of the history of women religious in the Frankish Kingdom will be undertaken in the next chapter, we will investigate here whether or not the status of deaconesses was confused with that of professed widows and whether or not deaconesses were absorbed into nunneries. Of greatest importance from a historical perspective is the relationship between the abolition of feminine ministry and the concept of ritual purity. The latter became a basic argument for the sixth-century Merovingian church in its fight against clerical marriage.

WOMEN IN PASTORAL CARE

Unlike the pagan cults, the early Christian church prescribed neither celibacy nor marriage for its presbyters. The ideal of virginity and sexual abstinence advocated by Paul (1 Cor. 7:32–34) became the norm for the Latin church only in the fourth century. For the first three centuries after the establishment of Christianity, the married and the celibate served together in charismatic ministry. Indeed, a married man was better equipped than a single man to furnish pastoral care in those embattled years. His wife and daughter provided auxiliary services in the small congregations, which may be best characterized as extended families.[8] Clement of Alexandria, writing around 200, sanctioned marriage for laymen, deacons, priests, and bishops alike, extolling the virtues of women as helpmates to their husbands.[9] Only in the third century, when the ascetic ideal came to influence not only Christian communities but also pagan sects, was Paul's proclamation that marriage was a servitude

to the flesh and earthly things, a burden that both husband and wife had
to bear, taken more seriously. Two leading churchmen of the time,
Origen and Tertullian, painted an even more derogatory picture of
marriage, singling out women as burdens upon their husbands.[10]

The disparagement of marriage in general and women in particular
became increasingly prevalent in the writings of fourth and fifth century
Latin fathers. As the Western church began to press for sexual abstinence in higher orders, apologists began to compare the wives of clerics
to Eve. For example, an anonymous treatise about the seven ecclesiastical grades, composed around 420, warned priests not to give power
over their souls to their wives because, like Adam placed in paradise,
they too might be beguiled.[11] Tirades about woman's role as temptress,
henceforth appearing regularly in conciliar legislation, papal decretals,
sermons, and treatises, encouraged the identification of women with
sexuality and sin.[12]

Even more detrimental to women in religious service was the call
for cultic purity, which was introduced into papal decretals in the late
fourth century. By personally embracing the ascetic ideal, the wife of a
clerk could invalidate the argument that she was a temptress and a moral
liability to her husband, but there was nothing she could do to counter
the argument that the mere touch of her hands was polluting. The
church's concern for cultic purity was sometimes reinforced by, and at
other times confused with, the ascetic ideal of sexual abstinence. The
two together served as powerful weapons against clerical marriages and
feminine influence in parish affairs.

The first official proposal for clerical continence was advanced by
the Spanish provincial synod held at Elvira around 306.[13] Perhaps because it emphasized asceticism and not ritual purity, the proclamation
remained ineffective. Indeed, it met with considerable opposition. The
Council of Nicaea in 325, under the leadership of Paphnutius, rejected
the requirement of chastity as a burden too heavy for most men to bear
and defended marriage as an honorable state.[14] The Council of Gangra
(340–345) reaffirmed this decision by excommunicating those who
refused to partake of the sacrament performed by a married priest.[15]
Without mentioning either Elvira or subsequent councils, Popes Damasus (366–384) and Siricius (384–399) upheld the requirement of clerical
abstinence as the official policy of the Latin church.[16] By invoking the
need for ritual purity, they established a new rationale for the continence of the clergy, which was then proclaimed by the Council of
Carthage in 390.[17]

Defenders of clerical marriage vainly tried to argue for the consummation of Mary's and Joseph's union after the birth of Christ. Mary's

perpetual virginity found powerful advocates in Jerome and Augustine.[18] The Council of Carthage declared in 401 that at the time of ordination, clergy in higher orders had to take a vow to abstain from sexual relations with their wives for the rest of their lives.[19]

Nevertheless, marriage was not considered an impediment to ordination. A man who had been married only once to a woman who had not been previously married was eligible for ordination to the diaconate and higher grades.[20] Although an ordained minister could not marry,[21] celibacy of the clergy was not yet prevalent. Nor was a married minister's vow interpreted in the fifth century as obliging him to sever his family ties. Only in the sixth century, in the newly founded Frankish Kingdom, did the church adopt a stricter policy. It began to press for celibacy by insisting on actual separation of the ministers of the altar from their wives, rather than sexual abstinence.

Ambivalent as the Latin churchmen may have been about marriage in general and women in particular, they did not ignore the mutuality of the marriage contract. Gallo-Roman synods in the pre-Frankish period required that the wife of a man being ordained to higher ranks not merely consent to her husband's pledge but also take a vow herself.[22] By doing so, the wife acquired the honored status of a woman religious. Consecrated to God and sharing her husband's home and duties, albeit not his bed, the wife of a priest, deacon, or bishop could devote her full energy to auxiliary services in the parish.[23] The last Gallican council upholding this tradition was held in 506 at Agde, which had not yet come under Frankish domination. Convened by Caesarius of Arles, a staunch advocate of the mutuality of the marriage contract, it stipulated that ordination was to take place only after husband and wife "pariter conversi fuerint."[24] By insisting that both husband and wife take a religious vow before the husband was ordained, the Gallican councils minimized the papal call for ritual purity and stressed, instead, the ideal of asceticism as the basis for priesthood.

The mutuality of the marriage bond was a fundamental principle of Christian social theory. Paul had defined this bond as giving husband and wife power over each other's body (1 Cor. 7:1–5). In keeping with the patristic belief that men were sexually more aggressive than women, Augustine had advised husbands to take the initiative in the observance of sexual abstinence.[25] However much they believed in the value of continence, the fathers did not condone abstinence without mutual consent even as a temporary measure on the eve of holidays and during Advent and Lent.[26] Justinian's legislation that a marriage was automatically dissolved if one of the partners entered a monastery met the stern opposition of Pope Gregory I (590–604). Neither a husband nor a wife,

Gregory insisted, had the right to take a vow of abstinence without the permission of his or her partner.[27]

Gregory's ruling on the reciprocity of the marriage contract was apparently not communicated to the Frankish church. The power that men exercised over their wives under Germanic law, including the right to dissolve their marriages unilaterally, was extended in the Merovingian kingdom to cases involving the vow of continence. As before, if a married man was ordained to a higher clerical office, he had to promise to abstain from marital relations with his wife. The evidence suggests, however, that his wife was not asked to take a vow of continence. The missals circulating in the Merovingian kingdom did not include prayers for the blessing of priests' and deacons' wives, although these ceremonies were incorporated into the rituals of ordination in the ninth century, when the Carolingian church came to follow more closely the Roman liturgy.[28] Furthermore, none of the sources indicates that the wives of Frankish priests and deacons wore a special habit, which Pope Gregory I required as the symbol of their commitment to a life of sexual abstinence.[29]

On the other hand, under the double standards governing marital relations in the Frankish Kingdom, a married woman could not embrace religious life without her husband's permission. Although consecrated a deaconess, Saint Radegund had to resort to Saint Germain's mediation to obtain release from her marital obligations to her polygynous husband.[30] Other women did not fare as well. Gregory of Tours relates that, with citations from canon law, he opposed the haughty words of Bertegund, who, when asked to become the abbess of Saint Martin of Tours, told her husband: "Go home and govern our children. I will not return to you, for the married will not see the kingdom of heaven."[31] The so-called *Excarpsus Cummeani,* a penitential of Irish inspiration that enjoyed considerable popularity in eighth-century Francia, subjected a woman to penance if she took a vow of abstinence without her husband's permission.[32] The bishops assembled at Compiègne in 757 declared that, if a woman veiled herself without her husband's consent, her husband had the right to reclaim her and resume conjugal relations.[33]

Instead of making the ordination of a married man contingent upon his wife's approval, the Merovingian councils assumed that a husband had the unilateral right to renounce intercourse with his wife. Ostensibly to protect ritual purity, the councils imposed constraints upon him and degraded the status and freedom of his wife. The legislation amounted to a de facto requirement of clerical celibacy in the Frankish church. Deprived of any role in parish affairs, women associating with clerks became subject to accusations of polluting the sacraments and bringing the wrath of God upon the people.

The Frankish councils initially tried to deter clerks from resuming sexual relations with their wives by invoking the threat of deposition. Extending the rule of continence also to subdeacons, the Council of Orléans in 538 cited Pope Innocent I's letter to Victricius of Rouen. "What shame shall be his who returns to sacrifice, defiled by sexual desire," the Pope had written.[34] The bishops, meeting at Clermont three years earlier, had been even more ingenious. Using Pope Leo I's plea that clerks should transform their matrimonial ties into a brother and sister relationship, these bishops executed a legal tour de force by drawing the conclusion that clerical incontinence was a form of incest. If a clerk had intercourse with his wife, and particularly if he begot children, he was guilty of incest and had to be deposed.[35] In 567 the Council of Tours charged incontinent married clerks with Nicolaitic heresy, also punishable with deposition. The call for ritual purity played an important part in the council's deliberations. "How does one who consecrates the Body of the Lord," the bishops asked, "dare to commit such a crime?"[36]

As a further precaution, the councils forbade clerics free association with their wives. In 541, the Council of Orléans enjoined married priests and deacons to sleep in separate rooms from their wives. The Council of Tours held in 567 reiterated this rule, adding that the wife of a priest, deacon, or subdeacon must constantly be in the company of a slave girl. Bishops, according to the same council, were to maintain separate residences for their wives and should never be alone; even when they slept, they should have subordinate clerks present in order to avoid all suspicion. In keeping with this law, the Council of Mâcon (581–583) ordered that no woman should enter the chamber of a bishop without the company of two priests or at least two deacons.[37] The first indication that the wives of lesser churchmen were expected to live apart from their husbands dates from 583, when the Council of Lyons requested priests and deacons to refrain from seeing their wives daily.[38] By this time, the wives of deacons and priests were apparently no longer allowed to share the homes of their husbands.

The banishment of deacons', priests', and bishops' wives from the presence of their husbands had a dual consequence. It may have ostensibly removed a source of temptation from the clerks' lives, but it also decreased the influence of women in parish affairs. Avitus of Vienne's remark that priests' wives, even when chaste and harmless, were obstacles in their husbands' paths illustrates the thinking that prompted this restrictive legislation.[39] No one bothered about the subsequent fate of these women, who had the dubious and empty honor of being called *diaconissae*, *presbyteriae*, and *episcopiae*, designations that reflected the honor previously accorded clerks' wives.[40]

The complaint registered by Saint Columban, an Irish missionary who visited Frankland at the end of the sixth century, that the clergy in those regions lived either openly or clandestinely with their wives,[41] as well as the letters on the same subject that Pope Gregory I addressed to the Frankish clergy, leave no doubt that ecclesiastical sanctions were defied by both clerks and their wives.[42] The *Burgundian Penitential,* making special provisions for infanticide committed by married clerks, corroborates this defiance.[43]

In addition, Gregory of Tours testified that even wives of bishops were reluctant to leave their husbands and that some openly rebelled against their husbands' abstinence. The only explanation that the wife of Felix of Nantes could imagine for being banished from his bed was that he had found another woman. Seeking to expose his infidelity, she burst into his chamber at night, only to find sitting on his chest a lamb, the miraculous symbol of his chastity, according to Gregory.[44] More conventional but equally edifying was the outcome of Susanna's intrusion into her husband's chamber. Priscus apparently welcomed her visit. For their impudence, Gregory informs us, both were struck with divine punishment. The bishop had epileptic fits, and Susanna, possessed by a demon, went insane.[45]

Women not lacking in virtue or self-control also resisted separation from their husbands. Confident in their mutual chastity, the wife of Simplicius, demonstrating greater tenacity than tact, refused to leave her husband. But her presence in the episcopal residence created such a scandal that a mob besieged it. Only by voluntarily proving her virginity with the ordeal by fire did the determined woman save herself and her husband from violent death.[46] Other women more meekly accepted their role as a single parent and head of a household.[47] Some, like the wife of the priest Namatius, found solace and fulfillment in charitable works and the building of churches and oratories.[48]

The power of a churchman's office might compensate him for the lack of female companionship, but his wife faced only a life of deceit and loneliness. Never entirely above suspicion, the wives of churchmen were forced to lead self-effacing and unproductive lives. Whatever their personal inclinations and preferences, they were not allowed to remarry, not even as widows. The precedent for this last restriction on clerical wives had been set in 400, when the Council of Toledo had refused communion until her deathbed to the remarried widow of a deacon, priest, or bishop. The logic behind this legislation was that the wife of a deacon, priest, or bishop had pledged herself to a life of continence at the time of her husband's ordination.[49] The Frankish councils subjected the wives of churchmen to the same rule,[50] even though they did not require wives to take the pledge on which the Toledo legislation was based. The Council of Mâcon in 585 went even further, ordering that, if the widow of a deacon, priest, or bishop contracted a second marriage, her union was to be dissolved and she was to be confined to a monastery until the end of her life. Moreover, the council extended this canon to the widows of exorcists, lecturers, and acolytes, even though these officials were not bound by the rule of continence.[51]

The threat of deposition deterred many a man ambitious for an ecclesiastical career from contracting a marriage. Rather than marry, clerics frequently resorted to a more convenient and less formal arrangement with women who functioned ostensibly as their housekeepers. Consecrated virgins, vowed widows, and even maidservants served the purpose, as one can see from the proceedings of the Council of Tours held in 567. Rejecting the excuse that clerks needed clothing and their homes kept in order, the council argued that it was better for them to work with their hands than to keep "serpents" in their homes.[52] Although the Frankish councils prescribed that churchmen could have in their households only females who were their near blood relatives, they usually punished those who were caught with degradation, not deposition.[53] Indeed, the Council of Orléans, held in 538, declared that a married priest was not to be deposed if he had a child from a concubine, or lived openly with a concubine after the death of his wife.[54]

The penitentials also treated the incontinence of a cleric with his own wife as a more serious offense than fornication with a woman to whom he was not married. For example, the *Burgundian Penitential* prescribed five years of penance for fornication by priests and deacons. If a deacon had "adulterous relations" with his wife, the length of his penance remained the same, but for the first two years he had to live on bread and water. For incontinence with his wife, a priest had to perform seven years of penance, with the first three of these on bread and water.[55]

The Merovingian church apparently felt less threatened by clerical concubines than by clerical wives. Concubines might cause embarrassment or even scandal, but the hierarchy could deal even more arbitrarily with them than with wives. The concubines of clerics were held in such public contempt that neither the state nor their own families would protect them. Exile was their fate if the church took action against them.[56] But they fared worse in the hands of their own families. Gregory of Tours reported that a freewoman who went to live with a priest was burned alive by her enraged relatives. Her seducer, a priest, suffered no harm, although the woman's relatives held him prisoner until the archbishop ransomed him for twenty gold shillings.[57]

The presence of concubines in the households of clerks reinforced the arguments of those who wanted to depict women as wanton creatures and temptresses. The Council of Tours held in 567 compared women to snakes that shed their skins in order to appear more appealing.[58] Used as scapegoats by the church to explain the incontinence of the clergy, women came to be blamed for all kinds of misfortunes associated with ritual impurity. The Bavarian Code declared that "a deacon or priest could live only with his mother, daughter, or sister, because the natural bond hindered schemes of wicked crime and affection in these women and extolled them to persevere in chastity." Any other woman was not allowed to dwell in a deacon's or priest's house "for fear that, deceived by her, he should be polluted when offering God a sacrifice, on account of which the people were to perish and be struck by plague."[59]

The insidious argument that women caused plagues and famines by corrupting priests, who then offered sacrifices displeasing to God, served to destroy clerical marriages. The same argument was also used in the battle against the feminine diaconate. In addition, the Merovingian bishops reasserted atavistic taboos about the impurity of women in their efforts to remove them from ecclesiastical offices.

WOMEN AND THE DIACONATE

The controversy over the diaconate of women in the first two centuries centers on the title *diakonos* given to Phoebe in the Epistle to the Romans (16:1), which had been translated by Jerome as "in ministerio Ecclesiae." Gryson has argued that the title did not designate a precise function in the middle of the first century A.D. Phoebe's contribution, according to Gryson, was offering shelter to Christian travelers and making her home available for meetings of Christians. Other scholars, however, have interpreted this passage to mean that Phoebe, and others like her, were the apostles' co-workers.[60] Nevertheless, historians do agree that, by the third century, deaconesses were performing specific liturgical functions. The *Didascalia* makes it clear that deaconesses assisted bishops and priests in baptizing female catechumens, giving religious instruction to women, and nursing sick women.[61] In the East, during the fourth century, deaconesses came to be recognized as full members of the clergy. Their importance is confirmed by conciliar legislation, the attention the Eastern fathers paid to their activities, and references to them in inscriptions.[62]

The duties of deaconesses differed from those of deacons. Allowed to serve only women, deaconesses were limited to functions that, because they required prolonged or intimate contact with women, were deemed unsuitable for priests and deacons. Deaconesses, moreover, were subject to strict rules of celibacy, whereas married men were admitted to equivalent or higher ecclesiastical grades without being required to take a perpetual vow of continence.

The Western hierarchy was less inclined to admit women to its ranks. Some of the most influential churchmen of the fourth century expressed opposition to the very idea of women performing even minor clerical functions. The prominent role of women in the Priscillian heresy, which made its appearance in Spain and Aquitaine around 370, served as a convenient excuse for opposing the presence of women in the clergy. Ambrosiaster, writing in Rome in the late fourth century, spoke with distaste of the "foolish audacity" of the Cataphrygians, who ordained deaconesses, even though the apostle had ordered women to remain silent in churches (1 Cor. 14:34).[63] The Cataphrygians were the followers of Priscillian and were accused not only of ordaining deaconesses but also of holding Manichaean beliefs, practicing sorcery, and engaging in orgies with women.

An educated layman with connections in the highest circles in both Spain and Aquitaine, Priscillian has aptly been described by Henry Chadwick as "an early evangelist" whose teachings approached gnostic dualism. Preaching intense study of the Bible, renunciation of the pleasures of the flesh, and the equality of men and women as receptacles of the Holy Spirit, Priscillian attracted among his followers influential and educated women,[64] particularly in Aquitaine, where the regimen of asceticism had become popular among the wealthy.[65] Priscillian also earned the hatred of the self-indulgent clergy in Spain and Aquitaine. Rumors spread that he had impregnated the daughter of the poetess Euchrotia, one of his female disciples. Even Jerome denounced the female company Priscillian kept as "an example of misguided females giving patronage to heretics." Priscillian's confession, during his trial at Trier in 381, to having held nocturnal vigils with (loose) women and to praying while naked, as well as his subsequent execution together with two of his male followers and Euchrotia (who had accompanied him to Trier in an attempt to use her connections on his behalf), supported the charge that he had encouraged women to play an improper role in the sect.[66] The tragic end of the affair also helped to perpetuate the myth that the exclusion of women from clerical and pastoral functions was the mark of orthodoxy.

Two councils were convened in the West to extirpate Priscillian's teachings, one at Saragossa in 380 and another at Nîmes from 394 to 396. The second council warned against women who preached, taught men, and exercised Levitic ministry. The bishops assembled at Nîmes clearly stated that, in their own churches, women did not hold these offices. They did mention that in some churches women were serving as deaconesses, but they did not know the location of these churches.[67]

After the Council of Nîmes, there was complete silence on deaconesses for about fifty years, until 441, when the Council of Orange ordered that "henceforth deaconesses were not to be ordained and those who had been were to accept priestly benediction as ordinary people by bowing their head."[68] We may conclude from this proclamation that, sometime between 394 or 396 and 441, the ordination of deaconesses had become common practice in the churches of Gaul. We do not know who these women were and what function they performed. They may have been the wives of churchmen; some evidence suggests that, in fifth and early sixth century Gaul, wives of clerks in higher offices were ordained deaconesses.[69] In any event, we do know that, by 441, the Gallican church had ordained deaconesses who regarded themselves as equals to the male clergy, and hence refused to bow their heads to priestly benediction as lay people. The bishops assembled at Orange were apparently determined to abolish the feminine diaconate, to humiliate the women who had already been ordained, and to assert the exclusivity of male authority in the church.

A further clue to the fate of women in the ecclesiastical hierarchy of late fifth-century Gaul comes from the *Statuta ecclesiae antiqua*, compiled around 475 by Gennadius of Marseilles. Although Gennadius relied extensively on the *Apostolic Constitutions*, a late fourth-century Syriac collection of Greek canons and liturgy, he did not copy it indiscriminately but, rather, used the technique of paraphrasing to adapt it to the Western ecclesiastical tradition.[70] Gennadius' position on the ministry of women struck a compromise between the intransigence of the Council of Orange and the open-mindedness of the Eastern fathers. Like the *Apostolic Constitutions*, the *Statuta* made it clear that women could not teach men or baptize. The function of female ministers was to act as intermediaries between the male hierarchy and female believers and to prepare members of their own sex for baptism. Probably out of deference to the pronouncement of Orange, Gennadius referred to women's clerical office as a ministry and not as a diaconate, mentioning only election and not ordination to the office. Conspicuously absent from his compilation was the simile of the *Apostolic Constitutions*, which compared deacons to Christ and deaconesses to the Holy Ghost.

We may assume, therefore, that the position of women in the clerical hierarchy had been degraded to a nonordained level by this time. On the other hand, the office was not yet identified or confused with the religious order of widows. In complete accord with the *Apostolic Constitutions,* Gennadius noted that both consecrated virgins (*sanctimoniales*) and widows were eligible for the office and that the function of female ministers was distinct from that of widows, who, receiving a stipend from the church, were expected to persevere in the *opus Dei,* that is, in prayer and self-denial.[71]

The *Statuta ecclesiae antiqua,* though widely used, could not overcome the prejudices against feminine ministry in the Frankish church. Indeed, historical circumstances were less favorable to the participation of women in clerical and pastoral functions in the Merovingian kingdom than they had been in fifth-century Gaul. The political power that the Merovingian bishops gained from the patronage of their kings enhanced the effectiveness of their opposition to the feminine diaconate. The socio-economic advantages of a clerical career attracted a sufficient number of men to enable the church to dispense with the services of women in auxiliary pastoral and liturgical functions. Most importantly, the disparaging tone of Germanic laws—their emphasis on women's biological function and their tendency to treat women as sex objects and mere chattel—created a climate favorable to conciliar legislation that, though not unprecedented, became increasingly systematic and devastating in its sexist intent. During the sixth century, opposition to the feminine diaconate was no longer justified on the basis of heresy, nor was the haughtiness of deaconesses used as an excuse. Rather, the argument centered on the very nature of women, which was held to represent a threat to the ritual purity of the church in a variety of nefarious ways.

The battle against female ministers opened in the Merovingian church in 511, when three Frankish bishops learned that two Breton priests, Lovocatus and Catihernus, were celebrating the Eucharist with *conhospitae* or cohostesses. Acting as traveling evangelists, these priests and their female assistants journeyed through the countryside, saying mass and distributing communion in the huts of peasants. The bishops were disturbed that the *conhospitae* were both polluting the sacrament by offering the chalice to the communicants and sleeping under the same roof with the priests, even though they were not blood relatives. We do not know if the women thus disparaged were either the priests' wives or deaconesses. The bishops referred to them as *mulierculae,* a derogatory term used to designate women of dishonorable status and one that the bishops might have deliberately chosen to cast aspersion on the virtue of the female assistants.[72]

During the first quarter of the sixth century, some Frankish bishops could still be persuaded to impart consecration to the feminine diaconate, despite the prevailing opposition to the ministry of women. The deaconesses can be identified by name. One was Helaria, the daughter of Remy, the saintly bishop of Reims. The other was Saint Radegund (521–587), whose escape from the amorous clutches of her polygamous husband culminated in the drama of her consecration by Saint Medard. The account of Radegund's activities as a deaconess and her biographer's choice of words in describing her consecration (she put on the habit of a nun and, by the altar, Saint Medard laid his hands on her) indicate that her status was identified with that of a professed widow who had dedicated herself to a life of abstinence, charity, and prayer.[73]

The absorption of the feminine diaconate into the religious order of widows was accomplished by councils held at Epaon in 517 and Orléans in 533. The legislation of Epaon at first tended toward identifying the religious widowhood with the diaconate of women. But the council managed to check that tendency by asserting that "deaconess" was a mere title and by abrogating "the consecration of widows, called deaconesses," commanding that henceforth widows who wished to lead a religious life were to be given only a benediction as penitents.[74] The aim of this restriction was to ensure that widows did not claim clerical status by virtue of their consecration as deaconesses. Even the honorary title of deaconess seems to have provoked the anger of the Frankish bishops. Farther north where married women, possibly the wives of clerks, held the title, the Council of Orléans in 533 ruled that:

> Women who, until now, against canonical interdiction, had received benediction to the diaconate are to be excommunicated if they are proved to have resumed marital relations. After due admonishment by the bishop who took notice of their sin, if they dissolved their foul union, they might be restored to communion after a period of suitable penance. It is resolved, however, that henceforth, because of the fragility of the female sex, no woman is to be given benediction to the diaconate.[75]

The bishops assembled at Orléans hoped to accomplish two objectives with this circuitous argument. First, they wanted to disqualify, once and for all, women from clerical office, and, second, they wanted to degrade the status of widows in the Frankish church. Henceforth, widows wishing to devote their lives to the service of God could not receive a public benediction. They could take only a private vow of continence, which was nevertheless binding for life. The Council of Tours in 567 justified this by recalling as common knowledge that Epaon had abolished consecration of "widows called deaconesses."[76]

Antifeminist legislation in the sixth century went beyond excluding women from the clerical hierarchy, abolishing the title of deaconess, and degrading the status of professed widows. A synod held at Auxerre between 561 and 605 asserted that women by nature were impure. Hence, they had to be veiled in the presence of the sacraments and could not touch anything that was consecrated. There were some earlier precedents for this legislation. Paul had declared that women should cover their heads when praying (2 Cor. 11:5), and the Council of Laodicaea (mid-fourth century) and Pope Gelasius I had warned that women must be kept apart from the altar area. The Frankish bishops combined and extended these precepts by ordering that women could not receive the Eucharist in their hands or touch the altar cloth, and they must be veiled when they took communion.[77]

THEORY AND PRACTICE IN THE SEVENTH CENTURY

Although the Frankish bishops were effective in excluding women from clerical offices and in barring them from participation in pastoral functions by accusing them of incontinence, heresy, pollution, and pride, they did not altogether succeed in discouraging women from claiming active roles in the life of the church. Deprived of the opportunity to serve as deaconesses and share the duties of their husbands as deacons,' priests,' and bishops' wives, more and more women, as we shall see in the next chapter, turned their energies to founding nunneries and developing them into centers of learning, devotion, and liturgy. The convents became more than a retreat for worship and prayer: they provided nuns and abbesses with an opportunity to exercise quasi clerical functions.

In the seventh century, if the silence of the synods accurately reflected the situation, the campaign against women for polluting the sacraments and seducing the clergy subsided. The earlier legislation was neither rescinded nor uniformly enforced. In part, this may be attributed to the absorption of women aspiring to pastoral ministry into the new monastic foundations. There is also sufficient evidence to indicate that the attention of many of the leading bishops shifted from clerical discipline to asceticism. Instead of insisting upon their own authority and the exclusion of women from the hierarchy, bishops readily cooperated with women in the propagation of the monastic way of life.

Concerns about the ritual impurity of women were not forgotten, but they did not prevent women in nunneries from exercising quasi-clerical functions. A penitential, the so-called *Judgment of Clement*, com-

posed between 700 and 750, extended the sixth-century prohibition
against women touching the Eucharist and the clerical vestments to the
unconsecrated host, the linen, and the chalice upon the altar. It also
denied women access to the chancel, the area around the altar.[78] In the
seventh century these rules were not observed. Nuns assisted priests in
the distribution of the sacraments and looked after the altar by keeping
the altar cloth and vessels clean. In double monasteries, abbesses exercised authority over both nuns and monks; they heard confessions and
gave benediction to both female and male members of the community.[79]

The idea that women could be consecrated deaconesses was kept
alive by Fortunatus' *Life of Saint Radegund,* which was read and copied
by subsequent generations.[80] During the second half of the seventh
century, the anonymous biographer of Blessed Sigolena of Albi, paraphrasing from Saint Radegund's *Life,* wrote that Sigolena had been
consecrated deaconess before she founded Troclar.[81] In a charter from
the Rhineland, dated 636, the donor referred to his sister as deaconess.[82] Although we cannot exclude the possibility that the consecration
of women to the diaconate was resumed in the late Merovingian kingdom, particularly in the border regions, these two documents do not
provide definite proof for such a conclusion. The deaconess living near
the Rhine may simply have been the wife of a deacon. Further,
Sigolena's *Vita* is unreliable as a source, having been copied indiscriminately from earlier lives. No surviving document supports Schäfer's
hypothesis that deaconesses were absorbed into institutes of canonesses,[83] a designation that came to be applied, in any event, only in the
late eighth or early ninth century.

There is even less information about priests' and deacons' wives
during this period. They simply did not command the attention of
seventh and early eighth century bishops. The synods reiterated the
basic precept that priests and deacons could not marry and could share
their homes only with their nearest blood relatives.[84] A woman living
with a clerk in higher orders, if she was not a near blood relation, was
treated as an adulteress.[85] Thus, the wife of a priest or a deacon, if she
chose to remain with her husband, ran the risk of public humiliation and
severe punishment as if she were a mere concubine. On the other hand,
there is sufficient evidence to suggest that the councils did not insist on
the enforcement of celibacy and that the church did not monitor the
lives of priests and deacons.

During the seventh century, we find married men in the highest
echelons of the Frankish church handing down bishoprics to their
sons.[86] Certainly among lesser clerics the rule of continence was disregarded. Saint Boniface remarked that it was not uncommon to find

clerics in bed with several concubines each night.[87] He also complained
to Pope Zachary about the persecutions he suffered from unchaste
priests and deacons, as well as fornicating clerics, when he tried to
uphold the requirement of clerical celibacy in the Frankish Kingdom.[88]
A capitulary issued by Charlemagne between 769 and 771 suggests that
the behavior of some priests differed little from that of laymen. Some
priests had several wives, shed the blood of Christians and pagans, and
refused to obey the canons.[89] Even bishops flouted the requirement of
abstinence. Bishop Clemens, born a Scot, resisted attempts to remove
him from office for having fathered two children while a bishop. Losing
the battle in the end, he was stripped of office and placed in chains.[90]

CAROLINGIAN REFORMS

The movement for ecclesiastical reform initiated by the Anglo-Saxon
missionary Saint Boniface called for the reassertion of episcopal authority. Supported by Carloman and Pepin, and later by Charlemagne and
Louis the Pious, the Carolingian bishops went beyond this initial goal
by reorganizing the clergy as a corporate body distinct from and superior to the laity. Thus, the priesthood was set apart from the laity, and
its authority through the sacraments was emphasized. Because ritual
purity under episcopal leadership was an essential aspect of this program, the councils insisted upon clerical celibacy and the exclusion of
women from any ecclesiastical authority or active participation in sacred
rites.

In tones reminiscent of their sixth-century predecessors, the Carolingian bishops reaffirmed the disability of women to perform clerical
functions and persuaded the rulers to include these admonitions in the
royal capitularies. In 789 Charlemagne issued the order that abbesses
could not bless male members of their congregations by laying hands
and making the sign of the cross on their heads, nor could they veil nuns
with priestly benediction.[91] Even nuns were forbidden to approach the
altar, touch the sacred vessels, and help distribute the body and blood
of Christ.[92] If altar linens had to be washed, they were to be removed
by clerics and turned over to women at the altar rails. Similarly, offerings
brought by women were to be received by priests at the altar rail.

Synod after synod forbade clerks to live with women other than
their closest blood relations—a mother, sister, or niece, with some synods substituting an aunt for a niece.[93] The goal was not to prevent clerks
from sleeping with their wives, as in the seventh century, but to transform the clergy into a celibate body. As the emphasis shifted from
asceticism back to ritual purity, the church abandoned the techniques

of persuasion and example and resorted once again to legal and juridical constraints. The cathedral clergy was organized into chapters of
canons, according to the plan of Chrodegang of Metz, and discipline
was tightened.[94] The church censured as adulterers both married
priests and deacons who had resumed sexual relations with their wives
and unmarried clerics who had fornicated. Clerical incontinence became a criminal offense, equal to theft and perjury, punishable with loss
of office and inheritance.[95] Recidivists were incarcerated and subjected
to two years of penance.[96] The punishment of a priest was particularly
severe; he was to perform penance for two years on bread and water
after being publicly flogged and deprived of his office.[97]

The female accomplices of incontinent clerks were also subjected
to increasingly severe punishment. Women who had frequented places
where priests resided and worked were now to be tried in court.[98] In
particular, the wives of churchmen had to guard themselves from any
suspicion. As in the late Roman church, the wives of men who were to
be ordained to higher offices were required to take a vow of continence.
The blessing of priests' and deacons' wives, which was included in
ninth-century ceremonies of ordination,[99] reflected the influence of
Rome and the reassertion of the mutuality of the conjugal bond, an
essential aspect of the Carolingian program of reform. It also had the
definite advantage of enabling the Carolingian bishops to subject the
wives of priests to the strict discipline that they were trying to impose
on all women religious. According to a capitulary issued by Charlemagne in 779, a woman who, after taking a religious vow, fornicated or
resumed conjugal relations was to be confined to a convent.[100] The
frequent warnings that the councils issued against clerics visiting convents and the investigation ordered in 836 of nunneries, "which appear
to be whorehouses in some places,"[101] suggest that the cloistering of
women did not solve the problem of clerical incontinence.

The cloistering of women religious, on the other hand, solved, at
least temporarily, the problem of clerical wives. Treating the wives of
churchmen in higher orders as if they were mere concubines did not
conform with the Carolingians' beliefs on the sanctity of monogamous
unions and the distinction between marriage and concubinage. By re-
quiring a vow of chastity from the wives of clerks at the time of their
husbands' ordination and then cloistering them if they did not keep this
vow, the Carolingian church avoided the more difficult question on the
relationship between married clerks and their wives. It also avoided
acknowledging that the status of wives of churchmen in higher orders
differed from that of adulteresses.[102]

By the middle of the ninth century, women aspiring to spiritual leadership or pastoral care had to be content with living in a convent or as recluses. If they chose to remain in the world, they were suspected of being the devil's agents. In 847, the prophetess Theoda of Mainz was condemned as an irrational woman engaged in soothsaying:

> At this time, from the country of the Alemans, a woman named Theoda, a pseudoprophetess, came to Mainz, creating no small turmoil for the parish of Bishop Salomon with her soothsaying. She claimed to know, as though it had been divinely revealed to her, the exact day on which the world would be consumed and other secrets known to God alone. She preached that the last day of the final year was close upon us. Whence many of both sexes were filled with fear and went to her offering gifts and commending themselves to her prayers. What is more serious, they turned from doctrines of the church preached by clerks of the holy orders to follow her as though she were a teacher sent from heaven. She was brought before bishops at St. Albans (Mainz) and her assertions were diligently examined. She confessed that a certain priest had suggested these things to her and that she had said such things, the cause of complaint. The synod judged that she should be publicly flogged. Whereupon with shame she gave up the ministry of preaching that she had irrationally seized upon and presumed to claim for herself against the custom of the church, and, perplexed, she put an end to her soothsaying.[103]

Although later in the ninth century Saint Liutberga also preached and prophesied, she did so as a recluse with episcopal sanction. Her humility and submissiveness to the hierarchy had been carefully scrutinized before she was allowed to practice an individualistic form of religious life. Her activities, moreover, took place within the strict confines of a woman's role. She gave instruction to women of the neighborhood in the art of working with wool. Only as her fame grew did she begin to preach and prophesy to those who came to visit her cell.[104] The humiliation of Theoda and the testing of Liutberga marked the final stages of the long battle against the active participation of women in the church, which the Frankish episcopate had begun to wage three centuries earlier. Henceforth women would appear in ministerial roles only in heretical sects.

The efforts of the Carolingians to keep women religious locked in convents and clerks segregated from the company of women, on the other hand, did encounter increasing resistance during the second half of the ninth century. With the empire divided and power devolving on the great feudatories, the episcopate could not take concerted action to enforce clerical and monastic discipline. As a last desperate effort to uphold the ritual purity of the clergy, the Council of Mainz in 888 banished even close blood relations from the homes of priests, citing the scandalous conduct of priests who had impregnated their own sisters.[105] This legislation did not prevent Hatto, Abbot of Reichenau, from attributing to the fourth-century saint Verena the role of a housekeeper to a priest of Zürzach before her withdrawal from the world as a recluse. In his description of Verena's daily activities in the priest's household, Hatto mentioned that she carried the offering of wine to the altar. Writing in 888, more than five hundred years after Verena's death, Hatto undoubtedly used as models the women religious of his own time who served in clerical households and churches.[106] For example, Saint Maura, while dwelling in her father's house, devoted much thought and effort to the cathedral of Troyes and its bishop. Her death around 861 left Bishop Prudentius bereft not only of a beloved disciple but also of a glorified housekeeper. The composition of her biography enabled Prudentius to express his sorrow:

> Who poured the oil into the lamps? Maura! Who gathered the curtains? Maura! Who bought the sacerdotal vestments with her own money? Maura! I value more the linen garment she gave me than I do either gold or topaz. She spun, wove, and whitewashed it herself and begged me with utmost humility to wear it while I was celebrating the mass.[107]

Churchmen in the lower echelons became even bolder. The Synod of Worms in 868 felt obliged to explain that priests were to abstain from their wives and were not to beget children, thus acknowledging once again that priests' wives were not mere concubines.[108] In 893 a Gallic priest petitioned the Synod of Châlons to acknowledge the validity of his public marriage to one Grimma. Although the synod rejected his request, it suspended him only temporarily from communion.[109] Moreover, the Synod of Mainz in 852, as well as Pseudo-Isidore and Nicholas I, declared sacraments offered by unchaste priests to be valid.[110]

Even the title of deaconess reappeared in the latter half of the ninth century. In 868, the Council of Worms reissued canon fifteen of Chalcedon, which stipulated that women over forty could be ordained to the diaconate.[111] This legislation may have been prompted by the desire of the church to find a suitable title for queens and princesses who withdrew to a monastery that already had a ruling abbess. The title may have served lay abbesses who, like lay abbots, held monasteries as benefices from the king and presided over communities that were not under

Benedictine Rule. A late ninth-century gloss of the same canon makes it evident that the title of deaconess was associated with the office of the abbess by that time.[112] Around 940, Bishop Atto of Vercelli explained without hesitation that a deaconess was an abbess, although he conceded that in earlier times deaconesses had held an ecclesiastical office. At the time of the conversions, Atto said, deaconesses had baptized women.[113]

The legislation against women as helpmates of priests was apparently difficult to enforce. The efforts of the Frankish church were, however, not in vain. Neither in the seventh nor in the late ninth century were women able to restore the positions they had lost during the previous hierarchical reorganizations. Indeed, even in the tenth century, when clerical concubinage once again became common, women outside the convent appeared only in traditional feminine roles and made no attempt to claim a share in pastoral or ministerial functions.

Ritual purity served as the rationale both for excluding women from the clerical hierarchy and for eliminating their influence from parish affairs as the wives of priests. The belief that women were particularly sinful and that their presence both directly and indirectly constituted an obstacle to ritual purity led to the organization of the clergy into an exclusively male hierarchy. The conciliar legislation on this from the sixth century provided Carolingian churchmen with a series of precedents that could be used to restrict further the role of women in the church.

In the seventh century, when the ascetic spirit prevailed, women fared better. Instead of propagating mysogynistic sentiments in order to strengthen episcopal domination and to enhance the authority of the male hierarchy, the monastic reformers recognized the spiritual equality of women. Both male and female leaders of monasticism sought to segregate the sexes to improve the circumstances for prayer and contemplation. In the previous century, Saint Caesaria had advised Saint Radegund to expose herself to the company of men as rarely as possible if she wished to guard her chastity, "for you cannot fight lust if you do not flee from the presence of men."[114]

Finally, it must be emphasized that the legislation of the Frankish bishops on the spiritual and physical impurity of women was not without precedent. The same arguments were presented by fourth-century Gallican councils when they tried to reduce the female diaconate to a mere title and by popes when they requested clerks to relinquish female companionship. The political situation and socio-psychological attitudes in the Frankish Kingdom, however, were relatively more favorable than in the late Roman Empire to the enforcement of antifeminist legislation. The episcopate could unite more readily and could count on royal cooperation, especially under the Carolingians. The emphasis that the Germanic laws placed on the biological function of women encouraged their restriction to private roles and lent support to the bishops' efforts to exclude women from clerical and pastoral functions.

7

The Search for Spiritual Perfection and Freedom

The pursuit of spiritual perfection through monasticism was the one area of religious life open to women after the female diaconate was abolished and the status of priest's wife degraded in the sixth century. Feminine monasticism originated in early Christianity and, like its masculine counterpart, developed into a movement with the official recognition of the church. Monasticism (from the Greek verb *monazein* "to be alone") was not an option that women could pursue in antiquity. Except for a few prophetesses or priestesses, women in ancient societies were expected to marry, bear and raise children, and look after the household. Contemplation, a reflective mode of existence, was an essential aspect of monasticism and the direct opposite of the active life, the life of service required of women as wives and mothers.

Christianity initiated a new era not only in the history of monasticism but also in the history of feminism. Accepted as fully equal to men in their spiritual potential, Christian women could transcend biological and sexual roles and seek fulfillment in religious life. The description of Jesus' visit to the house of the two sisters, Martha and Mary, proclaimed this revolutionary doctrine (Luke 10:38–42). While Martha busied herself with serving the guests, Mary "sat at the Lord's feet and listened to his teaching." Annoyed with her sister and also with Jesus, Martha spoke up: "Lord, do you not care that my sister left me to serve alone? Tell her then to help me." But the Lord answered her: "Martha, Martha, you are anxious and troubled about many things; one thing is needful. Mary has chosen the good portion, which shall not be taken from her."

Women were among the hermits who appeared in the desert beginning in the second century. The earliest monasteries included communities of women engaged in prayer and contemplation. In the fourth century, the women in Jerome's circle took the initiative in establishing the first monastic communities in the West. As the church developed a male-dominated hierarchy, monasticism offered a special appeal to women, for it permitted them to retain a degree of influence in the church and participate actively in the service and worship of God. That monasticism served as a liberating force in the lives of women has not been adequately understood or sufficiently emphasized. From Andreas Capellanus' *Art of Courtly Love* to Diderot's *Nun,* men have written about the fraudulent and pathological aspects of women's monastic experience. Historians have singled out celibacy as the source of misogyny, which led to the isolation of women and the curtailment of their activity in the church. At the other end of the spectrum, some surveys either make short shrift of women's contributions to monasticism or treat women religious and their communities as imitators of and parasites upon monks.[1]

The purpose of this chapter is to present a more balanced analysis of feminine monasticism in the Frankish Kingdom from the sixth to the ninth century. It will not attempt to trace systematically the history of feminine institutions, which would require a separate monograph.[2] Rather, it will examine the social circumstances and the psychological attitudes that prompted women to eschew marriage and seek a contemplative life. The extension of legal rights to married women in the Carolingian period, which was paralleled by restrictions not only on opportunities for women to engage in God's service but also on their activities in the monasteries, is particularly relevant. One must inquire whether this policy was inspired by organizational concerns or by the ideal of asceticism. A comparison with the attitudes of the Irish and Anglo-Saxon missionaries toward women religious should clarify the Frankish bishops' motives. Finally, this chapter will address the question of whether or not convents lost their appeal when feminine monasticism became closely supervised and strictly regimented by the Carolingian hierarchy.

REBELLION AND OBEDIENCE

Lacking autobiographies, we must turn to eulogies of feminine chastity, biographies, and chronicles to gain an understanding of the motives that led Merovingian and Carolingian women to embrace the religious life. Although hagiographies often distort facts about the lives of their protagonists by copying indiscriminately from earlier sources, even the most unreliable ones reflect ideals and, to some extent, the prevalent behavior at the time of their composition.

The most eloquent and perhaps the most sensitive expression of sixth-century perceptions of the advantages of virginity and sexual continence for women was formulated by Venantius Fortunatus. His long poem dedicated to Agnes, abbess of the monastery of Holy Cross at

Poitiers, not only spoke of the heavenly rewards awaiting the virgins who chose Christ as their bridegroom but also depicted in vivid metaphors the tribulations of married women. Fortunatus did not shrink from describing the temptations of sexual intercourse, stressing that salvation hangs on a thin thread when, with the panting of the breath and the heaving of the body, the womb swells with excitement and the serpent of voluptuousness grows. Nor did he mince words in enumerating the pains of childbirth, the mother's sorrow when her child is born dead, or when she sees her infant die on her breast, and, finally, the insecurity and desolation of widowhood.[3]

Fortunatus had a better understanding of feminine psychology than the Western fathers. Although he used Ambrose for his description of the discomforts of women in intercourse, childbearing, breast-feeding, and nurturing,[4] he also probed beyond the mere physical aspects of women's experience. Writing at a time when the wishes of women were of little consequence, Fortunatus took pains to describe the feelings of women. His insight into a woman's inner life undoubtedly came from his close friendship with Saint Radegund and her nuns at Poitiers. In explaining what prompted women to wrench themselves free from sex roles and to embrace monastic life, he pointed with great sensitivity to the traumas of marriage and childbirth, and of a child's or a husband's death.

Merovingian chronicles and saints' lives confirm Fortunatus' observations. They tell us about women such as Saint Monegund, who took a religious vow after the death of her children,[5] or Saint Rictrud, who renounced secular life when her brothers murdered the man whom she had married against their wishes.[6] They provide case histories of widows who, like Itta, acquiesced to their daughters' request to build convents to which they withdrew with their daughters.[7] "Freed of the law of her husband," the wealthy widow Eustadiola constructed a nunnery for herself and her maidservants, according to her biographer.[8] Another seventh-century matron, Sigolena of Albi, offered her husband all her worldly goods in order to "gain the freedom of her body," and would have lived with him happily ever after in chaste marriage. When his unexpected death ended this convenient arrangement, the young widow, only twenty-four years old, had considerable difficulty in convincing her parents that she did not wish to remarry, but she ultimately persuaded her elderly father to build a convent for her.[9]

The sexual double standard to which married women were subjected and the fear of childbearing probably influenced the decision of widows to avoid remarriage, and prompted the attempts of married women to seek release from the marriage. Saint Radegund (ca. 518–

587) had an even more dramatic motivation. First captured as war booty and then won in a judicial contest by her polygamous husband, Radegund decided to leave Clothar I when she learned that he had ordered the murder of her own brother:

> From the king she went directly to blessed Medard of Noyon, earnestly beseeching him to consecrate her to God once she changed her habit. Royal officials, however, embarrassed the blessed man to the extent of dragging him violently from the altar in the basilica so that he would not veil the king's wife. . . . When the saint perceived this, she entered the sacristy, put on the habit of a nun, and proceeded to the altar, where she addressed the blessed Medard, saying: "If you refuse to consecrate me, fearing more a man than God, you will be held responsible for the soul of one of your sheep, O Pastor!" Shaken by her entreaty, as if he were struck by thunder, he laid his hands on her and consecrated her deaconess.[10]

When Clothar persisted in his efforts to reclaim her, she appealed to Saint Germain. A shrewd observer of human nature and a clever diplomat, Saint Germain obtained from the king not only Radegund's freedom but also material assistance for her to build a nunnery at Poitiers.[11]

Young virgins of prominent families, often not more than twelve or fourteen years of age, were equally resolute in their spiritual purpose and defied their parents in order to avoid wedlock. The father of Saint Burgundofara dragged her from a basilica where she had hidden when he wanted to betroth her.[12] The legend surrounding Saint Austroberta follows the same pattern: apprehensive that her father would force her to marry, Austroberta fled, taking her younger brother with her.[13] With courage and initiative, these young girls and others like them earned the sympathy and respect of churchmen. When an influential bishop or abbot interceded on the aspiring contemplative's behalf, her parents usually relented and founded a nunnery for her.

Not every Frankish saint had to assert her religious calling against antagonistic forces. In hagiographies written in the eighth century, the tension between parents and daughters was frequently resolved by a relative or a friend. Afraid to announce her spiritual vow to her parents, Saint Bertila of Chelles had the good fortune of gaining as her champion Audoen (Dado), bishop of Rouen (614–684), a promoter of monasticism and one of the most powerful men in the Merovingian kingdom.[14] Monastic life had become so popular among the young by this time that it was not unusual for several children in a family to take vows, reinforcing each other's intention. Although married, Waldtrud, recognizing that the celestial visions of her younger sister Aldegund were a manifest sign of her vocation, persuaded their parents to send Aldegund to a convent. Later, Waldtrud herself embraced monastic life by founding Mons.[15]

In the ninth century, a new pattern of behavior emerged in hagiography. Beside the stereotype of the virgin or widow who had to rebel against the authority of her family, or request the intercession of an influential churchman, a third type of consecrated woman appeared: the obedient daughter of pious parents who took a vow of chastity at their request. Or she married and bore and raised children, postponing her religious calling until her children were grown.

The legendary story of the sisters Herlinda and Renilda illustrates this new ideal of feminine behavior. The two girls, offered to God for the remission of their parents' sins, were sent to a convent at an early age to receive a religious education. Obedient and virtuous, they did not fail to live up to parental expectations. In the monastery their mother and father eventually built at Eyck, the sisters provided an inspiration in piety and religious service to young women throughout the region.[16] The life of Saint Hathumoda, more reliable as a factual account, illustrates the tendency of parents of many children to encourage the younger ones to remain celibate.[17]

A different kind of obedience was exacted from an only daughter. To provide a role model for this kind of filial behavior, the biographer of Salaberga, writing in the early ninth century, some 150 years after her death, deprived the saint of her virginity, inventing two husbands and five children for her. Salaberga's purported marriages were arranged by her father "against her wishes," the biographer was careful to say. Her first union ended abruptly with the death of her husband two months after the nuptials. For two years she remained a widow, contemplating entrance to Remiremont, only to be thwarted in her objective by a new suitor, Baldwin (surnamed Baso). Although this young man also had a religious vocation, he was as conscious of his social obligations as was Salaberga. Pressured by his parents and ordered by the king, Baldwin married Salaberga for the sake of procreating children. The union, fruitless at first, was eventually blessed by five children, each dedicated to God by the parents. When her obligation to bear and raise children had been finally met, Salaberga was able to fulfill her wish of founding and leading a convent.[18]

These three patterns of behavior—rebellion against parents or husbands, tension and accommodation through the intercession of an influential man, and dutiful obedience—correspond roughly to three different phases in the history of feminine monasticism. In the sixth century, when nunneries were few in number, women wishing to devote themselves to the service of God had to be steadfast in their purpose to escape sex roles. During the seventh and eighth centuries, when nunneries were being built throughout the kingdom, women attracted to religious life could find support in their own families, even though some had to rely on outside mediation. Finally, the Carolingian reforms, which, on the one hand, urged the strict cloistering of women and, on the other hand, enhanced the dignity of married women, made religious life a less attractive alternative to marriage than it had appeared to women in previous centuries.[19]

THE HEROIC AGE OF FEMALE ASCETICISM

Feminine monasticism in sixth-century Gaul was a spontaneous movement, growing against great odds, primarily through the initiative of women. In central and northern Frankland, where there were no monasteries to serve as models, feminine asceticism was a grass-roots movement. Single, married, and widowed women of all ages, ranging from mere children to elderly matrons, offered their services to God. They shared one characteristic—a vow of chastity, often taken in opposition to their family. Some formed communities around churches and oratories, while the majority continued to live at home, placing themselves under the protection of a local church and wearing a veil as the mark of their vocation.

In the south, where Christianity had deeper roots and a network of monasteries had developed, a few nunneries were in existence at the beginning of the sixth century. Of the female communities established in pre-Merovingian times, not all survived the Germanic invasions.[20] The convent founded by Cassian at Marseilles,[21] Baume-les-Dames (Balma) established by Romanus in the Jura Mountains,[22] and the community of more than sixty nuns organized by Leonian at Vienne continued.[23] More influential than these older convents was Saint Jean of Arles, which Caesarius built for his sister at the beginning of the century.[24]

The need to guard the autonomy, privacy, and freedom of female contemplatives was well understood by Caesarius. He not only insisted on the community's exemption from episcopal governance and its economic self-sufficiency, but also prohibited the nuns from associating with and providing services, such as weaving, sewing, and cooking, for people in the outside world.[25] These proved to be sufficiently attractive features to prompt the adoption and adaptation of Caesarius' Rule by later foundations farther north.[26] Popular as this rule proved to be, the convent founded by Caesarius did not become the center of female monasteries. Although his successor, Aurelian, sponsored a second community of nuns at Arles, new convents were slow to appear in the south.[27] In 543, Duke Ansemund and his wife, Ansleutana, established a proprietary monastery for their daughter Remilia in the suburbs of Vienne.[28] A similar community was organized at Toulouse only toward the end of the sixth century, when the widow Beretrud attached a convent to Saint Saturnin.[29] Other southern cities, such as Narbonne, had no female convents.

In central and northern Frankland, feminine monasticism exhibited greater vigor, although the first communities were formed only toward the middle of the sixth century. Gregory of Tours reports that, in the absence of a nunnery, Saint Papula, disguising herself as a man, joined a male institution.[30] Other women remained at home, but dedicated their lives to the service of God.[31] This ancient form of asceticism had been practiced by both men and women in Gaul at least since the fourth century.[32] Women appear to have been more numerous than men in the ranks of lay religious, probably because they could not enter the clergy.[33] Gregory of Tours did not fail to mention the scandalous behavior of two lay women religious,[34] but spoke with respect of those who persisted in their vows. For example, in his *Life of the Fathers,* he celebrated a certain Georgia, who persisted in fasting and praying and died a virgin at the age of sixty.[35]

The childhood pastimes of Saint Radegund are a good example of the daily life of professed virgins and widows. Odd as Radegund's activities may seem today, they represented an attempt to imitate the services women religious rendered in churches and oratories. Educated at Athies, a royal villa, until she reached the appropriate age to be taken by Clothar I as one of his wives, Radegund was taught to read and write. She was impressed by the lives of martyrs and decided to follow their example. With the help of a young clerk, Samuel, she gathered poor children, fed them from her own table, and honored them by washing their hands and hair. Then, with Samuel carrying a wooden cross and Radegund marching behind him chanting psalms, the clerk and the virgin led the ragged procession to the oratory. There, Radegund proceeded to act as "the good housekeeper," polishing the floor with her own robe and collecting the dust around the altar in her own kerchief.[36] The widowed queen Clotild engaged in similar pursuits. After her husband's death, she went to Tours, where she devoted the rest of her days to service at the basilica of Saint Martin, according to Gregory of Tours.[37]

The first feminine communities in central Gaul came into existence around oratories and basilicas, the gathering place of women religious.

Ingitrud established a cloister in the courtyard of Saint Martin of Tours.[38] Saint Martin-de-Jumellos, originally an oratory in the suburb of Amiens, was a nunnery in the days of Gregory of Tours.[39] Néris near Montlucon developed in a similar manner.[40] Saint Pierre-le-Vif of Sens was also connected with a basilica.[41] Unlike the nunneries in the south, these communities either burgeoned spontaneously through feminine initiative or were sponsored by women. Bishop Aunacharius' (561–605) foundation in Saint Martin's basilica at Auxerre probably also represented an attempt to build a convent for women religious already working at the basilica.[42] Nunneries occasionally evolved around the cell of a recluse. At Chartres, Saint Monegund's retreat became the nucleus for a female community. When Monegund left the city because she could no longer endure the crowds that her fame as a healer attracted, she went to Tours and founded another nunnery there. The latter, Gregory of Tours was careful to say, had only a few members and better suited Monegund's wish to spend the rest of her days in "integral faith and prayer."[43]

Sixth-century monastic foundations for women were, as a rule, built in places where the nuns were safe from attack, or at least could be readily defended. Caesarius had originally established the convent for his sister, Caesaria, in the suburb of Arles, but he moved it within the walls after the city was attacked by the Franks and Burgundians in 508.[44] In addition, nuns could be readily supervised if their nunneries were located in cities. Even in this heroic age of monasticism, convents served as prisons. For example, Gregory of Tours reports that King Gunthram had his widowed sister-in-law incarcerated at Arles, in the monastery founded by Caesarius.[45] Regarded as helpless and defenseless creatures whose virtue and lives had to be protected by men, Merovingian women were not allowed to lead a solitary life in uninhabited places. Gregory of Tours mentioned with astonishment the rumor of two virgins withdrawing to an impenetrable forest on a hill near Tours.[46] Yet, at the same time, male communities were developing around the retreats of saintly hermits in the wilderness of Frankland with such rapidity that, by the end of the sixth century, there was a tight network of Christian culture in the area bordered by the rivers Garonne, Rhone, and Somme. Because feminine communities were not organized in the countryside, their number remained relatively low in comparison to male communities.[47]

By the end of the sixth century, feminine abbeys existed in all the urban centers of central Gaul. In addition to those already mentioned at Amiens, Auxerre, Chartres, Poitiers, Sens, and Tours,[48] there was also one at Autun,[49] another at Lyons,[50] and probably one at Le Mans.[51]

As at Arles and Vienne, two female communities were functioning at Tours.[52] Convents for women in smaller villages, such as Néris,[53] were exceptions. Some probably had only a brief existence. A small convent established by Queen Clotild at Chelles, according to Gregory of Tours, was abandoned by the mid-seventh century and had to be rebuilt by Queen Balthild. Yet another rural convent, Les Andelys, near Rouen, also reported to be Clotild's foundation, was resuscitated by Audoen, Columban's disciple, in the seventh century.[54]

The vitality of feminine asceticism should not be measured merely in terms of the number of nunneries. The concern expressed by sixth-century councils over the status of professed virgins and widows living in the world indicates that many women were practicing asceticism outside the walls of convents.[55] Undoubtedly some chose this form of life in order to escape from an unwanted union, while others undertook a true religious vocation.

The rewards of this alternate way of life included a degree of dignity and autonomy unavailable to married women, but the risks were also great. A woman faced the danger of rape and abduction, often sanctioned by kings, as well as the possibility of excommunication and exile if she failed to make a heroic effort to resist her abductor. The same bishops who, in 567 at the Council of Tours, put the final seal on the abolition of the diaconate of women, made every effort to protect women religious from rape and abduction, and to prevent them from abandoning their religious commitment. Legislating strict sanctions against men who deflected women from their purpose of serving God rather than a husband, the council recalled that Roman law punished with death those who had raped and subsequently married consecrated virgins and vowed widows. Noting that vestal virgins were buried alive if they lost the grace of virginity, the council admonished women who had changed their dress in honor of the Redeemer to expect an equally grave sentence if they failed to persevere in their resolution.[56]

The severity of this council was not without precedent. In 538, the Council of Orléans had used Innocent I's image of a vowed virgin as Christ's betrothed and of a veiled virgin as Christ's bride to excommunicate as adulteresses those who had consented to live with their ravishers. If the culprit had not been veiled, she was in a somewhat better position: she was required to perform penance only for a limited time and not until death.[57] A widow's vow was equally binding for life, even though it could not be solemnized by a priestly blessing.[58] The notion that a religious habit was the symbol of the vow of chastity was stressed not only by Tours but also by later sixth-century councils.[59]

The bishops needed royal support to enforce these declarations, but only Clothar I went so far as to declare that "no one should dare to marry a nun."[60] A few years earlier, when one of his wives, Radegund, had been consecrated a deaconess, Clothar had not professed the same respect for a woman's religious vow.[61] Moreover, Clothar's brothers and descendants continued to sanction the abduction of professed virgins and widows. The Frankish bishops' efforts succeeded only in the following century. At the Council of Paris held in 614, Clothar II not only pledged to relinquish the practice of his predecessors but also ordered capital punishment for the abductors of women religious. Even if such a nefarious union was concluded in a church, the couple was to be separated, both parties were to be exiled, and their property was to be distributed among the nearest kin.[62]

Clothar II's edict heralded a new epoch when women no longer needed steadfast courage and stubborn determination, as in the sixth century, to lead an ascetic life. During the course of the seventh century, enough female monasteries came into being to offer refuge and shelter for women seeking to escape from abductors and irate parents. The abbess of Saint Jean of Arles did not hesitate to rescue the orphaned Rusticula, kidnapped by an eager suitor when she was only five.[63] Saint Burgundofara's father ultimately acquiesced to her religious calling when she entered a monastery.[64] Although men occasionally snatched their brides from convents, it was more difficult to abduct a woman from a community than from a private home; public opinion and the laws censured this conduct more severely. The Bavarian Code, issued in the early eighth century, ordered those who had abducted women from monasteries not only to return them but also to pay double indemnity to the institution if they did not wish to be exiled.[65]

The Council of Clichy, meeting in 626, still found it necessary to reiterate the threat of excommunication against those abducting women religious with royal permission.[66] By the end of the seventh century, kings no longer authorized these actions. The growth of monasteries increased respect for self-abnegating women, prompting kings to take all women religious under their protection. Entrance into a convent by this time was routinely offered as a choice to widows seeking an equal status with virgins and as a form of penance to lapsed women religious.[67]

THE FLOWERING OF FEMALE MONASTICISM

At that time, throughout the provinces of Gaul, the troops of monks and crowds of virgins under the rule of the blessed fathers Benedict and Columban began to multiply not only in the fields, towns, villages, and castles but also in the desert of the hermits, whereas only a few monasteries were found in these places before this time.[68]

These observations, although written by Saint Salaberga's biographer in the early ninth century, present an accurate picture of the religious revival in the Frankish Kingdom generated by the arrival of Saint Columban in the late sixth century.[69]

In keeping with the spirit of Irish Christianity, dominated both morally and administratively by monasticism rather than by clericalism, Saint Columban did not harbor prejudices against women. Instead of shunning their company, he sought their friendship. Instead of emphasizing their impurity, he recognized their spiritual equality. He accepted the hospitality of Theudemada, a lady of great wealth who led a religious life.[70] Acting as the spiritual adviser to married women, he baptized and blessed their children. The women thus honored proved to be enthusiastic supporters of monasticism, encouraging the religious vocation of their children and embracing the ascetic life themselves.[71] A case in point is Flavia, whose husband, Waldelen, was duke of Upper Burgundy. Approached by the young couple to pray for them so that their marriage might be blessed by children, Columban made them promise that they would offer their firstborn to God's service. Her wishes granted, Flavia not only sent her oldest son, Donatus, to Columban's foundation at Luxeuil, but when widowed she built Jussanum at Besançon. "Surrounding the convent with fortifications, she established many nuns there," wrote Ionas, Saint Columban's biographer.[72]

Saint Columban's example inspired a new attitude toward women among his Frankish collaborators and disciples, many of whom were trained at Luxeuil, the center of the Irish movement. Influential because of high birth and their positions as abbots and bishops, these men cultivated spiritual friendships with women and sought feminine cooperation in building a network of monasteries throughout the kingdom. As a result of their efforts, men and women began to work together in partnership, promoting the contemplative life and discovering a practical solution to the problem of instituting female communities outside the cities. To protect nuns, help them run their vast establishments, and provide sacerdotal services, these enterprising men and women attached a contingent of monks to some of the newly founded communities. They created thus a new institution, the double monastery, which had some precedents in the East and in Ireland. They also set up separate, affiliated communities for men and women in close proximity to each other.

In these new monasteries women were not overshadowed by higher ranking men. Rather, they collaborated with men and acted as spiritual leaders. The double monasteries, as Mary Bateson has aptly expressed it, provided the female element of the ruling class with something to rule.[73] Usually double monasteries were governed by an abbess, and the affiliated institutions by an abbot and an abbess. In keeping with the penitential practices the Irish introduced to continental monasteries, abbesses heard confession three times a day and gave absolution and benediction to members of their community. They performed, therefore, quasi-sacerdotal functions in addition to the normal administrative, disciplinary, and spiritual duties of their office. Under female leadership, some of the double houses became famous centers of learning and devotion; they attracted members from as far as England and served as models for the double monasteries of that island. Neither total segregation of the sexes nor strict cloistering was practiced in these communities. Nuns and monks occupied separate living quarters, but, in the scriptoria and the schools, and during the divine service, the two sexes shared common functions.

The rule compiled for nuns, probably by Waldebert of Luxeuil (629–670), indicates that women did not live as parasites on men in the double monasteries. Nuns were required to perform manual labor. In addition to cooking, cleaning, serving, spinning, and sewing, activities traditionally associated with women, fishing, brewing, and building the fire were among the daily assignments of nuns. Work outside the monastery was always undertaken by teams of three or four, and special liturgical rites were prescribed for those going off to work in the morning and coming home in the evening.[74]

Faremoutiers-en-Brie (Evoracium) was probably the first double monastery. It was established around 617 by Burgundofara under the guidance of Eustachius, abbot of Luxeuil. At an impressionable age, when she was not more than ten, Burgundofara had met Saint Columban and received his blessing. This experience left such a deep mark on her that she resisted her parents' attempts to force her to marry a few years later. Probably through her brother Chagnoald, a monk at Luxeuil, she appealed to Eustachius. Coming in person to her rescue, Eustachius took her to Meaux, where she was veiled and consecrated. The abbot then assigned two of his monks, Chagnoald and Waldabert, to help her build a nunnery and to instruct the new community in the principles of religious life. Eventually a second house was added for the monks, and Burgundofara presided over both.[75]

Habendum-Remiremont, founded around 620 by the Austrasian magnate Romarich with the help of Amatus, one of Eustachius' pupils, had a different form of organization, at least initially. Established on the property of Romarich in the Meuselle Valley, it was planned as a joint community of monks and nuns rather than as a nunnery with monks attached to it. Amatus' authority as the first abbot may have been superior to that of his coabbess, Mechtafled. On the other hand, the size of the feminine community was not only substantial from the very beginning, with eighty-four nuns serving under Mechtafled, but remained so. Although similar data on the size of the male community are missing, the number of monks declined sufficiently by the time the fourth abbot died for the abbess to assume sole governance. Eventually the community of monks was completely dissolved.[76]

Joint supervision by an abbot and abbess did not become the prevalent form of government in the Frankish double monasteries. It remained in use only at affiliated institutions, such as Pavilly and Jumièges. Founded by Saint Filibert, Jumièges at first housed both monks and nuns. When the community grew in size, Filibert built Pavilly for the women and installed an abbess. Although the two houses retained a close relationship, they were too far apart to constitute a single institution.[77]

The government of a double monastery by an abbot was an exception. Dom Schmitz's characterization of double monasteries as usually falling into this pattern needs correction.[78] Jumièges was a real double monastery only for a brief period, as a fledgling institution, before the foundation of the sister house. The other outstanding example, Bèze, was not planned as a double institution but became one in 657 when Abbot Waldelen admitted his sister Adalsind and her nuns from neighboring Dorniaticum. Citing injuries and threats by men as her reason for wishing to join her brother's community, Adalsind accepted Bèze's rule, turning over Dorniaticum with all its possessions and subjecting herself and her nuns to Waldelen's authority as abbot.[79]

Frankish double monasteries normally were governed by abbesses. Laon, one of the largest convents, with three hundred nuns, was established around 641 on the model of Remiremont and had a single superior, Saint Salaberga.[80] Jouarre, originally a male convent built by the monk Ado around 630, was put under the authority of an abbess when it was transformed into a double monastery by Bishop Faro of Meaux. From his sister's convent at Faremoutiers, Faro brought the nun Theudechild to run the enlarged community.[81] Around 658 or 659, when Queen Balthild reconstructed the ruins of a convent at Chelles as a monastery, she requested from Jouarre a nun capable of assuming command. Initially only a few priests were attached to Chelles to provide for the sacramental needs of the sisters, but, as the fame of the

abbey grew under the capable leadership of Bertila, an increasing number of men sought admission. By the time Bertila died around 704,
Chelles was a true double monastery, characterized by her biographer
as a Christian community "fratrum sive sororum."[82]

The double monasteries developing farther north, between the
Somme and the Meuse, fall into the same pattern; they were either
governed by an abbess or were under joint female and male guidance.
Gertrud ruled Nivelles, which was founded by her mother, Itta, with the
help of Saint Amand around 640.[83] Aldegund single-handedly directed
Maubeuge, which she had organized in 661.[84] On the other hand, at
Marchiennes, established around 647, the nuns were supervised by
Rictrud, and the monks had their own abbot, Ionas.[85] By the ninth
century, the abbess exercised authority over both sexes at Marchiennes.
At Hasnon, built around 670, the founder, John, governed the men, and
his sister, Eulalia, presided over the women.[86]

Some of the double monasteries began as nunneries, with the community of monks being added at a later date. Notre-Dame of Soissons
was instituted as a feminine convent in 666. A few years later, when
Sigrada, Leodegar of Autun's mother, was living there, the community
also included brothers.[87] Hamaye, probably the oldest nunnery north
of the Somme,[88] and Avenay at Reims followed a similar pattern.[89] We
also know that Saint Jean of Arles and Holy Cross of Poitiers invited
monks to live in their burial churches.[90]

Although double monasteries were popular, their number remained relatively small.[91] Only the wealthiest foundations could support a community of nuns and monks.[92] Feminine convents affiliated
with masculine houses were also not very numerous.[93] On the other
hand, nunneries mushroomed in the cities and suburbs.

Without a systematic study of Merovingian nunneries to yield statistics, it is not possible to ascertain whether or not the imbalance between
male and female institutions was redressed by the seventh century. That
this may have been the case in the cities is suggested by the monastic
history of Metz. Only male communities existed in that city in the sixth
century. But two of the three convents that developed there in the
seventh century were nunneries, namely Sainte Glossindis and Saint
Pierre-aux-Nonnaines.[94] In other towns as well—at Noyon,[95] Clermont,[96] Bourges[97]—more than one female community sprang up during this period of religious enthusiasm.

Various factors prompted the development of several nunneries in
the same town. Often one house was within the walls and the other
in the suburb.[98] The size of the endowment undoubtedly limited the
number of members an established community was willing to accept.

Laon, with three hundred nuns, a figure stated in the life of Saint Salaberga, was an exception. Remiremont had eighty-four nuns and Pavilly only twenty-five.[99] Many convents were probably even more modest in size.

In addition, the proprietary church system encouraged the proliferation of small nunneries. Under this arrangement, the founder retained control over the convent's administration and landed property.[100] Many of the seventh-century female houses, established by wealthy widows, doting parents, and bishops devoted to their mothers and sisters, fall into this pattern. For instance, Flavia's Jussanum and the female communities at Bourges were proprietary nunneries.[101] This type of institution usually remained quite small, representing no more than an extended household, that is, an aristocratic house turned into a family cult center.[102] As opposed to the prestige of the greater houses, a proprietary convent offered the comfort of familiar faces and surroundings. Members did not suffer from homesickness, an emotion Leodegar of Autun thought his mother, Sigrada, experienced at Soissons. Writing to her from prison, Leodegar tried to console her with the suggestion that the brothers and sisters of the monastery had replaced her family and servants.[103] The presence of close blood relations, sisters and aunts, in a larger community undoubtedly eased the adjustment to the new surroundings, and was often the determining factor in an aristocratic woman's choice of a convent. To discourage the formation of kinship circles in double monasteries, Waldebert's Rule stressed spiritual sisterhood as the essence of communal life.[104]

Many opportunities were available to women who wished to embrace celibate life in the seventh century. The call to asceticism, sounded throughout Frankland by the Irish missionaries, found an enthusiastic response among both sexes. In all walks of life, men and women renounced marriage, devoting their energies to the service of God. As in previous centuries, some professed virgins and widows continued to live in the world, looking after the poor and acting as housekeepers in churches, but the chance to communicate and live with other women holding the same interests and beliefs held an even greater attraction. Religious communities provided a supportive environment and an atmosphere of calm where women could live, work, and pray. By serving God and each other in humility, actively participating in the liturgy, and exercising their intelligence and administrative talents, they could achieve a level of accomplishment in their lives not available to them in the outside world.

Life in small proprietary nunneries, which observed rules of varying laxity, or may not have observed any at all, was not very different from that in the great aristocratic households. Relatively free to come and go as they pleased, members could leave the community at will. The effort of the Council of Paris in 611 to impose stability on monks and nuns alike was not sustained. Even Waldebert, although intending his compilation for larger institutions, envisioned the readmission of a female monastic to the same community.[105]

In the double monasteries and larger communities, discipline was strict and the nuns were kept busy. Under rules combining Caesarian, Columban, and Benedictine elements, daily activities were carefully regulated.[106] In addition to assigned chores, everyone had to engage in prayer, liturgical services, and devotional readings at certain times of the day. Not only communal affairs such as meals but also private and personal matters were subject to rules. For example, places in the dormitory were assigned according to age, with younger sisters alternating with older ones to avoid the possibility of frivolity and carnal temptation.[107] Even washing hair was a communal activity to be undertaken every Saturday.

Some members served in administrative offices as dean, wardrobe mistress, cellarer, and portress. Others acted as librarians, scribes, and teachers.[108] Seventh-century foundations functioned also as boarding schools for both sexes, accepting as pupils even "infantes," children below the age of six.[109] A purely contemplative existence was pursued only by those choosing to endure the rigors of solitude as recluses. Although Gregory of Tours spoke of special cells being set aside for recluses in monasteries, seventh-century sources do not mention anyone leading this type of life.[110]

Lesser women, the protégés and servants of the founders and abbesses, were admitted to both the double monasteries and smaller convents. Eustadiola, her biographer relates, built her nunnery for herself and her slaves ("suisque puellis").[111] Queen Balthild instructed the Saxon slaves ("viros et puellas") whom she had redeemed and kept in her own household to join monasteries.[112] The rules did not limit membership to women of the upper classes. Both Caesarius' Rule and Aurelian's adaptation of it envisioned poor as well as wealthy women among the sisters of a community. Aurelian's Rule clearly stated that freedwomen could be accepted as postulants if they had their master's permission. Caesarius' Rule stressed that noble origin or wealth was not to be taken into consideration in the selection of an abbess. The royal princesses at Holy Cross of Poitiers challenged in vain the leadership of the abbess Leubovera, who was not of royal blood.[113] Only in the late eighth century did the requirement of an entrance fee become customary both in female and male communities.[114]

Nevertheless, social distinctions were not altogether obliterated in the convents. Saint Radegund's hagiographer made a point of mentioning the punishment the queen inflicted from heaven upon Vinoberga, her maidservant ("famula"), who dared to sit upon the throne after she had died. For three days and nights smoke and flame billowed from the girl's body. Only after she had confessed her sin and prayed with the congregation for forgiveness did the saint relent and relieve the girl's agony.[115]

MONASTICISM UNDER THE CAROLINGIANS

When the Anglo-Saxon missionaries arrived on the continent in the early eighth century, they found in the Frankish Kingdom a network of monasteries, which they then extended to the lands east of the Rhine. They introduced the Benedictine Rule into these new foundations, subjecting abbots and abbesses to strict episcopal control. Although some bishops jealously guarded their prerogatives of supervising female communities,[116] the convents under Caesarius' Rule, the communities established in the wake of the Irish revival, and the houses to which Balthild granted immunity were free from episcopal control.

When Saint Boniface turned his attention to the state of the Frankish church, he first proposed the reform of all monasteries according to the Benedictine norm.[117] As the reforms progressed, all forms of religious life were brought under episcopal control. Although Boniface's intent was to apply the same rules to both male and female communities,[118] later synods tended to interpret the rules more strictly for women than for men. The extension of episcopal jurisdiction over the monasteries was carried out with the help of the new dynasty. In fact, increased episcopal authority was the bishops' reward for cooperating in the creation of the Carolingian "Reichskirche." In this new structure, the monasteries lost their former independence, and their resources became subject to royal exploitation.[119] As advisers of kings and close associates of bishops, abbots were able to mitigate the constraints placed upon their communities. But female communities, caught between the highhanded treatment of bishops and the financial exactions of kings, declined in power and influence.

It was not the intention of the Anglo-Saxon missionaries to slight women religious or diminish the prestige of their institutions. Like their Irish predecessors, the Anglo-Saxons held nuns in high regard. They maintained correspondence with abbesses in England, requesting material assistance, books, and helpers.[120] The women who responded to their call founded and led feminine communities east of the Rhine. Even

though Boniface and his companions appreciated the contributions of
their female coworkers, they were careful to guard the prerogatives of
the male clergy. Boniface spoke of both monks and nuns as "the knights
of Christ,"[121] but he also questioned Pope Zachary on whether or not
it was proper for nuns to engage in the liturgical rite of washing each
others' feet.[122] It did not bother Boniface that monks performed the
same ceremony; monks were eligible to participate in the clerical hierarchy and many indeed were priests. As bishops, the Anglo-Saxons
supervised feminine communities more closely and interpreted the
Benedictine Rule more rigorously for female than for male monastics.
For example, Bishop Lull excommunicated Abbess Sitha for allowing
two nuns to take a voyage without asking his permission. Yet the Council
of Verneuil held in 755 acknowledged that monks may travel when
ordered by their abbot.[123]

In 742, when Boniface initiated reforms in the Frankish areas, he
called for the observation of Benedictine Rule by monks and nuns
alike.[124] Thirteen years later, in 755, when the Council of Verneuil
convened, it became evident that the imposition of the Rule was not an
easy matter. The precise instructions for bishops, if a monastery failed
to accept the rule, included excommunication of the recalcitrant community; individual nuns were to be imprisoned and subjected to forced
labor if they failed to conform. That uncooperative monks might be
coerced in this manner was not considered.[125]

The Council of Verneuil also declared that women who had veiled
themselves and men who had tonsured themselves were either to join
a monastery "sub ordine regulari," or to live under the supervision of
bishops "sub ordine canonica."[126] Around the same time, between 751
and 766, Chrodegang of Metz undertook the compilation of a set of
regulations for canons attached to the basilicas of Metz.[127] Rules for
canonesses were assembled for the first time in 813,[128] even though,
beginning with the Council of Frankfurt in 796, abbesses had been
routinely offered the choice between Benedictine profession or a
canonical life.[129] If an abbess chose the latter, both she and the nuns in
her charge were to observe the regulations of the councils. That these
regulations were not altogether consistent, or that their texts were not
readily available, did not bother the reforming councils.

As the reorganization of monasteries under episcopal authority
progressed, women who wished to lead a religious life came under
increasing pressure to join a community. By the late seventh century,
widows and virgins who wished to be veiled were ordered into convents.[130] Probably in an attempt to protect these women from hasty
veiling, Charlemagne ruled that the ceremony could be performed only

when a woman reached age twenty-five.[131] This did not mean that a private vow of chastity ceased to be binding. Although the symbol of a private vow, the black dress, was now designated as only quasi religious, a woman wearing this dress could be ordered by the bishop to a nunnery if she came under suspicion of having broken the vow.[132]

During the second phase of the Carolingian reforms, when the emphasis was shifting to the unique sacramental and juridical powers of the priesthood, the church became even less tolerant of women religious outside convents. In 829, the Council of Paris declared that women who had veiled themselves were evil; they tempted and trapped priests and were to be barred from churches. A widow had to wait thirty days after her husband's death to be veiled, and then had to join a convent. Priests could veil widows only with the consent of bishops.[133] The Council of Paris also put the final seal on earlier legislation limiting the function of women religious to the lighting of candles and the ringing of church bells. The status of these women, the council declared, was not different from that of ordinary laymen.

> It is against divine law and canonical instruction for women to intrude on the other side of holy altars, to touch impudently the consecrated vessels, administer for priests sacerdotal vestments, and, what is even worse, more indecent and more inappropriate, to distribute the body and blood of the Lord to the people. . . . It is certainly amazing that women, whose sex by no means makes them competent, despite the laws, were able to gain license to do things that are prohibited even to secular men.[134]

The foundation of a small proprietary nunnery no longer provided a viable alternative to those who did not wish to give up their independence while leading a religious life. New foundations were not encouraged,[135] except in recently conquered lands. Moreover, the Carolingian policy of transforming monasteries into royal abbeys in order to gain access to their resources, a policy closely linked with the program of bringing all monasteries under episcopal governance, called for the consolidation of communities with only a few members.[136] Many of these were nunneries. In 789, Charlemagne ordered that "the very small monasteries where nuns reside without a rule be combined into one regular congregation at a place designated by the bishop."[137] The execution of this project apparently took several decades. A capitulary issued in 829 expressed continued concern about the existence of small monasteries,[138] and Hrabanus Maurus encouraged a fellow bishop to dissolve a "monasteriola nonnarum" and transfer to another convent the nuns who did not live according to the rule.[139]

As small nunneries were gradually eliminated and the status of women religious living in the world degraded, the only choice available to women who did not wish to marry was to join either a Benedictine convent or an institute of canonesses. But the institutes of canonesses came to resemble Benedictine houses when specific guidelines for the life of canonesses were finally issued in 813 by the Council of Châlons. Although the council declared that women who lived according to the canons and called themselves canonesses constituted a separate order —presumably the feminine counterpart of the order of canons—canonesses were to lead a more austere life than canons.[140] Three years later, in 816, when the Council of Aix expanded these guidelines into a rule, the *Institutio sanctimonialium,* little difference between the obligations of Benedictine nuns and canonesses remained.

Because of the alleged weakness of their sex, female members of the canonical order were to be strictly cloistered.[141] Whereas canons were allowed to manage both ecclesiastical and personal property,[142] canonesses had to delegate this task to an outsider.[143] Canonesses were required to cover their faces in public and to wear a veil in church,[144] and they were to be carefully guarded from all contact with men.[145] Even abbesses could meet men only in the presence of other sisters.[146] Conversations with relatives and servants had to be monitored by three or four reliable members of the community.[147]

The cloistering of religious women was an issue that had weighed heavily on the minds of earlier Carolingian churchmen as well. Abbesses, and certainly other members of the community, were allowed to leave the monastery only if they were summoned by the king, according to the Council of Verneuil held in 755.[148] The reiteration of similar and even greater restrictions by practically every reforming synod indicates that the cloistering of nuns was not as strictly enforced as the hierarchy may have wished.[149] Like their Anglo-Saxon sisters, Frankish women religious were apparently accustomed to going on pilgrimages, at least until 796 or 797, when the Council of Friuli ordered them not to.[150] In so doing, the council may have had in mind the Anglo-Saxon nuns who never reached Rome but ended up, according to Saint Boniface, in one of the many brothels that lined the roads to Italy.[151] Similar considerations—the desire to prevent sisters from leaving the convent and to guard them against temptation—prompted council after council to inveigh against nuns wearing male attire,[152] and to caution against unnecessary visits by men, including bishops, canons, and monks.[153] In imposing on canonesses the strict cloistering required by the Benedictine Rule, the Carolingian churchmen were undoubtedly motivated by a desire to protect the safety and chastity of women, but they ultimately restricted the ascetic life sought by women.

An extension of the effort to avoid the danger of close association of the sexes within the convents was to prohibit nuns and canonesses from educating boys.[154] Even hospices for the poor and pilgrims had to be located outside the convent, adjacent to the church where the clergy attached to the monastery officiated.[155] Abbesses of both types of monasteries, for Benedictines and canonesses, lost not only their freedom of movement but also their former influence. Although emperors and kings periodically summoned them, undoubtedly to discuss the disposition of monastic resources,[156] abbesses, unlike abbots, did not participate in reforming assemblies. Moreover, they were denied participation in functions that could be construed as quasi sacerdotal. Forbidden to give benediction to the opposite sex, they could not consecrate members of their own community.[157] Although the belief that canonesses were members of the clergy lingered,[158] the councils abolished all functional distinctions between canonesses and nuns. Apart from ringing church bells and lighting candles,[159] nuns and canonesses could participate in the work of the church only by praying, singing, reciting psalms, celebrating the canonical hours,[160] tending the sick and poor women,[161] and educating girls.[162]

Once the councils had established that all women religious were to be cloistered, with their activities supervised by bishops, and that nuns and canonesses were to perform similar functions, the reformers stopped pressing for the imposition of the Benedictine Rule in feminine houses. In 816, a year after the Council of Aix issued the *Institutio sanctimonialium,* another Aachen assembly was held to formulate detailed rules for Benedictine monks.[163] No attempt was made to adapt the Benedictine Rule for use by nunneries. Whereas monks were sent to Inde to be trained in Benedictine observances, Louis the Pious did not designate a model Benedictine abbey for the training of women. Although Louis did offer the same economic incentive to both feminine and masculine houses to adopt the Benedictine Rule, a list of forty-eight Benedictine royal abbeys compiled in 819, the *Notitia de servitio monasteriorum,* included only five nunneries.[164] Yet, two years earlier, an important royal monastery not listed in the *Notitia,* Remiremont, had opted for the Benedictine Rule.[165] We can only conclude that the reformers did not bother to list all feminine Benedictine abbeys because they were not pressing the imposition of the Benedictine Rule on female communities.

To determine the relative proportion of Benedictine nunneries and institutes of canonesses, more research on the history of individual houses is needed. The terminology of donations and grants of immunity from royal exactions is not sufficiently precise to warrant Schäfer's hypothesis that institutes of canonesses dominated in the ninth century.[166] The restriction imposed by the *Institutio* and the economic advantages that abbesses could obtain under Benedictine Rule may have prompted abbesses to choose the latter course. The fact that the *Institutio sanctimonialium* is extant in only four ninth-century manuscripts suggests that it was not widely followed.[167] The testimony of Bishop Alderic, that he consecrated 103 "monachas" and 17 "canonicas" in the diocese of Le Mans between 832 and 857,[168] indicates that, at least in that region, more women joined Benedictine convents than institutes of canonesses.

The immediate effect of Carolingian policies on double monasteries is clearer. Double monasteries did not disappear, but the community of monks was transformed into a community of canons. This development did not necessarily parallel the transformation of the female community into an institute of canonesses. The *Translatio S. Baltechildis,* in 833, described Chelles as having a "clergy of men and women," which probably meant that both houses had relinquished the Benedictine Rule.[169] On the other hand, the nuns of Holy Cross of Poitiers observed the Benedictine Rule and had canons living at Sainte Radegonde, their affiliated institution.[170] Notre-Dame of Soissons under Benedictine observance had a chapter of canons by 872.[171] Royal appropriations of the property of female communities made the presence of monks as supervisors of agricultural labor superfluous. It was far less expensive to support a few canons than a community of monks. The canons were priests and administered to the sacramental needs of the sisters. The new arrangement had disadvantages as well. Canons were less likely than monks to share with the sisters a sense of common endeavor. They were not cloistered and enjoyed a greater freedom of movement than the sisters. Although they were economically dependent on the abbess, they did not come under her jurisdiction. Their clerical status, moreover, gave them the magisterial authority that abbesses had formerly exercised.

The transformation of a double monastery into a community of nuns, or canonesses with a chapter of canons attached, ended a period in the history of Western monasticism when feminine and masculine communities had been considered fully equal and coordinate institutions. Henceforth it became more difficult for male and female ascetics to draw inspiration from each other for their parallel, albeit autonomous, pursuit of spiritual perfection. Nuns and canonesses had to depend for religious guidance on men in the "sacred orders," whereas monks could rely solely on members of their own community.

The strict cloistering of nuns and canonesses on the one hand and the shrinking economic resources of monasteries on the other considerably tempered women's enthusiasm for monastic life in the ninth century. Undoubtedly, the improved legal position of married women also contributed to the waning of women's interest in an ascetic life. In the highest echelons of society, fewer ladies preferred the convent to marriage. We do not hear of ninth-century princesses running away from eager suitors or ardent husbands and clamoring for admittance to convents.

In comparison to the numerous female saints among the Merovingians, there were only a few under the Carolingians. The tight controls placed by ninth-century bishops on all forms of female asceticism seem to have inhibited women's aspirations for heroic sanctity. Women who were sanctified by the Carolingians either were connected with monastic foundations in newly conquered lands or were associated with domestic virtues, like Saint Liutberga.[172] This suggests that the Carolingian bishops may have considered elevation to sainthood a reward for socially constructive behavior.

Although the wives and daughters of Carolingian kings held the lands of the great feminine abbeys as part of their dowry or inheritance,[173] they chose the convent as a place of dwelling only when they needed shelter in old age or adversity. Charlemagne's daughters withdrew to monasteries when, after their father's death, their brother Louis the Pious forced them to leave the court.[174] Louis the Pious appointed his widowed mother-in-law as abbess of Chelles,[175] and the dowager empress Engelberga joined before her death the nunnery she had founded at Piacenza.[176] Judith of Bavaria found refuge at Notre-Dame of Laon until her husband could clear her name.[177] Nunneries were also used as places of refuge by women with estranged or irate husbands. Avenay sheltered Theutberga until Lothar II was forced to drop his charges of incest and reclaimed her.[178] Andelau provided protection to Queen Richardis when Charles the Fat accused her of adultery.[179] Conversely, princes used nunneries as prisons for troublesome women. When Tassilo, duke of Bavaria, was exiled and forced to enter a monastery, his daughters were sent to nunneries.[180] The stepsons of Judith of Bavaria imprisoned her at Holy Cross of Poitiers,[181] and Charles the Bald confined his own daughter, named Judith after her grandmother, to Notre-Dame of Senlis.[182] Both male and female communities functioned as asylums for the handicapped, retarded, and mentally disturbed. Ninth-century accounts of miracles abound with cures of blind nuns or nuns possessed by demons.[183] The cloister was thus used both to shield female ascetics and to segregate women considered undesirable, socially dangerous, or unproductive, whether priests' wives, lapsed "sanctimoniales," or other women.

Increasingly used as a shelter, a prison, an old-age home, and exploited as a source of income for princesses and queens, nunneries lost their aura of heroic sanctity during the ninth century. The criteria for admission increasingly emphasized wealth rather than religious calling. Only in exceptional cases would a woman of humble background be admitted. The *Miracles of Austroberta,* composed in the ninth century, reports that the saint interceded on behalf of a poor girl. Refused admission to Pavilly on the ground that she was an unfree dependant of the monastery, the girl maintained a vigil at the saint's tomb, only to be forcibly removed by the abbess. This might have sealed the fate of the girl had not the abbess been suddenly struck by an illness, which was interpreted by the community as the saint's punishment for her haughtiness. Duly repentant, the abbess sent for the girl and accepted her as a postulant.[184]

The outstanding characteristic of ninth-century abbesses was, not their holiness, but their business acumen. Ermentrud, abbess of Jouarre, exemplified the aggressive economic policy that abbesses had to pursue, despite the strict cloistering imposed on them. Through her family connections she obtained important relics for Jouarre. Once her monastery became a place of pilgrimage, she secured through the empress, her namesake and the proprietress of Jouarre, a grant of immunity from Charles the Bald with attendant rights of a marketplace and coinage.[185] Not only Benedictine abbeys, such as Jouarre, but also institutes of canonesses were granted privileges of this kind by Charles the Bald and his successors. In 877, for example, Nivelles obtained by royal grant a piece of land, the income from which was to be reserved exclusively for members of the convent.[186] Under Louis the Pious, this grant would have been issued only to a Benedictine monastery.

Once the economic incentive to observe the Benedictine Rule ceased, more and more Benedictine nunneries, such as Remiremont, were transformed into institutes of canonesses. By the end of the ninth century, the attempt to cloister canonesses had been abandoned. As royal control disintegrated and power devolved into the hands of the great aristocratic families, the episcopate could not enforce its legislation. What the Carolingians had sown, the late ninth-century aristocracy reaped. Local families took over the exploitation of monastic revenues, with their daughters administering convents as lay abbesses. Under their leadership, rules were eased; Benedictine abbeys were transformed into institutes of canonesses, and strict cloistering was no longer required.[187]

The freer life led by canonesses and their abbesses better suited the function of political leadership that all monasteries had to undertake by the end of the ninth century, in addition to the traditional economic, cultural, and social roles they had played earlier. Providing a more desirable alternative to married life, these communities attracted powerful women as members. In the tenth century, abbesses once again arrogated for themselves the title "diaconissa,"[188] and at least one was addressed as "metropolitana."[189] Despite their titles, the superiors of tenth-century feminine communities did not attempt to play clerical and quasi-clerical roles. Nor did they attempt to assert spiritual leadership over men. Although abbesses led a much freer life than their ninth-century predecessors, their power was based on the control they exercised over the monastery's extensive holdings rather than on their religious authority.

Resistance to women religious living in the world diminished by the end of the ninth century. While cautioning against the hasty veiling of widows, the Council of Mainz in 888 offered veiled widows the choice of joining a monastery or remaining in their own homes.[190] Nor were veiled virgins forced to enter a convent. Thus, nuns appeared once again as the helpers of priests, although their activities remained strictly limited to housekeeping tasks, such as maintaining order in the church, keeping the lights burning, and producing altar clothes and priestly vestments. They were also encouraged to contribute their own wealth to the church.[191]

The Carolingian effort to cloister women religious proved to be premature. It represented an ideal ill-suited to the political and social realities of the next two centuries, and was revived only in the late eleventh century by the Gregorian reformers. Nevertheless, women religious never recovered the clerical functions they had exercised as deaconesses in the sixth century and as abbesses in the seventh century.

Even though the Carolingian bishops had managed to eliminate female leadership roles in the church, restricting women to the domestic and private spheres and subjecting them to male authority, they could not prevent women from making their presence felt as contemplatives. One of these contemplatives was Saint Liutberga. The widowed Countess Gisla chose Liutberga from a convent, attracted by her intelligence and sweet disposition, as a companion. After her patroness's death, Liutberga was entrusted with the management of the vast estates of the descendants of Count Hessi of Saxony. Although the family prospered under her care, her long vigils and visits to churches after nightfall annoyed the reigning count. When, as a result of his outbursts, she announced her intention to become a recluse, he influenced the bishop against her. Eventually she was permitted to attach herself as a recluse to the convent of Wendhausen, where she supported herself by giving instruction in the art of wool dyeing. Her influence soon expanded beyond this. Great men and women and even prelates from distant places visited her, seeking her counsel and listening to her elevated discourse.[192]

Others, like Hathumoda, asserted feminine presence in the church by insisting on asceticism as the essence of monastic life. As the first abbess of Gandersheim, founded between 852 and 853 by her parents, Hathumoda could have organized the community as an institute of canonesses. She chose instead the more rigorous Benedictine observance, cloistering the sisters and forbidding them to have private cells, keep servants, and eat apart from the community.[193] At the same time, Hathumoda took pains to establish a tradition of scholarship that was to nourish the talents of the dramatist and poet Hroswitha in the next century.

Different as their backgrounds, experiences, and accomplishments were, Liutberga and Hathumoda represented the same feminine type, the self-reliant female contemplative of the Middle Ages. In comparison with women religious of late antiquity, even the women in Jerome's circle, Liutberga and Hathumoda were far more independent. They did not labor in the shadow of great men. In an age of waning spirituality and asceticism, each in her own way acted as a religious reformer. Liutberga demonstrated that recluses could be both spiritually and socially useful, whereas Hathumoda provided an example of feminine initiative in the pursuit of monastic perfection. Making the most of the roles to which women religious were restricted by the second half of the ninth century, Liutberga and Hathumoda and others like them transcended these roles. Reaching out beyond themselves, they demonstrated that women could excel at spiritual leadership.

8

Scholarship in Women's Communities

Monasteries of women, like male religious institutions, were centers of civilization and culture in the early Middle Ages.[1] A great deal has been written about the development of early monasteries and the daring and dedication of monks, hacking their way through the European forests and bringing cultivation and books wherever they went. The monks' schools, libraries, and scriptoria have been rightly acclaimed as bulwarks of culture against the forces of ignorance that seemed almost to engulf western Christendom between 500 and 800. In comparison, little attention has been paid to the role that nuns played in the preservation of learning between late antiquity and the Carolingian Renaissance of the ninth century. There are no current histories of the cultural contributions of early medieval nunneries.[2] The only study correcting the neglect of the sisters' share in scholarship is Bernhard Bischoff's study of the Cologne manuscripts copied by nuns.[3] The purpose of this chapter is to integrate Bischoff's findings into a broader treatment of the intellectual pursuits and spiritual influence of Merovingian nuns and to investigate the impact of the Carolingian revival of learning on communities of women.

NUNS AS SCHOLARS, TEACHERS, AND SCRIBES

Although nunneries never rivaled their male counterparts in number or in size in the Merovingian kingdom, they kept pace with them in standards of learning and scholarship. The first rule issued for nuns in Gaul, Caesarius of Arles's *Regula sanctarum virginum,* included the requirement that the sisters should be old enough to be taught to read and write. Moreover, in a letter to his sister, Caesarius noted that a certain part of the day should be set aside for the "divina lectio," the reading and listening to the reading of the Scriptures and devotional works.[4] Subsequent rules for women—Aurelian of Arles's Rule, written in the mid-sixth century, Donatus of Besançon's Rule, issued between 630 and 655, and the *Regula cuiusdam patris ad virgines,* probably composed by Waldabert of Luxeuil (629–670) for the nuns of Faremoutiers—all

upheld similar criteria, thus establishing a way of life in female monasteries that paralleled that of monks.[5] Nuns who learned slowly were
subject to the rod, the standard punishment for lazy monks.[6]

Beyond the elementary skills of reading and writing, the education
of both sexes was largely limited, at least until the ninth century, to a
solid knowledge of the Bible, the works of the fathers of the church, and
some acquaintance with canon and civil law. Evidence that nuns con-
formed to this pattern is plentiful. Caesaria, abbess of Saint Jean of Arles
in the sixth century, advised Radegund and the sisters of Holy Cross at
Poitiers "to read and hear assiduously the divine lessons . . . to gather
from them precious daisies for your ears and make from them rings and
bracelets."[7] Her words must have been well received, for Radegund,
according to her biographer, stayed awake at night to read the Scriptures. Fortunatus, moreover, testified that the Greek fathers were read
in her convent.[8] A century later, Gertrud of Nivelles was renowned for
having committed to memory the entire library of divine laws and for
being able to lecture on the obscure mysteries of scriptural allegories.[9]

The accomplishments of the two eighth-century nuns, Herlinda
and Renilda of Eyck, might have been exaggerated by their ninth-
century biographer. In addition, it is possible that the nunnery at Valenciennes, where they were allegedly educated, did not exist during this
period. Whatever the facts about Herlinda and Renilda of Eyck, the
most interesting part of their biographer's account is his insistence that
the girls were sent to Valenciennes to study

> divine doctrines, human arts, religious studies, and sacred letters.
> Whatever they were taught through books and lectures, they had
> memorized. . . . In the aforesaid monastery, they acquired a thor-
> ough knowledge of the diverse forms of divine office and ecclesias-
> tical ceremonies, that is, of the reading and modulation of chants
> and psalter, and, what is even more admirable in our times, of
> copying and illuminating. . . . In the same way, they were instructed
> in every skill of those arts which are usually produced by the hands
> of women, that is, in spinning and weaving, making designs and
> interlacing in gold, and embroidering flowers in silk.[10]

That the production of fine cloth and needlework, the traditional occupation of women, was regarded by some as a less desirable pursuit than
the spiritual and intellectual labor of nuns is evident from Caesarius of
Arles's remark that abbesses should encourage praying and reading
rather than needlework among their nuns. According to Caesarius,
temptations to vanity were inevitable when nuns were allowed to give

too much attention to embroidering and other fine arts.[11]

To educate nuns, books and teachers were needed. When Gertrud became abbess of Nivelles, a monastery founded by her mother, Itta, around 640, she sent to Rome for books and to Ireland for monks "to teach her and the sisters divine laws in the form of poetry."[12] The Irish monasteries, with the ancient tradition of oral learning, were at that time the most distinguished centers of scholarship.[13] Soon, however, some of the Frankish double monasteries were equally famous as centers of devotion and learning. The biographer of Saint Bertila, the first abbess of Chelles (ca. 658/59–705), writing around the middle or late eighth century, remarked that "kings from across the seas from various parts of Saxony beseeched her to send her disciples as teachers and to establish similar monasteries for men and women." Bertila obliged them by dispatching several chosen women and devout men with many volumes of books.[14]

In the eighth century, when the Anglo-Saxons emerged as the leading educators in the Latin West, their missionaries kept in close touch with the nuns of their native land. The English sisters supplied them not only with money and altar cloths but also with books. For example, to impress the heathen Germans, Saint Boniface asked Eadburga, the abbess of Thanet, to transcribe for him in golden letters Saint Peter's Epistle.[15] A more modest manuscript, Apponius's commentary on the Song of Songs, copied in the eighth century by an English nun Bertila and addressed to an "incletus iuvenis," is preserved in the Municipal Library of Boulogne-sur-Mer.[16]

Nor was the influence of Anglo-Saxon nuns on continental education limited to the help they gave missionaries. Some Anglo-Saxon nuns actually became missionaries themselves, heeding Saint Boniface's call for a mission of nuns "to teach the clerks and the children of the nobility the message of celestial sermons." Among the learned women who joined him, Tecla and Lioba established at Kitzingen and Bischofsheim the first nunneries in German lands.[17]

The cultural contributions of the more closely cloistered Frankish sisters, although equally impressive, were perhaps not as dramatic and certainly not as widely publicized. In communities under the stringent Rule of Caesarius, nuns functioned as teachers as a matter of course; the presence of men in the convent was tolerated only for the celebration of mass and the administration of the sacraments.[18] Even in the double monasteries, where the sexes were not as strictly segregated, the teachers were usually women. When Queen Balthild founded Chelles between 657 and 659, she turned for educational guidance to the abbess of Jouarre, not to Irish monks, as Gertrud had. Responding to this

request, Theudechild sent some of her nuns under the leadership of
Bertila.[19]

Other double monasteries also served as coeducational schools.
We know of two Merovingian princes who were raised at Chelles.[20] The
warm gratitude that Paschasius Radbertus, abbot of Corbie (844–851),
expressed to the nuns who had educated him at Soissons attests to the
quality of instruction in female communities.[21] When the Carolingian
reformers decided to cloister women more strictly, and with this end in
mind barred boys from nunneries, coeducation in nunneries was apparently so widespread that the order for its abolition was incorporated in
an imperial capitulary.[22]

In monasteries women acted also for the first time in history as
librarians. Caesarius of Arles in his rule enumerated among monastic
officers the custodian of books.[23] This was an important office, entrusted only to responsible members of the community. Books were
scarce and were carefully guarded as valuable property. Their theft was
not uncommon, as the threats of God's wrath or even anathema invoked
against thieves at the beginning or end of volumes indicate.[24]

Some of the books in monastic libraries were legacies or gifts. For
example, Eckhard, count of Autun and Mâcon, in his will of January 876
bequeathed five manuscripts to three members of Faremoutiers. He left
a copy of the Gospels and a Life of Saint Antony to the abbess Bertrada,
a psalter and a volume of prayers to his sister Adana, and a book on
gynecology to his sister-in-law, Tetrada.[25] At the death of these women,
the manuscripts probably became part of the convent's collection.
Other books were specifically ordered for the monastic library by the
abbess, probably in consultation with the librarian.

Thanks to the painstaking scrutiny of Bernhard Bischoff and other
scholars, a few eighth and ninth century manuscripts commissioned by
nuns have been identified. For example, Jerome's Commentary on Jere-
miah was copied in 805 for an abbess Hlottildis, who might be Theotil-
dis of Remiremont, according to Bischoff.[26] Notations in manuscripts
about their destination and location are usually too cryptic to be useful.
The scribe of a ninth-century collection of penitentials merely remarked
that he had compiled the volume for a congregation of nuns "ad lapi-
dum fluminis," a river that Bischoff, on the basis of the script, has
proposed to be the Main.[27] In the Autun Gospels copied with commentaries in 754, the scribe identified himself as Gundoinus and explained
that he was induced to produce the book by a certain "domina Fausta"
in honor of Saint John and Saint Mary. Because the paleographical
evidence points to a scriptorium at Autun, and there was in the city a
convent dedicated to Saint John and Saint Mary, Lowe has concluded

that Fausta was the abbess of that institution.[28] A further example of a volume copied for nuns is in the rich manuscript collection of the Laon Municipal Library. Codex 113, a ninth-century collection of sermons and documents bearing on theological controversy and religious persecution of orthodox Christians under the Vandals, includes an anonymous treatise, *Liber de quatuor virtutibus, hoc est caritatis, continentiae, patientiae et penitentiae*, which was dedicated to "dominae meae dilectae" and was written for the edification of her community. The sermon on the birth of Saint John in the collection suggests that perhaps it was destined for the same community as the Autun Gospels.[29]

The Laon manuscript gives us an insight into the range of readings of an average Frankish nun. The sermons include Saint Augustine's Oration in his *Soliloquiorum*, two discourses on the birth of Christ and one on his resurrection, and an interesting exposition in rhythmic prose on the parable of the bleeding woman. There are two poems, Sedulius Coelius' verse on the birth of Christ and, in a later hand, the first four lines of a hymn by Aurelius Prudentius Clemens, as well as several dogmatic writings on the Monothelite controversy and a short tract on clerical life, commonly attributed in the Middle Ages to Saint Jerome.[30] If we add to this list the titles of the books that were bequeathed to or copied for nuns, it becomes evident that the libraries of Frankish convents were not limited to the volumes of the Bible, psalters, and missals. The nuns also had access to commentaries on the scriptures, saints' lives, religious poetry, sermons, patristic writings, penitentials, and books of medicine.

The correspondence of Alcuin with Gisla and Rotrud, Charlemagne's sister and daughter, who had both retired to Chelles, confirms the breadth of the Frankish nuns' interest in books. It was to them that the eminent scholar and teacher turned for criticism of his unfinished commentary on the Gospel of Saint John. They urged him to complete it, asking him in the meantime to explain for them certain difficult passages in Saint Augustine and to supply them with Saint Jerome's letter to "the Roman women." Reciprocating their interest, Alcuin not only encouraged them to read biographies of the fathers, saints' lives, and Pope Gregory's *Dialogues*, but also sent them Bede's works.[31]

Some of the manuscripts in the libraries of the Frankish female communities were copied by nuns. Until quite recently, the accomplishments of Frankish nuns as scribes were unknown. The feminine names that appear in some eighth and ninth century manuscripts had traditionally been dismissed by scholars as attempts on the part of women readers to immortalize themselves, or as garbled versions of masculine names.[32] But the paleographical evidence assembled by Bernhard Bi-

schoff leaves no doubt that the nine nuns who had identified themselves
in the Cologne manuscripts were professional scribes. In addition to the
Cologne manuscripts they copied for Hildebald of Cologne (783–819),
Bischoff has located in various libraries seventeen codices that were
written by the same group.[33] Although he proposed Chelles as the
scriptorium where the nine nuns were active, he has provided evidence
that books were copied in other convents as well.

The existence, possibly at Laon, of a scriptorium where women
worked as scribes is indicated by an eighth-century collection of Isidore
of Seville's works, entitled in the codex *Liber rotarum,* now housed in the
Municipal Library of Laon. The codex concludes with the declaration
written in cursive: "ego Dulcia scripsi et susscripsi istum librum rotarum." On the basis of its distinctive "az" type of script, Lowe has related
the codex to other manuscripts, including Cambridge CCC MS 334,
which was copied by a male scribe, Fortunatus. We can presume, therefore, that in Dulcia's scriptorium men and women collaborated in the
production of books.[34] The possibility that this scriptorium was at
Notre-Dame-de-la-Profonde, the convent at Laon founded by Saint
Salaberga, is suggested by the similarity of Dulcia's script with that used
at Luxeuil. Salaberga's mentor was Waldebert of Luxeuil. Furthermore,
in a fragment of a manuscript with the same "az" type of script, there
are marginal notations by Martin Hiberniensis, a scholar who was teaching at the Laon cathedral school in the ninth century.[35]

Another manuscript pointing to an integrated scriptorium in the
vicinity of Meaux is an eighth-century copy of Augustine's *De Trinitate*
in the Municipal Library of Cambrai. The codex contains the name
MA-DAL-BER-TA enclosed within an initial I. Two initials resembling
this I, with the name David, appear in the famous Sacramentary of
Gellone, copied in the late eighth century in the region of Meaux and
now housed at the Bibliothèque Nationale. Despite some earlier attempts to account for the feminine ending in the Cambrai manuscript
as a scribal error, most modern scholars agree that it was copied in the
scriptorium of a double monastery in the vicinity of Meaux, either at
Faremoutiers or at Jouarre.[36]

Bischoff has also discovered the existence of a scriptorium at Würzburg, where a nun named Abirhilt and possibly another named Gunza
were working.[37] To this list we must add the scriptorium at Remiremont, where, in the ninth century, the nun Caecilia had the honor of
recording her abbess's donation and where the convent's *Liber memorialis*
was undoubtedly also written.[38] Yet another nunnery, the one at which
Eugenia worked, has remained unidentified. A ninth-century scribe, she
proudly signed her name with Greek letters in the copy she made of

Priscian's grammar, now at the Bibliothèque Nationale.[39]

Further study of early medieval manuscripts will undoubtedly disclose more details about the activities of nuns as teachers, librarians, writers, and scribes. Even with the data now available to us, we can conclude that nuns played a significant role in the cultural life of the Frankish Kingdom. The ninth-century artist, illuminating the so-called First Bible of Charles the Bald, did not engage in flights of fancy when he depicted Saint Jerome dictating his translation of the Bible to both men and women.[40] He modeled the women, with scrolls in their hands on Jerome's right, and the men, with books in their laps on Jerome's left, after the learned nuns and monks of the early Middle Ages. Pictures in other ninth-century manuscripts also attest that the scholarly woman surrounded by scrolls was a standard feminine paradigm.[41]

MEROVINGIAN NUNS AS AUTHORS

Women in religious communities made a significant contribution to Merovingian literature. Although modest in scope and pragmatic in focus, as Pierre Riché has demonstrated, Merovingian writings exerted a lasting influence on hagiography and devotional literature.[42] While Merovingian legal texts were the products of episcopal and royal courts, saints' lives, hymns, and prayers were closely connected both in their inspiration and composition with the monasteries. Nuns left an imprint on this type of literature by introducing feminine ideals into hagiography and leaving a record of their own mystical experiences.

The learned Bollandists, who began editing saints' lives in the seventeenth century, and the distinguished German scholars, who reedited them in the nineteenth century, assumed that the anonymous biographies of male and female saints surviving from Merovingian times had been composed by men. The only work in which the author had identified herself as a woman and a nun, Baudonivia's *Life of Saint Radegund,* was dismissed as an exception. Influenced by Krusch's remark that her style was barbarous,[43] scholars have tended to disparage her work as mere compilation, especially in comparison to Fortunatus' skillful and dramatic *Vita* of Radegund that Baudonivia intended to supplement.[44]

That the biographer of Saint Wynnebald, who was also entrusted with the task of putting into writing the verbal account of the saint's pilgrimage to the Holy Land with Saint Willibald, was a nun of Heidenheim has been demonstrated by Bernhard Bischoff.[45] The cryptogram of Hugeburc's name, appearing in the earliest extant manuscript, might have been deciphered earlier if scholars had paid attention to Saint Boniface's testimony that the Anglo-Saxon nuns who came with him to the continent were avid readers and talented writers. The missionary's correspondence makes it clear that his close friend, Saint Lioba, was only one of the several Anglo-Saxon nuns who turned to the composition of religious poetry.[46]

The possibility that Frankish nuns may also have made a contribution to the meager literary production predating the Carolingian Renaissance and that their writings may be buried among the anonymous hymns, chronicles, and saints' lives in early medieval manuscripts has not been seriously considered. Only recently, as the high standards of learning in Frankish female convents have gained recognition, have scholars begun to pay closer attention to evidence that suggests feminine authorship. An awareness of Gisla's erudition (Charlemagne's sister and a nun at Chelles) led the German scholar Hoffman to trace to her convent the composition of the *Annales Mettenses*.[47]

The older version of Saint Balthild's life, the A *Vita,* was also composed at Chelles by a nun of the community.[48] The intimate details the A *Vita* gave of Balthild's activities and death, as well as the prominent place it accorded to the bishop of Paris in the circle of Balthild's friends, leaves no doubt that this version was written at Chelles, not long after Balthild's death in 679, by someone who knew the queen quite well.[49] A reference in the preface to the "dilectissimi fratres," at whose behest the work was composed, convinced scholars that the author was a monk of Chelles.[50]

A careful scrutiny of the A *Vita,* however, reveals that Chelles was not a double but a single female community when Balthild lived there. The text does not mention the presence of monks. Although there were priests at the bedside of the dying Balthild,[51] their function was purely sacramental. They were summoned to entrust her "blessed soul to God."[52] The fact that, when the priests arrived, Balthild told the sisters to leave indicates that the priests and the nuns did not constitute a monastic community.[53] An entirely different picture emerges from the *Vita* of Bertila, the first abbess of Chelles, who was installed in that office by Balthild herself and under whose leadership Balthild later lived at Chelles. Composed in the second half of the eighth century, the *Vita Bertilae* depicted the monastery as a double institution with a substantial number of monks and nuns.[54] Rather than dismissing one of the lives as an unreliable source, we can resolve the discrepancy in their stories by considering the time of their composition. The *Vita Bertilae* reflects changes that occurred after Balthild's death. Bertila, who outlived Balthild by twenty-six years (dying around 705), invited monks to join the community after the death of her patroness.[55]

The authoress of Balthild's A *Vita* may have finished her composition after the first monks were admitted to Chelles. I doubt, however, that the "dilectissimi fratres," to whom she dedicated her work, were the new brothers. Rather, as Nelson suggested, they were probably the monks of Corbie, which was also founded by Balthild and where Balt-hild's friend, Theudefrid, continued to serve as abbot for some time after her death.[56]

The corrected and revised version of Balthild's life, the B *Vita,* which was composed in the early ninth century, may also have been the work of a woman. Because it referred to Balthild's testament in the convent's archives, the editor concluded that the author was the convent's "bibliothecarius." But the learned librarian could just as well have been a woman. Neither external nor internal evidence in this later version, nor for that matter in the *Translatio S. Baltechildis,* which was composed shortly after 833, excludes the possibility of female authorship.[57]

Female authors writing about women introduced feminine values and ideals into hagiography. They replaced the ideal of the asexual female saint, the "virago," whose greatest accomplishment was the imitation of male virtues, with a heroine who relied on female attributes to achieve sanctity. The conventional *topoi* of monastic lives—humility, piety, and self-denial—appeared also in the compositions of Baudonivia and the nun of Chelles. Radegund, according to Baudonivia, served meals to pilgrims and washed and dried the face of the sick with her own hands.[58] Balthild also, according to the authoress of her *Vita,* sought menial jobs at Chelles, such as cooking and the cleaning of latrines.[59] But the characterization of the two saints as mother figures, peace-makers, and promoters of dynastic cult centers was an unusual theme in hagiography. It represented the assimilation into religious life of the nurturing and mediatory roles women were expected to play as daughters and wives in Merovingian society. Although women transcended their biological and sexual roles in religious communities, they did not reject the attitudes associated with these roles. On the contrary, they elevated feminine psychological traits to a spiritual plane.

Writing between 609 and 614,[60] Baudonivia was the first to emphasize typically female attributes, which do not appear either in Fortunatus' *Vita* of Radegund or in the other sources that Baudonivia used. Her aim was to compose a guide for her fellow nuns. Not wishing to repeat "those things that the blessed father, Bishop Fortunatus, has written about," she concentrated on the second phase of Radegund's life, when the saint lived in a cell adjacent to the convent she had built at Poitiers.[61] The prototype of the ideal nun that Baudonivia presented to her sisters was not, however, a self-effacing and sexless abstraction.

In contrast to Fortunatus' portrayal of Radegund as the withdrawn wife and reluctant queen whose main objective was to transcend her femininity and escape from her husband, Baudonivia described Radegund as an outgoing and emotional woman, who was as concerned about the affairs of the convent as about the developments in the kingdom.[62]

The childless Radegund in Baudonivia's *Vita* assumed the responsibilities of motherhood, nurturing and disciplining the spirit of the sisters with boundless energy:

> When the lesson was read, with pious solicitude caring for our soul, she said: "If you do not understand what is read, it is because you do not ask solicitously for a mirror of the soul?" Even when the least [of us] out of reverence took the liberty to question her, she did not cease with pious solicitude and maternal affection to expound what the lesson contained for the good of the soul.[63]

An extension of Radegund's role as mother was her function as "domina," which she discharged with strictness and kindness even after her death. She punished severely her former servant, Vinoberga, for sitting on her throne, but then took pity on her after she had prayed for mercy.[64]

Radegund's attempts to act as a peacemaker and her efforts to set up the convent as an intermediary between royalty and divinity were also interpreted by Baudonivia as expressions of her feminine concerns. While the love of peace was not an entirely new motive in hagiography,[65] this was the first time that a female saint assumed the role of peacemaker as a family obligation. The conventional notion that the love of associates in the monastery obliterated the memory of parents and husband, one that Baudonivia dutifully introduced,[66] did not prevent her from making clear that Radegund retained close ties with her husband's kin:

> Because she loved all the kings, she prayed for the life of each and instructed us to pray without interruption for the stability [of their kingdoms]. Whenever she heard that they had turned against each other with hatred, she was greatly shaken and sent letters to the one and the other [imploring them] not to wage war and take up arms against each other but to conclude peace so that the country should not perish. In the same way, she sent great men to give salutary advice to the illustrious kings so that the country should be made more salubrious both for the king and the people. She imposed continuous vigils upon the congregation and instructed us with tears in her eyes to pray for the kings without interruption.[67]

The relic that Radegund obtained from the Byzantine emperor played an important part in her scheme to develop the convent into an agency of intercession on behalf of kings. Baudonivia recalled that Radegund had regarded the piece of the true cross "as an instrument whereby the salvation of the kingdom would be secured and the welfare of the country assured."[68]

The appearance of the same dual theme in Balthild's *Vita*—Balthild's motherly disposition, her sense of mission as peacemaker between the warring kingdoms, and the extension of this mission to Chelles, which under her guidance became the source of concord between God and the court—suggests the direct influence of Baudonivia. The nun of Chelles probably had access to Baudonivia's *Vita Radegundis* in the convent's library while she composed Balthild's life toward the end of the seventh century. It would be wrong, however, to accuse her of imitation. Balthild, like Radegund and all Merovingian wives and mothers, was socialized to serve in the family and the broader aristocratic structure as a mediatrix of conflicts. The biographer, being a woman herself, found this role admirable. Baudonivia's work, serving as her model, encouraged her to interpret Balthild's actions in the context of this feminine role.

The Chelles authoress stressed the motherly aspects of Balthild's activities as a queen. She looked after the young men in her court as an "optima nutrix," and treated the poor as a "pia nutrix."[69] When she described Balthild's rule as regent, she emphasized that Balthild was an instrument of divinely ordained harmony between the warring kingdoms.[70] Finally, when she spoke of Balthild's plans for Chelles, she made it clear that Balthild knew only too well that the congregation had to offer prayers not only for the king and queen but for the royal officials as well. With the magnates running the kingdom, the help of God had to be obtained for a broad constituency if Chelles was to serve as a dynastic cult center.[71]

While some female hagiographers translated attitudes associated with feminine roles in secular society into ideals of sanctity, another seventh-century nun, Aldegund, found her own voice and gave expression to her own spiritual experiences. Born around 639, Aldegund founded Maubeuge and served as its first abbess.[72] She began having visions as a child and as an adult had almost nightly communications with the divine. According to the author of her *Vita*, who claims to have been educated at Maubeuge and to have known her personally, Aldegund left a record of her visions by dictating them to Subnius, abbot of the neighboring Nivelles. Passages from the book were read aloud to the sisters, and the author personally was asked by Aldegund to act as a reader. Although no manuscript of this original version of Aldegund's visions is extant, the *Vita* claims to provide a summary of its contents.[73]

Visions serving as premonitions of impending death or as assurances of salvation at the time of death were common themes in early medieval hagiography. Christ as the bridegroom appeared in Baudonivia's *Life of Radegund,* promising the saint that she would be one of the brightest diadems in his crown.[74] The dying Balthild saw Mary welcoming her to an altar, which had stairs behind it flanked by angels and leading up to heaven.[75] Aldegund's visions, covering a broader range of incidents, brought together many strands of early medieval mysticism, imprinting feminine values upon this type of spirituality.

In her first vision, Aldegund saw Christ calling her to monastic life.[76] Some of her later experiences were in the form of encounters with the devil, who appeared to her as a roaring lion and a rapacious wolf, images that were probably patterned after Saint Anthony's temptations.[77] Aldegund's firm "virilitas" in resisting the demon was a variation on the "virago" motif in Roman literature.[78] She was always given consolation after the temptations, a foretaste of the mysteries of heaven. Christ, the Holy Ghost, angels, and blessed souls advised her not only on how to achieve salvation but also explained to her the sense of mystic phenomena. Angelic messengers and their reassuring words were conventional topics in saints' lives. Even Aldegund's vision of a beautiful young girl sent from heaven by the Blessed Virgin had its parallel in Pope Gregory I's *Dialogues.*

Although the imagery and symbolism of Aldegund's visions were inspired by earlier models, the message the heavenly envoys brought to her was new. Instead of advising Aldegund to abstain from laughing and joking and to hold her tongue if she wanted to join the circle of celestial virgins, the young girl sent by Mary spoke about the commandment of love: "You shall love the Lord God with all your heart and with all your soul, and with all your powers, and your neighbor as yourself." (Matt. 22:37).[79] Love was also the advice that Saint Peter gave to Aldegund when he informed her that she would soon be summoned to heaven:

> Why are you bewildered? I am Peter the Apostle who has the power to bind and to loose and was sent to you by Jesus Christ. O chaste [virgin], you are counted among the blessed! The Lord desires your departure. . . . Do not fear; whoever fears is not perfect in love; "but perfect love casts out fear, for fear has to do with punishment" (John 4:18).[80]

Unlike the visions of female saints described by men, Aldegund's experiences were not designed to instruct women on overcoming the weaknesses of their sex. As in the saints' lives written by women, Aldegund's message was intended to draw the lesson of love. By penetrating the nature of women's religious impulses and spiritual experiences, female authors of the seventh century became eloquent witnesses to the true meaning of evangelical piety at a time when the church emphasized rituals as the way to salvation. They revealed that the women who sought an active part in the spiritual and monastic experiments of the seventh century were not weak in mind or spirit, but could live fully the message of the Gospels and imitate Christ.

CAROLINGIAN RESTRICTIONS

The significant literary creativity of women in Merovingian monasteries was not sustained in the Carolingian period. Although nuns continued to act as scribes, book collectors, teachers, and librarians, they were not known to be active in Carolingian literary scholarship. A careful scrutiny of the contents, themes, and imagery of the anonymous saints' lives and devotional literature composed in Carolingian times may reveal the authorship of nuns.[81] It would, however, be foolish to expect discoveries of female contributions to the new branches of literature that resulted from the Carolingian revival of learning. The new literary products, the textbooks, Biblical commentaries, sermons, theological treatises, letters, encomia, and moral instructions addressed to kings, and the interpretations of canon and civil law were written by men. The Carolingian revival of learning, which began at Aachen under the sponsorship of Charlemagne and was later introduced into the cathedral and monastic schools, bypassed the communities of women.

The active interest in books and learning exhibited by the female members of his own family was not taken into account by Charlemagne in his legislation on education. The general instructions Charlemagne issued on standards of scholarship in 789 specified that "psalms, musical notations, songs, computations, grammars in each monastery and bishopric . . . and, whenever it was needed, the Gospels, the Psalter and the Missal were to be written by men who had reached the age of majority."[82] Although this legislation was not uniformly enforced, it did cast aspersions on the performance of nuns as scribes and scholars. In addition, the strict cloistering of women religious, which began under Charlemagne and continued under Louis the Pious, limited the opportunities for nuns to keep abreast of the new learning. Nuns, unlike monks, were not trained in the new schools. Abbesses were not allowed to go to the leading centers of learning to master the new skills. The restriction that convents could educate only girls undoubtedly served to justify the exclusion of nuns from the mainstream of education and intellectual life. The Carolingian program of learning had as its purpose the creation of an elite that was literate in Latin, well-versed in Christian doctrine, and familiar with the Roman liturgy. Because women could neither preach nor participate in the liturgy, there was no need to introduce this new program in female communities.

These circumstances explain why the only authoress known to us in the ninth century was not a nun but a secular woman. The motherly instinct of Dhuoda was stronger than her embarrassment at her ungrammatical Latin. The desire to leave a moral guide for her son, who was taken from her in infancy, overcame Dhuoda's painful awareness that she was pursuing the craft of men.[83] It is equally noteworthy that a nun as writer reappeared in the tenth century, when the restrictions imposed by the Carolingians on female communities were no longer observed. In an era that has been called the darkest of the dark centuries, when literary activity had reached such a low ebb that in all western Europe historians are hard pressed to list the names of more than a half a dozen writers, a woman religious achieved fame by producing enduring classics of devotional and secular literature. Hroswitha of Gandersheim, a prolific author equally talented in prose and poetry, composed plays, legends, histories, and epic poems. Her works apparently were not popular in the Middle Ages: few manuscript copies remain in existence. But, rediscovered in the sixteenth century, they have been translated into many languages and continue to be read today.[84]

Flexible monastic structures, such as those which existed in Merovingian times, were more congenial for female creativity than the rigid Carolingian nunneries. The strict cloistering of women religious and the separation of the sexes in the monastic schools of the ninth century were not conducive to the realization of the intellectual potential of women. Rather, they resulted in the exclusion of women religious from the mainstream of education and led to the perpetuation of the misogynistic myth that, compared to men, women had weaker minds.

Conclusion

The fusion of Germanic and Roman populations in the early Middle Ages was beneficial to women. Improvement in the position of women occurred at a time when their cooperation was essential for the creation of a new society. Women made the most of the opportunities for self-assertion and achievement that were available to them. But the social and psychological climate was not conducive, and would not be for many centuries to come, for women to take the initiative to press for further rights.

The legal and social advancement of women in the early Middle Ages, although less dramatic and less rapid than the emancipation of women in the last one hundred years, was significant. However oppressed they appear in the light of modern criteria, medieval women were far more visible, vocal, and powerful than their sisters in antiquity. Double standards governed sexual relations. Discrimination against women was not eliminated from secular laws and was incorporated into the church's legislation. Nevertheless, compared to women in antiquity and primitive Germanic societies, early medieval women had achieved considerable legal and social rights.

Women living in the *Regnum Francorum* were the first to experience the increase in female rights and the expansion of feminine roles. With no legal or religious obstacles standing in the way of intermarriage between the Frankish newcomers and the Gallo-Roman population, the mutual influence of Germanic and Roman customs in family law and matrimonial arrangements resulted in the amelioration of women's status. Women in families of Roman descent were no longer treated as perpetual minors. They no longer had to produce three offspring to be eligible to plead and testify in court as they had in the late Roman Empire. As widows, they could manage their own property without the help of a tutor and could act as guardians for their minor children. In addition, the exclusion of women from the inheritance of landed property was relaxed in the Frankish codes. In line with the Germanic tradition, married women were active partners with their husbands even when subject to Roman law. At the same time, marriageable girls in

Germanic families were no longer sold. The former brideprice was transformed into a *dos,* a settlement providing for the woman's economic security. In the case of women of Gallo-Roman descent, the natal family continued to supply a dowry, and brides also received a gift from their groom before the consummation of the union.

Although the laws and customs in lands under Frankish domination emphasized the biological function and sexual nature of women, they did not deprive women of opportunities to find personal fulfillment in a variety of roles. Frankish women could sublimate their sexual drives and motherly instincts in ways not available to women in ancient societies. Their labor, moreover, was not as exploited as it had been in primitive tribal societies. Queens had access to power not only through their husbands but also through churchmen and secular officials whom they patronized. As widows, acting as regents for their sons, they could exercise political power directly. The wives of magnates issued donations jointly with their husbands, founded monasteries, endowed churches, cultivated interfamilial ties, transmitted clan ideology to their children, supervised the household, and administered the family's estates when their husbands were away. Whether they contracted a formal union or entered into a quasi marriage, their children could inherit. As widows, they acted as guardians of their minor children, arranged their marriages, and, in the absence of sons, wielded economic power as well. In the dependent classes, women shared their husbands' work, produced textiles and articles of clothing both for their familys' and the lords' use, and were instrumental in bringing about the merger of the free and slave elements in society.

For those who wished to free their bodies, souls, and brains from male domination and devote their lives to the service of God, Christianity provided an alternative way of life. Although, in relation to the total population, women in religious life remained a small minority even in the seventh and eighth centuries, when many female communities were founded, their roles, social functions, and cultural contributions have an importance for the history of women that outweighs their numbers. This alternative way of life was available not only to the unmarried but also to widows. Monasteries served as a place of refuge for married women as well. The rich and the poor, at least until the late eighth century, were accepted as members. Women from all walks of life, as well as relatives, friends, and dependants of the foundress and abbess, were invited to join the new congregations. Freed from the need to compete for the attention of men, women in these communities sustained each other in spiritual, intellectual, scholarly, artistic, and charitable pursuits. Writings by early medieval nuns reveal that female ideals and modes of conduct were upheld as the way to salvation and as models of sanctity in the monasteries led by women. By facilitating the escape of women from the male-dominated society to congregations where they could give expression to their own emotions, ascetic ideals, and spiritual strivings, Christianity became a liberating force in the lives of women. Historians have often overlooked this and concentrated on the misogynistic sentiments perpetuated by the male hierarchy.

We must distinguish, however, two different traditions within Christianity. One was the tradition of the organized church, which reflected the prejudices of the patriarchal societies where Christianity was born and propagated. The other was the contemplative and prophetic tradition, which kept alive the principle of equality proclaimed in the Gospels. Sometimes both traditions appeared in the works of the same author. Prejudices against women were already articulated in some of the Pauline Epistles. But, as long as Christianity remained a revolutionary sect, with its adherents forming a state within the state, the dominant message of the Gospels was not forgotten. In the early Christian communities, men and women were subject to the same moral precepts, and women served as auxiliaries to men in the propagation of the faith, pastoral care, and the administration of the sacraments. Only in the fourth century, when Christianity became first a favored and then an exclusive state religion, did the male hierarchy begin to disqualify women from auxiliary ecclesiastical functions. Particularly in the West, where the active participation of women in religion came to be associated with heresy, Eve's role in the Fall and the ritual impurity of women were used as excuses not only for excluding women from the diaconate, but also for enforcing celibacy on the ministers of the altar.

Concentrating its efforts on the creation of a celibate male hierarchy, the Merovingian church waged an active war against deaconesses and priests' wives. To preach the parity of women and condemn the double standards governing marital and extramarital relations was not consonant with this campaign. Misogamy and misogyny were linked where this served a strategic purpose for the hierarchy. Women who tried to exercise active ministry were humiliated and ridiculed. Those married to clerks in higher orders suffered the denigration of their virtue and the defamation of their characters if they tried to remain with their husbands.

Female monasticism, on the other hand, at least in the sixth and early seventh centuries, a period of conciliar activity, was not yet sufficiently widespread to warrant much attention. Although a local sixth-century synod called for the subordination of monasteries, male and female, to episcopal authority, its declaration failed to gain support from either the hierarchy or the kings. Some bishops, disturbed by the independence of female communities, founded rival institutions subject to male control, or established a policy of harassment by withholding sacramental services from nuns. But there was a sufficient number of influential churchmen in the sixth and seventh centuries, when monasticism was beginning to spread in the lands under Frankish domination, who did not share this haughty, authoritarian attitude toward women. Inclined to the contemplative life and not motivated by considerations of rank and power, they acted as spokesmen for women seeking an autonomous existence and safeguarded female communities from encroachments by men.

Female monasticism as envisioned by Caesarius of Arles, Columban, and the monks of Luxeuil, who assisted in the establishment of the double monasteries, kept alive the Gospel's promise that women had the same spiritual potential as men. The rules for female communities that these men composed or helped to formulate were predicated on the principle that women could and indeed needed to develop their own independent form of spirituality. The same group of men did not hesitate to denounce the asymmetry of sexual relations as contrary to Christian morality.

It is tempting to speculate on what would have happened if the independent forms of female monasticism had been allowed to grow in Carolingian times and sexual double standards had been gradually eliminated through the preaching of the Christian ideal of equality. What kind of creativity might have burst forth from the communities of women if their members had not been so strictly cloistered that they were unable to participate in the Carolingian revival of learning? What kinds of influence might women of the aristocracy have exercised on politics and culture if the Carolingian legislation had not emphasized that women's concern was the family and domesticity?

The imposition of the Benedictine Rule, advocated by Saint Boniface, gave the Carolingian bishops the opportunity to bring all forms of religious life, male and female, under episcopal control. But, unlike the monks and canons who were incorporated into the Carolingian "Reichskirche," nuns and canonesses were isolated from the mainstream of religious, political, and intellectual life. They were also deprived of the last vestiges of quasi-clerical functions, which women had continued to exercise after the abolition of the female diaconate in the sixth century. The precipitous drop in the number of women saints in the ninth century suggests that female sanctity did not thrive in a culture that rigidly specified and limited the role of women in religion.

The Carolingian clerical hierarchy, now part of a tightly organized state religion, looked upon the enforcement of monogamy as the means by which secular society could be transformed according to Christian ideals. But this transformation, as the monk Hrabanus Maurus clearly perceived, involved much more than the repression of divorce and the definition of a legitimate marriage and its impediments.

The fundamental problems of sexual promiscuity and the sexual exploitation of women were not solved by the Carolingian legislation. Sanctions against divorce, which were included in conciliar proclamations and royal capitularies, made the position of aristocratic wives more secure. The glorification of women as wives and mothers, which appeared at this time in ecclesiastical writings, enhanced the dignity of married women. Significant as these gains were for the eventual emancipation of women, they appear less impressive when weighed against the broader consequences of the imposition of monogamy. The stability of marriage may have increased, but there is some evidence to suggest that it was accompanied by an increase in the abuse of wives, at least in the ninth century. The restructuring of the aristocratic family and the emphasis on the duties of the aristocratic wife as housekeeper, manager, and mother served, moreover, to remove noble women from political and cultural concerns into a private life of nurturing and housekeeping. Rather than sharing her husband's power, a wife in the ninth century was expected to relieve him of his domestic burdens and administer selflessly to his material, physical, and spiritual needs.

More importantly, the enforcement of marital indissolubility weakened the overall economic power of women, hardened social distinctions by putting an end to social mobility in the upper echelons of society, encouraged an attitude of superiority among the wives of the aristocracy, and reduced women who had sexual relations outside of marriage to social outcasts. As marriage became an irrevocable step and men were no longer able to practice polygyny or serial monogamy, fewer women could acquire landed wealth through marriage.

More than ever before, the matrimonial arrangements of the aristocracy were subordinated to the political and social interests of the family. Women of the dependent classes and even women of free birth, whose families lacked important connections, could no longer aspire to marry men of higher rank. The *Friedelehe,* or quasi-marriage that had ensured upward mobility in the Merovingian period, was now treated as a form of concubinage. A concubine could be abandoned at will; she had no legal status and could make no economic claims. Rather than protecting concubines and their offspring, the church held these women responsible for premarital and extramarital sex, which the introduction of monogamy did not eradicate. The idealization of married women as helpmates and mothers and the disparagement of concubines as whores and sorceresses created a new social division among women. On one side there were the respectable wives, and on the other, disreputable, loose women. The characterization of women in terms of two extreme sexual stereotypes, the chaste and self-effacing Mary and the impure and bold Eve, a theme that had appeared in patristic writings, could now be associated with real women. The responsibility for the success of monogamous unions was placed on women. The sanctification of the domesticated wife and dutiful mother provided an incentive for supreme efforts of selflessness on the part of married women. The association of sorcery with women's capacity for sexual enchantment served, on the other hand, to inhibit women's sexual drives outside of marriage.

The obvious conclusion from this study is that the position of women in Frankish society was not static. It differed in each social group and fluctuated within each group under the impact of different historical forces. Political dislocation and the resulting realignment of kinship ties and familial structure had a profound effect on the lives of noble women, while economic developments had a more immediate impact on peasant women. Circumstances permitting the upward and downward mobility between social groups within the same society favored women in the lower classes, but limitations on upward social mobility did not necessarily increase the power of upper class women outside the conjugal unit.

In the period following the accession of the Carolingian dynasty, when close cooperation between the church and the monarchy temporarily strengthened the power of each, women of the aristocracy faced a decline in the number of social options available to them. Excluded from institutions of authority, they were relegated to more passive, sexually determined roles both in secular life and in the monasteries. The greater security and dignity noble women gained as wives as the result of the introduction of lifelong monogamy served to enhance their dependency on men, facilitating the differentiation of domestic and public activities along sex lines.

Conversely, in the Merovingian period, when both royal and ecclesiastical authority had been feeble and decentralized, women could exercise considerable power as members of the landed aristocracy and as heads of monasteries. For all the sexual asymmetry, women were less marginal in Merovingian than in Carolingian society. Ambition in a woman was tolerated as long as she did not appear too independent and achieved her goals by using her sexual power, social connections, and wealth. It is symptomatic of the extensive opportunities women had for the assumption of leadership positions in Merovingian society that the name of Jezebel was associated with two dowager queens, Brunhild and Balthild, women of exceptional political skill and achievement. Under the Carolingians, in contrast, when women of the aristocracy were limited to domesticity and the cloister, those suspected of exercising undue sexual influence, like Louis the Pious's wife Judith and Lothar II's mistress Waldrada, were the ones who were compared to the wicked biblical queen.

The fact that in the period of political decentralization, following the final collapse of the dream of a Christian empire in 887, women once again became active in politics and cultural life suggests a pattern. Under feudalism, by virtue of their right to hold and inherit property, women of the aristocracy exercised private jurisdiction, had knights under their command, and participated in deliberative assemblies. Female religious communities regained their autonomy and were reintegrated into the mainstream of life in both the feudal principalities and the hegemonial German monarchy. Although they did not regain the influence they had in the double monasteries, abbesses once again assumed leadership positions, wielding political and religious power, and nuns distinguished themselves as teachers, scholars, writers, and mystics.

The suppression of women was not an endless story in medieval times. Women made a dynamic and creative contribution not only to social but also to cultural, political, and religious life whenever church and state were decentralized. Comparative studies of women's position in other societies where these conditions prevailed and were then eliminated, for example, in England before and after the Conquest, or in France during and after the Hundred Years War, will undoubtedly refine this observation.

In a broader European context, the work of feminist historians has revealed a complementary pattern, suggesting that, in periods of political or ecclesiastical advances, women's progress was stifled. For example, Joan Kelly Gadol's analysis of women's role reflected in Renaissance literature indicates that women's subordination was increased when, with the help of early capitalism, princes established "signorie" in Italy. Gadol's thesis that "events that further the historical development of men . . . have a quite different, even opposite effect on women"[1] should be kept in mind when looking at the ebb and flow of the power of institutions and women's participation in them. The ascent of institutions in which women had a limited role or none at all resulted almost invariably in the constriction of female roles. This can be readily discerned in Frankish society, where there were only a few institutions: the monarchy, the hierarchical church, the monastery, and the family. In

Merovingian times, when aristocratic families and monasteries were dominant elements, the role of women was open-ended and their contributions to all aspects of life were extensive. In Carolingian times, when kings triumphed over the aristocracy and bishops over the monasteries, the scope of women's activities was more narrowly delineated and women's involvement outside the home and convent was curtailed.

The causes for the liberation and oppression of peasant women must be sought, not in an institutional balance of power, but in economic and demographic developments shaping the structure of the family in the lower echelons of society and determining the place of women in the labor force. Although the information this study has yielded on the life and activities of peasant women is meager and sketchy, it permits the generalization that women's sphere of influence and scope of activity were more constant and stable in the dependent classes than in the ranks of the landowning aristocracy.

With the exception of natural disasters, such as bad harvests and epidemics, there were no major economic dislocations in the Frankish society until the second half of the ninth century, when the Viking raids destroyed a burgeoning network of commerce and devastated the land along the great rivers. The decimation of the population by natural disasters and raids made, however, the participation of women in the labor force even more necessary. Labor shortages, which had already resulted in vacant lands without tenants in the late Roman Empire, remained acute throughout the Merovingian and Carolingian periods. New lands had to be brought under cultivation, first north of the Loire, the area of heavy Merovingian settlement, and then in the regions east of the Rhine, which were conquered and colonized by the Carolingians. These conditions favored the inclusion of women in the labor force as domestic workers and artisans, skills for which they commanded a high value in the legal codes, and as cultivators. In the latter capacity women could earn an economic and social position higher than that of their husbands.

The manorial regime was based on the assumption that men would cultivate the land. Nonetheless, women of free status and enterprising spirit could establish themselves as tenants by taking advantage of the need of landowners to find a substitute for slave labor. Offering to marry unfree laborers, they could obtain from the lord of these men a guarantee of their own free status and that of their children, and also the recognition of their right to the land they cultivated. A freewoman, married to an unfree man, and a tenant in her own right, undoubtedly commanded respect from her husband and children. That arrangements of this kind were not uncommon and were regarded with favor by landowners is indicated by Charlemagne's legislation, which encouraged the assimilation through intermarriage of the various groups of people of different ranks on the royal estates into a general peasant class with common social and legal characteristics.

Although we know more about the history of early medieval women in the ruling classes, further research is needed in many areas. The systematic gathering of genealogical data by the Deutsches Institut in Paris, which eventually will be made available to researchers in computerized form, will undoubtedly generate studies on the economic power of women and the marriage strategies of the landowning classes in specific regions and periods. Another subject that would lend itself to systematic record collecting is the history of female monasticism. An intensive investigation of the number, size, membership, and endowment of female communities would deepen our understanding of the economic power, social function, and spiritual and cultural influence of female communities. Finally, regional studies, particularly on the history of women in Italy and Spain, are needed for a comparative analysis of the variety of roles women played, the social, spiritual, and intellectual contributions they made, and the constraints they suffered in the early Middle Ages.

The insights about women in the early Middle Ages provided by this study will undoubtedly be tested both in narrower contexts and from broader perspectives. This is as it should be. Only such a dual method, which lies at the heart of historical analysis, will enable us to chart womankind's progress and reversals during the formative period of European history.

APPENDIX

The source of this list is K. F. Werner's table in "Die Nachkommen Karls des Grossen." I have included only five generations and only those persons whose age at death could be approximated within ten years. In the case of married women for whom only the dates of marriage and death, and not of birth, exist, it was assumed that they entered into the union between 12 and 18. (See chapter 5, note 24, for the range of age at marriage for Carolingian queens and princesses.)

ABBREVIATIONS

ca	circa
m	married
c	became a concubine
*	not included in my genealogical chart 3
betr.	betrothed
( )	Numbers in parentheses represent the average used in my calculations.

MEN	Approx. Age	WOMEN	Approx. Age*
First Generation			
Charlemagne	72	Hildegard 758–783	25
		Fastrada m783–794	23/29 (26)
		Liutgard c794, m796–800	17/24 (21)
Second Generation			
Pepin the Hunchback ca 768–811	43	Adalhaid 773–774	1
Charles the Younger 772/3–811	38/39 (38.5)	Rotrud ca 775–810	35
		Bertha 779/80–ca 823	43/44 (43.5)
Carloman 777–810	33	Hildegard 782–783	1
Louis the Pious 778–840	62	Theudrada ca 785–844/53	59/68 (63.5)
Lothar 778–779/80	1	Ermengard m794–818	36/42 (39)

Drogo 801–855	54	Judith m819–843	36/42 (39)
Hugh 802/6–844	38/42 (40)		
Theuderic 807–818	11		

Third Generation

*Louis abbot of St. Denis ca 800–867	67	Kunigund m815–835	32/38 (35)
Bernhard ca 797–818	21	Adalhaid ca 797–810	13
Nithard 800–845	45	Atula ca 800–810/814	10/14 (12)
*Ricbodo 800/805–844	39/44 (41.5)	Gundrada ca 800–810/814	10/14 (12)
Arnulf 794–841	47	Alpais ca 794–852	58
Lothar I 795–855	60	Gisla 819/22–874	52/55 (53.5)
Pepin I 797–838	41	Ermengard m821–851	42/48 (45)
Louis II ca 806–876	70	Emma m827–876	61/67 (64)
Charles II, the Bald 823–877	54	Ermentrud ca 830–869	39
		Richild c869, m870–910/14	44/46 or 48/50 (47.5)

Fourth Generation

*Pepin count ca 815–840	25	Hildtrud ca 826–865/66	39/40 (39.5)
Eberhard ca 806–861/71	55/65 (60)	Gisla ca 830–860	30
Louis II ca 825–875	50	Engelberga, betr. 851–896/901	58/62 or 63/67 (62.5)
Lothar II ca 835–869	34	Waldrada c855–868?	25/31 (28)
Charles 845–863	18	Theutberga m855–875	32/38 (35)
*Pepin II ca 823–864	41	Hildegard 828–856	28
*Charles 825/30–868	33/38 (35.5)	Liutswind c850–891	53/59 (56)
*Ramnulf 815–866	51	daughter of Count Ernust m861–879	30/36 (33)
Carloman 830–880	50	Liutgard m876/77–885	22/23 or 24/25 (23.5)
Louis III 835–882	47	Richardis m862–900	50/56 (53)
Charles the Fat 839–888	49	Ingeltrud 837/40–870	30/33 (31.5)

Eberhard ca837–840	3	*Anna m915–936	36
Unruoch 840–874	34	Judith ca844–870	36
Berengar I 840/45–924	79/84 (81.5)	Ansgard m862–879	29/35 (32)
Charles (of Aquitain) 847/48–866	18/19 (18.5)	Adelheid m875–901	38/44 (41)
		Rothild 871–928/29	57/58 (57.5)
Louis the Stammerer 846–879	33		
Drogo 872/73–873/74	1		
Pepin 872/73–873/74	1		
Charles 876–877	1		
*Franco bishop of Lüttich 820/25–901	76/81 (78.5)		

Fifth Generation

Pepin ca 845–893	48	Gisla ca 852/55–868	13/16 (14.5)
*Heribert ca 850–900/7	50/57 (53.5)	Ermengard ca 852/85–896	41/44 (42.5)
*Wulfhard ca 830–889	59	Gisla ca 860/65–907	42/47 (44.5)
Hugo 855/60–895	35/40 (37.5)	Bertha ca 863–925	62
		*Ellinrat m870/75–914	51/57 or 56/62 (56.5)
*Adalhard ca 830–890	60	*Oda m888–903	27/33 (31)
*Ramnulf II 845/50–890	40/45 (42.5)	Hildegard 878/81–895	14/17 (15.5)
*Arnulf of Carinthia ca 850–899	49	Gisla 880/85–910/15	25/35 (30)
*Hugo 855/60–880	20/25 (22.5)	Aelftrud m884–929	57/63 (60)
*Louis ca 877–879	2	Frederuna m907–917	22/28 (25)
*Baldwin II 863/65–918	43/45 (44)	Eadgifu m919–951	44/50 (47)
*Rudolf ca 865–896	31		
Louis III 863/65–882	17/19 (18)		
Carloman 866–884	18		
Charles III, the Simple 879–929	50		

ABBREVIATIONS

AS	*Acta Sanctorum,* ed. Joannes Bollandus. Nov. ed. J. Carnandet et al.
Bruns	Herm. Theod. Bruns, *Canones apostolorum et conciliorum saeculorum IV. V. VI. VII.* 2 vols. Berlin, 1839.
CCL	*Corpus christianorum. Series latina.*
Codex Theod.	*Theodosiani libri XVI cum Constitutionibus Sirmondianis,* ed. Th. Mommsen and P. M. Meyer. 3 vols. Berlin, 1905.
CSEL	*Corpus scriptorum ecclesiasticorum latinorum*
JE	Philipp Jaffé, ed. *Regesta pontificum romanorum.* Ed. sec.
JK	S. Loewenfeld, K. Kaltenbrunner, P. Ewald. 2 vols. Leipzig, 1885–1888.
	JK=First part (Jaffé-Kaltenbrunner); JE=Second part (Jaffé-Ewald).
Mansi	J. D. Mansi et al. *Sacrorum conciliorum nova et amplissima collectio*
MIÖG	*Mitteilungen des Instituts für österreichische Geschichtsforschung*
MGH	*Monumenta Germaniae historica*
Auct. ant.	*Auctorum antiquissimorum*
Capit.	*Legum Sectio II: Capitularia regum francorum*
Conc.	*Legum Sectio III: Concilia*
Epist.	*Epistolae*
Mer. et kar. aevi	*Merowingici et karolini aevi*
Kar. aevi	*Karolini aevi*
Epist. sel.	*Epistolae selectae in usum scholarum*
Form.	*Legum Sectio V: Formulae*
Leg.	*Legum* (folio edition)
Legum Sectio I	*Legum Sectio I:Legum nationum germanicarum*
Libri mem.	*Libri memoriales*
Poet.	*Poetarum latinorum medii aevi*
Script.	*Scriptorum*
Script. rer. lang.	*Scriptores rerum langobardorum*
Script. rer. mer.	*Script. rerum merovingicarum*
PG	J. P. Migne, *Patrologia graeca*
PL	J. P. Migne, *Patrologia latina*
ZSSR	*Zeitschrift der Savigny-Stiftung für Rechtsgeschichte*
germ. Abt.	*germanische Abteilung*
kan. Abt.	*kanonische Abteilung*

NOTES

INTRODUCTION

1. L. Stouff, "Étude sur le principe de la personnalité des lois depuis les invasions barbares jusqu'au XIIᵉ siècle," *Revue bourguignonne de l'enseignement superieur*, 4, 2 (1894), 1–65, 273–310. F. L. Ganshof, "L'étranger dans la monarchie franque," *Société Jean Bodin, Recueils*, 10 (1958), 19–20.
2. Jacob Grimm, *Deutsche Rechtsalterthümer* (Göttingen, 1828); 4th rev. ed. in 2 vols. (Leipzig, 1899); Karl von Amira, *Germanisches Recht*, 4th ed. rev. Karl August Eckhardt, vol. 2 (Grundriss der germanischen Philologie, 5,2; Berlin, 1967).
3. R. Schröder, *Geschichte des ehelichen Güterrechts in Deutschland. Erster Teil: Die Zeit der Volksrechte*, vol. 1 (Stettin, 1863); Julius Ficker, *Untersuchungen zur Erbenfolge der ostgermanischen Rechte*, vols. 1–4 (Innsbruck, 1891–1896); Heinrich Brunner's articles on these subjects have been collected in his *Abhandlungen zur Rechtsgeschichte*, ed. K. Rauch, 2 vols. (Weimar, 1931).
4. R. Köstler, "Raub-, Kauf- und Friedelehe bei den Germanen," *ZSSR germ. Abt.*, 63 (1943), 92–136; and Gerda Merschberger, *Die Rechtsstellung der germanischen Frau* (Mannus-Bücherei, 57; Leipzig, 1937), are examples of this bias.
5. Jean Baptiste Brissaud, *Manuel d'histoire du droit français; sources, droit public, droit privé . . .* , (Paris, 1898–1904), 5 parts; new ed., Jacques Brissaud (Paris, 1935); Emile Chénon, *Histoire générale du droit français public et privé des origines à 1815*, vol. 1 (Paris, 1926); Louis-Maurice-André Cornuey, *Le régime de la "dos" aux époques mérovingienne et carolingienne* (Alger, 1929); A. Lemaire, "La 'dotatio de l'épouse' de l'époque mérovingienne au XIIIᵉ siècle," *Revue historique de droit français et étranger*, 4th ser., 8 (1929), 569–580.
6. François L. Ganshof, "Le statut de la femme dans la monarchie franque," *Société Jean Bodin, Recueils*, 12 (1962), 5–58. Max Conrat, *Breviarium Alaricianum, römisches Recht im fränkischen Reich in systematischer Darstellung* (1903 rpt. Aalen, 1963).
7. See in particular, Jean Gaudemet, "Le legs du droit romain en matière matrimoniale," *Il matrimonio nella società altomedievale* (Settimane di Studio del Centro Italiano di Studi sull'Alto Medioevo, 24; Spoleto, 1977), pp. 139–189; Giorgio Picasso O.S.B., "I fondamenti del matrimonio nelle

collezioni canoniche," ibid., pp. 191–231; Pierre Toubert, "La théorie du mariage chez les moralistes carolingiens," ibid., pp. 233–285; Raoul Manselli, "Il matrimonio nei penitenziali," ibid., pp. 287–319; Cyrille Vogel, "Les rites de la célébration du mariage: leur signification dans la formation du lien durant le haut moyen age," ibid., pp. 399–472; Gabriella Rossetti, "Il matrimonio del clero nella società altomedievale," ibid. pp. 473–567; Charles Verlinden, "Le 'mariage' des esclaves," ibid., pp. 569–601; Gérard Fransen, "La rupture du mariage," ibid., pp. 604–630.

8. Lina Eckenstein, *Woman under Monasticism* (Cambridge, 1896).

9. K. Heinrich Schäfer, *Die Kanonissenstifter im deutschen Mittelalter* (Kirchenrechtliche Abhandlungen, ed. Ulrich Stutz, 43–44; Stuttgart, 1907); idem, "Kanonissen und Diakonissen, Ergänzungen und Erläuterungen," *Römische Quartalschrift*, 24 (1910), 49–90.

10. Dom Philibert Schmitz, *Histoire de l'Ordre de Saint Benoît*, vol. 1, 2d ed. (Maredsous, 1948); vol. 7 (Maredsous, 1956).

11. Friedrich Prinz, *Frühes Mönchtum im Frankenreich* (Munich, 1965).

12. Mary Bateson, *Origin and Early History of Double Monasteries* (Royal Historical Society, Transactions, n.s. 13; London, 1899).

13. Ferdinand (P. Stephanus) Hilpisch, *Die Doppelklöster, Entstehung und Organisation* (Münster, 1928). See also chapter 7, n. 73.

14. Eduard Hlawitschka, *Studien zur Äbtissinnenreihe von Remiremont (7.–13. Jh.)* (Saarbrücken, 1963); Jean Jacques Hoebanx, *L'Abbaye de Nivelles des origines au XIVe siècle* (Mémoires de l'Académie Royale de Belgique, Classe des Lettres et des Sciences Morales et Politiques, 46; Brussels, 1952).

15. Bernhard Bischoff, "Die kölner Nonnenhandschriften und das Skriptorium von Chelles," in his *Mittelalterliche Studien*, vol. 1 (Stuttgart, 1966), 16–34.

16. Roger Gryson, *Le ministère des femmes dans l'Église ancienne* (Recherches et synthèses, Section d'histoire, 4; Gembloux, 1972); idem, *Les origines du célibat ecclésiastique du premier au septième siècle* (Recherches et synthèses, Section d'histoire, 2; Gembloux, 1970).

17. George H. Tavard, *Woman in Christian Tradition* (Notre Dame, Ind., 1973), lists recent studies on these two subjects.

18. Haye van der Meer, *Women Priests in the Catholic Church? A Theological-Historical Investigation*, trans. Arlene and Leonard Swidler (Philadelphia, 1973); Martin Boelens, *Die Klerikerehe in der Gesetzgebung der Kirche, unter besonderer Berücksichtigung der Strafe. Eine rechtsgeschichtliche Untersuchung von den Anfängen der Kirche bis zum Jahre 1139* (Paderborn, 1968).

19. Pierre Riché, "La femme à l'époque barbare," in *Histoire mondiale de la femme* (Paris, 1965), vol. 1, 27–46; "La femme à l'époque carolingienne," in ibid., 47–54.

20. G. Tellenbach, K. Schmid, J. Wollasch, and their pupils are known as the "Freiburg school"; their methodology is analyzed in G. Tellenbach, *Zur Bedeutung der Personenforschung für die Erkenntniss des früheren Mittelalters*

(Freiburger Universitätsreden, n.f. 25; Freiburg, 1975). A volume of essays by this group was edited by G. Tellenbach, *Studien und Vorarbeiten zur Geschichte des grossfränkischen und frühdeutschen Adels* (Forschungen zur oberrheinischen Landesgeschichte, 4; Freiburg i.B., 1957). A detailed bibliography and discussion of methodology is provided by Karl Schmid, "Programmatisches zur Erforschung der mittelalterlichen Personen und Personengruppen," *Frühmittelalterliche Studien*, 8 (1974), 116–130. For a summary and bibliography of recent research on medieval nobility, see Timothy Reuter's introduction to his edition and translation of essays by European scholars entitled *The Medieval Nobility: Studies on the Ruling Classes of France and Germany from the Sixth to the Twelfth Century* (Europe in the Middle Ages, Selected Studies, 14; Amsterdam, New York, Oxford, 1979), pp. 1–16; 331–366. The volume includes a translation of Karl Ferdinand Werner's study of Carolingian family names entitled "Important Noble Families," pp. 137–202; the article was originally published as "Bedeutende Adelsfamilien im Reich Karls des Grossen," in *Karl der Grosse: Lebenswerk und Nachleben*, vol. 1, ed. Helmut Beumann (Düsseldorf, 1965), 83–142. E. Hlawitschka's two most important studies on Frankish families are "Die Vorfahren Karls des Grossen," in *Karl der Grosse: Lebenswerk und Nachleben*, vol. 1, 51–82; and *Lotharingien und das Reich an der Schwelle der deutschen Geschichte* (Schriften der *MGH*, 21; Stuttgart, 1968).

21. Eugen Ewig, "Studien zur merowingischen Dynastie," *Frühmittelalterliche Studien*, 8 (1974), 15–59, in particular, 38–49, 52–58.

22. Janet L. Nelson, "Queens as Jezebels: The Careers of Brunhild and Balthild in Merovingian History," in *Medieval Women*, ed. in honor of Rosalind M. T. Hill (Studies in Church History, Subsidia 1; Oxford, 1978), pp. 31–77.

23. David Herlihy, "Land, Family and Women," *Traditio*, 18 (1962), 89–120 (reprinted in *Women in Medieval Society*, ed. S. Stuard [Philadelphia, 1976], pp. 13–45); "Life Expectancies for Women in Medieval Society," in *The Role of Woman in the Middle Ages*, ed. R. T. Morewedge (Albany, 1975), pp. 1–22; Emily R. Coleman, "Medieval Marriage Characteristics: A Neglected Factor in the History of Medieval Serfdom," *Journal of Interdisciplinary History*, 2 (1971), 205–219.

24. Archibald R. Lewis, *The Development of Southern French and Catalan Society, 718–1050* (Austin, 1965).

25. Diana Owen Hughes, "From Brideprice to Dowry in Mediterranean Europe," *Journal of Family History*, 3 (1978), 262–296.

26. Marie-Louise Portmann, *Die Darstellung der Frau in der Geschichtsschreibung des früheren Mittelalters* (Basler Beiträge zur Geschichtswissenschaft, 69; Basel, 1958); Maria Stoeckle, *Studien über Ideale in Frauenviten des VII–X Jahrhunderts* (Munich, 1957).

27. JoAnn McNamara and Suzanne Wemple, "Marriage and Divorce in the Frankish Kingdom," in *Women in Medieval Society*, ed. S. M. Stuard (Phila-

delphia, 1976), pp. 95–124; "The Power of Women through the Family in Medieval Europe: 500–1100," *Feminist Studies*, 2 (1973), 126–141 (reprinted in *Clio's Consciousness Raised: New Perspectives on the History of Women*, ed. Mary Hartman and Lois Banner [New York, 1974], pp. 103–118); "Sanctity and Power: The Dual Pursuit of Medieval Women," in *Becoming Visible: Women in European History*, ed. R. Bridenthal and C. Koonz (Boston, 1977), pp. 90–118.

CHAPTER 1

1. Tacitus, *Germania* 18, trans. H. Mattingly (Harmondsworth, 1960), pp. 115–116.
2. Tacitus, *Germania* 20. E. A. Thompson, *The Early Germans* (Oxford, 1965), has analyzed the evidence provided by Caesar and Tacitus on the social organization of the Germanic tribes. For a bibliography on matrilineal descent, see ibid., pp. 17, n. 1, and 34, n. 2.
3. Tacitus, *Germania* 20.
4. Ibid. 7.
5. Ammianus Marcellinus, *History*, 15. 12; rev. ed. J. C. Rolfe, vol. 1 (Cambridge, Mass., 1963), 195.
6. Tacitus, *Germania* 8.
7. Ibid. 15, 25.
8. Thompson, *The Early Germans*, pp. 51–52, in particular, 51, n. 3. Thompson argues that Tacitus's comments referred to the chiefs and their *comites*, who worked no land, but who were wholly supported by the rest of the population.
9. M. I. Finley, ed., *Slavery in Classical Antiquity* (Cambridge, 1960), pp. 191–203. Finley has examined the evidence relating to slavery among the Germans.
10. Tacitus, *Germania* 20.
11. Ibid. 18. Caesar, *Bellum Gallicum* 6.21, ed. O. Seel (*C. Iulii Caesaris Commentarii*, vol. 1; Leipzig, 1961), 190.
12. Tacitus, *Germania* 19. On the grave in the peat bog, see Malcolm Todd, *Everyday Life of the Barbarians* (London, 1972), pp. 30–31; on the savage penalties inflicted upon adulterous females among the Anglo-Saxons, see Sonia Chadwick Hawkes and Calvin Wells, "Crime and Punishment in an Anglo-Saxon Cemetery," *Antiquity*, 49 (1975), 118–122.
13. Saint Boniface, in a letter (no. 73) to King Aethelbald of Mercia (746–747), described how the Saxons on the continent executed an adulteress's partner. *Die Briefe des heiligen Bonifatius und Lullus*, ed. M. Tangl (*MGH Epist. sel.*, 1; Berlin, 1955), p. 150.
14. "Il se peut aussi que cette dote soit justement le prix." Noel Senn, *Le contrat de vente de la femme en droit matrimonial germanique* (Portentruy, 1946), p. 7; Louis-Maurice-André Cornuey, in *Le régime de la "dos,"* agrees. A similar view was expressed by Frances B. Gummere, *Founders*

of England (New York, 1930), p. 145; and Todd, *Everyday Life of the Barbarians,* p. 30.

15. Hughes, "From Brideprice to Dowry," p. 267, n. 14. For a bibliography of earlier works that accept Tacitus's statement, see Senn, *Le contrat de vente,* pp. 1–7.

16. Grimm, *Deutsche Rechtsalterthümer,* 4th ed., vol. 1, 420–421; Ficker, *Untersuchungen,* vol. 3, 403–415; H. Meyer, "Friedelehe und Mutterrecht," *ZSSR germ. Abt.,* 47 (1927), 198–286.

17. R. Köstler, "Raub-, Kauf- und Friedelehe bei den Germanen." An extremist, Gerda Merschberger went so far as to say that thinking the Germans had practiced *Kaufehe* was "rassfeindlich." *Die Rechtsstellung der germanischen Frau,* p. 47.

18. Noel Senn, *Le contrat de vente.*

19. Karl von Amira, *Germanisches Recht,* ed. Eckhardt, vol. 2, 73–74. See also vol. 1, 198.

20. S. Kalifa, "Singularités matrimoniales chez les anciens germains: le rapt et le droit de la femme à disposer d'elle-même," *Revue historique de droit français et étranger,* 48 (1970), 199–225.

21. Brideprice, as noted above on p. 12, refers to the settlement the groom paid to the bride's kinsmen. This term will be used only when the entire settlement was retained by the bride's kin. The payment from the bridegroom or his kin, whenever in whole or in part turned over to the bride, will be called the bridegift. The designation of this kind of settlement as bridewealth has been criticized by anthropologists. J. R. Goody and S. J. Tambiak, in *Bridewealth and Dowry* (Cambridge, 1972), defined bridewealth as a gift from the husband's kin to the wife's male kin that is not turned over to the bride and does not form a part of the conjugal property. The settlement that Tacitus and the Germanic codes describe does not fit this definition.

22. Nineteenth-century historians, influenced by J. J. Bachofen, saw in *Friedelehe* evidence that the Germans had once lived in a matrilineal society. See in particular L. Dargun, "Mutterrecht und Raubehe," *Untersuchungen zur deutschen Staats- und Rechtsgeschichte,* 16 (1883), 23–76.

23. Ficker, *Untersuchungen,* vol. 3, 409–410.

24. Sarah B. Pomeroy gives a balanced view of the position of women in the late Roman Republic and early Empire in *Goddesses, Whores, Wives and Slaves: Women in Classical Antiquity* (New York, 1975), pp. 149–230. The frustrations of Roman women were explored by M. I. Finley in his "The Silent Women of Rome," *Horizon,* 7 (1965), 57–64, reprinted in his *Aspects of Antiquity: Discoveries and Controversies* (London, 1968), pp. 129–142. Marilyn Arthur has upheld the thesis that "in Rome, as the nuclear family became more important to the state, misogyny reappeared." " 'Liberated Women': The Classical Era," in *Becoming Visible: Women in European History,* ed. R. Bridenthal and C. Koonz (Boston, 1977), p. 85. J. P. V. D. Balsdon, in his *Roman Women: Their History and Habits* (New

York, 1963), attributes female emancipation to the rise of the empire. See Arthur and Pomeroy for further secondary and primary sources.

25. *Digesta* 50.17.2: "Women are to be excluded from all civil and public offices; and therefore they cannot be judges or act as magistrates, nor can they undertake pleas, nor intervene on behalf of others, nor act as procurators." *Corpus iuris civilis*, ed. P. Krueger, vol. 1 (Berlin, 1928), 920.

26. For detailed accounts of the legal position of women under the republic and the empire, see the articles of Robert Villiers, "Le statut de la femme à Rome jusqu'à la fin de la Republique," and Jean Gaudemet, "Le statut de la femme dans l'Empire romaine," both in *Société Jean Bodin, Recueils*, 11 (1959).

27. Pomeroy, *Goddesses*, p. 150.

28. S. B. Pomeroy, "Married Women in Rome," *Ancient Society*, 7 (1976), 224–225. See also P. E. Corbett, *The Roman Law of Marriage* (Oxford, 1930).

29. Villiers, "Le statut," pp. 183–189.

30. Gaudemet, "Le statut," p. 195.

31. Ibid., p. 215.

32. Edoardo Volterra has pointed out that marriage in postclassical law was no longer founded on the continuing will but, rather, on the initial will of the partners. "La conception du mariage à Rome," *Revue internationale des droits de l'antiquité*, 3d ser., 2 (1955), 378.

33. M. K. Hopkins, "The Age of Roman Girls at Marriage," *Population Studies*, 18, 3 (1965), 309–327. The consent of a girl if she did not protest was assumed, *Digesta* 23.1.7.1: "intellegi tamen semper filiae patrem consentire, nisi evidenter dissentiat Iulianus scribit . . ." S. B. Pomeroy states that "in reality it is the consent of the woman's relatives, not that of the woman herself, that makes the marriage consensual" ("Married Women in Rome," p. 220). As John T. Noonan has pointed out, "Roman law itself, while making consent central to marriage, did not employ the doctrine to prevent parental decision making" ("Marriage in the Middle Ages: The Power to Choose," *Viator*, 4 [1973], 426).

34. Balsdon, *Roman Women*, p. 176.

35. *Digesta* 25.7.1; not 21.7.1 as Balsdon has it in his *Roman Women*, p. 231.

36. On the famous *lex Julia* of 18 B.C., regulating adultery and fornication, see *Codex Iust.* 9.9, ed. P. Krueger, vol. 2 (Berlin, 1954), 374; and G. Rotondi, *Leges publicae populi Romani* (Milan, 1912), pp. 443–447 (reprinted in Hildesheim, 1962). In *Digesta* 48.5.6.1 and 48.5.21(20), Ulpian condemned double standards; see also *Digesta* 48.5.14(13).5.

37. Pomeroy, *Goddesses*, p. 193.

38. Ibid., p. 170.

39. Ibid., pp. 170, 212.

40. Balsdon, *Roman Women*, p. 57.

41. Pomeroy, *Goddesses*, p. 170.

42. *Codex Theod.* 3.16.1 (issued by Constantine in 331) and 3.16.2 (issued by Honorius and Theodosius in 421), ed. Th. Mommsen, vol. 1 (Berlin, 1905), 155–157. On these laws and divorce in general, see B. Biondi, *Il diritto romano cristiano,* vol. 3 (Milan, 1954), 167–173; and McNamara and Wemple, "Marriage and Divorce in the Frankish Kingdom," p. 98.

43. *Codex Iust.* 5.26.1: "constante matrimonio concubinam penes se habere"; issued by Constantine in 329. In 336 Constantine forbade marriage between people of different ranks under the pain of loss of citizenship; see *Codex Theod.* 4.6.3 = *Codex Iust.* 5.27.1.

44. Constantine in 337 asked that the marriage "publice contestatione firmatur" (*Codex Iust.* 5.17.7). Theodosius and Valentinian called for "pompa, celebritas, sollemnitas, fides amicorum," although they acknowledged the validity of "nuptiae furtivae" (*Codex Theod.* 3.7.3 = *Codex Iust.* 5.4.22). The proof for the legitimacy of an offspring was defined as "honesta celebratio" and "legitima coniunctio" (*Codex Theod.* 4.6.7). Theodosius and Valentinian admitted the validity of a marriage without an exchange of gifts *(donatio ante nuptias),* as long as the marriage was "inter pares honestate" (*Codex Theod.* 3.7.3 = *Codex Iust.* 5.4.22).

45. *Codex Theod.* 3.7.1.

46. Hopkins, "The Age," pp. 319, 322–323. The modal age at marriage of Christian girls, according to Hopkins, was somewhat higher, between fifteen and eighteen.

47. The following discussion on early Christian views on the relationship between the sexes comes in part from the article that I collaborated on with JoAnn McNamara, entitled "Sanctity and Power: The Dual Pursuit of Medieval Women."

48. Acts 1:14; 5:14; 7:3; 9:2, 36, 39; 12:12; 16:14–15; 17:4, 12.

49. Elaine Pagels, "When Did Man Make God in His Image? A Case Study in Religion and Politics," *The Scholar and the Feminist,* 3 (1976), 31–44. On the position of women in the early church, see also Johannes Leipoldt, *Die Frau in der antiken Welt und im Urchristentum,* 2d ed., rev. (Leipzig, 1955), pp. 171–219; and Haye van der Meer, *Women Priests,* pp. 10–45.

50. Else Kähler, *Die Frau in den paulinischen Briefen* (Zürich, 1960), pp. 45–83. On the authorship of 1 Cor. 14:34, see G. Fitzer, *Das Weib Schweige in der Gemeinde: Ueber den unpaulinischen Character der Mulier-taceat-Verse in I Korinther 14* (Theologische Existenz Heute, n.s. 110; Munich, 1963). On First Timothy in particular and on the pastoral Epistles in general, see M. Dibelius, *Die Pastoralbriefe,* 3d ed. H. Conzelmann (Handbuch zum Neuen Testament, 13; Tübingen, 1953). Most Catholic scholars consider 1 Cor. 14:34 authentic. See also van der Meer, *Women Priests,* p. 15, and "Pastoralbriefe," H. Haag, ed., *Bibellexikon,* 2d ed. (Einsiedeln, 1968), pp. 1316–1324.

51. Anne Yarbrough, "Christianization in the Fourth Century: The Example of Roman Women," *Church History,* 45 (1976), 149–165. She argues against the thesis of P. R. L. Brown, "Aspects of the Christianization of

the Roman Aristocracy," *Journal of Roman Studies,* 51 (1961), 4. Brown holds that Jerome's group was instrumental in converting the Roman aristocracy to Christianity. According to Yarbrough, these women fled the world—they did not try to convert it.

52. The question of the feminine diaconate will be treated in greater detail in chapter 6.

53. Lev. 15:19; *Didascalia et constitutiones apostolicae,* ed. Fr. X. Funk, vol. 1 (Paderborn, 1905), 373, 379. On the whole issue, see Peter Browe, *Beiträge zur Sexualethik des Mittelalters* (Breslau, 1932), pp. 1–14.

54. Jerome, *Comm. in Zach.* 3.13 (*PL* 25, 1517).

55. Jerome, *Comm. in Ezech.* 6.18 (*PL* 25, 173).

56. In the same letter, addressed to Augustine of Canterbury, Gregory also insisted that expectant and menstruating women were not to be disqualified from accepting baptism and entering churches: *Registrum epistularum* (*MGH Epist.* 2, 331–339); included by Bede in *History of the English Church and People,* 1, 27, trans. by Leo Shirley-Price (Baltimore, 1955), pp. 76–81. P. Browe has assembled evidence that the Eastern church continued to bar menstruating women from communion (*Beiträge,* p. 9).

57. See, for example, Jerome, *Letters and Select Works* 22, trans. W. H. Freemantle (A Select Library of Nicene and Post-Nicene Fathers of the Christian Church, 2d Ser., 6; New York, 1893), p. 30: "Death came through Eve, but life has come through Mary." Patristic views on women and the relationship between the sexes have not yet been systematically studied; only Augustine's ideas have been analyzed in depth. See Kari Elisabeth Børresen, *Subordination et equivalence: Nature et role de la femme d'après Augustin et Thomas d'Aquin* (Oslo, 1968). For a general treatment, see H. Rondet, "Éléments pour une théologie de la femme," *Nouvelle revue théologique,* 79 (1957), 923–925; H. Borsinger, *Rechtstellung der Frau in der katholischen Kirche* (Zürich, 1929); René Metz, "La femme en droit canonique médiéval," *Société Jean Bodin, Recueils,* 12 (1962), 59–113.

58. *Apostolic Constitutions* 3.5, in *Ante-Nicene Christian Library,* ed. James Donaldson and T. T. Clark, vol. 17 (Edinburgh, 1870), pp. 95–96.

59. Tertullian, "The Apparel of Women," in his *Disciplinary, Moral and Ascetical Works,* trans. R. Arbesmann et al. (New York, 1959), pp. 117–119.

60. Ambrose, *Traité sur l'Évangile de s. Luc,* 2.28, ed. and trans. G. Tissot, vol. 1 (Sources chrétiennes, 45; Paris, 1956), 83; and translated in Tavard, *Woman,* p. 104.

61. Augustine, *Quaestionum in Heptateuchum libri vii* 153 (*CSEL* 28, 2; 80).

62. *Quaestiones Veteris et Novi Testamenti* 45.3 (*CSEL* 50, 83). On this text see R. Metz, "La femme," p. 73, n. 1.

63. Ambrosiaster, *Comm. ad Corinthios Primam* 7.11 (*CSEL,* 81/2, 74–75); Jerome, *Epist. 77: Ad Oceanum* 3 (*PL* 22, 691); Augustine, *De adulterinis conjugiis,* 1.8 (*PL* 40, 456); *De nupt. et conc.* 1.10 (*CSEL* 42, 222). Ambrose acknowledged that women could also separate from their adulterous

husbands: *De Abraham* 1.4.25 (*CSEL* 32-1, 519); but he disapproved of remarriage while the other party was alive: *Expositio Evangelii secundum Lucan* 8.6 (*CSEL* 32-4, 394); *De Abraham* 1.7.57 (*CSEL* 32-1, 541). Matthew 19:9, according to Catholic interpreters such as G. H. Joyce, can be interpreted as an "exceptive clause," allowing of divorce *a mense et thoro* but not of divorce a *vinculo,* and also as "an interpolation devoid of authenticity" (*Christian Marriage,* 2d ed. rev. [London, 1948], p. 288). Like St. Augustine, Catholic interpreters solve the difficulty posed by Matthew 19:9 by placing the emphasis on Matthew 5:31–35; Mark 10: 10–12; Luke 16:18. On the question of divorce, see also Ignaz Fahrner, *Geschichte der Ehescheidung im kanonischen Recht* (Freiburg, 1903).

64. *Conc. Arel.* (314), 11 (10) (*CCL* 148, 11); *Conc. And.* (453), 7 (*CCL* 148, 138); *Conc. Venet.* (461–491), 2 (*CCL* 148, 152).

65. Caesarius of Arles, *Sermones* 32.4, 42, 43, ed. G. Morin, vol. 1 (*CCL* 103.1; Turnhout, 1953), pp. 141–142, 184–194; trans. M. M. Mueller, *Saint Caesarius of Arles: Sermons and Admonitions on Various Topics,* vol. 1 (New York, 1956), 161–162, 208–220.

66. Caesarius of Arles, *Sermones* 19.5; 44.2 (Mueller 1, 102, 221; Morin 1, 141–142, 184–194).

67. Caesarius of Arles, *Sermones* 1.12 (Mueller 1, 13; Morin 1, 9). In addition to the sermons cited in the previous note, Caesarius dealt with the question of abortion and contraception also in *Sermones* 51.4 and 52.4 (Mueller 1, 258–259, 261; Morin 1, 229, 231–232). On the whole question, see John T. Noonan, *Contraception: A History of Its Treatment by the Catholic Theologians and Canonists* (Cambridge, Mass., 1967).

CHAPTER 2

1. See Introduction, note 1, for references.

2. Karl von Amira lists the various editions and the most important studies of these laws; see *Germanisches Recht,* ed. Eckhardt, vol. 1, 30–31, 35, 54–56, 60–61. I used the *Monumenta Germaniae historica, Legum Sectio I* (cited as *MGH Legum Sectio I,* followed by volume and part). English-speaking readers should refer to the translations of Katherine Fischer Drew, *The Burgundian Code* (Philadelphia, 1972) and *The Lombard Code* (Philadelphia, 1973). Although the Lombard code will not be discussed here, it may be consulted for analogous customs. For the *Lex Romana Visigothorum,* which is not included in the *Monumenta,* I relied on G. Haenel's edition (Leipzig, 1849) and M. Conrat's *Breviarium Alaricianum,* henceforth cited as Haenel and Conrat, respectively. Prefaces in the *MGH* edition assign dates to the codes. The commonly held view that the *Lex Romana Burgundionum* was issued by Gundobad has been challenged by W. Roels, *Onderzoek naar het gebruik van de angehaalde bronnen van Romeins rech in de Lex Romana Burgundionum* (Anvers, 1958), pp. 9–12. See also F. Beyerle, "Volksrechtliche Studien II: Die süddeutschen Leges

und die merowingische Gesetzgebung," *ZSSR germ. Abt.,* 49 (1929), 299–301, and "Die beiden süddeutschen Stammesrechte," ibid. 73 (1956), 84–140. Beyerle argued that both the Aleman and Bavarian Codes were compiled under Dagobert I (623–639). Eckhardt, in his revised edition of Amira, asserted that the Aleman *Pactus* was compiled in the seventh century, whereas the codification of the *Lex Alamannorum* was issued between 709 and 712 (*Germanisches Recht,* vol. 1, 57–59). The first version of the Bavarian Code, according to Eckhardt, was published in the second quarter of the eighth century. On the date of the Ripuarian Code, see F. Beyerle, "Volksrechtliche Studien I: Die Lex Ribuaria," *ZSSR germ. Abt.,* 48 (1928), and "Volksrechtliche Studien III: Das Gesetzbuch Ribuariens," ibid., 55 (1935); and Eckhardt's view in his revised edition of Amira, *Germanisches Recht,* vol. 1, 45–47. On the date of the Salic Code, I am following K. A. Eckhardt, *Pactus Legis Salicae. I. Einführung und 80 Titel Text* (Göttingen, 1954), pp. 159–161, and his introduction to his edition in *MGH Legum Sectio I,* 4/1, xxxix. The code was reissued by Pepin (*Lex Salica* in one hundred titles) and revised by Charlemagne in 798. Another compilation of the *Lex Salica* in seventy titles was issued by Charlemagne at Aachen in 802 or 803 and reissued around 830 upon the request of Everard of Friuli.

3. Primarily obtained from J. M. Pardessus and L. G. O. de Brequigny, eds., *Diplomata, chartae, epistolae . . .,* vols. 1–2, Paris, 1843–49.

4. The earliest among the collections of *formulae,* edited by K. Zeumer (*Formulae merowingici et karolini aevi;* hereafter cited as *MGH Form.*) are the *Formulae Marculfi* and the *Formulae Andecavenses.* The former is based on Salic law, the latter on the Visigothic compilation of Roman law. Alf Uddholm dates the former collection prior to 690 (*Formulae Marculfi: Études sur la langue et le style* [Uppsala, 1953]). Heinz Zatschek argues that the collection by Marculf was compiled between 700 and 720 ("Die Benutzung der *Formulae,* MÖIG, 42 [1927], 165–267). Even older is the *Formulae Andecavenses;* according to Zeumer, it existed in 676 without the last three items (*MGH Form.* 3).

5. Among narrative sources, in addition to chronicles I have relied extensively on saints' lives. The older view that most of the Merovingian lives were compiled centuries after the death of the saints, which was held by W. Levison and B. Krusch, editors of the texts in *MGH Scriptores rerum merovingicarum,* volumes 5–6, has been challenged by modern scholars. For example, see Pierre Riché on the life of Saint Rusticula, *Analecta Bollandiana,* 72 (1954), 369–377, and E. Dekkers on the life of Saint Geneviève in *Clavis patrum latinorum* 2104 (Sacris erudiri, 3; Steenbrugis, 1961). See also L. Van der Essen, *Étude critique et littéraire sur les Vitae des saints mérovingiens de l'ancienne Belgique* (Paris, 1907). On early medieval archaeology of Gaul, Edouard Salin, *Manuel des fouilles archéologiques,* vol. 1 (Paris, 1946), is very useful. For a bibliography of more recent works, see Lucien Musset, *The Germanic Invasions,* trans. E. and C. James (University Park, Pa. 1975), and Franz Irsigler, *Untersuchungen zur*

Geschichte des frühfränkischen Adels (Rheinisches Archiv, 70; Bonn, 1969), pp. 186–220.

6. My references are to C. de Clercq's edition of *Concilia Galliae* (*CCL* 148A; Turnhout, 1963).

7. *Liber hist. franc.* 36 (*MGH Script. rer. mer.* 2, 246).

8. See below, note 40.

9. Horst W. Böhme, *Germanische Grabfunde des 4. bis 5. Jahrhunderts zwischen unterer Elbe und Loire: Studien zur Chronologie und Bevölkerungsgeschichte* (Münchner Beiträge zur Vor- und Frühgeschichte, 19; Munich, 1974).

10. O. Doppelfeld, "Das fränkische Frauengrab unter dem Chor des kölner Domes," *Germania*, 38 (1960), 89–113. E. Salin, *La civilisation mérovingienne; d'après les sépultures, les textes et le laboratoire*, (4 vols.; Paris, 1949–59), vol. 4, 77–118. Salin discusses the magical powers attributed to crystal balls and amulets hanging from belts, and to their Christian equivalents, the small silver containers holding dust from the tomb of a saint or some other relic. Peter Lasko gives a sketch of the burial attire of Queen Aregund, the wife of Clothar I (*The Kingdom of the Franks* [New York, 1971], p. 57). Tables 26–27 in Hermann Ament, "Zur archäologischen Periodisierung der Merowingerzeit," *Germania*, 55 (1977), 136–137, show the difference in the nature of the artifacts buried with men and women. On this subject, see also E. Salin, *La civilisation*, vol. 2, 228. Gregory of Tours, *Hist. franc.* 8.21 (*MGH Script. rer. mer.* 1, 339), described the burial of a noble lady with "grandibus ornamentis et multo auro" in the basilica of Metz.

11. *Lex Alam.* 49 (*MGH Leges I,* 5/1, 108). On this see David Herlihy, "Life Expectancies for Women," p. 8.

12. *Pactus Alam.* 17, *Lex Alam.* 48, 61 (*MGH Legum Sectio I,* 5/1, 25, 108, 129). *Lex Bai.* 4.30 (*MGH Legum Sectio I,* 5/2, 335).

13. *Lex Bai.* 4.30 (*MGH Legum Sectio I,* 5/2, 335): "Si autem pugnare voluerit per audaciam cordis sicut vir, non erit duplex conpositio eius, sed sicut fratres eius ita et ipsa accipiat."

14. *Leges Burg.* 92.2 (*MGH Legum Sectio I,* 2/1, 111); Drew, *The Burgundian Code*, p. 82.

15. *Pactus legis Sal.* 24.8–9 (*MGH Legum Sectio I,* 4/1, 92); *Lex Sal.* 31–33, 69, 78, 90.1–2 (*MGH Legum Sectio I,* 4/2, 70–72, 114–116, 124, 156). The *Lex Rib.* 12–13 (*MGH Legum Sectio I,* 3/2, 78–79) also establishes 600 *solidi* as the *wergeld* for women of childbearing age, whereas the *wergeld* of a young girl or a women over forty was 200 *solidi.* If a pregnant woman was wounded but did not miscarry, she was entitled to a compensation of 200 *solidi;* if she aborted, to 600 *solidi,* or to 2,400 *solidi* if she aborted a girl. If she died, her family could claim 900 *solidi* as compensation. Moreover, the same law was extended to cover Roman and semifree women as well. Even slaves were covered, although in their cases the fine was lower: *Capitula Legi Sal. addita* 3.104.4–11 (*MGH Legum Sectio I,* 4/1, 260–261).

16. Herlihy, "Life Expectancies for Women," p. 8.

17. See chapter 1.

18. Avitus of Vienne, *Poematum de Mosaicae historiae gestis 3* (*PL* 59, 340B). In a similar vein, Desiderius, Bishop of Cahors, wrote to Abbess Aspasia in *Epist.* 1.4 (*MGH Epist.* 3, *Mer. kar. aevi* 1, 201): "Absit enim, ne, sicut Eva seducta est per serpentem, ita tu ad redivivas miserias cupias revertere."

19. Ambrose states in *De Abraham* 2.11.78 (*CSEL* 32.1, 631): "ad admixtionis usum vir muliere vehementior sit."

20. Double standards in marriage were denounced by Caesarius in several of his sermons: *Sermones* 32, 41, 42, 43 (Morin 1, 141–142, 184–194; Mueller 1, 161–162, 208–220). He characterized women as flesh in *Sermones* 120.1 (Morin 1, 501; Mueller 2, 194).

21. Defensor Locogiacensis monachus, *Scintillarum liber* 13.9 (*CCL* 117, 1): "Tenera res in feminis fama pudiciae est et quasi pulcherimus cito ad levem narciscet aurem, leveque flatu conrumpitur, maxime ubi aetas consentit ad vicium et maritalis deest auctoritas."

22. *Additio ad Concilium Matisconense* 2 in *Cartulaire de Saint-Vincent de Mâcon*, ed. M. C. Ragut (Mâcon, 1864), p. cclv, and also in Gregory of Tours, *Hist. franc.* 8.20 (*MGH Script. rer. mer.* 1, 338). I am indebted to Pierre Riché, for having called my attention to this passage, which is not included in either Maassen's or de Clercq's edition of the Merovingian councils (Riché, "La femme à l'époque barbare," p. 36). See also G. Kurth, "Le Concile de Mâcon et l'âme des femmes," in his *Études franques,* vol. 1 (Paris, 1919), pp. 161–167.

23. *Vita s. Balthildis* 4 (*MGH Script. rer. mer.* 2, 485–486). Her biographer also called attention to Clotild, Ultrogotho, and Radegund as examples for married women (c. 18, ibid., 505–506).

24. *Leges Burg.* 100 (*MGH Legum Sectio I*, 2/1, 113): "Quaecumque mulier Burgundia vel Romana voluntate sua ad maritum ambulaverit, iubemus, ut maritus ipse facultatem ipsius mulieris, sicut in ea habet potestatem, ita et de omnes res suas habeat."

25. *Lex Rom. Burg.* 37.2 (*MGH Legum Sectio I*, 2/1, 155); *Lex Rom. Vis.* 3.7.3 (Haenel 318; Conrat 109).

26. *Lex Rom. Burg.* 22.6 (*MGH Legum Sectio I*, 2/1, 145). According to P. D. King, children in the Visigothic Kingdom reached *perfecta aetas* at twenty, when they were released from the power of their relatives (*Law and Society in the Visigothic Kingdom* [Cambridge, 1972], p. 229).

27. M. K. Hopkins has shown that pagan girls usually married between twelve and fifteen and Christian girls later, between fifteen and eighteen ("The Age," pp. 319–320.) Although we do not have sufficient data to calculate the average age when a girl was given in marriage in the sixth century, Merovingian saints' lives suggest that the pagan pattern prevailed. Daughters of the aristocracy were sometimes betrothed even before they reached twelve. Rusticula was four years old, according to Fortunatus in *Opera poetica* 4.26, 28 (*MGH Auct. ant.* 4/1, 95, 100); see also

Riché's article, note 5 above. Rusticula may have been an exception; others were engaged just before they reached puberty. For example, Anstrud was twelve at the time of her engagement; see *Vita Anstrudis* 2 (*MGH Script. rer. mer.* 6, 67). On the age of the menarche and marriage, see also chapter 5, note 11.

28. On the *legitima aetas* of boys, see Ewig, "Studien," pp. 17–24.

29. King, *Law and Society,* p. 229. See also pages 228–233 for a general discussion of the power that parents and relatives had in the betrothal of minors.

30. D. O. Hughes's argument that the transfer of the *mundium* was not the mark of a valid marriage is well taken ("From Brideprice to Dowry," p. 280.) The *mundium* (as she suggests in note 18 with references to secondary sources) may have been losing its force. But it certainly was exercised over minors by parents or guardians and over married women by husbands. Those who held the *mundium* did not have full judicial power but only a right of protection over the person and his or her property. On the transformation of the brideprice into a bridegift see below, note 92.

31. For secondary literature and discussions on the value and influence of the Roman *donatio ante nuptias,* see below, note 91.

32. The value of the legal *dos* varied from code to code. Under Salic law, the groom had to pay 52½ *solidi,* under Ripuarian law 50 *solidi.* The Aleman *dos* assigned in some manuscripts was 40 *solidi,* in others 400 *solidi.* Even the 40 *solidi* was a considerable settlement, representing the value of almost seven horses (the code set the maximum price of a horse at 6 *solidi: Lex Alám.* 62 [70].1 [*MGH Legum Sectio I,* 5/1, 131]). The 50 *solidi* assigned by the Ripuarian Code represented the price of four stallions (at 12 *solidi* each) or of thirteen mares (at 3 *solidi* each): *Lex Rib.* 36.11 (*MGH Legum Sectio I,* 3/2, 90). As we will see below, wealthy families demanded much more than a legal *dos* from the groom.

33. Gregory of Tours, *Hist. franc.* 10.16 (*MGH Script. rer. mer.* 1, 428), described the engagement of a niece of the abbess of Saint-Croix at Poitiers: "coram pontefice, clero vel senioribus pro neptae sua orfanola arras accepisse." In his *Liber vitae patrum* 20.1 (*MGH Script. rer. mer.* 1, 741), he referred to the *sponsalia* of Saint Leobard: "dato sponsae anulo, porregit osculum, praebet calciamentum, caelebrat sponsaliae diem festum." On engagement and marriage ceremonies, see K. Ritzer, *Formen, Riten und religiöses Brauchtum der Eheschliessung in den christlichen Kirchen des ersten Jahrtausends* (Liturgiewissenschaftliche Quellen und Forschungen, 38; Münster, 1962).

34. Gregory of Tours, *Hist. franc.* 4.46 (*MGH Script. rer. mer.* 1, 180–182).

35. *Leges Burg.* 52.1–4 (*MGH Legum Sectio I,* 2/1, 85–86) discusses a specific case. The widow Aunegild, who promised herself with the consent of her parents to Fredegisil, ran off with Balthamodus. Although the judges thought that such cases should be punished with the loss of property and death, they showed mercy to the couple, in consideration of Easter

holidays. Aunegild had to pay to Fredegisil her *wergeld,* 300 *solidi,* and Balthamodus was to pay his own *wergeld* of 150 *solidi,* unless he could prove by *compurgatio* that, when he ran off with Aunegild, he was unaware that she had been pledged to another.

36. *Lex Rom. Burg.* 27 (*MGH Legum Sectio I,* 2/1, 147).

37. *Pactus legis Sal.* 65a (*MGH Legum Sectio I,* 4/1, 234); *Lex Bai.* 8.15 (*MGH Legum Sectio I,* 5/2, 359–360); *Lex Alam.* 52 (53) (*MGH Legum Sectio I,* 5/1, 110).

38. Gregory of Tours, *Hist. franc.* 3.27 (*MGH Script. rer. mer.* 1, 163). On Visigard, see O. Doppelfeld and R. Pirling, *Fränkische Fürsten im Rheinland* (Düsseldorf, 1966), pp. 18, 89. Her son was buried with her in the Cathedral of Cologne (see note 10, above)

39. Caesarius of Arles, *Sermones* 43.8 (Mueller 1, 219; Morin, 194). Fortunatus, *De vita sanctae Radegundis* 2 (*MGH Script. rer. mer.* 2, 365).

40. Gregory of Tours, *Hist. franc.* 10.5 (*MGH Script. rer. mer.* 1, 413): "Unde non sine pudore discessum est." See Léon Duquit, "Étude historique sur le rapt de seduction," *Nouvelle revue historique de droit français et étranger,* 2 (1886), 587–625, in particular, 591–593.

41. *Pactus legis. Sal.* 13.12–13 (*MGH Legum Sectio I,* 4/1, 63); 15.1–2 (ibid., 70). If she was abducted while on the way to be married, her *sponsus* received the same compensation as a husband, 200 *solidi:* 13.14 (ibid., 63). *Lex Rib.* 39 (35) 1–2 (*MGH Legum Sectio I,* 3/2, 91) contains a similar provision, although it does not cover engaged women. Childebert's decree appended to the *Pactus legis Sal.* as *Capitulare* 6, 2.2 (*MGH Legum Sectio I,* 4/1, 268), was a "selbstständiges Reichsgesetz für Austrasien," according to W. A. Eckhardt, "Die Decretio Childeberti und ihre Überlieferung," *ZSSR germ. Abt.,* 84 (1967), 1. The *Capitula Legi Sal. addita* 5, 130.2 (*MGH Legum Sectio I,* 4/1, 266), issued by Chilperic, also contained this precept. Rape was punished with death or loss of citizenship by Roman law: *Codex Theod.* 9.24.2; *Lex Rom. Burg.* 19.1 (*MGH Legum Sectio I,* 2/1, 142). Under the influence of Roman law, the Visigothic Code punished with death the abduction of a *sponsa* if she was raped. If she was not, the *raptor* forfeited all his property, or was sold as a slave, and the proceeds were shared by the betrothed couple: *Leges Vis.* 3.3.5 (*MGH Legum Sectio I,* 1, 142). See King, *Law and Society,* pp. 227–228, n. 1. Other codes did not include the death penalty, but imposed heavy fines: *Lex Alam.* 50.1–2, 51, 53.1–2 (*MGH Legum Sectio I,* 5/1, 110–111); *Leg. Burg.* 12.1–2 (*MGH Legum Sectio I,* 2/1, 51): *Lex Bai.* 8.7, 16 (*MGH Legum Sectio I,* 5/2, 356–357, 360).

42. *Lex Bai.* 8.17 (*MGH Legum Sectio I,* 5/2, 361): "Si quis liberam feminam suaserit quasi ad coniugium et in via eam dimiserit . . . cum XII solidi componat." *Lex Bai.* 8.15 (ibid., 359) punished a man with 24 *solidi,* "postquam sponsaverit alicuius filiam legitime, sicut lex est, et eam dimiserit."

43. *Lex Bai.* 8.8 (*MGH Legum Sectio I,* 5/2, 357): "Si quis cum libera per

consensum ipsius fornicaverit et nolet eam in coniugium sociare: cum
XII solidi componat quia nondum sponsata nec a parentibus sociata sed
in sua libidine maculata."

44. German historians usually describe *Friedelehe* as a union that the woman
enters according to her own will and that does not include the transfer
of her *mundium* to her husband. For example, Hlawitschka and Schmid
used this definition to describe Waldrada's union with Lothar II (Hlawitschka, *Lotharingien*, p. 17; Karl Schmid, "Ein karolingische Königseintrag im Gedenkbuch von Remiremont," *Frühmittelalterliche Studien*, 2
[1968], 103). Others are more cautious; for example, K. Ritzer (*Formen*,
p. 156, n. 16) remarked that much about *Friedelehe* remains to be cla-
rified. See also above, chapter 1, notes 22–23. I could not find any text
proving that the conclusion of a *Friedelehe* involved a contract or ceremony. Those who hold the contrary contrast *Form. Sangallenses miscellaneae* 12 (*MGH Form.* 385), drawn up between 885 and 887, in which
the father declares that he gives his daughter on condition that her
husband "ne eam obprimat servitute famularum," with *Marc. Form.* 2
(*MGH Form.* 87), composed in the seventh century, where the wife refers
to herself as "ancilla tua" and to her husband as "domne et iugalis
meus." Despite the differences in language, the two *formulae* do not
denote two different types of unions, in my opinion. The ninth-century
formula reflects the translation of the Christian concept of marriage into
secular legislation (described below, chapter 4). In practical terms, this
meant that a man was to treat his wife as his equal rather than as his
inferior. Thus, rather than proving that a *Friedelfrau* enjoyed a better
position than a wife, the two *formulae* show that, by the ninth century,
an evolution in the proper treatment of a married woman had taken
place.

45. King, *Law and Society*, p. 231.

46. *Leges Burg.* 44.1–2 (*MGH Legum Sectio I*, 2/1, 74). The compensation of 15
solidi in this law was less than the brideprice required if he wanted to
return her after she had lived with him: *Leges Burg.* 61 (ibid., 93).

47. For example, Pseudo-Chrysostom, *Opus imperfectum in Matthaeum* 1.22.2
(*PG* 56, 802): "Matrimonium non facit coitus sed voluntas." Cited by
Nicholas I, *Responsa ad consulta Bulgarorum* . . . (JE 2812 [2123]; Mansi
15, 101; *MGH Epist. 6, Kar. aevi* 4, 570). Augustine expressed this more
subtly in *De nupt. et conc.* 1.11 (*PL* 44, 420): "conjux vocatur ex prima
fide desponsationis, quam concubitu nec cognoverat nec fuerat cog-
niturus"; paraphrased by Isidore, *Etymol.* 19.7 (*PL* 82, 365). Ambrose
states in *De institut. virg.* 42 (*PL* 16, 316): "non enim defloratio virginitatis facit conjugium, sed pactio conjugalis."

48. *Conc. Aurelianense* (511), 2 (*CCL* 148A, 5): "si ad ecclesiam raptor cum rapta
confugerit et femina ipsa violentiam pertulisse constiterit, statim libere-
tur de potestate raptoris. . . . Sin vero . . . puella raptori aut rapienda
aut rapta consenserit, potestate patris excusata reddatur et raptor a

patre superioris conditionis satisfactione teneatur obnoxius." *Conc. Aurelianense* (541), 22 (ibid. 137): "Ut nullus per imperium potestatis filiam conpetere audeat alienam, ne coniugium, quod contra parentum uoluntate impiae copulatur, uelut captiuitas iudicetur. Sed si, quod est prohibitum, admittitur, in his, qui perpetrauerint, excommunicationis seueritas pro modo pontificis inponatur." *Conc. Turonense* (567), 21 (20) (ibid. 187): "cum non solum domni gloriosae memoriae Childebertus et Chlotcharius reges constitutionem legum de hac re custodierint et seruauerint, quam nunc domnus Charibertus rex successor eorum praecepto suo roborauit, ut nullus ullam nec puellam nec uiduam absque parentum uoluntatem [*sic*] trahere aut accipere praesumat." The royal order in question is *Chlotharii I regis constitutio* (about 560) 7 (*MGH Leg. I, 2*). See also *Conc. Parisiense* (556–573), 6 (*CCL* 148A, 208) and above, notes 40–41.

49. Gregory of Tours, *Hist. franc.* 9.33 (*MGH Script. rer. mer.* 1, 288).
50. Hucbald, *Vita s. Rictrudis* 1.11 (*AS* 12 Maii; 3, 83). Although Rictrud died in 668 and her life was composed in 907, Van der Essen (*Étude critique*, pp. 261–262) regards the life as a reliable source.
51. *Marc. Form.* 2.16; *Form. Salicae Lind.* 16 (*MGH Form.* 85, 277).
52. *Lex Rom. Burg.* 37.2 (*MGH Legum Sectio I*, 2/1, 155): "Quod si pares fuerint honestate persone, consensus perficit nuptias, sic tamen ut nuptialis donatio sollenniter celebretur; aliter filii exinde nati legitimorum locum obtinere non poterint." The source of this was Majoram's decree, "Nullum sine dote fiat conjugium," and the provision reserving a certain portion of the patrimony for legitimate children: *Codex Theod.* 2.22.1–2; *Codex Iust.* 5.27.3. To his illegitimate children a man could leave only one-eighth of his patrimony if he also had legitimate children, according to *Lex Rom. Burg.* 37.4 (*MGH Legum Sectio I*, 2/1, 156). The *Lex Rom. Vis.* C 3.7.3 (G. 4 pr) (Haenel 318; Conrat 109) specified that the marriage was valid when concluded by individuals of equal status, and did not consider the lack of *donatio nuptialis* and official celebration of the marriage as impediments to the recognition of the marriage as valid. See also Ervig's addition to the Visigothic Code: *Leges Vis.* 3.1.9 (*MGH Legum Sectio I*, 1, 131): "Ne sine dote coniugium fiat." King has pointed out that this "hardly justifies the view that the *dos* was essential for lawful marriage," *Law and Society*, p. 226, n. 3. A. Lemaire has argued that it was essential. See his "Origine de la règle 'Nullum sine dote fiat coniugium,' " in *Mélanges Paul Fournier* (Paris, 1929), p. 42. On consent and "nuptialis donatio," see also, J. Gaudemet, "Le legs du droit romain en matière matrimoniale," pp. 150–156.
53. On the inheritance rights of illegitimate children, see H. Brunner, "Die uneheliche Vaterschaft in den älteren germanischen Rechten," in his *Abhandlungen*, vol. 2, 165–197. Lombard law drew some distinctions between illegitimate and legitimate children; on this, see Hermann Winterer, "Die Stellung des unehelichen Kindes in der langobardische Ge-

setzgebung," *ZSSR germ. Abt.,* 87 (1970), 32–56. But the *Lex Bai.* 15.9
(*MGH Legum Sectio I,* 5/2, 428) made it clear that if a man had *multas
mulieres* and all were free, their children were to divide the patrimony
equally. The sons he had by an *ancilla,* a slave girl, were to receive a
portion only if the legitimate heirs wished to give them something.

54. The *Lex Rom. Burg.* 37.5–6 (*MGH Legum Section I,* 2/1, 156–157) is the only
     code to make no distinction between a freeman or freewoman. Both
     were punished with enslavement if they contracted this kind of union.
     Pactus legis Sal. 13.7–10 (*MGH Legum Sectio I,* 4/1, 61–62) punished with
     death the *puer regius* or *letus* who married a freewomen; she was punished
     with enslavement. Similarly, if a freeman married someone else's slave,
     he was reduced to servitude. But if he married a *litam alienam,* he only
     had to pay a fine of 30 *solidi.* If he claimed that the relation was a casual
     one, he was fined only 30 *solidi* if she was *regis ancilla,* 15 *solidi* if she was
     ancilla aliena (15.1–4; ibid., 93–94). *Capitula Legi Sal. addita* 3, 98.1 (ibid.,
     255) punished with loss of property women who married their own
     slaves. Under Ripuarian law, if a freeman married an *ancillam regis, seu
     ecclesiasticam, vel ancillam tabularii,* their children followed the mother's
     status. Only if he married an ordinary slave girl was he reduced to
     servitude. A freewoman was punished with enslavement unless she
     chose to have the slave killed: *Lex Rib.* 16.14–18 (*MGH Legum Sectio I,*
     3/2, 112). *Leges Burg.* 35.1–2 (*MGH Legum Sectio I,* 2/1, 69) punished
     with death both the freewoman and the slave, although her relatives
     could take pity on her and deliver her into servitude to the king. As to
     the union between a freeman and a slave girl, the code concerned itself
     only with rape, which was punished with 12 *solidi* (30.1; ibid., 66). Bavar-
     ian law handled the whole problem under the rubric of fornication; *Lex
     Bai.* 8.2–13 (*MGH Legum Sectio I,* 5/2, 354–358). Under Visigothic law,
     relations between a freewoman and her slave were most severely pun-
     ished: both were flogged and burnt and their children were deprived of
     the right of inheritance: *Leges Vis.* 3.2.2 (*MGH Legum Sectio I,* 1, 133–
     134). If he was a *servus alienus,* she was to be punished with lashings and
     loss of her freedom; the same fate awaited a freeman who cohabited with
     someone else's slave (3.2.3; ibid., 134–135). But the code did not punish
     a man who had sexual relations with his own *ancilla.* On the succession
     of children from unions between a freeman and slave girls, see Heinrich
     Brunner, "Die uneheliche Vaterschaft in den älteren germanischen
     Rechten," in his *Abhandlungen,* vol. 2, 165–197.

55. *Pactus legis Sal.* 13.11 (*MGH Legum Sectio I,* 4/1, 62–63); *Leges Burg.* 36
     (*MGH Legum Sectio I,* 2/1, 69); *Leges Vis.* 3.5.1, 2, 5 (*MGH Legum Sectio I,*
     1, 159–161, 163–164). On Visigothic incest laws, see also King, *Law and
     Society,* p. 233, n. 3. Jean Fleury, in his *Recherches historiques sur les empêche-
     ments de parenté dans le mariage canonique des origines aux Fausses Décrétales*
     (Paris, 1933), traced the increasingly intransigent policy of the church
     Beginning with the Council of Orléans in 511, canon 18 (*CCL* 148A

9–10), through all the later councils of the sixth century, the Frankish bishops condemned incest in all its forms. On Theudebert I, see *Epistola* 17 of Saint Caesarius, in his *Opera omnia,* ed. Morin, vol. 1, 31–32. By the late sixth century, the Frankish kings had incorporated the church's incest prohibitions into their own legislation: *Decr. Childeberti* 1.2 (*MGH Capit. reg. franc.* 1,15), issued in 596, decreed the death penalty for a man who married his father's wife or his wife's sister. According to Fredegar, Clothar II ordered the execution of a son of a *major domus* because he married his stepmother: *Chron.* 4.54 (*MGH Script. rer. mer.* 2, 147). See also *Lex Alam.* 39 (*MGH Legum Sectio I,* 5/1, 98–99); *Lex Bai.* 7.1 (*MGH Legum Sectio I,* 5/2, 347–348).

56. On Saxon law, see Ganshof, "Le statut," pp. 10–29, in particular, 18. *Pactus legis Sal.* 44.6–9 (*MGH Legum Sectio I,* 4/1, 169–171) provided for a token payment, the *reipus* or ring money, by the suitor of a widow to her relatives, without stating whether they were relatives on the woman's or on the dead husband's side. The same provision is found in *Lex Sal.* 79.3–6 (*MGH Legum Sectio I,* 4/2, 126). Some historians have found in these laws traces of an earlier form of matrimony, according to which the wife remained under the power of her own relatives. It is possible, however, that the payment went to the dead husband's relatives. Heinrich Brunner summarizes the conflicting interpretations in "Zu Lex Salica tit. 44: De Reipus," in his *Abhandlungen,* vol. 2, 67–78. In opposition to the German interpretation that these were the wife's relatives, Brunner has supported the French view that they were the relatives of the husband. A French scholar, Joseph Balon, recently advanced the thesis that these laws are traces of an earlier matriarchal society, *Traité de droit Salique,* vol. 2 (Ius medii aevi, 3; Namur, 1965), 496.

57. Fredegar, *Chron.* 3.18 (*MGH Script. rer. mer.* 2, 99–100).

58. Gregory of Tours, *Hist. franc.* 3.22–23 (*MGH Script. rer. mer.* 1, 130–131): "amore eius capitur suoque eam copulavit stratu . . . mittens postea Arvernum Deoteriam exinde arcessivit eamque sibi in matrimonio sociavit." For the chronology, I am following Ewig, "Studien," p. 39.

59. Gregory of Tours, *Hist. franc.* 4.28 (*MGH Script. rer. mer.* 1, 164).

60. Gregory of Tours, *Hist. franc.* 4. 9 (trans. O. M Dalton, vol. 2, 117–118; *MGH Script. rer. mer.* 1, 147). The juxtaposition of "unico amore" *Hist. franc.* 4.3 (Ibid. 1, 143) with Ingund's comment suggests that Clothar I resorted to bigamy rather than repudiate Ingund, as Ewig contends ("Studien," pp. 29–36).

61. According to Ewig, Ingund was repudiated twice, first around 524 when Clothar I married Guntheaca, Clodomer's widow. After Clothar had left Guntheaca, he remarried Ingund around 530 and lived with her until 537, when he divorced her for a second time to marry Aregund ("Studien," pp. 29–36). To exonerate Clothar from the charge of polygamy, Ewig has proposed 540 as the date of Clothar's marriage to Radegund (Ibid., pp. 56–57). According to Ewig's hypothesis, between

537 and 540 Clothar would have repudiated not only Aregund but also Chunsinna, whose son Chramn was born around 540. This rapid exchange of wives between 537 and 540 stands in marked contrast with the staid life Clothar then would have led with Radegund, whose divorce from Clothar Ewig dates around 550. The key document on Radegund, Fortunatus's *De vita sanctae Radegundis* 3 (*MGH Script. rer. mer.* 2, 366), makes it clear that she engaged daily in ascetic observances while still married to Clothar: "plus participata Christo quam sociata coniugio." I doubt that Clothar would have tolerated this behavior, including her nightly vigils, if he had no other wife. Polygamy in the royal family did not mean that all consorts were present at the court; only the favorite or favorites of the moment were with the king; the others lived at their own residences. Whether a queen was temporarily neglected or permanently abandoned depended entirely upon the king's pleasure.

62. Gregory of Tours, *Hist. franc.* 4.26 (*MGH Script. rer. mer.* 1, 161–162): "reliquit Ingobergam et Merofledem accepit. Habuit et aliam puellam opilionis, id est pastoris ovium, filiam, nomine Theudogildem. . . . Post haec, Marcoveifa, Merofledis scilicet sororem, coniugio copulavit." Ewig lists Merofled with a question mark and Theudegild without one among abandoned wives in "Studien," p. 44. If this is a case of serial monogamy, it involved a rapid succession of wives. During six years of his reign as King of Paris (561–567), Charibert had four wives: Ingoberga, Merofled, Theudegild, and Marcoveifa. Gregory made it clear that Charibert had wed Marcoveifa in her sister's place ("in loco sororis") and that this marriage met with ecclesiastical censure: *Hist. franc.* 5.47 (*MGH Script. rer. mer.* 1, 162, 239). But Gregory failed to explain why Saint Germain found this union reprehensible. Was it because Marcoveifa was Charibert's sister-in-law, or was it because she wore a religious habit when Charibert met her? (Marriages to relatives by affinity and nuns were included among incest prohibitions.) Whatever caused the excommunication, Charibert disregarded it, keeping Marcoveifa as one of his queens. The other queen who seems to have remained at his side was Theudegild, for otherwise she would not have had in her possession the royal treasures that she offered to King Gunthram not long after Charibert's death.

63. Fredegar, *Chron.* 60 (*MGH Script. rer. mer.* 2, 109): "relinquens Fredegundem et alias quas habebat uxores." Gregory of Tours, *Hist. franc.* 4.28 (*MGH Script. rer. mer.* 1, 163): "Quod videns Chilpericus rex, cum iam plures haberet uxores. . . . Galsuendam expetiit." One of these "uxores" was Audovera, who had borne Chilperic three sons and two daughters. *Liber hist. franc.* 31 (*MGH Script. rer. mer.* 2, 292) attributed her repudiation to the trickery of Fredegund, who allegedly persuaded Audovera to stand as godmother for her own child. Chilperic, therefore, had to divorce her because he could not be married to his own child's godmother. But Fleury argues that the whole story was fabricated, because

the church forbade marriage with the godparent of one's child only in the eighth century (*Recherches,* p. 154).

64. Ewig remarks that the failure of the chroniclers to distinguish a *Friedelehe* from *matrimonium* led to confusion between marriage and concubinage, because a *Friedelehe* was not significantly different from concubinage ("Studien," p. 42). In Merovingian society, *Friedelehe* represented, in my opinion, a union in which the wife had less economic protection than in a marriage arranged by her parents. Like a concubine, she could build a power base for herself only through sexual and emotional subservience. Nonetheless, the chroniclers referred to a *Friedelfrau* as "uxor." The polygamous unions of kings, noted above, were undoubtedly concluded as quasi marriages.

65. Fredegar, *Chron.* 4.44 (*MGH Script. rer. mer.* 2, 142). On Bertetrud, see also *Gesta Dagoberti* 2 (*MGH Script. rer. mer.* 2, 401).

66. Fredegar, *Chron.* 4.53, 58, 59, 60 (*MGH Script. rer. mer.* 2, 147, 150–151). Apparently, Dagobert had the habit of keeping a wife in each of his residences. When he repudiated his first wife, he left her at "Romiliacuo villa," where he had married her. Although Nanthild shared her title with Vulfegund and Berechild, she managed to ensure the succession of her own son, Clovis, and the regency for herself (*Chron.* 4.79; ibid., 161). See also *Gesta Dagoberti* 22 (*MGH Script. rer. mer.* 2, 408).

67. *Liber hist. franc.* 44 (*MGH Script. rer. mer.* 2, 315).

68. *Leges Vis.* 3.4.9; 6.2 (*MGH Legum Sectio I,* 1, 150, 168): if her husband contracted marriage with another woman, the second wife was to be delivered for the vengeance of the insulted wife, but there was nothing to prevent a married man from sleeping with a freewoman or his own slave girl. Only if he slept with an *ancilla* belonging to another was he to be punished with lashes: *Leges Vis.* 3.4.15 (ibid., 156). Only the *Lex Rom. Vis.* 2.21.1 (Conrat 132) warned: "Eo tempore, quo quis uxorem habet, concubinam habere non potest."

69. Gregory of Tours, *Hist. franc.* 4.28 (*MGH Script. rer. mer.* 1, 163–164). Chilperic's first wife was Audovera. A later chronicle attributed her repudiation to the trickery of Fredegund; see note 63, above.

70. The documentation for this case has been assembled by H. Brunner, "Die uneheliche Vaterschaft in den älteren germanischen Rechten," in his *Abhandlungen,* vol. 2, 167. See also chapter 3, n. 14 on Carolingian genealogy.

71. *Lex Bai.* 15.9 (*MGH Legum Sectio* I, 5/2, 428–429).

72. Gregory of Tours, *Hist. franc.* 9.27 (*MGH Script. rer. mer.* 1, 382).

73. *Hist. franc.* 9.13 (trans. Dalton, vol. 2, 383; *MGH Script. rer. mer.* 1, 370).

74. Boniface, number 50, in *Die Briefe,* ed. Tangl, p. 82.

75. See above, note 41, and below, note 83.

76. *Poenit. Hubertense* 9, 12, 38; in F. W. H. Wasserschleben, ed., *Die Bussordnungen der abendländischen Kirche* (Halle, 1851), pp. 378, 379, 382. H. J. Schmitz assigned a ninth-century date to this penitential in his edition. *Die Bussbücher und das kanonische Bussverfahren* (Düsseldorf, 1898; reprint

Graz, 1958). But Gabriel Le Bras rejected the later date ("Pénitentiels," in *Dictionnaire de théologie catholique*, vol. 12 [Paris, 1933], pp. 1169–1170). See also Jean-Louis Flandrin, "Contraception, Marriage, and Sexual Relations in the Christian West," in *Biology of Man in History: Selections from the Annales*, ed. Robert Forster and Orest Ranum (Baltimore, 1975), p. 29.

77. *Pactus legis Sal.* 33.3 (*MGH Legum Sectio I*, 4/1, 118). Same as *Lex Sal.* 39.4 (*MGH Legum Sectio I*, 4/2, 88), which punished with 45 *solidi* those who called a freewoman a whore. *Lex Sal.* 64.2.2 (*MGH Legum Sectio I*, 4/2, 231), in the earliest version of the code, set the fine at 52½ for calling a woman a witch. In later versions, this law was expanded to include also the slanderous designation *meretricem*.

78. *Lex Alam.* 56.1 (*MGH Legum Sectio I*, 5/1, 115); *Lex Bai.* 8.3–4 (*MGH Legum Sectio I*, 5/2, 355). *Pactus legis Sal.* 20.1–4 (*MGH Legum Sectio I*, 4/1, 83–84), repeated in *Lex Sal.* 26.1–4 (*MGH Legum Sectio I*, 4/2, 66).

79. This is the usual view of German scholars, one that was expressed also by W. Rullkoetter, *The Legal Protection of Woman among the Ancient Germans* (Chicago, 1900).

80. *Miracula s. Austrebertae virginis* 22 (*AS* 10 Feb.; 2, 426) describes how the saint rescued a woman who threw herself into the river to save her honor. Austroberta apparently was the patron saint of victims of rape. Chapter 20 reports the story of a young woman who lost her sight when a black demon tried to rape her. Gregory of Tours, in *De virtutibus s. Martini* 3.37 (*MGH Script. rer. mer.* 1, 641), mentions that a woman was attacked at her loom. As a result, she lost her speech, but recovered it when she came to church and confessed she had been raped by a demon. On the suicide of a woman accused of adultery, see Gregory of Tours, *Hist. franc.* 5.32 (*MGH Script. rer. mer.* 1, 225).

81. *Lex Rom. Burg.* 21.1 (*MGH Legum Sectio I*, 2/1, 143); the source of this is *Codex Theod.* 3.16.1. *Pactus Alam.* 34.3 (*MGH Legum Sectio I*, 5/1, 33); *Form. Andecavenses* 57 (*MGH Form.* 24); *Marc. Form.* 2.30 (*MGH Form.* 94). The subject is discussed by Hubert Richardot, *Les pactes de séparation amiable entre époux* (Paris, 1930).

82. *Lex Rom. Vis.* C.3.16.1 (Haenel 94; Conrat 117): "In masculis etiam, si repudium mittant, haec tria crimina inquiri conveniet, si moecham vel medicamentariam vel conciliatricem repudiare voluerit." See also *Lex Rom. Burg.* 21.2 (*MGH Legum Sectio I*, 2/1, 143–144).

83. Under *Leges Burg.* 34.2–4 (*MGH Legum Sectio I*, 2/1, 68), if a man divorced his wife without cause, he had to pay her a sum equal to what he had given her as her bridegift, and he was fined 12 *solidi* as well. If he simply left her, she had the right to claim his whole property. He could divorce her without payment if he could prove that she had committed adultery, practiced witchcraft, or violated tombs. Similar provisions are contained in *Leges Vis.* 3.6.1 (*MGH Legum Sectio I*, 1, 166); *Lex Bai.* 8.1, 13 (*MGH Legum Sectio I*, 5/2, 352, 359); *Pactus Alam.* 35.1 (*MGH Legum Sectio I*, 5/1, 34). The killing of an adulteress caught in the act was permitted both

by Roman and Germanic laws: *Lex Rom. Vis.* 17.1–3 [*Pauli Sent.* 2.27.1]
(Haenel 372; Conrat 548); *Lex Rom. Burg.* 35 (*MGH Legum Sectio I,* 2/1,
146); *Leges Burg.* 68. 1–2 (*MGH Legum Sectio I,* 2/1, 95); *Lex Bai.* 8 (*MGH
Legum Sectio I,* 5/2, 352). Gregory of Tours, in *Hist. franc.* 8.19 (*MGH
Script. rer. mer.* 1, 338), reports the slaying of an adulteress by her husband. In another case he points out that it was the woman's kin who
burnt her alive: *Hist. franc.* 6.36 (*MGH Script. rer. mer.* 1, 276). On divorce
because of sterility, see Fredegar, *Chron.* 4.60 (*MGH Script. rer. mer.* 2,
151).

84. *Leges Burg.* 34.1 (*MGH Legum Sectio I,* 2/1, 68): "Si quae mulier maritum
suum, cui legitime est iuncta, dimiserit, necetur in luto."

85. *Lex Rom. Vis.* C.3.16.1 (Haenel 94; Conrat 117): "mulieri non licere
propter suas pravas cupiditates marito repudium mittere exquisita
causa, velut ebrioso aut aleatori aut muliercularia . . . sed in repudio
mittendo a femina haec sola crimina inquiri, si homicidam, vel medica-
mentarium vel sepulcrorum dissolutorem maritum suum probaverit." If
she could not, she was punished with exile. See also Conrat, pp. 116–
118; *Lex Rom. Burg.* 21.3 (*MGH Legum Sectio I,* 2/1, 144).

86. *Leges Vis.* 3.5.4 (*MGH Legum Sectio I,* 1, 163).

87. Gregory of Tours, *Hist. franc.* 2.12 (*MGH Script. rer. mer.* 1, 80). On the
power of dukes, see Archibald Lewis, "The Dukes in the *Regnum Francorum,*" *Speculum,* 51 (1976), 381–410.

88. *Liber hist. franc.* 35 (*MGH Script. rer. mer.* 2, 302–304).

89. Gregory of Tours, *Hist. franc.* 10.8 (*MGH Script. rer. mer.* 1, 414–416).

90. *Conc. Agathense* (506), 25 (*CCL* 148, 204); *Conc. Aurelianense* (533), 11 (*CCL*
148A, 100). Studies of the Merovingian bishops' position on divorce are
listed in chapter 4, note 4.

91. See H. Brunner, "Die fränkisch–romanische dos," in his *Abhandlungen,* vol.
2, 78–115; and A. Lemaire, "Origine de la règle 'Nullum sine dote fiat
coniugium,' " pp. 415–444. See also his "La 'dotatio de l'épouse.' "
A. Vandenbossche refuted the assertion that there was any relation
between the *donatio nuptialis* and the *wittemon* in *La dos ex marito dans la
Gaule franque* (Paris, 1953), pp. 140–141. For other studies, see F. Ganshof, "Le statut," p. 29, n. 69. On the *donatio ante nuptias,* see *Lex Rom.
Vis.* C.3.5.1–3; 3.5.8 (Haenel 78–80; Conrat 322, 324); *Leges Vis.* 3.1.5–6;
3.1.9 (*MGH Legum I,* 1, 126–129, 131–132); *Lex Rom. Burg.* 22, 37 (*MGH
Legum Sectio I,* 2/1, 144, 155–156). This *donatio* is to be distinguished
from the Roman *dos* brought by the wife. The *Lex Rom. Burg.* required
donatio nuptialis as essential for the validity of a marriage; see note 52
above.

92. This whole process has been traced by Louis-Maurice-André Cornuey, *Le
régime de la "dos."* It supersedes R. Schröder, *Geschichte des ehelichen Güterrechts in Deutschland,* vol. 1. See also E. Mayer-Homberg, *Die fränkischen
Volksrechte im Mittelalter,* vol. 1 (Weimar, 1912), pp. 318–323. On the
terminology designating Germanic marriage settlements, see Drew, *The
Burgundian Code,* p. 50, n. 2.

93. *Leges Burg.* 66.1–3; 69.1–2; 86.2 (*MGH Legum Sectio I,* 2/1, 94–95, 108). F. Beyerle believes that 86.2 is the least evolved of these laws because it allows the bride one-third of the *wittemon* only if her father did not give her the *malahereda,* the furniture and clothing necessary to run a household (*Gesetze der Burgunden* [Weimar, 1960], p. 170).

94. *Leges Vis.* 3.1.6 (*MGH Legum Sectio I,* 1, 130).

95. *Pactus legis Sal.* 101.2 (*MGH Legum Sectio I,* 4/1, 256–257). On the *reipus* or ring money, see note 56, above.

96. *Lex Alam.* 54.1–2 (*MGH Legum Sectio I,* 5/1, 112–113); *Lex Bai.* 15.8 (*MGH Legum Sectio I,* 5/2, 427); *Lex Rib.* 41 (37). 2 (*MGH Legum Sectio I,* 3/2, 95). The principle that a widow, if she had children, was entitled only to the usufruct of her *dos* was upheld also by the Burgundian Code: *Leges Burg.* 24.1; 62.2 (*MGH Legum Sectio I,* 2/1, 61, 93). The Roman code issued for the Visigoths specified that, in the case of the remarriage of widows with children, the bridegift went to the children, but a widow who did not have children "omne, quod quoquomodo percepit, pleni proprietate iuris obtineat": *Lex Rom. Vis.* C.3.8.2.2 (Haenel 84; Conrat 121–122).

97. *Lex Saxonum* 40; in *Leges Saxonum und Lex Thuringorum* ed. Claudius Freiherr von Schwerin (*MGH Fontes iuris germanici antiqui in usum scholarum,* 4; Hanover, 1918), pp. 27–28; *Die Gesetze des Karolingerreiches 714–911; III: Sachsen, Thuringen, Chamaren und Friesen,* ed. K. A. Eckhardt (Germanenrechte 2; Weimar, 1934), p. 24. The practice of giving a *dos* to the bride was not unknown to the Saxons. Article 47 of the code remarks that the East and Westphalians and the Angari give such a settlement to their wives.

98. *St. Leandri . . . de Institutione virginum et contemptu mundi ad Florentinam sororem liber,* in Lucas Holstenius, ed. *Codex Regularum monasticarum et canonicarum,* vol. 1 (Augsburg, 1759; reprint Graz, 1957), p. 408.

99. *Lex Alam.* 54.3 (*MGH Legum Sectio I,* 5/1, 113–114). See Cornuey, *Le régime de la "dos,"* pp. 127–131. Hughes upholds the importance of the *morgengabe* as the "symbol of a new, medieval view of marriage" in "From Brideprice to Dowry," p. 275. The codes and documents of practice convey the impression that the *dos* had a greater significance.

100. See H. Brunner, "Beiträge zur Geschichte des germanische Wartrechtes," in his *Abhandlungen,* vol. 2, 229–233. Brunner shows that the usufruct of one-third of her husband's patrimony was frequently turned over to the wife as her *dos.* But compare *Form. Andecavenses* 34 (*MGH Form.* 16): "Pro amore dulcitudinem suam aemitto tibi . . . sponsa mea illa, abiat, teniat, possediat, faciat quod voluerit;" and *Marc. Form.* 2.15 (*MGH Form.* 85): ". . . et in sua dominatione revocare vel quicquid exindae facire elegerit liberam habeat potestatem." These two were examples for drawing up a *libellum dotis.* The same principle was followed also in the *Epistola conposcionalis, Marc. Form.* 2.16 (*MGH Form.* 85–86), where the husband makes amends for having abducted his wife and settles property on her without any restrictions. Similar contracts were included in later collec-

tions: *Cartae Senonicae* 25; *Salicae Merkelianae* 15,17; *Form. Salicae Lind.* 7 (*MGH Form.* 196, 246, 248, 271). Other *formulae* granted the bride only the usufruct of land, such as *Form. Andecavenses* 54 (*MGH Form.* 23), and specified that she could not alienate the land, but had to leave it to the children she was expected to have; see also *Form. Sangallenses miscellaneae* 18 (*MGH Form.* 388).

101. *Lex Saxonum* 47 (Eckhardt, *Die Gesetze,* 3, 26; von Schwerin 29).

102. Gregory of Tours, *Hist. franc.* 9.20 (*MGH Script. rer. mer.* 1, 376).

103. *Lex Rom. Burg.* 10.1 (*MGH Legum Sectio I,* 2/1, 133): "Secundum Gai regulam patri matrive intestatis filii filieve aequo iure succedant." From *Codex Theod.* 9.25.2. See also Biondo Biondi, *Il diritto romano cristiano,* vol. 3, 339–341.

104. See J. Lalinde Abadiá, "La sucesión filíal en el derecho visigodo," *Anuario de historia del derecho español,* 32 (1962), 113–129; and King, *Law and Society,* p. 248. Both discuss this development in detail. On the equal successory right of women, see *Leges Vis.* 4.2.1 (*MGH Legum Sectio I,* 1, 74).

105. *Lex Thur.* 26–30 (von Schwerin 60–61; Eckhardt *Die Gesetze,* 3, 38–40). The fifth "generatio" in Germanic law corresponds to the seventh degree in Roman law. Ganshof proposed that the concession that a woman could succeed at all must reflect an attempt to correct the archaic nature of the law, "Le statut," p. 34.

106. *Lex Saxonum* 41, 44, 46, 47 (Eckhardt, *Die Gesetze,* 3, 24–26; von Schwerin 28–29).

107. *Pactus legis Sal.* 59.6 (*MGH Legum Sectio I,* 4/1, 223). The earliest version, namely, text A issued by Clovis, has only "de terra vero," whereas texts B and C have "de terra vero salica." I am following Ganshof's interpretation ("Le statut," pp. 34–35) that this indicates a total incapacity of women to hold land, one that in the B version was limited to Salic land. Text B was issued either by Theuderic I (511–533) or Theudebert I (533–548), rulers of the territory that later came to be known as Austrasia. Text C was issued in Burgundy between 567 and 596. On the dates of the text see *Pactus legis Salicae,* ed. Eckhardt (*MGH Legum Sectio I,* 4/1, XL). Chilperic's decree added to the *Pactus legis Sal.* 108 (*MGH Legum Sectio I,* 4/1, 262) stated that "quamdiu filii aduixerint terram habeant, sicut et lex Salica habet. Et si subito filii defuncti fuerint, filia simili modo accipiat terras ipsas."

108. *Leges Burg.* 14.1 (*MGH Legum Sectio I,* 2/1, 52); *Lex Rib.* 57 (56).4 (*MGH Legum Sectio I,* 3/2, 105); *Lex Alam.* 55 (*MGH Legum Sectio I,* 5/1, 114); *Lex Bai.* 15.8 (*MGH Legum Sectio I,* 5/2, 429).

109. *Leges Burg.* 51.3–5; 86.1 (*MGH Legum Sectio I,* 2/1, 84, 107).

110. *Pactus legis Sal.* 59.1–5 (*MGH Legum Sectio I,* 4/1, 222–223). The interpretation of these laws is subject to dispute. Nineteenth-century historians saw in these laws traces of an ancient matrilineal system of inheritance. This view was refuted by H. Brunner, "Kritische Bemerkungen zur

Geschichte des germanischen Weibererbrechts," in his *Abhandlungen,* vol. 2, 198–217. I am following his argument that these laws must regulate the succession of immovables because the last law in this group excluded women altogether from the inheritance of land. Text B inserted the father's sister after the mother's sister, which changed the sentence in the next clause ("et inde illis generacionibus") to mean that the relatives on the paternal (not on the maternal side) were to inherit. In text C the father could claim before the mother. Because of these changes, these laws came to regulate succession not only to immovables but also to land other than Salic land (on this see above, note 107).

111. *Leges Burg.* 53.1–2 (*MGH Legum Sectio I,* 2/1, 87–88).
112. On the jewelry and clothing of Merovingian woman, see note 11, above; on the household goods she received as her dowry, see note 116, below.
113. Gregory of Tours, *Hist. franc.* 4.28 (*MGH Script. rer. mer.* 1, 164).
114. *Liber hist. franc.* 13 (*MGH Script. rer. mer.* 2, 258).
115. Gregory of Tours, *Hist. franc.* 6.45 (*MGH Script. rer. mer.* 1, 284–285).
116. *Pactus legis Sal.* 100.2 (*MGH Legum Sectio I,* 4/1, 257): "... quia et achasium dedi ... et lectum stratum et lectaria condigna et scamno cooperto et cathedras, quae de casa patris mei exhibui, hic demitto." The furniture from the bride's trousseau was to remain in her husband's possession even if she died without leaving children, according to *Pactus Alam.* 34.1 (*MGH Legum Sectio I,* 5/1, 33).
117. *Pactus legis Sal.* 67 (*MGH Legum Sectio I,* 4/1, 238).
118. *Leges Burg.* 14.5–6 (*MGH Legum Sectio I,* 2/1, 53). Regardless of the number of brothers, she received the usufruct of a third portion.
119. *Lex Alam.* 54 (*MGH Legum Sectio I,* 5/1, 112): a widow had the right to claim "quidquid de sede paternica secum adtulit." On the rights of women divorced through no fault of their own, see above, note 83.
120. *Leges Burg.* 74.1 (*MGH Legum Sectio I,* 2/1, 98).
121. See H. Brunner, "Die fränkisch-romanische dos," in his *Abhandlungen,* vol. 2, pp. 78–116. Brunner has pointed out that a woman who had received land by a *libellum dotis* was not entitled by law to claim one-third of her husband's property as her dower. This law could be bypassed by donations or testamentary bequests, which usually stipulated that the woman was entitled to the usufruct of her husband's property only as long as she did not remarry; see, for example, *Marc. Form.* 2.7, 8, reiterated in *Form. Aug. B* 26, 27 (*MGH Form.* 79–80, 359).
122. Fredegar, *Chron.* 4.85 (*MGH Script. rer. mer.* 2, 164).
123. Gregory of Tours, *Hist. franc.* 8.39 (*MGH Script. rer. mer.* 1, 352).
124. B. Meyer, ed., "Das Testament der Burgundofara," *MIÖG,* 14, *Ergänzungsband* (1939), 11–12.
125. *Marc. Form.* 2.12 (*MGH Form.* 83).
126. *Form. Andecavenses* 41, 54 (*MGH Form.* 18, 23); *Marc. Form.* 2.7, 17 (*MGH Form* 79–80, 86–88).
127. Pardessus 442 (vol. 2, pp. 255–258).

128. The following deeds issued by women alone are listed by Pardessus (possibly spurious ones are marked with an asterisk): 127 (1, 94), 177* (1, 131), 179* (1, 135), 241 (1, 227), 328 (2, 105), 338* (2, 116), 361 (2, 148), 432 (2, 230), 447 (2, 356), 476 (2, 284), 477 (2, 433), 480 (2, 288), 491 (2, 299), 39 add. (2, 447), 516 (2, 328), 45 add. (2, 452), 554 (2, 365), 70 add. (2, 467), 75 add. (2, 472), 581 (2, 394), 82 add. (2, 476). See also O. Opet, "Geschlechtsvormundschaft," *MIÖG*, 3, *Ergänzungsband* (1890–94), 22, n. 2.

129. Gregory of Tours, *Hist. franc.* 9.33 (*MGH Script. rer. mer.* 1, 389).

CHAPTER 3

1. The degree of social mobility in the late Roman Empire is a subject of debate. For a brief bibliography, see Frank D. Gilliard, "The Senators in Sixth Century Gaul," *Speculum*, 54 (1979), 685–697. Although Gilliard admits that "the evidence does not allow a precise answer," he concludes that there was some social mobility in the late empire. The senatorial class in fifth and sixth century Gaul was a conglomerate of landholders, including the descendants of imperial *senatores*, municipal *curiales*, and parvenus: ibid., p. 694, n. 48. André Chastagnol denied this, arguing for the static stratification of the social system in the late empire ("Classes et ordres dans le Bas-Empire," in *Ordres et classes; Colloque d'histoire sociale, Saint-Cloud, 24–25 mai, 1967*, ed. D. Roche and C. E. Labrousse [Paris, 1976], pp. 49–57).

2. *Leges Burg.* Pref. 5; 2.2; 101.1–2 (*MGH Legum Sectio I*, 2/1, 31, 42, 114) made the distinction between *obtimates*, the nobility constituted by the king's officials *(consiliarii, domestici, maiores domus nostrae, cancellarii, comites, judices)*, the middle class *(populus mediocris)*, and the lower class *(minores personae* or *leudes)*. Slaves were also ranked, their *wergeld* ranging from 30 *solidi* for an unskilled slave to 200 *solidi* for a goldsmith. The *Pactus Alam.* 14.6–8 (*MGH Legum Sectio I*, 5/1, 24) also distinguished between a *baro de minofledis*, a *medianus Alamannus*, and a *primus Alamannus*. Franz Irsigler (*Untersuchungen*, pp. 82–221), traces the meaning of these social distinctions in the writings of Gregory of Tours, Venantius Fortunatus, and the law codes. He also discusses the historiography of Merovingian nobility in the nineteenth and twentieth centuries: Ibid., pp. 37–81.

3. Léopold Génicot, "La noblesse au Moyen Age dans l'ancienne 'Francie,' " *Annales*, 17 (1962), 1–22. Karl Bosl, "Castes, ordres et classes en Allemagne (d'après un choix d'exemples allemands)," in *Problèmes de stratification social: Actes du Colloque International (1966)*, ed. Roland Mousnier (Paris, 1968), pp. 13–29. See also Timothy Reuter's introduction to *The Medieval Nobility*, pp. 25–29.

4. For a detailed analysis, see Archibald Lewis, "The Dukes in the *Regnum Francorum*."

5. On cognate relations, see Karl Schmid, "Zur Problematik von Familie, Sippe und Geschlecht . . ." *Zeitschrift für Geschichte des Oberrheins*, 105

(1957), 1–62; J. Fleckenstein, "Fulred von Saint Denis und der fränkische Ausgriff in den süddeutschen Raum," in *Studien und Vorarbeiten zur Geschichte des grossfränkischen und frühdeutschen Adels*, ed. Gerd Tellenbach (Forschungen zur oberrheinischen Landesgeschichte, 4; Freiburg i, B., 1957), pp. 9–39; Karl Bosl, *Franken um 800: Strukturanalyse einer fränkischen Königsprovinz*, 2d ed. rev. (Munich, 1969), p. 73; W. Störmer, "Eine Adelsgruppe um die Fuldaer Abte Sturmi und Eigil und die Holzkirchener Klostergründungen Troand," in *Gesellschaft und Herrschaft . . . Festgabe für Karl Bosl zum 60. Geburtstag* (Munich, 1969); idem, *Früher Adel: Studien zur politischen Führungsgeschichte im fränkischen-deutschen Reich vom 8. bis 11. Jahrhundert* (Stuttgart, 1973).

6. Salin, *La civilisation mérovingienne*, vol. 1, 409. Salin analyzes these intermarriages on the basis of the male dolichocephalic and female brachycephalic skulls found in the cemetery of Muid (Ibid., p. 76).

7. Karl Friedrich Stroheker, *Der senatorische Adel im spätantiken Gallien* (Tübingen, 1948; reprint Darmstadt, 1970), p. 110. Stroheker demonstrated that Germanic names begin to appear in the ranks of Aquitanian, Narbonnais, and Lyonnais bishops only toward the end of the sixth century.

8. S. Corsten, "Rheinische Adelsherrschaft im ersten Jahrtausend," *Rheinische Vierteljahrsblätter*, 28 (1963), 84–129. Venantius Fortunatus wrote a poem about Bodegisil and another about Palatina: *Opera poetica* 7.5–6 (*MGH Auct. ant.* 4/1, 156–158). Palatina's father, Gallimacus (Gallomagnus), in addition to the position of *referendarius* (Gregory of Tours, *Hist. franc.* 9.38; *MGH Script. rer. mer.* 1, 392), held the office of bishop (Gregory of Tours, *Liber vitae patrum* 8; *MGH Script. rer. mer.* 1, 698).

9. Rolf Sprandel, *Der merowingische Adel und die Gebiete östlich des Rheines* (Forschungen zur oberrheinischen Landesgeschichte, 5; Freiburg, 1957). For more detailed information and a bibliography of primary sources, see Ulrich Nonn, "Eine fränkische Adelssippe um 600. Zur Familie des Bischofs Berthram von Le Mans," *Frühmittelalterliche Studien*, 9 (1975), 186–201; Ewig, "Studien," pp. 52–56.

10. Gregory of Tours, *Hist. franc.* 9.33 (*MGH Script. rer. mer.* 1, 388).

11. Ewig, "Studien," pp. 52–56.

12. R. Sprandel, *Der merowingische Adel*, p. 33, n. 5; A. Coville, "Les Syagrii," in *Recherches sur l'histoire de Lyon du Ve au IXe siècle* (Paris, 1928), pp. 3–29. A domna Siagria is mentioned also in the donation issued by Abo in 739, in *Monumenta Novaliciensia vetustiora* #2, ed. C. Cipolla, vol. 1 (Rome, 1898), 25; and *Cartulaires . . . dits cartulaires de Saint-Hugues*, A 22, ed. Jules Marion (Collection de documents inédits sur l'histoire de France, 8; Paris, 1869), p. 38.

13. Musset, *The Germanic Invasions*, p. 127.

14. E. Hlawitschka, "Zur landschaftlichen Herkunft der Karolinger," *Rheinische Vierteljahrsblätter*, 27 (1962), 1–17; idem, "Die Vorfahren Karls des Grossen," pp. 51–81.

15. *Liber hist. franc.* 48 (*MGH Script. rer. mer.* 2, 322–323). On Ansfled's marriage to Drogo, see ibid., 2, 323, n.3.

16. *Vita s. Geretrudis* 1–2 (*MGH Script. rer. mer.* 2, 454–455).
17. Gregory of Tours, *Hist. franc.* 3.31 (*MGH Script. rer. mer.* 1, 134–135). O. M. Dalton criticized some of Gregory's inaccuracies of this chapter, but not the episode in question, *The History of the Franks*, vol. 2 (Oxford, 1927), pp. 513–514.
18. On Audofled and Clotild, see Gregory of Tours, *Hist. franc.* 3.1, 10, 31 (*MGH Script. rer. mer.* 1, 109, 117, 134–135). On the marriages of Merovingian princesses, see Ewig, "Studien," pp. 46–49.
19. Caesarius of Arles, *Sermones* 43.4 (Mueller 1, 216; Morin 1, 191–192).
20. Gregory of Tours, *Hist. franc.* 9.8 (*MGH Script. rer. mer.* 1, 414).
21. See chapter 2, notes 40, 41, 48.
22. *Conc. Turonense* (567), 21 (20) and *Conc. Parisiense* (556–573), 6 (*CCL* 148A, 187, 208). See also chapter 2, note 48.
23. Gregory of Tours, *Liber vitae patrum* 9 (*MGH Script. rer. mer.* 1, 703): "Requiram puellam pulchram ingenuamque, cui copulatus solatium praebeas maternae viduitati."
24. *Lex Rom. Vis.* Nov. M. 4.1.2–3 (Haenel 302–304; Conrat 105–106).
25. Gregory of Tours, *Hist. franc.* 10.8 (*MGH Script. rer. mer.* 1, 414): "nobilem ex matre, patre inferiore."
26. *Vita s. Balthildis* A.3 (*MGH Script. rer. mer.* 2, 484–485). The story appears in both versions of her life; the older, A version, was written by someone who knew her personally, probably by a nun at Chelles. On the Erchinoald episode as a chastity motif, see Nelson, "Queens as Jezebels," p. 34, note 13 and p. 46. Balthild's change of heart when Clovis II proposed marriage to her is not sufficient evidence for the interpretation of the Erchinoald episode as mere fiction. Clovis was a king while Erchinoald was only a mayor.
27. Ewig, "Studien," p. 42.
28. Gregory of Tours, *Hist. franc.* 4.26 (*MGH Script. rer. mer.* 1, 160–162).
29. Gregory of Tours, *Hist. franc.* 4.25 (*MGH Script. rer. mer.* 1, 160). On Austrechild, see also Fredegar, *Chron.* 3.56 (*MGH Script. rer. mer.* 2, 56).
30. Gregory of Tours made it clear that Fredegund was Chilperic's former concubine and reported Rigunth's disparaging words in *Hist. franc.* 4.28; 9.34 (*MGH Script. rer. mer.* 1, 164, 389). On Fredegund's background, see *Liber hist. franc.* 31 (*MGH Script. rer. mer.* 2, 323). On the need for critical scrutiny in using the *Liber,* see Eugen Ewig, "Noch einmal zum 'Staatreich' Grimoalds," *Speculum historiale; Festschrift J. Spörl,* ed. C. Bauer et al. (Freiburg, 1965), pp. 454–457.
31. *Vita s. Balthildis,* A.2 (*MGH Script. rer. mer.* 2, 483): "forma corporis grata ac subtilissima et aspectu decora." On the background of these queens, see Ewig, "Studien," p. 40. On Bilichild, Theudechild, and Nanthild, see Fredegar, *Chron.* 4.35, 37, 58 (*MGH Script. rer. mer.* 2, 134, 138, 149–50). On Balthild's other suitor, see note 26, above; on her concern for slaves, see *Vita s. Balthildis,* A.9 (*MGH Script. rer. mer.* 2, 494).
32. Gregory of Tours, *Hist. franc.* 3.26 (*MGH Script. rer. mer.* 1, 132).
33. For example, *Vita Bavonis Confessoris Gandavensis* 2–3 (*MGH Script. rer. mer.*

4, 535–536) describes how the saint reformed under the care of his wife and, when she died, refused to remarry. For donations and wills by husbands, see chapter 2, note 126.

34. For example, Bertisinda and Raudoald were buried next to each other with one tombstone in the cemetery near the Chapel of Saint Aura at Mainz: Salin, *La civilisation mérovingienne*, vol. 2, 87.

35. Irsigler, *Untersuchungen*, pp. 203–204, n. 135 (with bibliography).

36. *Gesta Dagoberti* 13, 16 (*MGH Script. rer. mer.* 2, 404, 406). Sigihild's ultimate goal was to secure Dagobert's throne for her own son, Charibert. Her plans came to nought when Dagobert repudiated the sterile Gomatrud and married other women who bore him children. Fredegar, *Chron.* 4.56 (*MGH Script. rer. mer.* 2, 149).

37. Fredegar, *Chron.* 4.34 (*MGH Script. rer. mer.* 2, 134).

38. Fredegar, *Chron.* 4.71 (*MGH Script. rer. mer.* 2, 156). Gundoberga was related to the Franks through her mother, Theudolinda, of whom Fredegar speaks as coming from "ex genere Francorum." *Chron.* 4.34 (*MGH Script. rer. mer.* 2, 133). Theudolinda was the daughter of Garibald, Duke of Bavaria, and Vuldetrada, a Lombard princess. On the unions of Vuldetrada and Theudolinda, see Karl Bosl, "Der 'Adelsheilige.' Idealtypus und Wirklichkeit, Gesellschaft und Kultur im merowingischen Bayern des 7. und 8. Jahrhunderts," in *Speculum Historiale; Festschrift J. Spörl*, ed. C. Bauer et al. (Freiburg, Munich, 1965), p. 169; Reinhard Schneider, *Königswahl und Königserhebung im Frühmittelalter* (Stuttgart, 1972), pp. 29–32, 37–40.

39. Gregory of Tours, *Hist. franc.* 9.33 (*MGH Script. rer. mer.* 1, 388).

40. "acerbitatem ne te videant in luctu affici." *Epist. Austrasicae* 1 (*MGH Epist.* 3, *Mer. kar. aevi* 1, 112).

41. Gregory of Tours, *Hist. franc.* 3.1, 10 (*MGH Script. rer. mer.* 1, 109, 117). See also E. A. Thompson, *The Goths in Spain* (Oxford, 1969), p. 2.

42. Gregory of Tours, *Hist. franc.* 10.27 (*MGH Script. rer. mer.* 1, 438).

43. *Epist. Austrasicae* 27, 43, 44 (*MGH Epist.* 3, *Mer. kar. aevi* 1, 139, 149, 150). On Ingund's fate, see Gregory of Tours, *Hist. franc.* 6.40; 8.18, 21, 28; 9.16, 20, 24 (*MGH Script. rer. mer.* 1, 278–279, 337, 339, 341, 371, 378, 381).

44. *Gesta Dagoberti* 22 (*MGH Script. rer. mer.* 2, 408).

45. Gregory of Tours, *Hist. franc.* 5.34 (*MGH Script. rer. mer.* 1, 227).

46. See note 29.

47. Gregory of Tours, *Liber vitae patrum* 19.1 (*MGH Script. rer. mer.* 1, 737).

48. On infanticide, see *Vita s. Balthildis* 6 (*MGH Script. rer. mer.* 2, 488); and Mary M. McLaughlin, "Survivors and Surrogates," in *The History of Childhood*, ed. Lloyd De Mause (New York, 1974), p. 156, n. 102. On child abuse in antiquity and the early Middle Ages, see Lloyd De Mause, "The Evolution of Childhood," in ibid., pp. 1–73; and Richard B. Lyman, Jr., "Barbarism and Religion: Late Roman and Early Medieval Childhood," in ibid., pp. 75–100.

49. Gregory of Tours, *De virtutibus s. Martini* 2.24 (*MGH Script. rer. mer.* 1, 617).

Carl Haffler, "The Changeling: History and Psychodynamics of Attitudes to Handicapped Children in European Folklore," *Journal of the
History of Behavior Sciences,* 4 (1968), 55–61.

50. *Vita Odiliae* 2–9 (*MGH Script. rer. mer.* 6, 38–42). Although the biography
was composed in the ninth century, it reflects a long tradition. That
parents were ashamed of a daughter's blindness is evident also from
Saint Salaberga's life; her biographer made it clear that she was presented to Saint Eustachius only upon his urging. *Vita Sadalbergae* 4 (*MGH
Script. rer. mer.* 5, 53).

51. *Gesta Dagoberti* 2 (*MGH Script. rer. mer.* 2, 401): "Hic denique in annis
puerilibus positus, traditus est a genitore venerabili ac sanctissimo Ar-
nulfo Mettensium urbis episcopo, ut eum secundum suam sapientiam
enutriet." It was not unusual to turn a son over to a former enemy as
a hostage; see, for example, Gregory of Tours, *Hist. franc.* 6.26 (*MGH
Script. rer. mer.* 1, 265).

52. Clotild raised her orphaned grandsons; see Gregory of Tours, *Hist. franc.*
3.1, 18 (*MGH Script. rer. mer.* 1, 126–127).

53. *Epist. Austrasicae* 23 (*MGH Epist.* 3, *Mer. kar. aevi.* 1, 135–137).

54. Gregory of Tours, *Hist. franc.* 3.6 (*MGH Script. rer. mer.* 1, 113).

55. Gregory of Tours, *Liber vitae patrum* 8.1 (*MGH Script. rer. mer.* 1, 691).

56. *Epist. aevi mer. collectae* 17 (*MGH Epist.* 3, *Mer. kar. aevi* 1, 464).

57. *Vita s. Desiderii* 11 (*MGH Script. rer. mer.* 4, 570): "Ego infelix mater quid
agam cum fratres tui iam non sunt? Si tu discesseris, ego orbata absque
liberis ero. Sed tu, piissime pignus, mihi dulcissime, sic te iugiter prae-
cave, ut dum solatia fratrum perdidisti, te non perdas, ut ne, quod absit,
in interitum vadas." See also her two earlier letters (9 and 10; ibid., 569)
in which she exhorted her son to virtue and to live and speak well. The
best summary of the advice she gave to Desiderius is contained in the
following phrase: "regi sis fidelis, contubernales diligas, Deum semper
amas et timeas."

58. On this subject, see Mary M. McLaughlin, "Survivors and Surrogates," pp.
106–109.

59. *Vita s. Geretrudis* 2 (*MGH Script. rer. mer.* 2, 455–456).

60. *Vita s. Balthildis* 14 (*MGH Script. rer. mer.* 2, 500–501).

61. *Leges Burg.* 75.1–3; *Lex Rom. Burg.* 36 (*MGH Legum Sectio I,* 2/1, 107, 153).
Gregory of Tours, *Hist. franc.* 9.19 (*MGH Script. rer. mer.* 1, 373–374),
relates that Tranquilla left her sons after the death of her husband
Sichar and went to live with her kinsmen until she remarried.

62. After her consecration as deaconess, she resided "Suedas in villa, quam ei
rex dederat" and then subsequently "Pictavis . . . monasterium sibi per
ordinationem praecelsi regis Chlotharii construxit." Baudonivia, *De vita
s. Radegundis* 3, 5 (*MGH Script. rer. mer.* 2, 381).

63. Although Saint Monegund's life as a recluse was more austere than the life
of an ordinary woman, her activities were similar to those of married
women. According to Gregory of Tours, she baked her own bread after
she had taken a religious vow, and had next to her chambers a small herb

garden, "parvulum viridiarium." *Liber vitae patrum* 19.1 (*MGH Script. rer. mer.* 1, 737).

64. I have taken what follows from Gregory of Tours, *Hist. franc.* 5.21; 7.36; 8.2; 9.33; 10.12 (*MGH Script. rer. mer.* 1, 219, 317, 327, 387–389, 419). For studies on this family, see note 5 above.

65. On the residences of queens, see Carl Richard Brühl, *Fodrum, gistum, servitium regis. Studien den wirtschaftlichen Grundlagen des Königtums im Frankenreich und in den fränkischen Nachfolgestaaten . . . vom 6. bis zur Mitte des 14. Jahrhunderts* (Kölner historische Abhandlungen, 14; Cologne, 1968), p. 69. Gregory of Tours speaks of a "maiorem domus reginae" in *Hist. franc.* 9.30 (*MGH Script. rer. mer.* 1, 384) and of queens having men under their protection in 9.19 (ibid., 374): "regina Brunechildis in verbo suo posuerat Sicharium."

66. For example, both Childebert's mother, Brunhild, and queen, Faileuba, participated in the conclusion of the Treaty of Andelot with Gunthram, according to Gregory of Tours, *Hist. franc.* 9.11 (*MGH Script. rer. mer.* 1, 368). On the date for the treaty, see below, note 71. On the influence of queens in episcopal appointments, see Nelson, "Queens as Jezebels," pp. 53–55.

67. See note 66.

68. Their rivalry is the subject of a novel by M. Brion, entitled *Frédégonde et Brunehaut* (Paris, 1935).

69. Gregory of Tours, *Hist. franc.* 4.28, 51; 5.18, 39 (*MGH Script. rer. mer.* 1, 164, 186–187, 212, 231).

70. *Liber hist. franc.* 35 (*MGH Script. rer. mer.* 2, 302–303).

71. Gregory of Tours, *Hist. franc.* 6.46; 7.4–5, 19–20; 8.9; 10.28 (*MGH Script. rer. mer.* 1, 287, 293, 294, 301–302, 330–331, 439). The most direct statement by Gregory about the illegitimacy of Clothar is found in 8.31 (ibid., 347): ". . . ad filium, qui esse dicitur Chilperici . . ."

72. *Liber hist. franc.* 36 (*MGH Script. rer. mer.* 1, 246).

73. Gregory of Tours, *Hist. franc.* 8.31; 10.27 (*MGH Script. rer. mer.* 1, 347, 439).

74. Gregory of Tours, *Hist. franc.* 10.28 (*MGH Script. rer. mer.* 1, 439). For the chronology, I am following Eugen Ewig, "Die fränkischen Teilungen und Teilreiche (511–613)," *Akademie der Wissenschaften und Literatur, Abhandl. der Geistes- und Sozialwissenschaftlichen Klasse*, 9 (1952), 683.

75. Fredegar, *Chron.* 4.17 (*MGH Script. rer. mer.* 2, 128); *Liber hist. franc.* 37 (*MGH Script. rer. mer.* 2, 306).

76. Gregory of Tours eulogized her for her beauty, virtue, prudence, and amicability. He also described her banishment after Sigebert's death, her marriage to Prince Merovech, and her inability to receive Merovech in the East Kingdom where Chilperic allowed her to go upon the intercession of the magnates of that kingdom. *Hist. franc.* 4.27; 5.1–3, 14 (*MGH Script. rer. mer.* 1, 163, 191–193, 201–206). The anonymous author of the *Liber historiae francorum* blamed her for many atrocities; on these see B. Bachrach in the preface of his translation of the *Liber historiae*

francorum (Lawrence, Kansas, 1973), pp. 10–11. Ionas, *Vitae sanctorum: Columbani* 1.18 (*MGH Script. rer. germ. in usu schol.* 187), also stressed her ruthless drive for power. G. Kurth's essay entitled "La reine Brunehaut" (in *Études franques,* vol. 1, 265–356), remains useful in summarizing earlier scholarship, but needs to be supplemented with more recent research. Ewig ("Die fränkischen Teilungen" pp. 682–689) analyzes the influence Gunthram exercised in the East Kingdom and the close relationship between Brunhild and Childebert after 585 when Wandelen, Childebert's "nutritor," died. Janet Nelson ("Queens as Jezebels," pp. 41–43) argued convincingly that some of the officials during Childebert's minority were probably Brunhild's appointees and that with these she managed to silence the faction of the Austrasian nobility that opposed her. Nelson provides an overview of the conflicting interpretations of Brunhild's later policies, with the Germans favoring the interpretation that she promoted "Romantum" and the French depicting her as a "would-be despot." Ibid., p. 45, nn. 79, 81.

77. Nelson, "Queens as Jezebels," pp. 42–43.

78. Gregory I, *Registrum epistularum* 7.5, 55, 57; 8.4; 9.212, 213; 11.46, 48, 49; 13.7 (*MGH Epist.* 1, 382, 430, 431; 2, 5, 197–200, 318, 320–322, 371–375).

79. Gregory of Tours, *Hist. franc.* 9.11, 20 (*MGH Script. rer. mer.* 1, 374–377, 434–437). I am following Ewig's date for the treaty ("Die fränkischen Teilungen," p. 687). R. Schneider prefers the date 586 (*Königswahl,* pp. 124 and 125, n. 325).

80. Fredegar, *Chron.* 4.30, 34 (*MGH Script. rer. mer.* 2, 132–133). See also Ewig, "Studien," p. 40, nn. 144–145.

81. Gregory of Tours, *Hist. franc.* 9.38 (*MGH Script. rer. mer.* 1, 392–393).

82. Fredegar, *Chron.* 4.35 (*MGH Script. rer. mer.* 2, 134). Ewig dates this marriage between 601 and 602. See "Studien," p. 26.

83. On Protadius, see Fredegar, *Chron.* 4.27–29 (*MGH Script. rer. mer.* 2, 131–132). Brunhild had alienated the Orléanese and Burgundian nobility with her patronage of Protadius, according to Ewig, "Die fränkischen Teilungen," p. 691. Fredegar, in *Chron* 4.32 (*MGH Script. rer. mer.* 2, 133), blamed Brunhild and bishop Aridius of Lyons for the exile of Desiderius. The *Vita Desiderii* 2.2, 8 (*MGH Script. rer. mer.* 3, 638, 640–41) implicated her in the subsequent stoning of Desiderius. Janet Nelson examines the question, bringing in other sources, and absolves her of direct responsibility. See "Queens as Jezebels," pp. 56–57.

84. Ionas, *Vitae sanctorum: Columbani* 1.19 (*MGH Script. rer. germ. in usu schol.* 188).

85. Theuderic's death and Warnachar's betrayal are described in Fredegar, *Chron.* 4.38, 40–42 (*MGH Script. rer. mer.* 2, 140–142). The *Liber hist. franc.* 40 (*MGH Script. rer. mer.* 2, 310) gives the gory details of her execution. According to Nelson ("Queens as Jezebels," p. 59, nn. 154–155), this passage was influenced by 4 Kings 9:30–33. The biblical

passage also served as the source of inspiration for Ionas's description of her death in *Vitae sanctorum: Columbani* 1.29 (*MGH Script. rer. mer.* 4, 106).

86. Fredegar, *Chron.* 4.79 (*MGH Script. rer. mer.* 2, 161): Aega vero cum regina Nantilde, quem Dagobertus reliquerat.

87. In a donation jointly issued in 633 with Nanthild and their daughter Rathild, Dagobert I made it clear that she was his legitimate queen. See Pardessus 261 (vol. 2, p. 24): ". . . Nanthildis, regina Francorum, nostra legitima . . ." For her life, I am following Fredegar, *Chron.* 4.58, 60, 79, 83–84, 89, 90 (*MGH Script. rer. mer.* 2, 150, 151, 161, 163, 165–166); *Gesta Dagoberti* 22 (*MGH Script. rer. mer.* 2, 408); *Liber hist. franc.* 42 (*MGH Script. rer. mer.* 2, 315). For the chronology, see E. Ewig, "Die fränkischen Teilreiche im 7. Jahrhundert (613–714)," *Trierer Zeitschrift,* 22 (1953), 114–118.

88. On Clovis II's debauchery, see *Liber hist. franc.* 44 (*MGH Script. rer. mer.* 2, 315–316). On Balthild's activities and friendships, see Fredegar, *Chron. Cont.* 1 (*MGH Script. rer. mer.* 2, 168); *Liber hist. franc.* 43 (*MGH Script. rer. mer.* 2, 315); *Vita s. Balthildis* 5–10 (*MGH Script. rer. mer.* 2, 487–495); and F. Prinz, *Frühes Mönchtum,* pp. 128, 132, 136–137, 143, 168, 193, 274–276, 283, 293–296. On the circle of Audoen and Ebroin, see J. Fischer, *Der Hausmeier Ebroin* (Bonn, 1954); E. Vacandard, *Vie de Saint Ouen, évêque de Rouen (641–84)* (Paris, 1902); and F. Prinz, *Frühes Mönchtum,* pp. 125–126, 129. For literature on Waldabert of Luxeuil, see F. Prinz, *Frühes Mönchtum,* pp. 143, n. 118, 270–271; and on Filibert of Jumièges, see ibid., pp. 72, 131 n.59. Balthild had among her circle of friends many other influential churchmen, in particular Theudefrid of Corbie and Saint Leodegar. See F. Prinz, *Frühes Mönchtum,* 137 and 295.

89. *Vita s. Balthildis* A.4 (*MGH Script. rer. mer.* 2, 485–486): "ut domino et principibus se ostendat ut mater, sacerdotibus ut filia, iuvenibus seu adolescentibus ut optima nutrix." On Ebroin, see Fischer, *Der Hausmeier.*

90. L. Dupraz held that Balthild, with the help of Ebroin, tried to reunite Neustria, Austrasia, and Burgundy in *Le Royaume des Francs et l'ascension politique des maires du palais au déclin du VII siècle (656–680)* (Fribourg i. B., 1948), pp. 239 and 351. Fischer (*Der Hausmeier,* p. 87) attributed to her only a Neustro-Burgundian policy. Nelson ("Queens as Jezebels," pp. 48–49) rejected the thesis that Balthild imposed Childeric II on the Neustrians, arguing that the marriage of the seven-year-old prince with his cousin, Bilichild, in 662 and his rule over Neustria under the regency of his mother-in-law, Chimnechild, were arranged by Grimoald with the backing of the Austrasian nobility. An important element in the debate concerning Balthild's political maneuvers as regent is the date of Grimoald's death. If the Austrasian mayor of the palace was executed by Clovis II, as stated in *Liber hist. franc.* 43 (*MGH Script. rer. mer.* 2, 316), then he was executed before Clovis II died in 657. If "Chlodoveo" in the *Liber* is amended to read "Chlothario," Grimoald's execution could

be assigned to 662, shortly after the death of Grimoald's own son, Childebert, who had exiled Dagobert II in 661 and ruled Austrasia as Childebert III between 661–662. Those who favor this solution argue that only Grimoald's presence as the power behind the throne can explain why the Austrasian nobility tolerated Childebert's usurpation. Other scholars have rejected the suggested emendation. See L. Levillain, "Encore la succession d'Austrasie," *Bibliothèque de l'École des Chartes*, 105 (1945–46), 296–306; and Ewig, "Noch einmal zum 'Staatreich' Grimoalds," pp. 454–457. Nelson, on the other hand, argued in its favor ("Queens as Jezebels," p. 49, n.102). The execution of Grimoald by Clovis in 656 or 657 and Childebert's usurpation between 661 and 662, when Grimoald was already dead, make sense if one takes into account the power vacuum that was created by the deaths of Sigebert II and Clovis II in 656 and 657. After the death of Sigebert II in 656, a loyalist faction of the Austrasian magnates thwarted the plot of Grimoald to substitute his own son on the throne for the infant Dagobert II by delivering the overambitious mayor into the hands of Sigebert's half-brother, Clovis II. But the death of the Neustrian king the following year weakened the pro-Dagobert faction in Austrasia. By 661 Grimoald's son, Childebert, had sufficient support to exile Dagobert II and usurp the throne. When after a year of usurpation Childebert unexpectedly died, Balthild, who was regent in Neustria, stepped in. Instead of recalling Dagobert, she arranged the marriage of her second son, Childeric, with the exiled king's sister, Bilichild, and had Childeric II proclaimed King of Austrasia. The *Vita s. Balthildis* 5 (*MGH Script rer. mer.* 2, 487) leaves no doubt that she played an active role in Childeric II's accession: "Austrasii pacifico ordine, ordinante domna Balthilde, per consilium quidem seniorum receperunt Childericum, filium eius in regem Austri."

91. On the wide-reaching family connections of Theudefrid, Waldebert, and Filibert, who were named by Balthild's hagiographer as her friends (*Vita s. Balthildis* A. 7–8; *MGH Script. rer. mer.* 2, 491), see F. Prinz, *Frühes Mönchtum*, pp. 137, 173–174, in particular 174, n.114.

92. *Vita s. Balthildis* A.6–9 (*MGH Script. rer. mer.* 2, 488–494).

93. Eugen Ewig, "Das Privileg des Bischofs Berthefrid von Amiens für Corbie von 664 und die Klosterpolitik des Königin Balthild," *Francia*, 1 (1973), 62–114, in particular 107. Ewig thinks that the structural changes Balthild made in the church were abortive. Janet Nelson, in a more positive vein, suggests that the "Carolingians have reaped what Balthild had sown" in "Queens as Jezebels," pp. 67–71.

94. *Vita Balthildis* A.10 (*MGH Script. rer. mer.* 2, 495): "Nam et Franci . . . nec fieri permittebant, nisi commotio illa fuisset per miserum Sigobrandum episcopum, cuius superbia inter Francos meruit mortis ruinam. Et exinde orta intentione, dum ipsum contra eius voluntatem interfecerunt, metuentes, ne hoc ipsa domna contra eos graviter ferret ac vindicare ipsam causam vellet, permiserunt eam subito pergere ad ipsum monasterium." For an analysis and bibliography, see Nelson, "Queens as

Jezebels," pp. 63–64, in particular, nn. 174–178. The last document Balthild signed with Clovis was issued in September 663 or 664, according to Ewig, "Das Privileg," p. 106, n. 80. See Pardessus 336 (vol. 2, p. 114). For a summary of earlier scholarship on her retirement, see Ch. Courtois, "L'Avènement de Clovis II et les règles d'accession au thrône de chez les Mérovingiens," in *Mélanges Halphen* (Paris, 1951), pp. 155–164.

95. Gregory of Tours, *Hist. franc.* 6.4 (*MGH Script. rer. mer.* 1, 246).

96. Herlihy, "Life Expectancies for Women," p. 7. See also Jutta Barchewitz, *Von der Wirtschaftstätigkeit der Frau in der vorgeschichtlichen Zeit bis zur Entfaltung der Stadtwirtschaft* (Breslauer historische Forschungen, 3; Breslau, 1937).

97. Fortunatus, *Vita s. Amantii* 9 (*MGH Auct. Ant.* 4/2, 60–61). She probably sold wine she produced from crops on her own land. According to Johannes Schneider, the "pauperes" were small landholders. See "Die Darstellung der Pauperes in den Historiae Gregors von Tours: Ein Beitrag zur sozialökonomischen Struktur Galliens im 6. Jahrhundert," *Jahrbuch für Wirtschaftsgeschichte* (1966, pt. 4), p. 73. See also Gilliard, "The Senators in Sixth Century Gaul," p. 693, n. 43.

98. *Pactus Alam.* 17.1–7 (*MGH Legum Sectio I,* 5/1, 23): the *wergeld* of a freeman was 40 *solidi;* of a *litus* (semifree), 13 *solidi;* of a freewoman, 80 *solidi;* of a *lita,* 26 *solidi;* of a slave woman, 12 *solidi.*

99. *Leges Burg.* 30.1–2 (*MGH Legum Sectio I,* 2/1, 66) punished the rape of an *ancilla* with 12 *solidi;* if she was raped by a slave, he was to receive 150 lashes. *Lex Rib.* 39 (35). 3 (*MGH Legum Sectio I,* 3/2, 90) set the same punishment for the abduction of an *ingenuam* and a *mulierem* who "in verbo regis vel ecclesiastica est." *Pactus legis Sal.* 15.1–2, 5–6 (*MGH Legum Sectio I,* 4/1, 93–96) set the compensation payable to her master for fornication with *ancilla aliena* at 15 *solidi,* with *regis ancilla* at 30 *solidi.* If the transgressor was a slave and the girl belonged to a different master, he was to receive 300 lashes; if she died, he was to be castrated and had to pay 6 *solidi* to her lord. *Pactus legis Sal.* 130:1–2 (*MGH Legum Sectio I,* 4/1, 266) punished the rape of a *liberta* by a *libertus* with 20 *solidi.* *Lex Alam.* 75.1–3 (*MGH Legum Sectio I,* 5/1, 140) fined a man 3 *solidi* for the rape of a *vestiaria* or *publicula de genitio priore.* See also *Pactus Alam.* 32.1–5 (*MGH Legum Sectio I,* 5/1, 33). *Lex Bai.* 8.10–13 (*MGH Legum Sectio I,* 5/2, 357–358): if a slave fornicated with a married freedwoman, he had to pay 40 *solidi;* if she was not married, 8 *solidi;* if she was a married slave, 20 *solidi;* if she was an unmarried slave, 4 *solidi.*

100. *Pactus legis Sal.,* 104.10–11 (*MGH Legum Sectio I,* 4/1, 261) punished with 5½ *solidi* those who were instrumental in making an ordinary slave (*pulicella*) abort her child. If she was an *ancilla cellarium aut genitium,* the fine was 100 *solidi.*

101. *Leges. Burg.* 33.1–3 (*MGH Legum Sectio I,* 2/1, 67).

102. *Conc. Aurelianense* (541), 24 (*CCL* 148A, 138).

103. Gregory of Tours, *Hist. franc.* 6.45 (*MGH Script. rer. mer.* 1, 284): "familias

multas de domibus fiscalibus auferre praecepit." Some were "meliores natu," a designation that might indicate freemen.

104. *Lex Rib.* 61.11 (*MGH Legum Sectio I, 3/2, 112*): "generatio eorum semper ad inferiora declinentur." This law referred specifically to the union of a Ripuarian freewoman with an *ecclesiasticus, Romanus,* or *regius homo,* but the same principle was also upheld in articles 9–10, which regulated the status of children issued from unions between a *tabularia, regia, or Romana femina* and slaves. The principle that the children were to follow *deteriorem lineam* was incorporated into the Roman codes issued by Germanic kings. *Lex Rom. Burg.* 37.5 (*MGH Legum Sectio I, 2/1, 156*); *Leges Vis.* 3.2.3–4; 3.2.7; 9.1.15 (*MGH Legum Sectio I, 1, 135–136, 137, 361*). *Lex Rom. Vis.* C. 4.8.3 (Conrat 36; Haenel 114). In addition, the laws punished a freewoman who married an unfree man with the loss of her freedom. *Lex Rib.* 67.16, 18 (*MGH Legum Sectio I, 3/2, 113*). See also chapter 2, note 54.

105. Pardessus 170 (vol. 1, p. 138): "et ipse quatuor arpennos vineae colat monachis, et nihil amplius. Uxor sua Subfronia et filios, si habuerint, in libertate permaneant."

106. *Marc. Form.* 2.29 (*MGH Form.* 93–94): "servus meus . . . te absque parentum vel tua voluntate rapto scelere in coniugium sociavit . . . sed . . . convenit inter nos, ut, si aliqua procreatio filiorum horta fuerit inter vos, in integra ingenuetate [*sic*] permaneant . . . et sub integra ingenuitate super terra nostra aut filiorum nostrorum . . . commanere debeant et redditus terre, ut mos est, pro ingenius annis singulis dessolvant."

107. David Herlihy, "Life Expectancies for Women," and Appendix in *The Role of Woman in the Middle Ages,* ed. R. T. Morewedge, pp. 7–10, 21. He drew his information from *Cartulaire de l'Abbaye de Saint-Victor de Marseille,* ed. Benjamin E. C. Guérard, vol. 2 (reprint Paris, 1957), 633–656, and *Il regesto di Farfa compilato da Gregorio di Catino,* ed. Ugo Balzini and I. Giorgi (Rome, 1892).

108. Coleman, "Medieval Marriage Characteristics," pp. 205–219.

109. John Contreni at Purdue University is studying the demographic implications of early medieval archaeological data. According to Vern Bullogh and Cameron Campbell the cause for the sexual disproportion until the thirteenth century was an iron deficiency in the diet, which contributed to the early death of women: "Female Longevity and Diet in the Middle Ages," *Speculum,* 55 (1980), 317–325. I was unable to consult the latest study on early medieval nutrition by Massimo Montanari, *L'alimentazione contadina nell'alto medioevo* (Naples, 1980). The earlier death of women has been proven by statistical studies of skeletal remains in Hungarian graveyards. For a list of studies, see Eric Fügedi, "Pour une analyse démographique de la Hongrie médiévale," *Annales-Économies-Sociétés-Civilisations,* 24 (1969), 1299–1312. Salin remarked on the presence of numerous bodies of women and children in the graves: *La civilisation mérovingienne,* vol. 4, 455.

110. See note 108.
111. *Form. Andecavenses* 59 (*MGH Form.* 25): "aliqua femena [*sic*] . . . servo nostro . . . ad coiugium [*sic*] copulavit, et modo nos bona volumtate convenit, ut, quamdiu quidam in coiugio sunt copolati, ipsa femena per nos non debiat esse declinatam in servicio, et agnacio, se ex ipsis procreata fuerit, ad ingenuetatem capitis eorum debiant permanere ingenui . . . et peculiare, quod stante coniugio laborare potuerit, ipsa femena tercia parte exinde habeat." Charles Verlinden suggests that this was a remarkable concession, probably granted because the woman was living under Roman law and Roman law was influenced by canon law ("Le mariage des esclaves," p. 589).

CHAPTER 4

1. H. Brunner summarized succinctly the goal of aristocratic marriages in Merovingian times: "Für die Sippe was der Zweck der Ehe nicht die dauernde Lebensgemeinschaft zwischen Mann und Weib, nicht das *consortium omnis vitae, divini et humanis iuris communicatio,* sondern die Erhaltung und Vermehrung der Sippe durch die Erzeugung von Kindern." "Die Geburt eines lebenden Kindes . . ." in his *Abhandlungen,* vol. 2, 160.
2. Double standards of sexuality were condemned by Ambrose, *De Abraham* 1.4.25 (*CSEL* 32, 1, 519): "omne stuprum adulterium est, nec viro licet, quod mulieri non licet." See chapter 1, note 56, for passages from Augustine and Jerome upholding the mutuality of marriage contracts. Early Christian teachings on marriage have been analyzed by Herbert Preisker, *Christentum und Ehe in den ersten drei Jahrhunderten* (Neue Studien zur Geschichte der Theologie, ed. R. Seeberg, 23; Berlin, 1927). On patristic teachings on marriage, see L. Godefroy, "Mariage dans les pères. Le sacrement," in *Dictionnaire de théologie catholique,* vol. 9 (Paris, 1927), 2105–2109. Modern studies of Ambrose's and Augustine's views are listed in chapter 6, note 25.
3. Georges Duby, *Medieval Marriage: Two Models from Twelfth Century France,* trans. Elborg Forster (Johns Hopkins Symposia in Comparative History, 11; Baltimore, 1978).
4. *Conc. Aurelianense* (533), 11 (*CCL* 148A, 100). Joyce's conclusion that we do not have sufficient evidence to believe that the Merovingian bishops did not protest against divorce seems to rest on tenuous ground (*Christian Marriage,* p. 337). For a different interpretation, see Ignaz Fahrner, *Geschichte der Ehescheidung.* Merovingian and Carolingian conciliar legislation on marriage and divorce was analyzed also by A. Esmein, *Le Mariage en droit canonique,* 2d ed. rev., R. Génestal and J. Dauvillier (Paris, 1935); Pierre Daudet, *Études sur l'histoire de la juridiction matrimoniale* (Paris, 1933); and McNamara and Wemple, "Marriage and Divorce in the Frankish Kingdom," pp. 95–124. The oldest Frankish collection of canons, the pre-Carolingian *Vetus Gallica,* had only a few canons on marriage

and included Augustine's condemnation of remarriage after divorce as adultery according to celestial law: "non iure fori sed iure celi." On this, see Picasso, "I fondamenti del matrimonio nelle collezioni canoniche," pp. 200–201.

5. For a quick overview of Merovingian and Carolingian conciliar legislation on impediments to marriage, see G. Fransen, "La rupture du mariage," pp. 614–626. On incest legislation, see Fleury, *Recherches.* On the punishment of abduction and rape, see chapter 2, note 41. For further studies, see Ganshof, "Le statut," p. 44 and n. 117. Saint Caesarius of Arles and Saint Columban were among the most outspoken opponents of concubinage; see chapter 1, note 65, and chapter 3, note 84.

6. On Boniface's correspondence with Gregory II, Gregory III, and Zachary, see Boniface's letters, numbers 26, 28, and 77, in *Die Briefe,* ed. Tangl, pp. 45, 51, 159; *Epistolae* 26, 50, 51 (*MGH Epist.* 3, *Mer. Kar. aevi* 1, 276, 299). On Pope Gregory II's reply to Boniface, see William Kelly, *Pope Gregory II on Divorce and Remarriage: A Canonical-Historical Investigation of the Letter "Desiderabilem mihi," with Special Reference to the Response "Quod proposuisti"* (Analecta Gregoriana 203; Ser. Fac. Iuris Can. Sectio B, 37; Rome, 1976). On Pope Zachary's letter to Pepin, see JE 2277 (Mansi 12, 326; *PL* 89, 930).

7. *Pippini regis Capit.* (754–755), 1 (*MGH Capit.* 1, 31). Fleury connected this capitulary to the legislation of the assembly held at Compiègne in 757: *Decr. Comp.* (757), 1–4 (*MGH Capit.* 1, 37–39). *Recherches,* p. 180, n. 23.

8. *Conc. Vernense* (755) 15 (*MGH Capit.* 1, 36): "Ut omnes homines laici publicas nuptias faciant tam nobiles quam innobiles." A synod held in Bavaria between 740 and 750 declared: "Ut et nuptiae caveantur, ne inordinate neque inexaminate non fiant, neque quisquam audeat ante nubere, antequam presbytero suo adnuntiet et parentibus suis et vicinis, qui eorum possint examinare propinquitatem, et cum eorum fiat consilio et voluntate" (*Conc. Bai.* 12; *MGH Conc.* 2, 53). Charlemagne also prohibited clandestine marriages in his *Admonitio generalis* (789), 68 (*MGH Capit.* 1, 59) and *Capit. missorum* (802), 35 (*MGH Capit.* 1, 98). On the whole question, see Ritzer, *Formen,* pp. 260–261.

9. *Decr. Comp.* (757), 13, 17, 18 (*MGH Capit.* 1, 38–39).

10. *Capit. Harist.* (779), *Forma communis* 5; *Capit. de partibus Saxoniae* 20; *Capit. missorum* (802), 33 (*MGH Capit.* 1, 48, 69, 97).

11. Pope Stephen III reminded Charlemagne and Carloman that Pope Stephen II had persuaded their father not to divorce their mother Bertrada. *Codex Carolinus* 45 (*MGH Epist. 3, Mer. et kar. aevi* 1, 561–562; JE 2381). The older view, according to which Pepin's and Bertrada's union, beginning as a *Friedelehe,* was transformed into a "legitimate" union only after the birth of Charlemagne, has been refuted by K. F. Werner, "Die Geburtsdatum Karls des Grossen," *Francia,* 1 (1973), 117, n. 6, and 133. L. Oelsner discussed Pepin's marriage and his attempt to divorce Bertrada in order to marry Angla, the wife of a certain Theodrad (*Jahrbücher des fränkischen Reiches unter König Peppin* [Leipzig, 1871], pp. 495–496).

12. *Liber hist. franc.* 49 (*MGH Script. rer. mer.* 2, 324): "habensque Pippinus . . . filium ex alia uxore nomine Carlo." Fredegar, *Chron.* 4.103 (*MGH Script. rer. mer.* 2, 122): "igitur . . . Pippinus aliam duxit uxorem nobilem et elegantem nomine Chalpaida." Pepin also had a concubine. See E. Hlawitschka, "Die Vorfahren Karls des Grossen," p. 75, nn. 16–18, and Table.

13. Charles Martel had two wives: Chrodtrud (d. 725), the mother of Carloman, Hiltrud, and Pepin, and Swanahild, the mother of Grifo. He also had a concubine, possibly called Ruodhaid, the mother of Bernhard, Hieronymous, and Remigius. See Hlawitschka, "Die Vorfahren Karls des Grossen," nn. 31–33, and Table.

14. *Conc. Suessionense* (744), 9 (*MGH Conc.* 2, 35).

15. *Decr. Comp.* 6, 7, 16, 19, 20 (*MGH Capit.* 1, 37–39).

16. *Decr. Vermeriense* 4, 5, 9, 17 (*MGH Capit.* 1, 40–41).

17. *Marc. Form.* 2.30 (*MGH Form.* 94); reiterated in *Form. Senon.* 47; *Form. Turon.* 19; *Salicae Merkelianae* 18 (*MGH Form.* 94, 206, 248). See chapter 2, note 81, for further references.

18. *Penitentiale Egberti* 1.19, 26 (Mansi 12, 436, 438); *Exceptiones* 122–123 (Mansi 12, 424); also in Wasserschleben, *Die Bussordnungen*, pp. 231–247. Wasserschleben believed that it was composed in the Frankish Kingdom. On penitential literature in general, see P. Fournier and G. Le Bras, *Histoire des collections canoniques en occident depuis les Fausses Décrétales*, vol. 1, (Paris, 1931), 107; and H. J. Schmitz, *Die Bussbücher und die Bussdisziplin der Kirche* (Mainz, 1883; reprint Graz, 1958); C. Vogel, *Le pécheur et la pénitence dans L'Eglise ancienne* (Paris, 1960); idem, *Le pécheur et la pénitence au Moyen Age* (Paris, 1969). On the theory of marriage and divorce, see R. Manselli, "Il matrimonio nei penitenziali," pp. 303–311. For specific rules permitting divorce, see Daudet, *Études*, pp. 61–64. Magingoz, an eighth-century bishop of Würzburg, also permitted women to remarry: Boniface, *Epistolae* 134 (*MGH Epist.* 3, *Mer. kar. aevi* 1, 420).

19. *Conc. Romanum* (826), 36 (*MGH Conc.* 2, 582; *MGH Capit.* 1, 376): "Nulli liceat, excepta causa fornicationis, adhibitam uxorem relinquere et deinde aliam copulare; alioquin transgressorem priori convenit sociari coniugio." G. H. Pertz ed. *MGH Leg.*, Vol. 2, 2, 17, places it among spurious documents. But the council is not regarded as spurious by A. Dumas. See his article on Pope Eugenius II in *Dictionnaire d'histoire et de géographie ecclésiastique*, 15 (1963), 1347–1349. The same article 36 was promulgated by Emperor Lothar in *Excerpta canonum* 1 (*MGH Leg.* 1, 373).

20. *Admonitio generalis* (789), 43 (*MGH Capit.* 1, 56). It is included in *Dionysio-Hadriana*, but was probably obtained from the extracts of the *Dionysiana* sent to Pepin by Pope Zachary.

21. *Conc. Foroiuliense* 10 (*MGH Conc.* 2, 192; Mansi, 13, 849). The bishops relied on citations from Jerome and Matthew to decree: "Item placuit, ut resoluto fornicationis causa iugali vinculo non liceat viro, quamdiu

adultera vivit, aliam uxorem ducere, licet sit illa adultera; sed nec adul-
terae, quae poenas gravissimas vel poenitentiae tormentum luere debet,
alium accipere virum, nec vivente nec mortuo quem non erubuit de-
fraudare marito." This council was convoked by Charles to reform the
Italian church, according to H. Barion, *Das fränkisch-deutsche Synodalrecht
des Frühmittelalters* (Kanonische Studien und Texte, ed. A. M. Königen,
5–6; Bonn, 1931), p. 222, n. 24.

22. *Capit. missorum* (802), 22 (*MGH Capit.* 1, 103). The same principle was
reiterated by a member of Charlemagne's court, Theodulf, bishop of
Orléans (790–818), in his *Capitulare* (*PL* 105, 213).

23. Einhard, *Vita Caroli* 18 (*MGH Script.* 2, 453), excluded Himiltrud and her
son from the list of the emperor's wives and concubines, although he
later mentioned that Pepin the Hunchback was the son of a concubine.
Vita Caroli 20 (*MGH Script.* 2, 454). Pope Stephen III, in a letter to
Charlemagne, and Carloman *Codex Carolinus*, 45 (*MGH Epist.* 3, *Mer. kar.
aevi* 1, 561; JE 2831), expressed the belief that she was Charles's wife.
For an analysis of this letter, see Karl Schmid, "Heirat, Familienfolge,
Geschlechterbewusstsein," *Il matrimonio nella società altomedievale* (Setti-
mane di Studio del Centro Italiano di Studi sull'Alto Medioevo, 24;
Spoleto, 1977), pp. 112–114. For earlier interpretations, see S. Abel,
Jahrbücher des fränkischen Reiches unter Karl dem Grossen, 2d ed., B. Simson,
vol. 1 (Leipzig, 1888), 83; vol. 2 (Leipzig, 1883), 40, n. 1. Hellmann did
not include Himiltrud among Charles's legitimate wives. S. Hellmann,
"Die Heiraten der Karolinger," in his *Ausgewählte Abhandlungen zur His-
toriographie und Geistesgeschichte des Mittelalters,* ed. H. Beumann (Darm-
stadt, 1961), pp. 370–371. See also K. F. Werner, "Die Nachkommen
Karls des Grossen," in *Karl der Grosse: Lebenswerk und Nachleben,* vol. 4, ed.
W. Braunfels (Düsseldorf, 1967), 410, n. 14. E. Brandenburg challenged
the view that Pepin the Hunchback was treated as an illegitimate son in
Die Nachkommen Karls des Grossen (Genealogie und Landesgeschichte, ed.
H. F. Friedrichs, 10; Caroli Magni Progenies, 1; Leipzig, 1935; rpt.
Frankfurt, 1964).

24. *Codex Carolinus* 45 (*MGH Epist. 3, Kar. aevi* 1, 561–567; JE 2381). See also
notes 11 and 23 above.

25. Paschasius Radbertus, *Ex vita s. Adalhardi* 7 (*MGH Script.* 2, 525); trans.
A. Cabannis, *Charlemagne's Cousins* (Syracuse, 1967), p. 29. Another
source suggests that Charlemagne put the Lombard princess aside because she was bedridden and unable to bear a child. See the Monk of
Saint Gall (Notker the Stammerer), *De gestis Karoli Magni* 2. 17 (*MGH
Script.* 2, 759), trans. L. Thorpe, *Two Lives of Charlemagne,* Penguin classics (Baltimore, 1970), p. 162.

26. Werner, "Die Nachkommen," pp. 442–443, n. 1A, lists all these concubines with references.

27. Einhard, *Vita Caroli* 19 (*MGH Script.* 2, 454). H. Fichtenau, *The Carolingian
Empire,* trans. P. Munz (New York, 1964), pp. 42–43.

28. Werner, "Die Nachkommen," p. 444, n. 8.

29. Ibid., p. 444, n. 8. Werner cites the sources in support of Louis the Pious's paternity of Alpais (Elpheid), refuting R. Louis's thesis that she was Charlemagne's daughter. See René Louis, *Girart, comte de Vienne (819–877) et ses fondations monastiques* (Auxerre, 1946), pp. 14–16.

30. *Vita Hludowici* 1.8 (*MGH Script.* 2, 611); trans. A. Cabannis, *Son of Charlemagne: A Contemporary Life of Louis the Pious* (Syracuse, 1961), p. 39.

31. Nithard, *Historiarum* 2 (*MGH Script.* 2, 651); trans. B. W. Scholz, in *Carolingian Chronicles* (Ann Arbor, 1972), p. 130.

32. *Ordinatio imperii* (817) 15 (*MGH Capit.* 1, 273).

33. Jonas of Orléans, *De institutione laicali* 2.2 (*PL* 106, 171). Incorporating the distinction between legitimate and illegitimate children from Roman law (*Nov. Maiorani* 6.9; *Codex Theod.*, ed. Mommsen, vol. 2, 165–166), the *Cartae Senonicae* App. 1 (*MGH Form.* 28) permitted a man to leave his patrimony to his illegitimate children if he had no legitimate children. See also chapter 2, notes 51–53, and H. W. Klewitz, "Germanisches Erbe im fränkischen und deutschen Königtum," *Welt als Geschichte,* 7 (1941), 201–216.

34. *Salicae Merkelianae* 19 (from *Marc. Form.* 2.16); *Form. Salicae Lind.* 16 (*MGH Form.* 248, 277).

35. On Judith see *Vita Hludowici* 32.2; 37.2; 44.1–2; 52.1; 59.1–2; 61.3; 62.1; 63.2 (*MGH Script.* 2, 624–647); Cabannis, *Son of Charlemagne,* pp. 69, 77, 89–90, 102, 114–115, 119, 120, 123; *Annales Regni francorum* (819) (*MGH Script. rer. germ. in usum schol.* 150); Scholz, *Carolingian Chronicles,* p. 105; Nithard, *Historiarum,* 2, 3, 4 (*MGH Script.* 2, 651–652); Scholz, *Carolingian Chronicles,* pp. 130–131, 134; Paschasius Radbertus, *Vita Walae* 2.9, 21 (*MGH Script.* 2, 553–554; *PL* 120, 1643D–1644A); Thegan, *Vita Hludowici* 36 (*MGH Script.* 2, 597); *Annales Bertiniani* (830) (*MGH Script.* 1, 423); Agobard of Lyons, *Libri duo pro filiis et contra Judith uxorem Ludovici Pii* (*MGH Script.* 15, 274–279). Judith came from a wealthy family in Alamannia. Her father was Count Welf and her mother Heilwig (Eigilwi), a Saxon lady. She was less than twenty at the time of her marriage, while the emperor was twice her age. The worst charges against her were levied by Paschasius Radbertus and Agobard. Her own son, Charles the Bald, was apparently persuaded by the rumors; in 841 he attacked her purported lover Bernard and deprived her of all her fortune. She died at Tours in 841. Cabannis (*Son of Charlemagne,* p. 156) reported that a biography of Judith was being prepared as a dissertation at the University of Chicago by Mrs. Bernard Fischer. See also below, note 75.

36. *Conc. Parisiense* (829), 3.2 (*MGH Conc.* 2, 671; Mansi 14, 596). See also *Capit. pro lege habendum Worm.* 3 (*MGH Capit.* 2, 18), promulgated by Louis in the same year, and *Episcoporum ad Hludowicum imp. relatio* (829), 55 (*MGH Capit.* 2, 46). On the significance of the reforms of the four synods of 829, held at Toulouse, Mainz, Lyons, and Paris, see Barion, *Das fränkisch-deutsche Synodalrecht,* pp. 257–258.

37. According to P. Lauer, only after he was deposed in 833 was Louis urged

to forsake secular life (*Nithard: Histoire des fils de Louis le Pieux* [Les classiques de l'histoire de France au moyen age, 7; Paris, 1926], p. 11.)

38. *Vita Hludowici* 44 (*MGH Script.* 2, 633). She was called "an incestuous polluter of Pepin's father's bed." Cabannis, *Son of Charlemagne*, p. 89. Louis the Pious was Bernard's godfather, according to Thegan, *Vita Hludowici* 36 (*MGH Script.* 2, 597).

39. Jonas of Orléans, *De institutione laicali* 2.2 (*PL* 106, 170D): "Quidam laicorum amore libidinis superati . . . antequam ad copulam conubii accedant, diversissimis modis se corrumpunt." See also *De institutione laicali* (*PL* 106, 2.3, 4, 172, 177). *Episcoporum ad Hludowicum imp. relatio* (829), 54 (*MGH Capit.* 2, 45) warned married men "neque pellicem neque concubinam habere debeant."

40. Hrabanus Maurus, *Epistolae* 29 (*MGH Epist. 5, Kar. aevi* 3, 446–447).

41. The *meretrices* punished in Louis the Pious's *Capit. de disciplina palatii Aquisgranensis* (ca 820), 1, 3 and the woman referred to in the *Capit. Francica* 8 (*MGH Capit.* 1, 298, 334) were probably not professional prostitutes but women of questionable sexual conduct, namely, the concubines of court officials and servants. On this, see Leah L. Otis, "Nisi in Prostibulo: Prostitution in Languedoc from the Twelfth to the Sixteenth Century" (Ph.D. dissertation, Columbia University, 1980), pp. 19–21. Both the *Conc. Meld. Par.* (845–846), 78 and the *Conc. Mog.* (852), 14 (*MGH Capit.* 2, 419, 190), refrained from using disparaging terminology. The source of article 14 of the *Conc. Mog.* was *Conc. Tolet.* (400), 17 (Mansi 3, 1001).

42. *Conc. Meld. Par.* (845–846), 69 (*MGH Capit.* 2, 414–415) disregarded *Capit. ecclesiasticum* (818–819), 24 (*MGH Capit.* 1, 279), which addressed itself to the problem of the rape of a betrothed girl, citing the Council of Ancyra that the rapist must restore the girl to her fiancé and must undergo public penance, even if the girl had consented. The rapist and the girl could not marry under the pain of anathema, though she could marry her former fiancé if he agreed, or another man if she had not consented to the rape. *Capit. legibus addenda* 9 (*MGH Capit.* 1, 282), issued by Louis the Pious in 818 or 819, was more lenient with the rapist. It stipulated that he must pay the groom *(sponsus)* a *compositio* according to his law and sixty additional *solidi* to the king. If he refused payment, he could be exiled and could not keep the woman.

43. *Conc. Mog.* 10 (*MGH Capit.* 2, 189).

44. *Conc. Mog.* 12 (*MGH Capit.* 2, 189). See also note 41, above.

45. Fulrich was excommunicated by Hincmar. See Flodoard, *Historia ecclesiae Remensis* 3.10 (*MGH Script.* 13, 483); and P. Ewald, ed., "Die Papstbriefe der 'Brittischen Sammlung,'" *Neues Archiv,* 5 (1880), 385–386.

46. *Benedicti Capitularia* 3.463 (*MGH Leg.* 2, pars altera, 132); see also 3.179 (ibid., 113). For its sources, see E. Seckel and J. Juncker, "Studien zu Benedictus Levita," *ZSSR kan. Abt.,* 24 (1935), 40–61; J. Gaudemet, "Le legs du droit romain en matière matrimoniale," pp. 153–154. The same

passage was restated by Pseudo-Evaristus, *Epist.* 2 (*Decretales Pseudo-Isidorianae* ed. P. Hinschius [Leipzig, 1863], p. 87); in an abridged form, Herard of Tours, *Capitula* (Mansi 16, App. 677; *PL* 121, 770B), and Isaac of Langres, *Canones* 5, 6 (*PL* 124, 1094D–1095D). See also Ritzer, *Formen*, pp. 253, 273, and n. 467. Rudolf von Scherer discussed the broader problem of marriage in both sources in *Über das Eherecht bei Benedict Levita und Pseudo-Isidore* (Graz, 1879). The term *dotatio* in these texts referred to the bridegift provided or promised by the groom before the wedding. This seems to contradict Diana Hughes's thesis that the test of the validity of a marriage in the ninth century was the *morgengabe* ("From Brideprice to Dowry," p. 274). On the introduction of ecclesiastical benediction into the marriage ceremony, see C. Vogel, "Le rôle du liturge dans la formation du lien conjugal," *Revue de droit canonique*, 30 (1980), 7–27. For a systematic survey of papal decretals, Frankish conciliar legislation, and nuptial rites, see C. Vogel, "Les rites de celebration du mariage," pp. 420–437.

47. Hincmar, *De divortio* 4 (*PL* 125, 649A–B), from Pseudo-Evaristus, *Epist.* 2 (*Decretales Pseudo-Isidorianae*, p. 87). See also Hincmar, *De divortio* 21 (*PL* 125, 734B). Hincmar introduced consummation into the definition of marriage in the case of Stephen, a vassal of Charles the Bald. See his *Epist.* 22 (*PL* 126, 132C–153C). On Hincmar's views on marriage and divorce, see J. Gaudemet, "Indissolubilité et consommation du mariage, l'apport d'Hincmar de Reims," *Revue de droit canonique*, 30 (1980), 28–40.

48. Metz, *"La femme,"* 87.

49. Judith's eventful life has been treated by H. Sprömberg, "Judith, Königin von England, Gräfin von Flandern," *Revue belge d'histoire et de philologie*, 15 (1936), 397–428, 915–950. Even before she eloped with Baldwin, the twice-widowed Judith was the source of some embarrassment to her father. Married in 856, when she was only twelve, to the elderly King Aethelwulf of Wessex, Judith became a widow two years later, in 858. Instead of returning home, she then married Aethelwulf's son, Aethelbald; *Annales Bertiniani* (856), (858) (*MGH Script.* 1, 450–451). On her coronation and anointment in 856, see *Coronatio Iudithae* (*MGH Capit.* 2, 425–427), and Michael J. Enright, "Charles the Bald and Aethelwulf of Wessex," *Journal of Medieval History*, 5 (1979), 291–302. Her marriage to her stepson embarrassed her contemporaries, as is evident from the remark of Asser, Alfred the Great's biographer. Dorothy Whitelock analyzed the reaction to the marriage in England in *The Beginnings of English Society* (Hammondsworth, Middlesex, 1959), p. 150. She has included the passage from Asser in her *English Historical Documents, 500–1042* (London, 1955), p. 226. Whitelock's opinion that marriage to a stepson was Germanic practice has been rejected by Lorraine Lancaster, "Kinship in Anglo-Saxon Society," in *Early Medieval Society*, ed. Sylvia Thrupp (New York, 1967), p. 25. Although Germanic law did not pro-

hibit this type of marriage, canon law did. Disapproval in Frankish circles of Judith's second union is reflected in her retention in a monastery under the supervision of the bishop of Sens when she returned home after the death of Aethelbald. See *Annales Bertiniani* (862) (*MGH Script.* 1, 456): "sub tuitione paterna et regia atque episcopali custodia servabatur." See also note 53 to the text (*MGH Script.* 1, 451) for Ingulf's description of her second union as "scelus abhorrentium." On Judith's marriage to Baldwin, see *Annales Bertiniani* (862–863) (*MGH Script.* 1, 456, 462). See also Flodoard, *Historia ecclesiae Remensis* 3.12 (*MGII Script.* 13, 488–490; *PL* 135, 159); *Hludowici Karoli et Hlotharii II. Conventus apud Saponarias* (862), 5 (*MGH Capit.* 2, 160); and the letters of Pope Nicholas I, *Epist.* 7 to Charles the Bald, dated Nov. 862 (JE 2703); 8 to Judith's mother, dated Nov. 862 (JE 2704); 57 to the Synod of Soissons, dated April 863 (JE 2723); 60 to Charles the Bald, dated April 863 (JE 2722) in *MGH Epist.* 6; *Kar. aevi* 4, 272, 274, 360–361, 369. Hincmar explained in a letter to Nicholas, *Epistolae* 2 (*PL* 126, 26A; JE 2741), that in his opinion the couple had to perform penance before they could contract a legitimate marriage: "sic nobis secundum sacras regulas . . . visum fuerat . . . ut . . . prius . . . Ecclesiae quam laeserant satisfacerent, et sic demum quod praecipiunt jura legum mundalium exsequi procurarent." But overruled by the pope, Hincmar capitulated and accepted the legality of Judith's and Baldwin's union on the ground that the king "secundum leges saeculi eos uxoria conjunctione ad invicem copulari permisit."

50. Ninth-century marriage contracts make it clear that the union was concluded with the consent of both sets of parents: "utraque ex parte parentum nostrorum." *Form. Aug. B.* 24; *Form. Sangallenses miscellaneae* 18 (*MGH Form.* 357–358, 388). When asking for an annulment of his marriage on the ground of nonconsummation, Stephen testified that his betrothal had been concluded according to normal procedures, which included "consensu parentum et amicorum meorum." Hincmar, *Epist.* 22 (*PL* 126, 133). Louis the Pious married Ermengard "cum consilio et consensu patris," according to Thegan, *Vita Hludowici* 4 (*MGH Script.* 2, 591). The *Ordinatio imperii* (817), 13 (*MGH Capit.* 1, 272), issued by Louis the Pious, specified that, if he should die, his sons were to marry "cum consilio et consensu" of their senior brother. Louis personally made arrangements for the marriage of Pepin to the daughter of Count Theotbert; see *Vita Hludowici* 35 (*MGH Script.* 2, 626). Charles the Bald personally betrothed the daughter of the duke of Brittany to Louis the Stammerer; see *Annales Bertiniani* (856) (*MGH Script.* 1, 449).

51. He was persuaded to marry her by Count Stephen of Auvergne, according to the *Annales Bertiniani* (862) (*MGH Script.* 1, 457). See also Werner, "Die Nachkommen," p. 453, n. 35, and the genealogical table. Pope Nicholas's attempt to intercede on behalf of the younger Charles failed to move Charles the Bald: *Epistolae* 9 (*MGH Epist.* 6, *kar aevi* 4, 275; Mansi 15, 458; JE 2705). See also G. Eiten, *Das Unterkönigtum im Reiche*

der Merovinger und Karolinger (Heidelberger Abhandlungen, 18; Heidelberg, 1907), pp. 172–173.

52. A great deal has been written about Hincmar's silence when Louis the Stammerer repudiated his first wife, Ansgard, and married Adelheid. The documentation relating to Hincmar's reaction to the Stammerer's two unions has been assembled by Carl Richard Brühl, "Hinkmariana II: Hinkmar im Widerstreit von kanonischen Recht und Politik in Ehefragen," *Deutsches Archiv,* 20 (1964), 55–77; K. F. Werner, "Die Nachkommen," pp. 429–453; and E. Hlawitschka, *Lotharingien,* pp. 221–240. Their conclusion that Hincmar set aside canon law in this case may be modified by interpreting Hincmar's silence as a consequence of the stand he took on parental consent. In 862, Hincmar supported Charles the Bald's efforts to have the unions of his three children dissolved because each was concluded without his consent. Judith eloped with Baldwin, the Stammerer married Ansgard, and the younger Charles married the widow of Count Humbert. Charles the Bald pressed charges of abduction against Baldwin, but with his sons he relied on threats and persuasion. When Pope Nicholas overruled Hincmar, Charles the Bald yielded in the case of Judith and Baldwin, disregarding Hincmar's pleas that the couple should at least perform penance before they were recognized as husband and wife. Offended by the king's decision, Hincmar remained aloof when Charles the Bald pursued the dissolution of the unions of his two sons. The necessity of parental consent, a principle deeply rooted in secular custom, was eventually introduced into canon law and prevailed until the mid-twelfth century when Roland Bandinelli, the future Pope Alexander III, gave support to the idea that had been voiced by Pope Nicholas, namely, parental consent was not necessary for a valid marriage. See R. Metz, "La protection de la liberté des mineurs dans le droit matrimoniale de l'Église," *Acta Congressus internationalis juris canonici, Romae Pontif. Univ. Gregor., 25–30 Sept. 1950* (Rome, 1953), pp. 170–183. Jean-Louis Flandrin analyzes the tension between the church and the state that resulted from the former's position that marriages contracted without parental consent were valid in *Families in Former Times: Kinship, Household and Sexuality,* trans. Richard Southern (Cambridge, 1978), pp. 130–133.

53. Daudet (*Études,* p. 95), gave 855 as the date of Lothar's marriage; C. E. Smith (*Papal Enforcement of Some Medieval Marriage Laws* [Louisiana State University, 1940], p. 55), accepted the date 857. The date 857 is taken from Regino of Prüm's *Chronicon* (*MGH Script.* 1, 571), which is not as reliable as Hincmar's *De divortio* (*PL* 125, 619–772), the source used by Daudet. Smith failed to consult the two basic studies on the affair: Max Sdralek, *Hinkmar von Rheims kanonistisches Gutachten über die Ehescheidung des Königs Lothar II* (Freiburg i.B., 1881), and R. Parisot, *Le Royaume de Lorraine sous les Carolingiens, 843–923* (Paris, 1889), pp. 83–88, 143–324. More recently, the case engaged the attention of Brühl, "Hinkmariana II," pp. 55–77, and Joseph Prinz, "Ein unbekanntes Aktenstück zum

Ehestreit König Lothars II," *Deutsches Archiv,* 21 (1965), 249–263. On Waldrada's family, see F. Vollmer, "Die Etichonen," *Studien und Vorarbeiten zur Geschichte des grossfränkischen und frühdeutschen Adels,* ed. G. Tellenbach (Forschungen zur oberrheinischen Landesgeschichte, 4; Freiburg i.B., 1957), p. 176, n. 291; and E. Hlawitschka, *Lotharingien,* pp. 17–18. According to Werner ("Die Nachkommen," p. 450, n. 10), she died a nun at Remiremont in 868. See also notes 62 and 99, below.

54. See above, note 19.

55. Hincmar, *De divortio* praef. (*PL.* 125, 629C-D); *Annales Bertiniani* (858) (*MGH Script.* 1, 450).

56. Hincmar, *De divortio* 1 (*PL* 125, 630C–641D). For records of the two synods held in 860, see also *Synodus Aquensis I* (Ian.) and *Synodus Aquensis II* (Febr.) (*MGH Capit.* 2, 463–468), and *Hlotharii II Capitulare* (*MGH Leg.* 1, 467–468). The case can also be followed through the correspondence of Pope Nicholas (listed in note 58, below). In addition to Hincmar's treatise, two others are extant (Mansi, 15, 625–639); both are attributed by Sdralek to Adventius, bishop of Metz. According to E. Dümmler, two other bishops, Arnulf of Toul and Hogue of Utrecht, also wrote a treatise against the dissolution of the marriage (*Geschichte des ostfränkischen Reiches,* vol. 1 [Berlin, 1862], p. 476, n. 36). Dümmler may have had in mind the treatise submitted to the council held at Aix in 862 (Mansi, 15, 617–625).

57. *De divortio* (*PL* 125, 645A): "Vir autem et mulier . . . separari non possunt . . . nisi manifesta fornicationis causa. Et separati aut ita maneant, aut mutuo reconcilientur." See also *PL* 125, 644A and 655C.

58. *Epistolae* 16 (*MGH Epist.* 6, *Kar. aevi* 4, 330). For other letters by Nicholas on the subject of Lothar's divorce, see his *Epistolae,* 3, 5, 6, 10, 11, 16, 18, 19–21 (copies of 18), 22, 23–24, (indirect fragments), 25–26, 29–32, 35–39, 42, 44 (indirect), 45–49, 51, 52 (indirect), 53 (*MGH Epist.* 6; *Kar. aevi* 4, 268–351).

59. *Conc. Aquis.* (863), 3 (Mansi 15, 611–625).

60. The Synod of Metz was condemned for violation of the orders of the Apostolic See, and its acts were annulled "just like the robber synod of Ephesus." The pope reported these acts in a long series of letters to Charles the Bald, Louis the German, and the Frankish, German, and Lotharingian bishops. *Annales Bertiniani* (863) (*MGH Script.* 1, 460–461; JE 2747–2751).

61. See *Relatio de Theutbergae receptione scripta* (865) (*MGH Capit.* 2, 468–469). Nicholas I, *Epistolae* 45–49 (*MGH Epist.* 6, *Kar. aevi* 4, 319–334; JE 2870–2874).

62. *Annales Bertiniani* (868–869) (*MGH Script.* 1, 477, 482); Regino of Prüm, *Chronicon* (869) (*MGH Script.* 1, 581). Werner ("Die Nachkommen," Table) dates Waldrada's death April 9, 868. But Hincmar's comments for 869 imply that Lothar was still hoping for the permission to marry her (*Annales Bertiniani* [869] [*MGH Script.* 1, 481]).

63. *Vita s. Deicoli* 38 (*AS* 18 Jan.; 2, 572) and *Regesta Alsatiae aevi Merovingici et Karolini* 558, ed. A. Bruckner, vol. 1, (Strassbourg, 1949), 346.

64. She was first excommunicated by a synod held at Milan in 856, whose sentence was communicated to kings, bishops, and counts by Pope Anastasius (Mansi 15, 334, 384; JE 2673); for the second time by Anti-Pope Nicholas in the Roman synod of 863, c. 4 (Mansi 15, 651; JE 2747). Nicholas wrote to Hincmar and Charles the Bald in 860, to Ado of Vienne in 863, and to Louis the German in 867. *Epistolae* 1, 2, 18, 49 (*MGH Epist.* 6, *kar. aevi* 4, 267–268, 286, 333; JF 2684, 2685, 2750, 2874). Hincmar mentioned her case in *De divortio* (*PL* 125, 754–756), in a letter to Günther, *Epistolae* 24 (*PL* 126, 154–161), and in *Annales Bertiniani* (863), (865) (*MGH Script.* 1, 461, 469). See also *Annales Fuldenses* 4 (*MGH Script.* 4, 376–377); Regino of Prüm, *Chronicon* (866) (*MGH Script.* 1, 573), and *Conv. apud Saponarias* 4 (*MGH Capit.* 2, 160). For a summary of her case, see C. de Clercq, *La législation*, vol. 2, pp. 235–249 in passím, 252–262. She had two daughters by Boso and a son, Gottfried, by Wanger. On her children, see John VIII, *Epistolae,* 111, 129, 130 (*MGH Epist.* 7, *Kar. aevi* 5, 102, 114, 115); E. Dümmler, *Geschichte des ostfränkischen Reiches,* vol. 1, 459–460; E. Hlawitschka, *Franken, Alemannen, Bayern und Burgunder in Oberitalien (774–962)* (Forschungen zur oberrheinischen Landesgeschichte, 8; Freiburg i. B., 1960), pp. 158–162.

65. *Conc. Trib.* (895), 38, 39 (*MGH Capit.* 2, 235, 236).

66. *Conc. Trib.* (895), 41–48 (*MGH Capit.* 2, 237–240).

67. *Conc. Duziacense* (874) (Mansi 17A, 282–288).

68. *Conc. Colon.* (887), 6 (Mansi 18, 48) ordered separation of the couple in the case of endogamous unions; *Conc. Mog.* (888), 18 (Mansi 18, 69) ordered separation of couples related through spiritual bonds; *Conc. Met.* (888), 11 (Mansi 18, 80–81) dealt with cases involving abduction and incest.

69. Christianus Druthmarus, *Expositio in Mattheum* 62 (*PL* 106, 1413–1414): "sive sit gulosa, sive sit rixosa, sive infirma, tenenda est usque ad diem mortis, nisi ex consensu amborum relinquant saeculum. Quapropter antequam accipiat uxorem homo debet eam cognoscere in moribus et in sanitate, et non debet subito facere quod diu habet dolore. Sed si omnia facienda sunt cum consilio, istud amplius, quia seipsum traditurus est. . . . Quamvis multi septem causas considerent in accipiendis uxoribus, id est, generositatem, divitias, formam, sanitatem, sapientiam, mores, tamen duo amplius quaerenda sunt, sapientia et mores, quia si ista duo defuerint possunt alia deperire. Vidimus enim quasdam et nobiliter natas, et ditatas, ad tantam inopiam pervenisse propter incontinentiam morum, ut mendicando vitam finirent. Multas vero audivimus ob fornicationis malum occisas. Et e contrario alias, ignobilius natas, de paupertate ad divitias pervenisse propter suam sapientiam et morum continentiam."

70. Hincmar, *De divortio* (*PL* 125, 656): "Quid enim si temulenta fuerit, si

iracunda, si malis moribus, si luxuriosa, si gulosa, si vaga, si jurgatrix, et maledica, tenenda erit istiusmodi? Volumus, nolumus, tenenda erit." Paraphrased from Isidore of Seville, *De ecclesiasticis officiis* 2.12 (*PL* 83, 813B); Hincmar omitted: "si sterilis sit, si deformis, si aetate vetula, si fetida . . . si fatua . . ."

71. Sedulius Scottus, *De rectoribus christianis* 5 (*PL* 103, 300): "Is ergo perspicaciter procuret, ut non solum nobilem, pulchram ac divitem, sed et castam, prudentem quoque atque in sanctis virtutibus morigeram habeat coniugem." Inspired by *Proverbia graecorum*, in *Sedulius Scottus*, ed. S. Hellmann (Munich, 1960), and Cassiodorus, *Historia tripartita* 9.31 (*PL* 69, 1147–1148). Jonas of Orléans rated the qualities of a marriageable woman in the following order: "family, prudence, wealth, and beauty." *De institutione laicali* 2.12 (*PL* 106, 188D–189A); see also 2.5 (ibid., 179B).

72. *Ordinatio imperii* (817), 13 (*MGH Capit.* 1, 272): "de exteris gentibus nullus illorum uxorem accipere praesumat. Omnium vero homines propter pacem artius conligandam, ubicumque inter partes elegerint, uxores ducant."

73. Georges Tessier attributed to Charlemagne eleven female companions in *Charlemagne* (Paris, 1967), pp. 57–58. K. F. Werner identified only ten: "Die Nachkommen," Table. On Charlemagne's marriages, see also above, notes 23–25. On Fastrada, see Pierre Riché, *Daily Life in the World of Charlemagne*, trans. JoAnn McNamara (Philadelphia, 1978), p. 61.

74. On Ermengard, see Thegan, *Vita Hludowici* 4 (*MGH Script.* 2, 591). On Louis's mistress, see Werner, "Die Nachkommen," pp. 442–443, n. 6A; on her family, see Werner, "Bedeutende Adelsfamilien," p. 119.

75. On Judith's family, see J. Fleckenstein, "Über die Herkunft der Welfen," in *Studien und Vorarbeiten, zur Geschichte des grossfränkischen und frühdeutschen Adels,* ed. G. Tellenbach (Freiburg i.B, 1957), pp. 7–136; and above, note 35. A description of how a basileus selected his bride is found in the *Life of St. Philaret,* according to Charles Diehl, *Byzantine Empresses,* trans. H. Bell and Th. de Kerpely (London, 1959), p. 80; and René Guerdan, *Byzantium,* trans. D. I. B. Hartley (New York, 1962), pp. 34–35.

76. On Ermengard's family, see F. Vollmer, "Die Etichonen," pp. 137–184, and the genealogical sketch by G. Tellenbach, "Der grossfränkische Adel und die Regierung Italiens in der Blütezeit des Karolingerreiches," p. 57.

77. On Ringart, see Werner, "Die Nachkommen," p. 446, n. 11.

78. On the Welfs, see Fleckenstein, "Über die Herkunft der Welfen."

79. On Waldrada, see Vollmer, "Die Etichonen"; Werner, "Die Nachkommen," p. 450, n. 10; and note 99 below. On Theutberga's family, the Bosonids, see Tellenbach, "Der grossfränkische Adel und die Regierung Italiens," p. 63, and E. Hlawitschka, *Franken, Alemannen,* pp. 159–161.

80. See notes 51–52, above.

81. Ekkerhard IV, *Casuum s. Galli* 2 (*MGH Script.* 2, 92): "Eius generis prosa-
piae nec de matre nec de patre sum . . . ut virginitatem meam me cuidam,
vel ipsi regi quidem, deceat prostituere."

82. *Annales Bertiniani* (865) (*MGH Script.* 1, 470): "cujus filius et aequivocus
contra patris voluntatem filiam Adalardi despondit, unde satis animum
patris offendit." Charles the Bald reconciled father and son on the
condition that the young prince "iam ultra Adalardi filiae non copule-
tur." According to Werner, Louis III's illegitimate son, Hugo, was not
borne by Adalard's daughter but by a concubine: "Die Nachkommen,"
p. 451, n. 21. Louis's brothers also entered into unions that were not
legalized. Carloman's mistress, Liutswind, the mother of Arnulf, was of
noble birth, according to Regino, *Chronicon* (880) (*MGH Script.* 1, 591).
Charles III, the Fat, also had an illegitimate son, Bernhard, by an unknown concubine: Werner, "Die Nachkommen," p. 451, n. 23.

83. On Ermentrud, see Nithard, *Historiarum* 4.6 (*MGH Script.* 2, 671–672);
Nithard was critical of Adalard and hence also of the marriage. He noted
that Adalard "cared little for the public good. Again and again he advised Charles's father to distribute liberties and public property for
private use and . . . he ruined the kingdom altogether." Scholz, *Carolingian Chronicles*, p. 173. Nithard also added that Charles married Ermentrud because he believed that, with Adalard's help, he could win over
a large part of the people to himself. On Adalard, see Ferdinand Lot,
"Note sur le sénéchal Alard," *Le Moyen Age*, 21 (1908), 185–201; K. F.
Werner, "Untersuchungen zur Frühzeit des französischen Fürstentums," *Die Welt als Geschichte*, 18 (1958), 256–289; ibid., 19 (1959), 146-
193; esp. 272–275.

84. *Annales Bertiniani* (869) (*MGH Script.* 1, 486): "Carolus in villa Duciaco 7.
Idus Octobris certo comperiens, obisse Hirmentrudem uxorem suam. 2.
Non. Octobris in monasterio sancti Dionysii, ubi et sepulta est, ex-
equente Bosone, filio Buvini quondam comitis, hoc missaticum apud
matrem et materteram suam Theutbergam, Lotharii regis relictam,
sororem ipsius Bosonis nomine Richildem mox sibi adduci fecit et in
concubinam accepit; qua de re eidem Bosoni abbatiam sancti Mauritii
cum aliis honoribus dedit." *Annales Bertiniani* (870) (ibid., 486): "Et in
die festivitatis septuagesimae, praedictam concubinam suam Richildem
desponsatam atque dotatam in coniugem sumpsit."

85. *Annales Bertiniani* (876) (*MGH Script.* 1, 499): "Boso . . . filiam Hludowici
imperatoris, Hirmengardem . . . iniquo conludio in matrimonium sumpsit." Two years later (878) Boso persuaded Louis the Stammerer to
betroth his son Carloman to Boso's infant daughter (ibid., 508), but the
marriage never took place. On Boso, see W. Mohr, "Boso von Vienne
und die Nachfolgefrage nach dem Tode Karls d. K. und Ludwigs d. St.,"
Bulletin Du Cange; Arch. lat. med. aevi, 26 (1956), 141–165; and Hlawitschka, *Lotharingien*, p. 27. On the lineage of his mother, Richild, see Hlawitschka, *Franken, Alemannen*, pp. 47–73.

86. For example, in 846, Giselbert, a vassal of Charles the Bald, abducted the

daughter of Lothar I, and escaped with her to Aquitaine, where he married her. See *Annales Fuldenses* (846) (*MGH Script.* 1, 364). Hellmann remarked that the marriage was never recognized by the imperial family ("Die Heiraten," in his *Ausgewählte Abhandlungen,* p. 325, n. 1). Werner claims that the marriage was legitimized in 848 and that the couple had two sons, Giselbert and Reginar in "Die Nachkommen," p. 449, n. 8.

87. On Bernard of Plantevelue, see L. Auzias, "Bernard 'Le Veau' et Bernard 'Plantevelue,' " *Annales du Midi,* 44 (1932), 257–295, and J. Dhondth, "Le Problème des Bernards," in his *Études sur la naissance des principautés territoriales en France* (Brugge, 1948), pp. 293–314. Dhondth defended Auzias's identification of Bernard of Plantevelue against J. Calmette's arguments in *L'Effondrement d'un empire et la naissance d'une Europe* (Paris, 1941), pp. 134–138. See also L. Levillain, "De quelques personnages nommés Bernard . . ." in *Mélanges dédiés à la mémoir de Félix Grat,* vol. 1, (Paris, 1946), pp. 169–202, and Ferdinand Lot, "Études carolingiennes. Les comtes d'Auvergne . . . Les comtes d'Autun . . ." *Bibliothèque de l'École des Chartes,* 102 (1941), 282–291. William's wife Engelberga/Angilberga was probably the daughter whom Boso had pledged in 878 to Carloman. Carloman died in 884, when Engelberga was not more than eight years old; see above, note 85.

88. G. Tellenbach, *Königtum und Stämme in der Werdezeit des deutschen Reiches* (Quellen und Studien zur Verfassungsgeschichte des deutschen Reiches, 7, 4; Weimar, 1939), p. 56; cited in Dhondth, *Études,* p. 4.

89. In addition to the studies collected by Tellenbach in his *Studien und Vorarbeiten,* special mention should be made of the monographs of Hlawitschka: *Lotharingien* (1968); *Franken, Alemannen* (1960); *Die Anfänge des Hauses Habsburg-Lotharingen* (Saarbrücken, 1969). See also M. Mitterauer, *Karolingische Markgrafen im Südosten* (Vienna, 1963), and Werner, "Untersuchungen." Karl Brunner, *Oppositionelle Gruppen im Karolingerreich* (Veröffentlichungen des Instituts für Österreichische Geschichtsforschung, 25; Vienna, 1979), provides valuable genealogical information that will facilitate further study on medieval marriage patterns. It came to my attention after this book had gone to press.

90. Child marriages and marriages with great age differences between the parties were discouraged by Charlemagne, but his legislation was not reiterated by later Carolingians. *Capitula e conciliorum canonibus collecta,* 1 (*MGH Capit.* 1, 232); "nullus presummat ante annos pubertatis . . . puerum vel puellam in matrimonium sociare, nec in dissimili aetate, sed coaetaneos sibique consencientes." The only example of a younger boy married to an older woman that I found was that of Charles of Acquitaine (see above, n. 51), but that marriage was declared invalid.

91. R. Louis's remarks on Hugo's daughters, in his *Girart, comte de Vienne (819–877) et ses fondations monastiques,* must be supplemented by F. Vollmer's account of the Eticho clan ("Die Etichonen," pp. 163–171), and K. F. Werner's remarks on Bertha's brother-in-law, the seneschal Adalard ("Untersuchungen," pp. 154–156).

92. Aldhelm, *De sancta Opportuna* 1 (*AS* 22 Aprilii; 3, 63): "multi praepotentes viri, divitiis et varibus opibus referti, in matrimonium eam sibi conjungere satagebant. Promittebant ei auri et argenti immensa pondera, demonstrabant delectabilia mulierum ornamenta, gemmis et margaritis radiantia; offerebant servos et ancillas, et diversae facultatis praedia."

93. See Eckhard's testament in *Recueil des chartes de l'Abbaye de Saint-Benoît-sur-Loire* 25, ed. M. Prou and A. Vidier, vol. 1 (Paris, 1900), pp. 59–67.

94. Prudentius, *Vita s. Maurae virginis* 3 (*AS* 21 Sept. 6, 275): "Nihil secum frater Eutropius in conversione sua de rebus paternis attulit, ea unicae sorori suae ea intentione habendas relinquens, ut, ipsis mediantibus, nobiliores subiret thalamos."

95. Hincmar of Reims, *De divortio* (*PL* 125, 715): "ad nos saepe feminae veniunt, reclamantes quod juvenculi eis suam fidem promiserint, easque derisas reliquerint."

96. *Conc. Aquis.* (862) (Mansi 15, 625): "ut de mulieribus taceam, rarus ut nullus est vir qui cum uxore virgo conveniat."

97. Jonas of Orléans, *De institutione laicali* 2.2 (*PL* 106, 170D): "Quidam laicorum amore libidinis superati, quidam vero ambiendi honoris terreni cupiditate ducti, imo praestolandi tempus quo honores mundi nancisci valeant, interim in coeno luxuriae se volutantes, antequam ad copulam connubii accedant, diversissimis modis se corrumpunt." (Ibid., 172C): "summopere studendum est conjugii copulam adeuntibus, ut nec clanculo cum meretricibus, nec palam cum ancillulis, antequam uxorio vinculo se innectant, corrumpantur." The terms *meretrix* and *scorta* were used rather vaguely, referring to all so-called loose women, including actresses. Benedict III, *Epistola ad quendam Hucberti* (857) (*MGH Epist.* 5, *Kar. aevi* 3, 613): "cum scenicis mulieribus cotidie degere non dubitet, quae animas perdunt."

98. The case is discussed at length by Hincmar, *Epist.* 22 (*PL* 126, 132–153).

99. Her name was entered in the *Liber memorialis von Remiremont* (*MGH Libri mem.* 1, 24). See also *Vita s. Deicoli* 38 (*AS* 18 Jan.; 2, 572).

100. Regino, *Chronicon* (883) (*MGH Script.* 1, 594): "Bernarium nobilem virum sibique fidelissimum dolo trucidari iussit, pulchritudine illius captus uxoris, quam absque momento sibi in matrimonium iungit." Friderada's illegitimate daughter by Angilram (count of Flanders and chamberlain of Charles the Bald), was given in marriage to Count Richwin, who beheaded her because of her suspected adultery.

101. Hincmar, *De divortio* 15 (*PL* 125, 716C): "quia sunt feminae quae maleficio suo inter virum et uxorem odium irreconciliabile possint mittere, et inenarrabilem amorem iterum inter virum et feminam serere." He also describes the means used to achieve this effect (ibid., 717B-D).

102. *Cartae Senonicae* 22 (*MGH Form.* 194–195). See also F. Merzbacher, *Die Hexenprozesse in Franken,* 2d ed. (Munich, 1970).

103. Paschasius Radbertus, *Vita Walae* 2.9 (*MGH Script.* 2, 553–554). Judith's son, Charles the Bald, in dealing with witchcraft in his *Capit. Carisiacense* (873) 7 (*MGH Capit.* 2, 345), seems to have made a point of referring

to both men and women: "malefici homines" and "sortiariae."

104. *Annales Bertiniani* (834) (*MGH Script.* 1, 428): "Lotharius sororem Bernardi sanctimonialem in cupa positam, in Ararim fluvium demergi fecit." See also Thegan, *Vita Hludowici* 52 (*MGH Script.* 2, 601).

105. Jean-Louis Flandrin also characterizes marriage among the bourgeoisie in these terms in *Families in Former Times*, p. 181.

106. Although the church continued to disparage concubines as fallen women, it tolerated concubinage among the laity until the sixteenth century. For a perceptive sketch, see Jean-Louis Flandrin, *Families in Former Times*, pp. 180–184.

CHAPTER 5

1. *Annales Bertiniani* (866) (*MGH Script.* 1, 472): "Carolus eos petit, ut uxorem suam Hirmintrudem in reginam sacrarent, quod et ipso attestante in basilica sancti Medardi fecerunt, ut una cum eo illi coronam imposuerunt." See also P. E. Schramm, "Die Krönung bei den Westfranken und Angelsachsen von 878 bis um 1000," *ZSSR kan. Abt.*, 23 (1934), 117–242; Ritzer, *Formen*, pp. 256–257 and nn. 405–409; and P. Krull, *Die Salbung und Krönung der deutschen Königinnen und Kaiserinnen im Mittelalter* (Halle, 1911). On the incorporation of their names into the litany, see Ernst Kantorowicz, *Laudes regiae* (Berkeley, 1946). On their titles, see Thilo Vogelsang, *Die Frau als Herrscherin im hohen Mittelalter* (Frankfurt, 1954).

2. Einhard, *Vita Caroli* 18–19 (*MGH Script.* 2, 453–454).

3. *Capit. de villis* 16 (*MGH Capit.* 1, 84): "Voluimus ut quicquid nos aut regina unicuique iudici ordinaverimus aut ministeriales nostri sinescalcus et butticularius, de verbo nostro aut reginae ipsis iudicibus ordinaverit ad eundem placitum sicut eis institutum fuerit impletum habeant." See also articles 27 and 47 (*MGH Capit.* 1, 85, 87).

4. Hincmar, *De ordine palatii* 22 (*MGH Capit.* 2, 525). In his *Ad proceres* 13 (*PL* 125, 998D), Hincmar stressed that the king, with the queen and his sons, ruled through the ministers in spiritual and secular matters. Agobard of Lyons, some years earlier, wrote that Louis the Pious sought in his second wife, Judith, an "adiutrix in regimine et gubernatione palacii et regni," and proceeded to criticize Judith on the ground that, because she could not rule herself, she was incapable of caring for the palace and governing the kingdom. *Libri duo pro filiis et contra Judith uxorem Ludovici Pii* (*MGH Script.* 15, 275–277).

5. On the participation of queens at the side of their husbands in assemblies, see Brühl, *Fodrum*, pp. 67–69.

6. *Vita Hludowici* 31 (*MGH Script.* 2, 623); Thegan, *Vita Hludowici* 25 (*MGH Script.* 2, 596).

7. Dhuada, *Manuel pour mon fils/Dhuoda; introduction, texte critique, notes* 10.4, ed. Pierre Riché (Sources chrétiennes 225; Paris 1975), pp. 350–352: "Pro

utilitatibus domini et senioris mei Bernardi, ut meum erga illum in Marchis uel in multis locis, non uilesceret seruitium, nec a te uel a me se separasset." According to Riché, she finished the work in 843, the year before her husband was killed (ibid., p. 20). E. Bondurand argued that she began writing it shortly after the birth of her second son, Bernard, in 841. See Dhuoda, *Le Manuel de Dhuoda,* ed. E. Bondurand (Paris, 1887), p. 19. For a brief overlook, see Peter Dronke, *Women Writers of the Middle Ages* (Cambridge, London, New York, 1984), pp. 36–54.

8. *Capit. missorum de exercitu promovendo* (808), 4 (*MGH Capit.* 1, 137).

9. *Vita s. Liutbirgae* 1–7 (*MGH Script.* 4, 158–160). On the date of its composition, see Johanna Heineken, *Die Anfänge der sächsischen Frauenkloster* (Göttingen, 1909). See also *Vita Liutbirgae virginis (Das Leben der Liutbirg),* ed. O. Menzel (*MGH* Deutsches Mittelalter; kritische Studien des Reichsinstituts für ältere deutsche Geschichtskunde, 3; Leipzig, 1937); and W. Grosse, "Das Kloster Wendhausen, sein Stiftergeschlecht und seine Klausnerin," *Sachsen und Anhalt,* 16 (1940), 45–76. On Gisla's ancestors, husband, and children, see R. Wenskus, *Sächsischer Stammesadel und fränkischer Reichsadel* (Abhandlungen der Akademie der Wissenschaften in Göttingen, philol.-histor. Klasse, 3rd Ser., 93; Göttingen, 1976), pp. 178–179.

10. *Vita antiquior s. Glodesindis* 1 (*AS* 25 Iulii; 6, 203).

11. Both Pepin and Charlemagne prohibited the marriage of girls and boys before the age of puberty (see above, chapter 4, note 90). Pepin's and Charles's legislation probably referred to girls under twelve because, in the royal family, girls were regarded as nubile at age twelve. For example, Judith, the daughter of Charles the Bald, was twelve when she married Aethelwulf in 856 (see above, chapter 4, note 49). M. K. Hopkins ("The Age," pp. 310–313) cautions the reader that the opinion of ancient and late classical authors on the age of menarche probably reflected the experience of upper-class women. Hopkins accepts, nonetheless, their conclusion, as representative of "informed" opinion, that menarche occurred usually at thirteen or above. J. B. Post suggests that the age of menarche in the Middle Ages was similar to that of the twentieth century; menstruation normally appeared between the ages of twelve and fourteen ("Ages at Menarche and Menopause, Some Medieval Authorities," *Population Studies,* 25 [1971], 83–87). Girls were thought to mature earlier than boys, which may explain why girls married earlier. According to the so-called Pseudo-Egbert, *Poenitentiale* 1. 27 (*PL* 89, 408), girls matured at thirteen or fourteen, boys at fifteen. Peasant girls may have married somewhat later. Among peasants, boys and girls were believed to reach the age of marriage around the same time, at age fifteen. At this age, they came to be identified as *baccularius* and *baccularia* in the survey of serfs of Saint Victor of Marseilles, redacted probably between 813 and 814; on this see Herlihy, "Life Expectancies for Women," p. 5.

12. Einhard, *Vita Caroli* 19 (*MGH Script.* 2, 453–454). Although both boys and

girls in the royal family received instruction in reading and writing, their
education in practical matters differed; girls were taught spinning and
weaving, while boys were instructed in warfare.

13. *Vita s. Liutbirgae* 22, 35 (*MGH Script.* 4, 163, 164).

14. As Noonan has shown, the penitentials included condemnations of various
forms of contraception. *Contraception,* pp. 179–210.

15. *Vita Hludowici* Prol. (*MGH Script.* 2, 607). "Ademar . . . being of the same
age, was suckled with Louis" (Cabannis, *Son of Charlemagne,* p. 31). The
efficacy of breast-feeding as a form of contraception, an ancient belief
transmitted orally by mothers to daughters in European societies, is
questioned by doctors today. But Flandrin cites evidence from demographic sources on the prolongation of the sterile period, which always
follows confinement, in the case of nursing mothers. *Families in Former
Times,* pp. 198–203.

16. For biographical information on Carolingian queens, see the Table
in Werner, "Die Nachkommen," and Hellmann, "Die Heiraten der
Karolinger."

17. The ninth-century biographer of Herlinda and Renilda reports that the
girls were "secundum seculi dignitatem cum summa diligentia sub nu-
tricibus educatis." *Vita ss. Herlindis et Reinulae sive Reinildae* 3 (*AS* 22
Martii; 3, 384).

18. Sedulius Scottus, *Liber de rectoribus,* ed. Siegmund Hellmann (Quellen und
Untersuchungen zur lateinischen Philologie des Mittelalters, 1; Munich,
1906), p. 35.

19. *Vita Sadalbergae* 12 (*MGH Script. rer. mer.* 5, 56); *Vita s. Waldetrudis* 4–5 (*Acta
sanctorum Belgii selecta* 4, 441).

20. Caesarius, *Regula ad virgines* 5 and Donatus, *Regula* 6 stipulated six or seven
as the minimum age (Holstenius 1, 356, 380). When a child was presented as an oblate, the mother brought him or her to the altar, thus
symbolically expressing the relinquishment to God and the community
of her responsibility of raising the child; see, for example, *Cartulaire de
l'Abbaye de Redon* 266, ed. M. Aurélien de Courson (Collections de documents inedits, ser. 2,6; Paris, 1863), where the father makes the arrangements for his second son to become an oblate even though the mother
brings and presents the child. For children, even boys, following their
mother into a nunnery, see *De virtutibus s. Geretrudis* 11 (*MGH Script. rer.
mer.* 2, 469).

21. *Conc. Mog.* (888) 23 (Mansi 18, 70). This represented a compromise between the Salic and Ripuarian Codes. The *legitima aetas* of a boy was
fifteen under Salic law and twelve under Ripuarian law; see Ewig,
"Studien," pp. 17–24. On the education young people received in Charlemagne's court, see above note 12.

22. The distinction between an "infans" and a "puer" was drawn at age seven.
Ewig, "Studien," p. 29. On the age of oblates, see above, note 20. In
the twelfth century, vocational training began later, around age twelve.
Mary M. McLaughlin, "Survivors and Surrogates," p. 110.

23. *Capit. missorum* (786 or 792), 4 (*MGH Capit.* 1, 61).

24. Pepin's and Charles's legislation prohibiting marriages of boys and girls before the age of puberty (see chapter 4, note 90) tried to eradicate an ancient custom inherent in polygynous societies. By the 820s, as a result of the marriage strategy devised by the aristocracy under the strictures of monogamy, the age of marriage increased for men but not necessarily for women. According to the dates provided by K. F. Werner (see the genealogical table in "Die Nachkommen"), Charlemagne's sons married at sixteen (Louis the Pious) and eighteen (Carloman, later known as Pepin). Carloman's son, Bernhard, also married when he was eighteen, but Louis the Pious' sons and grandsons married later: Lothar I at twenty-six, Pepin I at twenty-five, Louis II, the German, at twenty-one, and Charles the Bald at nineteen. In the following generation the youngest age of marriage of a prince was twenty and the oldest forty-one. Among Lothar I's sons, Louis II married at twenty-six and Lothar II at twenty. Louis the German's sons were thirty-one (Carloman), forty-one (Louis III), and twenty-three (Charles III, the Fat). Charles the Bald's sons encountered parental opposition when they tried to marry at fifteen and sixteen. The second union of the Stammerer, with Adelheid (discussed in chapter 4), apparently concluded with Charles the Bald's approval, took place when he was twenty-nine. Gisla's and Eberhard's son, Berengar, was thirty-five or forty when he married.

    In four generations of Charlemagne and his descendants, the age of marriage for men has been recorded better than that for women. The available evidence nonetheless suggests that the wives and daughters of the Carolingians married between twelve and nineteen. Charlemagne's wife Hildegard was thirteen; Charles the Bald's first wife, Ermentrud, was twelve; Louis the Pious' second wife, Judith, was either eighteen or nineteen; his daughter Gisla was either fourteen or seventeen. We also know the age at marriage of Charles the Bald's two daughters: Judith was twelve and Rothild nineteen. For ninth-century views concerning the nubility of girls at thirteen or fourteen, see above, note 11.

25. The source for this is Werner, "Die Nachkommen." For a list of the people included in my tabulation, see Appendix 1.

26. K. J. Leyser, *Rule and Conflict in an Early Medieval Society: Ottonian Saxony* (London, 1979), pp. 49–59.

27. Herlihy, "Life Expectancies for Women," pp. 5–10.

28. On the correlation between poor diet and the shorter life span of women, see above, chapter 3, note 109.

29. Stoeckle (*Studien,* p. 62.) has remarked that, in Saxon lives, there was no contrast between marriage and virginity. The new type of Carolingian female saint did not battle with her parents, but accepted their wish to marry because of "caritas." František Graus has emphasized that Saint Salaberga's legend, which credits the saint with two husbands and five children (see below, chapter 7, note 18), was composed in Carolingian times; the fertile wife was not a topos in Merovingian hagiography (*Volk,*

Herrscher und Heiliger im Reich der Merowinger [Prague, 1965], p. 118).

30. Haimo of Auxerre, *In Epist. I ad Tim.* (*PL* 117, 791A-B): "Numquid salvabitur mulier amplius si permanserit in castitate? Utique sed si genuerit filios et eos in fide et religione . . . educaverit, atque ad perfectionem bonae vitae perduxit."

31. Peter Dronke traces Notker's imagery to a fusion of two dreams recorded by Saint Perpetua during her weeks in prison. *The Medieval Lyric,* 2d ed. (New York, 1977), pp. 41–43.

32. Ilene H. Forsyth, *The Throne of Wisdom: Wood Sculptures of the Madonna in Romanesque France* (Princeton, 1972), p. 66.

33. Salin, *La civilisation mérovingienne,* vol. 4, p. 392.

34. H. J. Turrin, *"Aureo flore* and the Question of Dating the Tradition of Marian Veneration in the Medieval West," *Mittellateinisches Jahrbuch,* 14 (1979), 76–88.

35. Haimo of Auxerre, *In Epist. ad Col.* 3 (*PL* 117, 762B), explained Col. 3:18, "mulieres, subditae estote viris," on the basis of Gen. 3:16, "sub viri potestate eris, et ipse dominabitur tui," adding that this subjection meant sexual subjection as well. When he declared that the Apostle had warned women not to follow the example of early Christian women who had abstained, because their abstinence might be interpreted as a rebellion against their husbands' authority, Haimo may have been playing with the words of 1 Pet. 2:18, "servi, subditi estote in omni timore dominis."

36. Hincmar, *De divortio* 5 (*PL* 125, 656D), remarked that, since a man is the head and the ruler of his wife, he ought to be punished more severely for adultery than his wife. Citing this passage, Jean Devisse attributed to the archbishop an attitude favorable to women in *Hincmar, Archévêque de Reims (845–882),* 3 vols. (Geneva, 1975–76), vol. 2, 401–402. More explicit on the absolute equality of men and women was Jonas of Orléans in his *De institutione laicali* 2.4 (*PL* 106, 176C–177B). As Pierre Toubert has noted, the Carolingian *specula conjugatorum* upheld the idea that marriage created a *societas* among the spouses. But their authors did not completely dismiss the notion that women, as daughters of Eve, were the source of sin. "La théorie de mariage chez les moralistes carolingiens," pp. 260–265. Even in the lives of female saints, one often finds the *locus comunis* that God must be praised for instilling in women virtues despite the weakness of their sex; see, for example, *Vita Aldegundis* 2 (*MGH Script. rer. mer.* 6, 86) and *Passio s. Maxellendis* 1 (*Acta sanctorum Belgii selecta* 3, 581).

37. Northilda's case was reported by Hincmar in *De divortio* 5 (*PL* 125, 655A-B).

38. Hincmar, *De divortio* 5 (*PL* 125, 657): "ad macellum illas duci faciant laniandas et coquorum suorum gladiis more vervecum atque porcorum mactari praecipiant [*sic*], vel ipsi etiam manu et mucrone proprio eas trucident." He repeated the idea in *Ad regem* 8 (*PL* 125, 1023).

39. *Conc. Trib.* (895), 46 (*MGH Capit.* 2, 239-40).
40. On Theutberga, see chapter 4, notes 53–62.
41. Regino, *Chronicon* (887) (*MGH Script.* 1, 597).
42. *Conc. Met.* (888), 10 (Mansi 18, 80).
43. The regulations relating to the status of widows in the capitularies and decrees of the councils have been traced by André Rosambert, *La veuve en droit canonique jusqu'au XIVe siècle* (Paris, 1923). Royal protection had already been extended to widows by the Merovingians: Clovis, *Ad episcopos* (507-511) (*MGH Capit.* 1, 1), and Clothar II, *Praeceptio* (584-628), 7 (*MGH Capit.* 1, 19); idem, *Edictum* (614), 18 (*MGH Capit.* 1, 23). The council held at St. Jean de Losne (670–673) under Childeric II specified that only widows who donned a religious garb were under royal tutelage (*Conc. Latunense* 12 [CCL 148A, 316; *MGH Conc.* 1, 218]). The Carolingians enjoined widows who took a religious vow to enter convents and appointed a *defensor* for those who remained in the world (*Conc. Parisiense* [829], 40–43 [*MGH Conc.* 637–638]). Following his coronation as king of the Lombards in 781, Charlemagne's son Pepin ordered the appointment of a *defensor* for every widow in *Pippini Italiae regis capitulare* (782–786) 5 (*MGH Capit.* 1, 192), and instructed judges to look after the interests of widows and hear their pleas without delay: *Capit. Mantuanum* (781?) 1; *Capit. Papiense* (787) 1; *Capit. italicum* (801) 2; *Capit. italicum* (801–810), 4; (*MGH Capit.* 1, 190, 198, 205, 209). In an appendix to the Bavarian Code, Charlemagne established a heavy fine of 60 *solidi* for those who disturbed the peace of widows, *Lex Bai. Additio* 7.1-2; 2.3 (*MGH Capit.* 1, 157–158). He instructed his *missi* throughout the empire to appoint to widows "bonos vicedomos et advocatos," *Capit. miss. spec.* (802) 20 (*MGH Capit* 1, 101). See also *Capit. miss. gen.* (802) 1, 5, 14, 40 and *Capit. miss. spec.* (802) 18, 19, 24 (*MGH Capit.* 1, 92, 93, 94, 98, 101, 104). The need for honest and just advocates for widows and for punishment of those who harassed widows was reiterated by Louis the Pious in *Capit. praec. ad leg. miss.* 3 and *Admonitio ad omnes regni ordines* (823-825), 8 (*MGH Capit.* 1, 189, 304). Councils also made several attempts to legislate in favor of widows. For example, the expeditious hearing of widows' pleas was ordered by the *Conc. Vernense* (755) 7 (*MGH Capit.* 1, 37). Priests were ordered to help widows before secular tribunals by the *Conc. Moguntinense* (813), 14 (*MGH Conc.* 2, 264), bishops were also so ordered by the *Conc. Cabillonense* (813), 11 (*MGH Conc.* 1, 276). The injunctions of later councils and capitularies concerned the behavior, rape, and abduction of widows: *Conc. Parisiense* (829), 64; *Conc. Aquisgranense* (836), 23 (*MGH Conc.* 2, 638, 723); *Conc. Parisiense* (846), 64 (*MGH Capit.* 2, 413); *Capit. apud Silvacum* (853), 21; *Capit. apud Carisiascum* (857), 2; *Admonitio domni Hlud.* 7 (*MGH Capit.* 2, 157–158, 272, 292).
44. Paschasius Radbertus, *Vita Walae* 26 (*MGH Script.* 2, 543).
45. Hincmar of Reims, *De divortio* 2 (*PL* 125, 644D): "sicut in adulescentulis viduis pervidemus, quae ideo post absolutionem virorum velamen sac-

rum suscipiunt, ut licentius pluribus abutantur." The *Conc. Remense* (813) 34 (*MGH Conc.* 2, 256) complained about the behavior of widows. The *Conc. Parisiense* (829), 43 (*MGH Conc.* 2, 639) restricted widows to monasteries if they wished to devote themselves to the service of God. See also Rosembert, *La veuve,* pp. 80–83.

46. *Translatio s. Baltechildis* 1 (*MGH Script.* 15/1, 284). For references on Heilwig's life and activities, see also B. Simson, *Jahrbücher des fränkischen Reiches unter Ludwig dem Frommen,* 2 vols. (Jahrbücher der deutschen Geschichte, 6; Leipzig, 1874–76), vol. 1, 146, 148; vol. 2, 31.

47. *Conc. Nemnetense* (895), 19 (Mansi 18, 171–172).

48. For example, a certain Benedicta appeared before a tribunal in Mâcon to defend herself against charges of breach of contract brought against her by another woman, Anastasia: *Cartulaire de Saint-Vincent de Mâcon* 15.

49. Herlihy, "Land, Family and Women," pp. 89–120.

50. On the basis of a chi-square test analyzing the difference between the proportions at the 95 percent confidence level, we can conclude that there is a statistically significant difference between eighth and ninth century donations by women.

51. Professor Herlihy was the first to note that "regional contrasts in the status of the woman are as pronounced as social differences." "Land, Family and Women," p. 110.

52. *Codex Laureshamensis,* ed. Karl Glöckner, 3 vols. (Darmstadt, 1929–36). Founded in 764 by Williswinda and her son, Cancro, count of the Upper Rhein, Lorsch was one of the favorite monasteries of the Carolingians. Even after it became a part of the Eastern Kingdom, Lothar II, king of Lotharingia, endowed it with property in the county of Ghent near Nijmwegen. One third of the monastery's holdings were in the county of Worms. In the county of Main, the monastery held the whole Mark Michelstadt, thanks to the generosity of Einhard. The best study of its early history is Daniel Neundörfer's *Studien zur ältesten Geschichte des Klosters Lorsch* (Arbeiten zur deutschen Rechts- und Verfassungsgeschichte, 3; Berlin, 1920). See also Hans-Peter Wehlt, *Reichsabtei und König dargestellt am Beispiel der Abtei Lorsch* (Veröffentlichungen des Max-Planck-Instituts für Geschichte, 28; Göttingen, 1970), and *Laurissa jubilans: Festschrift zur 1200-Jahrfeier von Lorsch, 1964,* ed. Hans Degen et al. (Lorsch, 1964).

53. Herlihy, "Land, Family and Women," p. 111. It is more appropriate to attribute the fluctuations of joint donations by men to the departing warrior's wish to provide for the welfare of his soul by turning over a piece of property to a brother, son, or friend with the proviso that it be given to a monastery if he did not return. Joint donations by men may also have been used to raise capital for equipping a warrior. Joint donations by men in the Lorsch cartulary were the lowest in Pepin's reign, not exceeding 4.7 percent; the percentage rose to 8.7 percent during Charles's reign as king, then fluctuated between 14.1 percent and 12.9

percent under Charles and Louis as emperors, respectively, and dropped to 8.8 percent thereafter. Only the difference in the proportion of male coactors in Pepin's as opposed to Charles's reign as emperor is significant when analyzed at the 95 percent confidence level. A close scrutiny of the documents reveals the appearance of *socii* as codonors under Charlemagne. We may thus attribute the increased proportion of male joint donations to Charlemagne's legislation encouraging small landowners to pool their resources when called to render military service. Legislation under Louis the Pious indicates that male members of a family, brothers in particular, chose not to divide their patrimony in order to take full advantage of this legislation; see *De capitulare Olonnense* (825), 6 (*MGH Capit.* 1, 330). Often such *socii* were maternal nephews and uncles; see *Codex Laureshamensis* 799, 911, 2121, 2528, 2984.

54. On the significance of these councils, see above, chapter 4, note 36.

55. *Capit. missorum* (802), 22 (*MGH Capit.* 1, 103).

56. *Conc. Parisiense* (829), 3.2 (*MGH Conc.* 2, 671); see also above, chapter 4, note 36.

57. *Codex Laureshamensis* 798, 556, 1880, 2310. According to K. F. Werner, Imma and Gerolt are not to be confused with Queen Hildegard's mother and brother ("Bedeutende Adelsfamilien," p. 111). Sometimes the donor distinguished between his property and property held jointly with his wife; see, for example, no. 365, issued by Hiltdibold and Ratrud in 805.

58. The two *libelli dotis,* added to the *Form. Aug.* B.24-25 (*MGH Form.* 357-358) under Louis the German's reign, gave the bride only usufruct of land. That this was the normal practice in the late ninth century is suggested also by *Form. Sangallenses miscellaneae* 16, 18 and *Collectio Sangallensis* 18 (*MGH Form.* 387–388, 406–407). *Form. Sangallenses miscellaneae* 12 (*MGH Form.* 384) contains also an earlier form of contract, a *carta dotis,* drawn up at the request of the bride's father, which stipulated that the title to the land belonged to the woman. In the seventh and eighth centuries, as seen in Marculf's compilation, the transfer of the ownership of land to the bride was normal practice; see *Marc. Form.* 2.15 (*MGH Form.* 85). In other words, by granting only usufructuary rights, the *dos* was transformed into a widow's dower.

59. Herlihy was able to assemble from the ninth century for southern France only 495 private transactions, but most of these are from the last quarter; only 37 documents survived from 801 to 825; 48 from 826 to 850; 118 from 851 to 875; and 292 from 875 to 900. Eighty-nine documents from the ninth century can be found in the *Cartulaire de Brioude,* ed. H. Doniol (Clermont-Ferrand, 1869), and *Le Grand Cartulaire de Saint-Julien de Brioude, essai de reconstruction,* ed. Anne Marie and Marcel Boudet (Saint Etienne, 1935). *Recueil des chartes de l'Abbaye de Cluny,* ed. A. Bernard and A. Bruell, vol. 1 (Paris, 1876), contains 66 charters dating from the ninth century. *Cartulaire de Saint-Vincent de Mâcon* contains 64 private

transactions that may be assigned to the ninth century. I have also included in my table charters dated by the editors approximately between 882 and 910 or between 886 and 927.

60. On the history of Auvergne and for relevant literature, see Lewis, *The Development of Southern French and Catalan Society*, pp. 107, nn. 76–79, pp. 181–184. For the history of Mâconnais, see P. de la Bussiere, *Le Baillage de Mâcon* (Mâcon, 1914). For a detailed bibliography, see Georges Duby, *La société aux XIe et XIIe siècles dans la région Mâconnais* (Paris, 1953), pp. xxx–xxxiii.

61. *Cart. Cluny* (893), 53. In 901, she exchanged serfs with Wigo and Leutaldus (ibid. 74). We know that a Leutbald was her vassal, because in 924 he made a donation to Cluny for her soul (ibid. 248). Some of the medieval chroniclers thought that she built Cluny; see Sigebert, *Chron.* 15 (*MGH Script.* 6, 344). Historians in the nineteenth century identified Countess Ava with Albana/*sive* Ave, wife of Count Guerin/Warinus of Mâcon, who acquired Cluny in 825 through an exchange with Bishop Hildebald (*Cartulaire de Saint-Vincent de Mâcon* 52). See, for example, P. Lorain, *Essai historique sur l'Abbaye de Cluny* (Dijon, 1839), pp. 18–19. M. Chaume suggested that she was the wife of Guerin of Velay, the brother of William the Pious in *Les origines du duché de Bourgogne*, vol. 1 (Dijon, 1927), 358, n. 1. E. Hlawitschka spoke of her as William's sister in *Lotharingien*, p. 118. In the document in question Ava speaks of William as her "frater," not "germanus," and refers to their "amabilem consanguinitatis propinquitatem."

62. See for example *Cart. Cluny* (897), 61, in which a certain Emma donates a piece of land to her brother Atto; ibid. (888), 33, in which King Rudolf donates land to his sister Adeleide; in *Cart. Brioude* (898), 231 Guitburga (Giburgia) makes a donation for the soul of her parents and her brother; in ibid. 294 (906) Rado does the same for the soul of his parents and his sister Agina.

63. We know that Benedicta was married to a certain Wulfradus (*Recueil des chartes de l'Abbaye de Saint-Benoît-sur-Loire* [889], 21). Three entries in the *Liber memorialis von Remiremont* (38r, 3 in hand 9; 43r, 15 in hand 5; and 50r, 7 in hand 19) list Benedicta's name among members of the kin of Vice-Count Leutald (Liutald/Leotald) of Mâcon, a vassal of William the Pious. The oldest of these entries (in hand 5) was made around 865 or 875, around the time Benedicta appeared at the *placitum* of Vienne (see note 48, above). All these entries include the name of two of the witnesses at Vienne: Humbert and Raculf. Although we need more research on the identity of this clan, we know that Raculf, Leutald, and Humbert (Umbert) were related. *Cart. Cluny* 139, issued between 910 and 927 by Umbert on his deathbed, was signed by "fratris ejus Letaldus." Moreover, the relationship between Leutald and Raculf, as Georges Duby has already remarked, is obvious from the fact that the grandsons of Raculf are named Leutald and Umbert (*La Société* p. 94,

n. 1). See also *Cartulaire de Saint-Vincent de Mâcon* 7, 8, 38. On Raculf and Leutald, who both appropriated the title Vice-Count of Mâcon, see René Poupardin, *Le Royaume de Bourgogne (888–1038)*, p. 214 (Bibliothéque de l'École des Hautes Études; Sciences historiques et philologiques, 163; Paris, 1907), p. 214, nn. 2–3, and p. 215, nn. 1–5; and Hlawitschka, *Lotharingien*, pp. 146–148, in particular, n. 116. See also above note 61, on a Leutald (Leutbald) who was Countess Ava's vassal.

64. The text in question is the *Cartulaire de l'Abbaye de Redon*. See also Arthur de la Borderie, *La Chronologie du cartulaire de Redon* (Rennes, 1901). On the history of Brittany, in addition to M. Aurélien de Courson's Prolegomena in the *Cartulaire*, see his *Histoire des peuples bretons dans la Gaule et dans les Iles Britanniques*, 2 vols. (Paris, 1846); Arthur de la Borderie, *Histoire de Bretagne*, 3 vols. (Rennes, 1896–99); A. Chaboseau, *Histoire de la Bretagne avant le 13. siècle* (Paris, 1926); the works listed by G. von Tevenar in "Bretonische Bibliographie," *Zeitschrift für keltische Philologie und Volksforschung*, 22 (1941), 77–92; and Jean Delumeau, *Histoire de la Bretagne* (Toulouse, 1969), pp. 117–152, in particular, 151–152.

65. In 846 the ruler of Brittany, Nominoe, broke all relations with the Frankish church, repudiating the authority of Tours as metropolitan see, and attributing that authority to Dol. On this, see de la Borderie, *La chronologie*, pp. 62–67. Even before the break with the Frankish church, Carolingian propagandists, bewildered by the customs of the Bretons, had claimed that their marital arrangements showed little influence of Christianity. See Ermoldus Nigellus, *Carmen in honorem Hludowici* 3 (*MGH Poetarum* 2, 42): "Christicolum retinet tantummodo perfida nomen, . . . coeunt frater et ipsa soror. Uxorem fratris frater rapit alter, et omnes incestu vivant."

66. For example, *Cart. Redon* 53 involves the sale of a piece of land held by Branoc, Iarnhitin, their sister Driken, her son Alvares, her daughter Iudita, and the children of Branoc and Iarnhitin, who were not named. *Cart. Redon* 121, a sale by Omnis of his share in a property, was signed by his sister Margithoiarn, his brother Benedic, and his nephew Ninan. *Cart. Redon* 29 reflects a family dispute over property inherited through the female line. Drogen apparently was left a piece of land by her "avunculus" (mother's brother), and her father and brother claimed a share in it. Courson, using Welsh codes, in particular the customs of Cambria collected around 940 by Hoel, son of Kadell, argued that such "blood land" was shared by brothers, cousins, and second cousins, but not by women. Courson interpreted a law that provided a daughter with half of her brother's share in their father's property as applicable only to movables and not land. *Histoire des peuples bretons*, vol. 2, 29–30. J. Weisweiler also stressed that a daughter inherited her father's land only if she did not have brothers, and then held the land only during her own life; upon her death, the property reverted to the male line. "Die Stellung der Frau bei den Kelten und das Problem des 'keltischen

Mutterrechts,' " *Zeitschrift für celtische Philologie,* 21 (1940), 227. The kinship system, communal tenure, and inheritance rights among the inhabitants of Brittany needs further study, which cannot be attempted here. On the basis of my evidence, I can only suggest that the Frankish occupation may have contributed to the disintegration of the system and resulted in the admission of women to the inheritance of "kin" or "blood" land, at least by testamentary bequest. *Cart. Redon* 241 supports this: "legaliter liceat unicuique nobili tam de suo alode quam de sua hereditate quicquid voluerit facere."

67. See, for example, *Cart. Redon* 184, which traces the genealogy of Arthiu, the wealthiest man in the region.

68. *Cart. Redon* 109.

69. *Cart. Redon* 181. The transaction was concluded in 834. We hear once more of Cleroc in *Cart. Redon* 28, a donation issued in 858 to the monastery where she identified herself as "religiosa femina." This transaction was approved by Omnis and Jarcun, her nephews, and by a priest, Anauhoiarn, but not by her husband. It is tempting to identify her husband, Anauuanoc, with the Anaunan who tried to murder the priest Anauhoiarn (*Cart. Redon* 202) and to speculate that the hostility between the two men was caused by jealousy harbored by a divorced husband. Anaunan is identified in *Cart. Redon* 202 as "clericus," possibly an editorial error in transcribing an abbreviation for "Clerocis conjunx." In *Cart. Redon* 203, a donation issued by Anaunan, he is not identified as a "clericus."

70. Women acting alone as vendors appear in *Cart. Redon* (7) 227, (42) 221, (63) 171, (71) 210, (73) 148, (86) 214, (94) 217, (110) 215, (214) 150, (234) 212; as sole buyers, in (13) 146, (66) 147, (82) 264, (207) 172, (213) 286, (228) 174.

71. The fact that the charters specify how the land was acquired by the principals and, if it was purchased, give the name of the previous owner also indicates that property acquired by purchase was considered a different type of legal entity from inherited land. *Cart. Redon* 244 distinguishes between "alodis," land acquired by purchase, and "hereditas," land that was inherited.

72. *Cart. Redon* 214.

73. For example, a certain Tehuuiu gave a piece of property to his wife Argantan because she was faithful; see *Cart. Redon* 152. The donation specified that she could do with it as she wished.

74. On Roiantken, see *Cart. Redon* 146, issued in 821; 147, issued between 821 and 826; 178, issued in 867; 174, in 864; 175, in 852 or 858; 36, in 864; and 236, in 875. (I am following de la Broderie's *La Chronologie.*) See in particular *Cart. Redon* 79, issued in 863, which was witnessed by her; 175, issued by her and witnessed by her husband, son, and brother; and 204, issued in 858 by her brother and witnessed by her husband and son.

75. Courson cites Welsh laws, according to which a girl received three settle-

ments, one at the time of her engagement, a second before she entered her husband's bed, and a third after the first night. *Histoire des peuples bretons,* vol. 2, 15. Courson equates these to the Germanic *arrha, dos,* and *morgengabe.* In *Cart. Redon,* reference is made only to the last. The other gifts, if they were known in Brittany, may have taken the form of practical objects, as Courson suggests. Even so, the *arrha* should not be considered a settlement; it was a token of the pledge given at the time of the engagement.

76. Coleman, "Medieval Marriage Characteristics," pp. 205–219.

77. Ludolf Kuchenbuch, *Bäuerliche Gesellschaft und Klosterherrschaft im 9. Jahrhundert* (Wiesbaden, 1978), pp. 76–94, 108–110.

78. *Admonitio generalis* (789) 82 (*MGH Capit.* 1, 61) forbade peasants to work on Sundays, enumerating the kind of work they usually performed. For instance, men were forbidden to work in the fields and forests, build houses, and go hunting, while women were not to engage in "opera textilia," which included the manufacturing of linen and wool in all stages, beginning with the shearing of lambs, and making clothing, as well as doing laundry. Every great household had a *genitium* where women were engaged in various phases of textile work. The care Charlemagne took to enumerate the supplies to be kept at the royal *genitia* and to order that the buildings where the *genitia* were located be kept in good repair and supplied with strong doors indicates the value that was attached to this type of work. See *Capit. de villis* (800?) 43, 49 (*MGH Capit.* 1, 87). Article 82 of the *Admonitio* was reiterated by the Council of Mainz in 852: *Conc. Mog.* 14 (*MGH Capit.* 2, 170). See Kuchenbuch, *Bäuerliche Gesellschaft,* p. 108, nn. 40–41.

79. *Capit. missorum Theodonis* 22 (*MGH Capit.* 2, 125).

80. Riché, *Daily Life,* pp. 101–105.

81. Leyser, *Rule and Conflict,* chaps. 5–6.

82. Lewis, *The Development of Southern French and Catalan Society,* pp. 123–124, 170–171, 391–392.

CHAPTER 6

1. Roger Gryson, in *Les origines du célibat ecclésiastique du premier au septieme siècle,* gives a summary of the controversy and a detailed bibliography. The first to point out that cultic purity was the real concern of those who advocated clerical celibacy was Heinrich Böhmer in "Die Entstehung des Cölibates," *Geschichtliche Studien Albert Hauck zum 70. Geburtstage, dargebracht von Mitarbeiter Kreise der Realencyklopädie für protestantische Theologie und Kirche* (Leipzig, 1916), pp. 6–24. Martin Boelens (*Die Klerikerehe,* p. 46) supports Böhmer, stating that the reason for the introduction of celibacy was the axiom "Der Beischlaf macht Kultusunfähig." The basic work in English is Henry C. Lea's *History of Sacerdotal Celibacy,* 3d ed. rev. (New York 1907). Other older works are still useful: F. X. Funk, "Cölibat

und Priesterweihe im christlichen Altertum," *Kirchengeschichtliche Abhandlungen und Untersuchungen,* 1 (1897), 121–155; E. Vacandard, "Les origines du célibat ecclésiastique," *Études de critique et d'histoire religieuse,* vol. 1 (Paris, 1905), 69–120; and idem, "Célibat ecclésiastique," *Dictionnaire de théologie catholique,* vol. 2, pt. 2 (Paris, 1905), 2068–2080. Among recent publications, see Jean Paul Audet, *Structures of Christian Priesthood: A Study of Home, Marriage, and Celibacy in the Pastoral Service of the Church,* trans R. Sheed (New York, 1967); J. E. Lynch, "Marriage and Celibacy of the Clergy: The Discipline of the Western Church; An Historico-Canonical Synopsis," *Jurist,* 32 (1972), 14–38, 189–212; and John T. Noonan, Jr., "Celibacy and the Fathers of the Church," in *Celibacy, the Necessary Option,* ed. George H. Frein (New York, 1968), pp. 138–151.

2. Samuel Laeuchli, *Power and Sexuality: The Emergence of Canon Law at the Synod of Elvira* (Philadelphia, 1972), p. 97.

3. Theodor Zahn, *Ignatius von Antiochen* (Gotha, 1873), pp. 580–585. For other opinions, see Gryson, *Le ministère des femmes dans l'Église ancienne,* pp. 10–17.

4. P. Joliot stressed that the diaconate was the only ecclesiastical office women ever held (*La condition juridique du religieux à travers l'histoire* [Bordeaux, 1942], pp. 58–60). Jean Daniélou noted that the Order of Widows was not clearly defined: "at the end of the fourth century it disappeared; it died of its own ambiguities." The Order of Deaconess, which grew as the Order of Widows declined, came to take its place. See *The Ministry of Women in the Early Church,* trans. Glyn Simon (London, 1961), pp. 18–20. Haye van der Meer interpreted the *Didascalia* and *Apostolic Constitutions* as attributing specific ecclesiastical functions to widows (*Women Priests,* pp. 50–51).

5. See K. H. Schäfer, *Die Kanonissenstifter im deutschen Mittelalter,* and the defense of his thesis, entitled "Kanonissen und Diakonissen, Ergänzungen und Erläuterungen." See also Wilhelm Levison's criticism of Schäfer's interpretation of *monialis* in "Recension: Schäfer, K. H. 'Die Kanonissenstifter'. . . ." *Westdeutsche Zeitschrift für Geschichte und Kunst,* 27 (1908), 491–512. Mary Pia Heinrich follows Schäfer, *The Canonesses and Education in the Early Middle Ages* (Washington, D.C., 1924).

6. A. Kalsbach upholds the former view in *Die altkirchliche Einrichtung der Diakonissen bis zu ihrem Erlöschen* (Quartalschrift für christliche Altertumskunde und für Kirchengeschichte, Supplementheft, 22; Freiburg, 1926). Hans Achelis attributes the Western opposition to the fear of Montanism in "Diakonissen," *Realencyklopädie für protestantische Theologie und Kirche,* vol. 4 (Leipzig, 1898), 616–620.

7. Van der Meer, *Women Priests,* p. 97.

8. Monastic chroniclers, such as the Venerable Bede, advanced the thesis that the celibacy of the clergy was of apostolic origin. Nineteenth-century Catholic historians accepted this. See, for example, G. Bickell, "Der Cölibat eine apostolische Anordnung," *Zeitschrift für katholische Theologie,*

2 (1878), 26–64; 3 (1879), 792–799. Although rejected by most Catholic authors of this century, it was upheld as recently as 1969, in H. Deen, *Le Célibat des prêtres dans les premiers siècles de l'Église* (Paris, 1969). On the historiography of clerical celibacy, see Anne Barstow, "The Defense of Clerical Marriage in the 11th and Early 12th Centuries" (Ph.D. dissertation, Columbia University, 1979).

9. Lynch, "Marriage and Celibacy," pp. 19–20.

10. Origen, *Fragments sur la Première aux Corinthiens* 34, ed. Claude Jenkins, *Journal of Theological Studies*, 9 (1907–1908), 501–502: Tertullian, *De exhortatione castitatis* 9–10 (*CCL* 2, 1027–1030).

11. Pseudo-Hieronymus, *De septem ordinibus ecclesiae*, ed. A. W. Kalff (Würzburg, 1935), p. 62: "Uxori tuae propter antiquam consuetudinem ac periculum sacerdotii, non des animam tuam in potestatem; ne forte in similitudinem Adae in paradiso positus confundaris." On the date of its composition, see Dom G. Morin, "Le destinataire de l'apocryphe hieronymien 'De septem ordinibus Ecclesiae,'" *Revue d'histoire ecclésiastique*, 34 (1938), 238–244.

12. Mary Daly elaborates on the neurotic projection of guilt upon women by the celibate clergy in *The Church and the Second Sex*, pp. 88–89.

13. *Concilios Visigothicos e Hispano-Romanos* 33, ed. José Vivés et al. (Barcelona, 1963), p. 7: "Placuit in totum prohibere episcopis, presbyteris et diaconibus vel omnibus clericis positis in ministerio abstinere se a conjugibus suis et non generare filios." Gryson argued against the widely accepted view that the Council of Elvira established the Western tradition in *Les origines*, pp. 127–170. On Elvira, see Laeuchli, *Power and Sexuality*.

14. The controversy was recorded by Socrates, *Historia ecclesiastica*, 1. 22 (*PG* 67, 102–103), and by Sozomen, *Historia ecclesiastica*, 1. 23 (*PG* 67, 926). Cassiodorus, in *Historia tripartita*, 2.14 (*CSEL* 71, 107), transmitted the episode to the Latin West.

15. *Conc. Gang.* 4 (Mansi 2, 1106); *Conc. Ancir.* (314), 10 (Mansi 2, 518) permitted deacons to marry after ordination, as long as they stated their intention to marry at the time of their ordination. Ancyra's rule became the basis of the Eastern discipline. See Petro B. T. Bilaniuk, "Celibacy and Eastern Tradition," in *Celibacy, the Necessary Option*, ed. George H. Frein (New York, 1968), pp. 32–72.

16. Damasus pronounced his views in an instruction he sent to the bishops of Gaul: *Ad episcopos Galliae* 2.5 (*PL* 13, 1184; JK 255), sometimes wrongly attributed to Siricius. See Dekkers, *Clavis patrum latinorum* 1632; E. C. Babut, *La plus ancienne décretale* (Paris, 1904). Siricius issued a similar decretal, *Cum in unum*, at a Roman council in 386, *Ad episcopos Africae*, 4 (*PL* 13, 1159A; JK 258).

17. *Conc. Carth.* (390), 2 (*CCL* 259, 13).

18. Bishop Bonosius of Sardica opened the argument, which was carried on by Helvidius, who insisted that Mary was the mother of Jesus' brothers.

A monk, Jovian, and then Vigilantius took up the struggle. Although their works were destroyed, we know their views from rebuttals by Jerome: *Adversus Helvidium* (*PL* 23, 183–206); *Adversus Jovinianum* (*PL* 23, 211–338); *Contra Vigilantium* (*PL* 23, 339–352). Augustine wrote three works in answer to Jovian's claims: *De bono conjugali* (*CSEL* 41, 187–231); *De sancta virginitate* (*CSEL* 41, 187–231); *De haeresibus* (*PL* 42, 21–50).

19. *Conc. Carth.* (401) in *Reg. Eccl. Carth. exc.* 70 and *Conc. Carth. V* 3 (*CCL* 259, 201, 356).

20. 1 Tim. 3:2 and 12 specified the monogamic condition, "unius uxoris vir," for eligibility to ecclesiastical office. Councils of the fourth and fifth century set the same requirement for the wife. See *Conc. Valentinum* (374), 1; *Conc. Arausicanum* (441), 24; *Conc. Turonense* (451), 4; *II Conc. Arelatense* (442–506), 45; *Conc. Andegavense* (453), 2; *Conc. Agathense* (506), 1, 43 (*CCL* 148, 38, 84, 123, 138, 145, 193, 211). Merovingian councils reiterated the same rules: *Conc. Epaonense* (517), 2; *Conc. Arelatense* (524), 3; *Conc. Aurelianense* (541), 10 (*CCL* 148A, 24, 44, 134).

21. On this, see *Conc. Aurelianense* (533), 8; *Conc. Aurelianense* (538), 7; *Conc. Incerti Loci* (post 614), 12 (*CCL* 148A, 100, 117, 288).

22. Pseudo-Hieronymus, *De septem ordinibus ecclesiae* 7 (*PL* 30, 164C): "Quod ea consentiente electus es a Domino." See also *II Conc. Arelatense* (442–506), 3 (*CCL* 148, 114): "conversam . . . uxorem."

23. Constantius clericus, in *Vita s. Germani* 22 (*MGH Script. rer. mer.* 7, 267), refers to a priest and his wife living under the same roof. The residence of a priest served as a hospice to travelers: *Vita s. Germani* 5 (ibid., 253). Audet (*Structures*, pp. 3–67) deals with home and marriage in the pastoral service of the early church." See also Henry G. Beck, *The Pastoral Care of Souls in South East France during the Sixth Century* (Analecta Gregoriana, 51; Rome, 1950).

24. *Conc. Agathense* (506), 16 (*CCL* 148, 201): "Sane si coniugati iuvenes consenserint ordinari, etiam uxorum voluntas ita requirenda est, ut sequestrato mansionis cubiculo, religione, praemissa, posteaquam pariter conversi fuerint, ordinentur." Included in *Decr. Grat.* D.77, c.6. (Friedberg, 1, 273)

25. Augustine dealt with sexual abstinence in *De nupt. et conc.* 1.11, 12 (*CSEL* 42, 224), but he warned: "Quibus vero placuit ex consensu ab usu carnalis concupiscentiae in perpetuum continere, absit ut vinculum inter illos coniugale rumpatur." Augustine's position on marriage was analyzed by Nicholas Ladomerszky, *Saint Augustin, docteur du mariage chrétien* (Urbaniana, 5; Rome, 1942). See also W. J. Dooley, *Marriage according to Saint Ambrose* (Catholic University of America, Studies in Christian Antiquity, 11; Washington, D.C., 1948).

26. Caesarius, *Sermones 44*.5 (*CCL* 103, 109); cf. *Poenitentiale Theodori* 1.14 (McNeill 95; Schmitz 1, 535); *Excarpsus Cummeani* (Schmitz 1, 623–624).

27. Justinian, Nov. 123.40 (*Corpus iuris civilis*, vol. 3, p. 622): "Si vero constante adhuc matrimonio aut vir solus aut uxor sola intravit in monasterium, solvatur matrimonium." Gregory I, in *Registrum epistularum* 11.30 (*MGH*

Epist. 2, 301), wrote: "... etsi mundana lex praecipit conversionis gratia utrolibet invito solvi posse coniugium, divina haec lex fieri non permittit." He went on to say that a husband may enter a monastery without his wife's permission only if she has committed adultery. In an earlier letter Gregory asserted that one partner alone could not enter a monastery, even if the other gave his or her consent; either both had to embrace monastic life, or both had to remain in the world. See *Registrum epistularum* 6.47 (ibid 1, 422). On this whole question, see T. P. McLaughlin, *Le très ancien droit monastique de l'Occident* (Archives de la France monastique, 38; Paris, 1935), p. 62, n. 1.

28. The wife's vow of continence was not included in the so-called *Sacramentarium Gelasianum,* which was copied at Chelles shortly before 750. See *Liber sacramentorum Romanae aecclesiae ordinis anni circuli,* ed. L. C. Mohlberg et al. (Rerum ecclesiasticarum documenta. Series maior, Fontes 4; Rome, 1960), p. xxxv. It appears in *Ordo* 36.27; see *Les ordines Romani* vol. 4, ed. M. Andrieu (Spicilegium sacrum Lovaniense. Études et documents, 28; Louvain, 1956), p. 200: "Similiter etiam feminae, diaconissis et presbiterissis quae eodem die benedicuntur."

29. Gregory I, *Registrum epistularum* 9.197 (*MGH Epist.* 2, 185–186).

30. Baudonivia, *De vita s. Radegundis* 4 (*MGH Script. rer. mer.* 2, 381).

31. *Hist. franc.* 9.33 (*MGH Script. rer. mer.* 1, 387).

32. *Excarpsus Cummeani* 3.38 (Schmitz 1, 626): "Mulieri non liceat votum vovere sine licentia viri, sed si voverit, dimitti potest et peniteat judicio sacerdotis." On the popularity of this penitential in the Frankish Kingdom, see McNeill and Gamer, *Medieval Handbooks,* p. 266, n. 6.

33. *Decr. Comp.* (757), 5 (*MGH Capit.* 1, 38).

34. *Conc. Aurelianense* (538), 2 (*CCL* 148A, 114–115). Innocent I, *Epistola ad Victricium* (Feb. 15, 404; *PL* 20, 475C–477A; JK 286), as Gryson has pointed out (*Les origines,* p. 157), was paraphrased from a decretal of Pope Siricius issued on Jan. 6, 386 (*PL* 13, 1157A–1162A; JK 258). See also Innocent's letter to Exuperius of Toulouse (JK 293).

35. *Conc. Claremontanum* (535), 13 (*CCL* 148A, 108). The passage is taken from Pope Leo I's letter to Rusticus of Narbonne (458 or 459): *Epist.* 167, 3 (*PL* 54, 1204A, JK 544). *Conc. Turonense* (567), 13, 12 (*CCL* 148A, 180) and *Conc. Matisconense* (581–583), 11 (*CCL* 148A, 225) reiterated Pope Leo's principle of chaste marriage.

36. *Conc. Turonense* (567), 20 (*CCL* 148A, 180). The charge of Nicolaitic heresy against married priests can be traced back to Clement of Alexandria's *Stromata,* where Clement described the Gnostic sect as the "Nicolaïtes." Gryson, *Les origines,* pp. 7–8. The threat of deposition on various grounds was invoked by the following Merovingian councils: *Conc. Claremontanum* (535), 13; *Conc. Aurelianense* (538), 2; *Conc. Aurelianense* (541), 17; *Conc. Aurelianense* (549), 4; *Conc. Turonense* (567), 13 (12); *Conc. Matisconense* (581–583), 11; *Conc. Lugd.* (583), 1; *Syn. Dioc. Autiss.* (561–605), 20 (*CCL* 148A, 108–109, 114–115, 136, 149, 180–181, 225, 232, 267–268).

37. *Conc. Aurelianense* (541), 17; *Conc. Turonense* (567), 13 (12); *Conc. Matisconense* (581–583), 3 (*CCL* 148A, 136, 180–181, 224). *Conc. Gerundense* (517), 6 (Bruns 2, 19) was the first to suggest that clerks in major orders live apart from their wives. It did not issue this as a command, but simply urged that they should have a clerk living in their household if they did not wish to separate from their wives.

38. *Conc. Lugd.* (583), 1 (*CCL* 148A, 232): "non solum lecto, sed etiam frequentatione quotidiana debeant de uxoribus suis sequestrari." C. de Clercq remarked that only bishops were required to maintain separate homes for a wife and children (*La législation religieuse franque*, vol. 1 [Paris, 1936], 95). He failed to notice that, if a priest lived in the same house with his wife, he could not avoid meeting her daily. Boelens (*Die Klerikerehe*, p. 57) was more perceptive.

39. Avitus of Vienne, *Epistolae* 1 (*PL* 59, 383): "personas hujusmodi non obesse nobis, sed impedire timendum est."

40. For *diaconissa*, see *Conc. Aurelianense* (533), 17–18; *Conc. Turonense* (567), 20 (*CCL* 148A, 101, 184); for *presbyteria*, see *Conc. Turonense* (567), 20 (ibid., 184); for *episcopia*, see *Conc. Turonense* (567), 14 (ibid., 181). Syn. dioec. Autiss. (561–605), 21, used the more common expression *presbytera* in referring to priests' wives (ibid., 268).

41. Columbanus, *Epistolae* 1 (*MGH Epist.* 3, Mer. aevi 1, 159): "Sunt enim . . . post in diaconatu adulterium absconsum, tamen dico cum clientelis." Note 1 on the text reads: "clienteles esse uxores, quas suscepturi sacrum ordinem aut religiosum statum legitime dimiserunt."

42. Gregory I, *Registrum epistularum* 9.213 (*MGH Epist.* 2, 198–199). See also his letter to Brunhilda, in *Registrum epistularum* 11.46 (*MGH Epist.* 2, 318–319).

43. *Poenitentiale Burgundiense* 19 (Schmitz 2, 321; McNeill 275). The Council of Clermont did single out the birth of a child as evidence of the clerk's guilt. See *Conc. Claremontanum* (535), 13 (*CCL* 148A, 108).

44. *Liber in gloria confessorum* 77 (*MGH Script. rer. mer.* 1, 794).

45. *Hist. franc.* 4.36 (*MGH Script. rer. mer.* 1, 171).

46. *Liber in gloria confessorum* 75 (*MGH Script. rer. mer.* 1, 793).

47. *Hist. franc.* 10.5 (*MGH Script. rer. mer.* 1, 413) describes the activities, as single head of the household, of Magnatrud, the widow of Badegysil, former bishop of Mans. She probably led the same kind of existence during her husband's episcopate.

48. *Hist. franc.* 2.17 (*MGH Script. rer. mer.* 1, 82). Wearing a black habit, she was mistaken for a poor widow.

49. *Conc. Tol.* 1.18 (Bruns 1, 206). Article 19 punished in the same manner the consecrated daughter of a priest, deacon, or bishop if she married.

50. *Conc. Aurelianense* (511), 13 (*CCL* 148A, 8); reiterated by *Conc. Epaonense* (517), 32 and *Syn. Dioc. Autiss.* (561–615), 22 (ibid., 32–33, 268).

51. *Conc. Matisconense* (585), 16 (*CCL* 148A, 246). Gryson remarked: "Assez curieusement, le deuxième concile de Mâcon étend l'interdiction du

remariage à la veuve de l'exorciste et de l'acolyte." *Les origines,* p. 196, n. 3.

52. *Conc. Turonense* (567), 10–11 (*CCL* 148A, 179).

53. The order that clerks could not have living with them women other than their relatives went back to canon three of the Council of Nicaea (325) (Mansi 2, 670). It was reiterated by the Gallican councils with slight variations: *II Conc. Arelatense* (442–506), 3 (*CCL* 148, 114): "aviam, (matrem), sororem, filiam, neptem vel conversam secum uxorem habere"; *Conc. Andegaverse* (453), 4; *Conc. Turonense* (461), 3; *Stat. eccl. ant.* (442–506), 27; *Conc. Agathense* (506), 10 (*CCL* 148, 137, 145, 171, 200). The following Frankish councils dealt with the problem: *Conc. Aurelianense* (511), 29 (*CCL* 148A, 12); *Conc. Claremontanum* (535), 16 (ibid., 109); *Conc. Aurelianense* (538), 4 (ibid., 115); *Conc. Aurelianense* (549), 3 (ibid., 149); *Syn. Asp.* (551), 2 (ibid., 163); *Syn. Turonense* (567), 11 (ibid., 179); *Conc. Matisconense* (581–583), 1 (ibid., 223); *Conc. Lugdonense* (583), 1 (ibid., 232); *Conc. Cabillonense* (647–653), 3 (ibid., 304); *Conc. Modog.* (662–675), 3 (ibid., 312); *Conc. Latunense* (673–675), 4 (ibid., 315); *Conc. Aug.* (663–680), 10 (ibid., 319).

54. *Conc. Aurelianense* (538), 10 (9) (*CCL* 148A, 115). On the other hand, if a married priest had a child by his wife, he was to be deposed, according to *Conc. Claremontanum* (535), 13 (ibid., 108).

55. *Poenitentiale Burgundiense* 12 (Schmitz 2, 321; McNeill 275): "sciat se adulterium commisse." But the preceding canon states: "Si quis vero fornicaverit quidem cum mulieribus si . . . diaconus V. an., si sacerdus [*sic*] .V. pen[e]teat." "Adulterium" was used to denote a sinful sexual relation: incest by *Conc. Epaonense* (517), 30 (*CCL* 148A, 31), homosexuality by *Conc. Turonense* (567), 15 (14) (ibid., 181), and concubinage by *Conc. Aurelianense* (538), 4 (ibid., 116); *Syn. Dioc. Autiss.* (561–605), 29 (ibid., 268); *Conc. Cabil.* (647–653), 3 (ibid., 304).

56. *Conc. Aurelianense* (541), 29 (*CCL* 148A, 139): "Si que mulieris [*sic*] fuerint in adulterio cum clericis deprehensae, . . . a civitatibus . . . repellantur."

57. *Hist. franc.* 6.36 (*MGH Script. rer. mer.* 1, 276).

58. *Conc. Turonense* (567), 10 (*CCL* 148A, 179).

59. *Lex Bai.* 1.12 (*MGH Legum Sectio I,* 5/2, 284–285).

60. Gryson, *Le ministère,* pp. 21–25; J. Forget, "Diaconesses," in *Dictionnaire de théologie catholique,* vol. 4, (Paris, 1911), pp. 685–703; H. Leclercq, "Diaconesse," in *Dictionnaire d'archéologie chrétienne et de liturgie,* vol. 4 (Paris, 1920), 725–733; G. G. Blum, "Das Amt der Frau im Neuen Testament," in *Novum Testamentum,* 7 (1964), 142–161. Van der Meer translates *diakonos* as "servant," but argues that Phoebe was Paul's co-worker, even though the term "did not really carry with it the sense of precise ministerial function which it will have later where women are concerned." *Women Priests,* p. 44.

61. *Didascalia et Constitutiones Apostolorum* 1 (Funk, p. 188).

62. Gryson has analyzed in depth the *Didascalia* and all the Eastern sources in

Le ministère, pp. 75–150. See also the list of fourth and fifth century inscriptions in the review of A. Kalsbach's monograph, *Die altkirchliche Einrichtung,* by Odo Casel, "Altchristliche Liturgie bis auf Konstantin d. Gr.," *Jahrbuch für Liturgiewissenschaft,* 11 (1931), 270–278.

63. Ambrosiaster, *Comm. 1 Tim.* (*CSEL* 81/3, 267–268).

64. I am following closely the analysis of Henry Chadwick, *Priscillian of Avila: The Occult and the Charismatic in the Early Church* (Oxford, 1976). It is noteworthy that one of the few surviving manuscripts of Priscillian's teachings (Würzburg, Univ. Bibl. M.p.th.q.3) was in the possession of a certain Bilihilt in the eighth century. Chadwick cites scholarly opinion suggesting that she may have been Saint Bilihild, the founder of Altmünster at Mainz. Ibid., p. 63.

65. Nora Chadwick, *Poetry and Letters in Early Christian Gaul* (London, 1955), attributes the literary activity of noble ladies in fourth-century Gaul to their education and their prestige as heiresses and wives. She also gives many examples of the close association these women had with religious leaders and the agreements of sexual abstinence they concluded with their husbands.

66. Jerome, *Letters and Select Works,* 133 (Freemantle, 273–274). The historian of the sect, Sulpicius Severus, while censuring the excessive punishment Priscillian and his followers suffered, helped to perpetuate the rumors by writing about nightly prayer services held by Priscillian's naked female disciples: Sulpicius, *Chron.* 2.50.8 (*CSEL* 1, 103): "nocturnos etiam turpium feminarum egisse conventus nudumque orare solitum."

67. *Conc. Saragossa* (380), 1 (Bruns 2, 13); *Conc. Neumausense* (394–396), 2 (*CCL* 148, 50).

68. *Conc. Arausicanum* (441), 25 (26) (*CCL* 148, 84): "Diaconae omnimodis non ordinandae; si quae iam sunt, benedictioni quae populo impenditur capita submittant." The terms "ordinatio" and "ordinare" denoted appointments to an ecclesiastical office, as is evident from *Stat. eccl. ant.* 90–97 (*CCL* 148, 181–183), and also other passages noted in the index of the same collection (*CCL* 148, 272–273). In the early church the ordination of deaconesses usually followed the same ritual as that for deacons. For exceptions, see A. Kalsbach, "Diakonissenweihe in Kan. 19 des Konzils von Nicea," *Römische Quartalschrift,* 32 (1924), 166–169; and Odo Casel, "Die Mönchsweihe," *Jahrbuch für Liturgiewissenschaft,* 5 (1925), 4–5.

69. See note 74, below. This certainly was the case in Italy, where Sergius, archbishop of Ravenna (743–752), consecrated his wife to the diaconate. See Agnellus, *Liber pontificalis ecclesiae Ravennatis* 154 (*MGH Script. rer. lang.* 377): "Quam, post regimen ecclesiae suscepit, eam Eufimiam sponsam suam diaconissam consecravit."

70. On the sources of this collection, see *Les Statuta Ecclesiae antiqua: Édition, études critiques,* ed. Ch. Munier (Bibliothèque de l'Institut de Droit Canonique de l'Université de Strasbourg, 5; Paris, 1960), pp. 125–146.

71. *Const. apost.* 2.26 (*PG* 1, 667A-B): "At diaconissa a vobis in figuram sancti Spiritus honoretur; quae absque diacono nihil agat, aut loquatur; sicut nec Paracletus a se quidquam loquitur aut facit, sed Christum glorificans, expectat illius voluntatem; ad haec, ut in Christum non creditur, nisi per Spiritus doctrinam, sic nulla mulier nisi per diaconissam ad diaconum et ad episcopum accedat." *Const. apost.* 3.6 (*PG* 1, 770): "Non igitur licere volumus mulieribus, ut in ecclesia doceant." *Const. apost.* 3.9 (*PG* 1, 782): "Quod non oportet, ut mulieres baptizent." *Const. apost.* 3.16 (*PG* 1, 798B): "Ac virum quidem suscipiat diaconus; mulierem vero diaconissa." *Stat. eccl. ant.* 37 (*CCL* 148, 172): "Mulier, quamvis docta et sancta, viros in conventu docere non praesumat." *Stat. eccl. ant.* 41 (*CCL* 148, 173): "Mulier baptizare non praesumat." *Stat. eccl. ant.* 100 (*CCL* 148, 184): "Viduae vel sanctimoniales, quae ad ministerium baptizandarum mulierum eliguntur, tam instructae sint ad officium, ut possint aperto et sano sermone docere imperitas et rusticanas mulieres, tempore quo baptizandae sunt, qualiter baptizatoris ad interrogata respondeant et qualiter accepto baptismate vivant." *Stat. eccl. ant.* 102 (*CCL* 148, 185): "Viduae, quae stipendio ecclesiae sustentantur, tam assiduae in Dei opere esse debent, quae et meritis et orationibus suis ecclesiam iuvent."

72. "Litterae trium episcoporum Gallicorum anno 511 scriptae," in J. Friedrich, ed., "Liber die Cenones der Montanisten bei Hieronymus," *Sitzungsberichte der bayerischen Akademie, philosofisch-historische Klasse* (1895), 207–221; reprinted in J. Mayer, ed., *Monumenta de viduis, diaconissis, virginibusque tractantia* (Florilegium patristicum, 42; Bonn, 1938), pp. 46–47; trans. Pierre de Labriolle, *Les sources de l'histoire du montanisme* (Fribourg, 1913), pp. 226–230. See also Labriolle's *La crise montaniste* (Bibliothèque de la Fondation Thiers, 31; Paris, 1913), pp. 499–507; and L. Gougaud, *Les chrétientés celtiques* (Paris, 1911), pp. 95–96; van der Meer, *Women Priests*, p. 98.

73. Remy of Reims, *Testamentum* (*CCL* 117, 477); Fortunatus, *De vita sanctae Radegundis* 12 (*MGH Script. rer. mer.* 2, 368): "veniens ad beatum Medardum Novomago, supplicat instanter, ut ipsam, mutata veste, Domino consecraret . . . manu superposita, consecravit diaconam." *De vita sanctae Radegundis* 15 (ibid., 369): "Nam ex illo tempore, quo, beato Medardo consecrante velata est."

74. *Conc. Epaonense* (517), 21 (*CCL* 148A, 29): "Veduarum consecrationem, quas diaconas vocitant, ab omni regione nostra paenitus abrogamus, sola eis paenitentiae benedictione, si converti ambiunt, inponenda." This kind of benediction, according to the Council of Orléans, could be given only to elderly women with the consent of their husbands, for it entailed lifelong sexual abstinence: *Conc. Aurelianense* (538), 27–28 (*CCL* 148A, 124).

75. *Conc. Aurelianense* (533), 17 (*CCL* 148A, 101): "Foeminae, quae benedictionem diaconatus actenus contra interdicta canonum acceperunt, si ad

coniugium probantur iterum devolutae, a communione pellantur. Quod si huiusmodi contubernium admonitae ab episcopo cognito errore dissolverint, in communionis gratia acta penitentia revertantur." *Conc. Aurelianense* 18 (*CCL* 148A, 101): "Placuit etiam, ut nulli postmodum foeminae diaconalis benedictio pro conditionis huius fragilitate credatur."

76. *Conc. Turonense* (567), 21 (20) (*CCL* 148A, 187): "solus propositus ille sufficere debet."

77. *Syn. Dioc. Autiss.* (561–605) 36–37, 42 (*CCL* 148A, 269–270). *Conc. Luodicense* 44 (Mansi 2, 581). Gelasius, *Epist.* 9, *Decr.* 26 (*PL* 59, 48; JK 636). Audet has traced back to the third century the belief that a certain distance must be maintained between the impure and the sacred (*Structures,* p. 13). See also van der Meer, *Women Priests,* pp. 94–95.

78. *Iudicium Clementi* 13 (Wasserschleben, 434; McNeill, 272).

79. See below, note 91.

80. The earliest manuscript of *De vita sanctae Radegundis* listed by the editor dates from the ninth century (*MGH Script, rer. mer.* 2, 360). But we know that hagiographers in the seventh and eighth centuries knew and used the work.

81. *Vita S. Sigolenae* 10 (*AS* 24 Iulii; 5, 632): "Eo sub tempore directam legationem ad Pontificem praedictae urbis suis miserunt parentes, ut ipsam, mutata veste, Domino consecraret. Qui eorum agnita voluntate, manu superposita consecravit diaconam." Wilhelm Levison has shown that, for this passage, the author used Fortunatus's *De vita sanctae Radegundis* 12 (*MGH Script. rer. mer.* 2, 368). "Sigolena," *Neues Archiv,* 35 (1910), 219–231. The author used other lives as well. Jean Verdon states that the details furnished by the author "ne peuvent-ils pas être retenus." "Recherches sur les monastères féminins dans la France du Sud aux IXe–XIe siècles," *Annales du Midi,* 88 (1976), 122. On the other hand, we cannot discard the possibility that Sigolena was consecrated a deaconess.

82. Deacon Grimo of Trier mentioned his sister Ermengunda, a deaconess, in a will. See *Urkundenbuch zur Geschichte der jetzt die preussischen Regierungsbezirke Coblenz und Trier bildenden Mittelrheinischen Territorien,* ed. H. Beyer, vol. 1 (Coblenz, 1860), 6.

83. *Conc. Incerti Loci* (post 614), 12 (*CCL* 148A, 288): "Presbyteri vel diaconi se nulla racione nubere praesumant." For precedents see above, note 21.

84. K. H. Schäfer, *Die Kanonissenstifter im deutschen Mittelalter.* For works supporting or refuting his thesis, see notes 5 above and 112 below.

85. See above note 53. *Conc. Incerti Loci* (post 614), 8 (*CCL* 148A, 287): "illa ut adultera condemnetur."

86. Friedrich Prinz, "Die bischöfliche Stadtherrschaft," *Historische Zeitschrift,* 217 (1973), 1–35, in particular 22–27.

87. Boniface, *Die Briefe,* 50–51, ed. Tangl, pp. 82–88. The first is by Boniface and the second is Zachary's reply.

88. *Conc. Romanum.* (745), prefatory letter (*MGH Conc.* 2, 39; JE 2273a, 2275).

89. *Karoli Magni Capitulare generale* 5 (*MGH Legum* 1, 33): "Si sacerdotes plures uxores habuerint . . . sacerdotio priventur."

90. Boniface, *Die Briefe* 59, ed. Tangl, p. 112.

91. *Admonitio generalis* (789), 76 (*MGH Capit.* 1, 60): "abbatissas contra morem sanctae Dei ecclesiae benedictionis cum manus impositione et signaculo sanctae crucis super capita virorum dare, necnon et velare virgines cum benedictione sacerdotali . . . quod omnino vobis . . . interdicendum esse scitote." Repeated verbatim in *Ansegesi capit.* 1.71 (*MGH Capit.* 1, 404).

92. *Conc. Parisiense* (829), 45 (*MGH Conc.* 2, 639): "contra legem divinam canonicamque institutionem feminas sanctis altaribus se ultro ingerere sacrataque vasa impudenter contingere et indumenta sacerdotalia presbyteris administrare, et, quod his maius, indecentius ineptiusque est, corpus et sanguinem Domini populis porrigere et alia quaeque, quae ipso dictu turpia sunt exercere . . . Miranda sane res est . . . ut quod viris saecularibus inlicitum est, feminae, quarum sexui nullatenus competit, aliquando contra fas sibi licitum facere potuerint." For sources for this, see note 77. In 820 Haito of Basel, in *Capitulare* 16 (*PL* 115, 13), wrote: "mulieres ad altare non accedant, nec ipsae Deo dicatae in nullo ministerio altaris intermisceantur. Quod si pallae altaris lavandae sunt, a clericis abstrahantur, et ad cancellos feminis tradantur. Similiter et presbyteri, cum oblata ab eisdem mulieribus offeruntur, ibidem accipiantur, et ad altare deferantur." Earlier, Theodulf of Orléans, in his *Capitula* 6 (*PL* 105, 193–194), ordered: "Feminae missam sacerdote celebrante, nequaquam ad altare accedant." In his second capitulary he was even more explicit; *Capitulare* (*PL* 105, 209): "quando missa celebratur, nulla femina ad altare praesumat accedere aut presbitero ministrare aut infra cancellas stare aut sedere." See de Clercq, *La législation,* vol. 1, 325.

93. *Conc. Germ.* (742), 7 (*MGH Conc.* 2, 4); *Conc. Suess.* (744), 8 (*MGH Conc.* 2, 35); *Conc. Risp. Fris. Salis.* (800), 17 (*MGH Conc.* 2, 210); *Conc. Mog.* (813), 49 (*MGH Conc.* 2, 272); *Karl. Capit.* (742), 7 (*MGH Capit.* 1, 26); *Admonitio generalis* (789), 4 (*MGH Conc.* 1, 54); *Capit. miss. gen.* (802), 24 (*MGH Capit.* 1, 96); *Capit. miss. spec.* (ca. 802), 3 (*MGH Capit.* 1, 102); *Conc. Worm.* (868), 9 (Mansi 15, 871); *Conc. Mog.* (888), 19 (Mansi 18, 69).

94. On the organization of the cathedral clergy into chapters of canons, see E. Morhain, "Origine et histoire de la règle canonique de s. Chrodegang," in *Miscellanea Pio Paschini,* vol. 1 (Lateranum, N.S. 14; Rome, 1948), 173–185. Chrodegang warned his canons against visiting women: "Nemo inter serpentes et scorpiones securus ingrediatur." Boelens, *Die Klerikerehe,* p. 82. Gabriella Rossetti has classified Carolingian legislation on clerical continence in two categories: councils ordering clerks of all grades to live in a "claustrum" and councils prohibiting subdeacons, deacons and priests to have women living in their homes even if these

women were near blood relatives. "Il matrimonio del clero," p. 530, n. 102.

95. *Capit. miss. gen.* (802), 5 (*MGH Capit.* 1, 108); *Capit. ad Lec. Can.* (802), 5 (*MGH Capit.* 1, 108); *Conc. Worm.* (868), 9–11 (Mansi, 15, 871); *Conc. Trib.* (895), 11a (*MGH Capit.* 2, 541). See also G. Rossetti, "Il matrimonio del clero," p. 530, n. 102.

96. *Conc. Liftinense* (743), 1 (*MGH Conc.* 2, 7): "Fornicatores et adulteros clericos, qui sancta loca vel monasteria ante tenentes coinquinaverunt, praecipimus inde tollere et ad poenitentiam redigere."

97. *Conc. Germ.* (742), 6 (*MGH Conc.* 2, 4): "Quisquis servorum Dei vel ancillarum Christi in crimen fornicationis lapsus fuerit, quod in carcere poenitentiam faciat in pane et aqua et, si ordinatus presbyter fuisset, duos annos in carcere permaneat et antea flagellatus et scorticatus videatur . . ." See also *Karl. Capit. Lift.* (743), 1 (*MGH Capit.* 1, 28); *Capit. miss. gen.* (802), 24 (*MGH Capit.* 1, 96): "honorem simul et hereditatem privetur."

98. *Conc. Meld. Par.* (845–846), 36 (*MGH Capit.* 2, 407): "neque mulieres quamcumque frequentationem habeant in locis, in quibus presbiteri aliquem recursum habuerint. Quodsi observare parvipenderint, ita ut transgressores et qui contra interdicta fecerint iudicentur." *Capit. Olonnense ecclesiasticum alterum* (825), 5 (*MGH Capit.* 1, 328) stated that women who lived with priests were to be ostracized.

99. See note 28, above.

100. *Capit. Francicum* (779), 18 (*MGH Capit.* 2, 38): "Item placuit de sanctimonialibus mulieribus qui se copulaverunt viris aut adulterio se polluerunt, ut disiugantur, et intrent in monasteria, tam viri quamque et feminae, cum rebus suis et cum illa compositione quam in publico dare debuerint."

101. On fornication in nunneries, see *Epist. Fuldensium fragmenta* C.6 (*MGH Epist.* 5, *Kar. aevi* 4, 525) and *Conc. Aquis.* (836), 2.12 (Mansi 14, 682), which ordered the investigation of nunneries "quae in quibusdam locis lupinaria potius videntur esse."

102. Boelens, refuted earlier interpretations of the Carolingians' silence on clerical marriages as a retreat from an uncompromising position of opposition. "Fornicatio," which was forbidden to clerks in higher orders by synod after synod, must be interpreted, according to Boelens, in a broad sense as referring to "jene unerlaubte Art von Beischlaf." *Die Klerikerehe*, pp. 87–88. For a summary of Carolingian legislation on the subject, see ibid., pp. 108–109.

103. *Annales Fuldenses* (847) (*MGH Script.* 1, 365). The characterization of Theuda as an "extravagant madwoman," an "eccentric heresiarch," by Jeffrey B. Russell seems excessive. See *Dissent and Reform in the Early Middle Ages* (Berkeley, 1965), pp. 108, 252.

104. *Vita s. Liutbirgae* 35 (*MGH Script.* 4, 164).

105. *Conc. Mog.* (888), 10 (Mansi 18, 67): "Quamvis enim sacri canones quas-

dam personas foeminarum simul cum clericis in una domo habitare permittant: tamen . . . saepe audivimus, per illam concessionem plurima scelera esse comissa, ita ut quidam sacerdotum cum propriis sororibus concumbentes, filios ex eis generassent." The following year, in a similar vein, Riculf, Bishop of Soissons, wrote that priests must be on guard against their mothers, aunts, sisters, and other near female relatives, "ne forte illud eveniat quod in sancta Scriptura legitur de Thamar, sorore Absalon . . . de Loth etiam qui filias suas . . . similiter corripit." *Statuta* 14 (*PL* 131, 20). Theodulf of Orléans, in *Capitula* 12 and *Capitulare* 6 (*PL* 105, 195, 209), also prohibited cohabitation with near blood relations, but on different grounds: once a woman lives in a priest's house, other women will come to visit her and tempt the priest. Theodulf's source was probably canon four of the Council of Friuli (796–797) (*MGH Capit.* 2, 178).

106. *Vita s. Verenae virginis* 2.9 (*AS* 1 Sept.; 1, 166): "et tulit Verena ampullam vini inter sacras manus suas, et afferebat ad altare ad manus sacerdotis . . . . Respondit presbyter, et ait ei: 'Si vis his nobiscum esse, mane in domo mea, et utere bonis meis;' commendavitque ei clavem cellarii sui, et omnia quae habebat." On the author Hatto, see Adolf Reinle, *Die heilige Verena von Zürzach: Legende, Kult, Denkmäler* (Ars docta, 6, Basel, 1948).

107. Prudentius, *Vita s. Maurae virginis* 4 (*AS* 21 Sept.; 6, 276).

108. *Conc. Worm.* 9 (Mansi 15, 871).

109. See the letter of Mantio, bishop of Châlons, to Fulcher, archbishop of Reims (*PL* 131, 23).

110. *Conc. Mog.* (852), 20 (*MGH Capit.* 2, 191). The council quoted *Conc. Gang.* 4 (Mansi 2, 1106), as did Pseudo-Isidore, *Decretales*, p. 265. Nicholas I's declaration, *Epist.* 99, 70 (*MGH Epist.* 6, *Kar. aevi 4*, 592; JE 2812) was cited around 1065, in *Tractatus pro clericorum connubio* (*MGH Libelli de Lite* 3, 591–592).

111. *Conc. Worm.* (868), 73 (Mansi 15, 882); Mayer, *Monumenta*, p. 51.

112. F. Maassen, "Glossen des canonischen Rechts aus dem karolingischen Zeitalter," *Akademie der Wissenschaften, Wien, phil.-hist. Klasse, Sitzungsberichte*, 84 (1876), 274. Schäfer ("Kanonissen," pp. 49–90), made full use of this gloss to support the thesis that the heads of the institutes of canonesses were deaconesses. His other evidence (ibid., p. 53, n. 4), the reference in the *Liber memorialis* of Remiremont to Ida, abbess of Remiremont and deaconess, is applicable only for a later period. Schäfer had access only to a description of the entry in A. Ebner, "Der liber vitae und die Nekrologien von Remiremont in der Bibliotheca Angelica zu Rom," *Neues Archiv*, 19 (1894), 47–83. E. Hlawitschka, one of the editors of *Liber memorialis*, lists Ida as the twenty-second abbess, living in the early tenth century. See *Studien*, p. 42. See also *Liber memorialis*, 13r, 32v.

113. *Epistola* 8 (*PL* 134, 114–115).

114. *Epist. aevi mer. collectae* 11 (*MGH Epist.* 3, *Mer. kar. aevi* 1, 452).

CHAPTER 7

1. As Elise Boulding remarked: "One of the many frustrations in trying to write the underside of history is that the rise of the monastic movement is written almost entirely in terms of men" (*The Underside of History* [Boulder, Colo., 1978], p. 368). Lina Eckenstein's *Woman under Monasticism* and her *The Women of Early Christianity* (London, 1935) may be supplemented by Eleanor Shipley Duckett, *The Gateway to the Middle Ages: Monasticism* (Ann Arbor, Mich., 1938), Sister M. Rosamond Nugent, *Portrait of the Consecrated Woman in Greek Christian Literature of the First Four Centuries* (Washington, D.C., 1941), and George H. Tavard, *Woman in Christian Tradition.* A more narrow focus is provided by René Metz, *La Consecration des vièrges dans l'Église romaine* (Paris, 1954). I was unable to consult the latest work on Carolingian monasteries by Jean Décarreaux, *Moines et monastères à l'époque de Charlemagne* (Paris, 1980). In his earlier work, Décarreaux dealt only with Radegund in some detail. See *Monks and Civilization from the Barbarian Invasions to the Reign of Charlemagne,* trans. C. Haldane (London, 1962).

2. See Introduction, notes 8–14, for relevant literature on the subject. Jean Verdon listed the nunneries that were still in existence in the ninth century. See "Recherches," pp. 117–138. He also noted that he is preparing a similar study on the nunneries of northern France (ibid., p. 118, n. 3).

3. Venantius Fortunatus, "De virginitate," *Opera poetica* 8.3, lines 327–384 (*MGH Auct. ant.* 4/1, 189–191).

4. Ambrose, *De virginibus* 1.6.25–27 (*PL* 16, 206–207) "plures generaverit, plus laborat. Numeret solatia filiorum, sed numeret pariter et molestias. Nubit et plorat . . . Concepit et, gravescit . . . quid recenseam nutriendi molestias, instituendi et copulandi." On the glories of virginity, see also Cyprian, *De habitu virg.* 22 (*CSEL* 3, 202–203); Jerome, *Adversus Helvidium* 20 (*PL* 23, 214A-B); *Epistolae* 22.2.1 (*CSEL* 54, 146); Augustine, *De sancta virginitate* 13 (*CSEL* 41, 245); *Epistulae* 150 (*CSEL* 44, 381). On the praises lavished on virgins in the high and later Middle Ages, see Matthäus Bernards, *Speculum virginum: Geistlichkeit und Seelenleben der Frau im Hochmittelalter* (Forschungen zur Volkskunde, 36, 38; Cologne, 1955), and John Bugge, *Virginitas: An Essay in the History of a Medieval Ideal* (International Archives of the History of Ideas, Ser. Min., 17; The Hague, 1975).

5. Gregory of Tours, *Liber vitae patrum* 19.1 (*MGH Script. rer. mer.* 1, 736). Gregory made it clear that she had married "parentum ad votum."

6. Hucbald, *Vita s. Rictrudis* (*MGH Script. rer. mer.* 6, 94). She died in 668, but her life was composed in 907; see Van der Essen, *Étude critique,* pp. 260–265.

7. *Vita s. Geretrudis* 2 (*MGH Script. rer. mer.* 2, 455–456). Gertrud was born in 626 and died in 658; when her father, Pepin, died in 640, she was fourteen years old, that is, of marriageable age.

8. *Vita s. Eustadiola* (*AS* 8 Iunii; 2, 132). She was a contemporary of Sulpicius, who died in 647; *Vita Sulpitii* (*MGH Script. rer. mer.* 4, 371–380). See also Dekkers, *Clavis patrum latinorum* 298.

9. *Vita s. Sigolenae* (*AS* 24 Iulii; 5, 630–637). See also above, chapter 6, note 81.

10. Fortunatus, *De vita sanctae Radegundis* 1.12 (*MGH Script. rer. mer.* 2, 368). Gregory of Tours, *Hist. franc.* 3.7 (*MGH Script. rer. mer.* 1, 115), also mentioned the murder of her brother.

11. On the history of Radegund's nunnery, first dedicated to Notre-Dame, and then named Sainte-Croix when Radegund obtained from the Emperor Justin a piece of the Cross, see, in addition to the sources cited in the previous note, her testament (Pardessus 192 [vol. 1, 151]) and the letter addressed to her by the Council of Tours held in 567 (*CCL* 148A, 195–199). Among secondary sources, see René Aigrain, *Sainte Radegonde* (Paris, 1918) and "Une abbesse mal connue de Sainte-Croix de Poitiers," *Bulletin philologique et historique* (1946–47), 197–202; Dom Pierre Monsabert, "Le testament de Sainte Radegonde," *Bulletin philologique et historique* (1926–27), 129–134; and Verdon, "Recherches," p. 120. Several articles deal with her in *Études mérovingiennes: Actes des Journées de Poitiers, 1952* (Paris, 1953): René Aigrain, "Un ancien poème anglais, sur la vie de sainte Radegonde," pp. 1–12; L. Coudanne, "Baudonivie, moniale de Sainte-Croix et biographe de sainte Radegonde," pp. 45–51; E. Delaruelle, "Sainte Radegonde, son type de sainteté et la chrétienté de son temps," pp. 65–74; Georges Marié, "Sainte Radegonde et le milieu monastique contemporain," pp. 219–225.

12. Ionas, *Vitae sanctorum: Columbani* 2.7 (*MGH Script. rer. mer.* 4/1, 122; *MGH Script. rer. germ. in usu schol.* 241–242). J. O'Carrol, "Sainte Fare et les origines," in *Sainte Fare et Faremoutiers* (L'Abbeye de Faremoutiers, 1956), pp. 4–35.

13. *Vita s. Austrebertae* 7 (*AS* 10 Feb.; 2, 420): "parentes ejus . . . arrhabone pro amore seculi recepto, tempus praefinitum et diem statuissent nuptiarium . . . illa in angustiis posita, cogitare coepit quid ageret. Moesta vero iter furtim arripuit, germano secum fratre, licet parvulo. assumpto." She was veiled around 656 and died between 681 and 704, according to the editor of her *Vita:* Pref. 1 (ibid., 418). Although her biographer claims to have been her contemporary, the *vita* was composed in the late eighth century; cf. Dekkers, *Clavis patrum latinorum* 2089.

14. *Vita Bertilae* 1 (*MGH Script. rer. mer.* 6, 101). According to the editor, W. Levison, the life was composed after the mid-eighth century, probably in the late eighth or ninth century (ibid. 6, 99).

15. *Vita Aldegundis* 2 (*MGH Script. rer. mer.* 6, 86). The prevailing opinion among scholars is that the first version of her life was composed before 850, in the late eighth century; for a summary of the literature, see E. de Moreau, *Histoire de l'Église en Belgique*, vol. 1, 2d ed. rev. (Brussels, 1945), 137–138. She died in 684, according to Van der Essen. *Étude critique*, pp. 219.

16. *Vita ss. Herlindis et Renildae* 3, 6 (*AS 22* Martii; 3, 384–385): "quoadusque filiae suae ad intelligibile tempus perductae fuissent, votis voverunt, absque ulla dilatione illas se tradituros divinis litteris imbuendas . . . in propria haereditate monasterium aedificarent, in quo electae filiae ipsorum pro peccatis suis immortali Domino funderent preces." Composed in the ninth century, according to Van der Essen, it contains legendary details about the life of the two sisters, who lived in the early part of the eighth century. *Études critique,* pp. 109–111.

17. Agius, *Agii Vita et obitus Hathumodae* 3 (*MGH Script.* 4, 167). She died in 874. Besides the monk Agius, her brother, she had two sisters, Gerberga and Christina, who also entered Gandersheim. Her older brother, Duke Otto, and her older sister, Liutgard, were married; see Heineken, *Die Anfänge,* and L. Zoepf, *Lioba, Hathumot, Wiborada: Drei Heilige des deutschen Mittelalters* (Munich, 1915); see also note 192, below.

18. *Vita Sadalbergae* 6, 10 (*MGH Script. rer. mer.* 5, 53, 55). She died shortly after the death of Waldabert of Luxeuil in 670. Her *vita* was probably composed in the first half of the ninth century, according to the editor, B. Krusch (ibid., 45). We know that she had dedicated herself to the service of God quite early in life, as soon as Eustachius cured her blindness: Ionas, *Vitae sanctorum: Columbani* 2.8 (*MGH Script. rer. mer.* 4/1, 122). See also chapter 5, note 29.

19. Jane Tibbetts Schulenburg's conclusions indicate a similar pattern: "In the sixth century, women comprised slightly over eight per cent of the total number of saints. . . . With the seventh century there is a substantial increase in the number of women saints. Approximately 15% . . . were women. . . . For the first half of the [eighth] century the percentage reached 23.5%. . . . [In the ninth century] . . . only 13.7% are women." "Sexism and Celestial Gynaeceum, 500–1200," *Journal of Medieval History,* 3 (1978), 120, 122, 123.

20. The community at Riez, which Sidonius Apollinaris mentioned in his *Carmina* 16.84 (*MGH Auct. ant.* 8, 241), may have been among those that did not survive the invasions. On Riez, see also E. Griffe, *La Gaule chrétienne à l'époque romaine,* vol. 2 (Paris, 1966), 260–65, with an explanation of the Sidonius reference in note 5, p. 263.

21. Before the foundation of Saint Jean, Caesaria lived at Marseilles, in a nunnery established by Cassian; see *Vitae Caesarii* 35 (*MGH Script. rer. mer.* 3, 470).

22. *Vita Romani* 1.15 (*MGH Script. rer. mer.* 3, 140). Romanus died at the end of the fourth century; see F. Prinz, *Frühes Mönchtum,* pp. 23–24. His life was composed in the sixth century; on its value as a source, see K. Weber, "Kulturgeschichtliche Probleme der Merowingerzeit im Spiegel frühmittelalterlicher Heiligenleben," *Studien und Mitteilungen des Benediktinerordens und seiner Zweige,* 48 (1930), 366–375.

23. *Vita Eugendi* 5 (*MGH Script. rer. mer.* 3, 156): "monachas vero procul intra urbem monasterioque conseptas ultra sexagenario numero admirabile ordinatione rexit et aluit." It later became a Benedictine abbey; see

Cartulaire de l'Abbaye de Saint-André-le-Bas de Vienne, ordre de Saint Benoît, ed. U. Chevalier (Vienne, 1869). A donation issued in 543 to another nunnery outside the city refers to this convent as the one where the donor's sister, Eubonia, is abbess. See Pardessus 140 (vol. 1, 107), and note 28, below.

24. *Vitae Caesarii* 1, 35 (*MGH Script. rer. mer.* 3, 470). For further literature, see F. Benoît, "Topographie monastique d'Arles au VIᵉ siècle," *Études mérovingiennes: Actes des Journées de Poitiers, 1952* (Paris, 1953), pp. 13–17; idem, "Le premier baptistère d'Arles et l'Abbaye Saint-Césaire," *Cahiers archéologiques*, 5 (1951), 31–59; F. Prinz, *Frühes Mönchtum*, p. 77, nn. 179–181; and L. Ueding, *Geschichte der Klostergründungen des frühen Merowingerzeit* (Historische Studien, 261; Berlin, 1935), pp. 56–64.

25. Caesarius of Arles, *Regula sanctarum virginum* 39, 46, 64, in *Opera omnia*, ed. G. Morin, vol. 2 (Maredsous, 1942), 112, 114, 119.

26. Saint Radegund adopted Caesarius's Rule for the convent Clothar built for her; Gregory of Tours, *Hist. franc.* 9.39 (*MGH Script. rer. mer.* 1, 395), and *Epistolae aevi mer.* 11 (*MGH Epist.* 3, *Mer. kar. aevi* 1, 450–453); also René Aigrain, "Le voyage de sainte Radegonde à Arles," *Bulletin philologique et historique* (1926–27), 119–127. Hope Mayo discusses various rules used in Frankish convents. See her "Three Merovingian Rules for Nuns" (Ph.D. dissertation, Harvard University, 1974). See also F. Prinz, *Frühes Mönchtum*, pp. 80–82, and note 106, below.

27. Aurelian founded Saint Mary of Arles around 548, incorporating many of Caesarius's points into its rule. A combination of the two rules was adopted by Bishop Ferreolus of Uzès for Ferreolac. For further literature, see Ueding, *Klöstergründungen*, p. 75; F. Prinz, *Frühes Mönchtum*, p. 80, n. 196; and Mayo "Three Merovingian Rules."

28. Pardessus 140 (vol. 1, 107). It was intended to serve as a burial convent with their daughter Remilia serving as abbess. According to Ado, *Chronicon* (*MGH Script.* 2, 317), the monastery was founded in 575 outside the walls. In the city there was another convent established by Leonian; Remilia was raised there. See also *Gallia Christiana*, vol. 16, 172, and note 23, above.

29. Gregory of Tours, *Hist. franc.* 9.35 (*MGH Script. rer. mer.* 1, 390).

30. Gregory of Tours, *Liber in gloria confessorum* 16 (*MGH Script. rer. mer.* 1, 756–757).

31. René Metz, "Les vièrges chrétiennes en Gaul au IVᵉ siècle," in *Saint Martin et son temps* (Studia Anselmiana, 46; Rome, 1961), pp. 109–132; idem, "La consécration des vièrges en Gaul des origines à l'apparition des livres liturgiques," *Revue de droit canonique*, 6 (1956), 321–339; idem, "La consécration des vièrges dans l'Église franque d'après la plus ancienne vie de Sainte Pusinne (VIII–IXᵉ siècle)," *Revue des sciences religieuses*, 35 (1961), 32–48. For studies on professed widows, see below, note 58.

32. Nora Chadwick, in her *Poetry and Letters in Early Christian Gaul*, gives examples of married couples in fourth-century Gaul renouncing sexual rela-

tions and dedicating their lives to divine service. Concerning virgins, see Metz's articles in the previous note.

33. Henry Neff Waldron, treated this form of religious life as the most common expression of lay *conversio*. On the basis of conciliar admonitions addressed to women converts, Waldron concludes that "avowed widows and professed virgins living in their own homes were the most common of all forms of *conversio*" ("Expressions of Religious Conversion among Laymen Remaining within Secular Society in Gaul: 400–800 A.D." [Ph.D. dissertation, Ohio State University, 1976], p. 338). He also notes that during the course of the eighth century male *conversi* abandoned tonsure, the outward mark of their *conversio,* and were no longer mentioned in ninth-century sources. This was not the case for virgins and widows dedicated to the service of God.

34. One was a washerwoman, "quae sub specie religionis veste mutata, concepit et peperit." The other, Marcoveifa, "religiosa veste habens," became a queen. *Hist. franc.* 2.1; 4.26 (*MGH Script. rer. mer.* 1, 37, 157).

35. Gregory of Tours, *Liber in gloria confessorum* 33 (*MGH Script. rer. mer.* 1, 768).

36. Fortunatus, *De vita sanctae Radegundis* 1.2 (*MGH Script. rer. mer.* 2, 365–366).

37. Gregory of Tours, *Hist. franc.* 2.43 (*MGH Script. rer. mer.* 1, 106): "Chrodechildis autem regina post mortem viri sui Turonus venit, ibique ad basilica Martini deserviens."

38. Gregory of Tours, *Hist. franc.* 9.33 (*MGH Script. rer. mer.* 1, 387): "in atrio sancti Martini."

39. Gregory of Tours, *De virtutibus s. Martini.* 1.17 (*MGH Script. rer. mer.* 1, 598): "In portam Ambiensi, in qua . . . oratorium a fidelibus est aedificatum, in quo nunc puellae religiosae deserviunt." See also Ueding, *Klostergründungen,* p. 129.

40. Gregory of Tours, *Liber vitae patrum* 9.2 (*MGH Script. rer. mer.* 1, 703). This nunnery grew up around the oratory built by Saint Patroclus. When he decided to withdraw to the woods, he left his cell to the virgins who had congregated there. See C. A. Bernouilli, *Die Heiligen der Merowinger* (Tübingen, 1900), pp. 99–100; Ueding, *Klostergründungen,* pp. 16, 126.

41. Two donations, forged in the eleventh century, claim that it was founded by Clovis and Clotild for their daughter Theodechild: see Pardessus 64 (vol. 1, 34), 335 (vol. 2, 112). See also M. Prou, *Étude sur les chartes de fondation de l'Abbaye de Saint-Pierre-le-Vif* (Paris, 1894), and H. Bouvier, "Histoire de Saint-Pierre-le-Vif à Sens," *Bulletin des sciences hist. et nat. de l'Yonne,* 45 (1892), 1–212. Ueding has argued that the cloister was founded by a Theudechild, the daughter of Queen Suavegotha, the wife of Theuderic I, *Klostergründungen,* pp. 198–204. This Theudechild was the sister of Theudebert I (534–548), rather than the daughter of Charibert, for whom Venantius Fortunatus composed an epitaph: *Opera poetica* (*MGH Auct. ant.* 4/1, 94). On the document listed in Pardessus as number 335, see Ewig, "Das Privileg," p. 92, nn. 48–50.

42. Prinz identifies it with Saint Martin-les-Marien. See *Frühes Mönchtum,* pp.

65–66. See also J. Wollasch, "Das Patrimonium beati Germani in Auxerre," *Studien und Vorarbeiten zur Geschichte des grossfränkischen- und frühdeutschen Adels*, ed. G. Tellenbach (Freiburg, 1957), p. 188. According to René Louis, it was affiliated with Saint Cosmas-Saint Damien, a male community, and the two formed a double monastery. See *Autessiodurum christianum: les églises d'Auxerre des origines au XIme siècle* (Paris, 1952), p. 16.

43. Gregory of Tours, *Liber vitae patrum* 19.2 (*MGH Script. rer. mer.* 1, 738): "Ibique paucas collegens monachas, cum fide integra et oratione degebat." According to Ueding, she died around 579 (*Klostergründungen*, pp. 25–26). F. Prinz has suggested that the Chartres community was organized according to the model of Saint Martin convents (*Frühes Mönchtum*, p. 37).

44. According to tradition, the first convent was at Aliscamps; see A. Malnory, *Saint Césaire, évêque d'Arles (503–43)* (Bibl. de l'École des Hautes Études, Sciences Philol. et Hist., 103; Paris, 1894), pp. 257–260; L. A. Constans, *Arles antique* (Paris, 1941), pp. 357–358; and the articles by F. Benoît, cited above, in note 24.

45. Gregory of Tours, *Hist. franc.* 4.26 (*MGH Script. rer. mer.* 1, 162).

46. Gregory of Tours, *Liber in gloria confessorum* 18 (*MGH Script. rer. mer.* 1, 757–758); the two virgins were Maura and Britta.

47. Further research is needed on the proportion of male and female communities in the sixth century. Ueding (*Klostergründungen*) listed fifty-nine monasteries for men and seventeen for women. See also Ch. Higounet, "Le problème économique: L'Église et la vie rurale pendant le très haut moyen âge," *Le Chiese nei regni dell'Europa occidentale* (Centro Italiano di Studi sull'Alto Medioevo: Settimana di studio, 7, 2; Spoleto, 1960), pp. 775–804. Higounet noted that three-fourths of the Merovingian monasteries were built in the country and one-fourth in the cities. Ibid., p. 785. Jean Hubert argues against the prevailing view that monasteries grew around hermitages. On the contrary, hermitages were attached to monasteries to permit members to engage periodically in complete solitude. "L'Érémitisme et archéologie," in *L'Eremetismo in occidente nei secoli XI e XII* (Milan, Univ. Catt. del Sacro Cuore, Contributi, Ser. 3, Var. 4; Studi medioevali: Misc. 4; Milan, 1965), pp. 469–475.

48. See notes 11, 38–39, 41–43, above.

49. Gregory I, *Registrum epistularum* 13.7, 12 (*MGH Epist.* 2, 371–372, 378–380). The second letter specified that the abbess was to be chosen by the king, with the consent of the nuns. Even though Autun did not emulate Arles in the election of the abbess, it had close relations with that convent. See F. Prinz, *Frühes Mönchtum*, p. 78.

50. Gregory of Tours, in his *Hist. franc.* 10.8 (*MGH Script. rer. mer.* 1, 415), mentioned a convent at Lyons from which Eulalius, count of Auvergne, had abducted a nun. Dedicated to Saint Peter, it was known as Sancti-Petri-Puellaris (Saint Pierre-aux-Nonnaines). Two donations that claim it was founded by King Gaudesil and his wife Teudelind are tenth and

twelfth century forgeries. See A. Coville, "La prétendue charte mérovingienne de Saint-Pierre de Lyon," and "L'Évêque Aunemundus et son
testament," in his *Recherches sur l'histoire de Lyon du Ve au IXe siècle (450–
800)* (Paris, 1928), pp. 251–266, and 366–416. For the two donations,
see Pardessus 196 (vol. 1, 156) and 324 (vol. 2, 101–102). The nunnery
was in existence in the early ninth century: Bishop Leidradus of Lyons,
in a letter to Charles the Great, dated 813, mentioned thirty-two nuns
living there under the Benedictine Rule, *Epist. variorum Carolo Magno
regnante scriptae* 30 (*MGH Epist.* 4, Mer. kar. aevi 2, 543). According to
Vita s. Boniti 37 (*MGH Script. rer. mer.* 6, 137), a woman called Dida was
the abbess in 705.

51. The sixth-century donations to Sancta Maria "juxta muros" are all forger-
    ies dating from the ninth century, according to Julien Havet, "Questions
    mérovingiennes VII: Les actes des évêques du Mans." *Bibliothèque de
    l'École des Chartes* 55 (1894), 5–60. See Pardessus, 108, 117, 128 (vol. 1,
    72–74; 80, 94–95). Ueding (*Klostergründungen,* p. 158) includes the con-
    vent among sixth-century foundations.

52. On Arles, see above, notes 24 and 27; on Vienne, notes 23 and 27; on
    Tours, notes 38 and 43.

53. See above, note 40.

54. On Chelles, see below, note 82. On Notre-Dame les Andelys, see *Vita s.
    Chrothildis* 11 (*MGH Script. rer. mer.* 2, 346). Bede mentioned Les Andelys
    among the Frankish convents to which English kings sent their daugh-
    ters to be educated. *Historia ecclesiastica gentis Anglorum* 3.8, ed. C. Plum-
    mer, vol. 1 (Oxford, 1896), 142. As F. Prinz has pointed out, Les Ande-
    lys was probably reorganized by Audoen of Rouen. See *Frühes Mönchtum,*
    pp. 296–297. See also Ph. Schmitz, *Histoire,* vol. 7, 19.

55. See chapter 6, notes 73–75.

56. *Conc. Turonense* 21 (20) (*CCL* 148A, 186), citing *Codex Theod.* 9.25.1 inter-
    pret. and 9.25.2 (Mommsen, vol. 1, 478–479), added the comparison to
    the vestal virgins.

57. *Conc. Aurelianense* (538), 19 (16) (*CCL* 148A, 121). The Council of Orléans
    (549), 19 (*CCL* 148A, 155) was somewhat more lenient, allowing absolu-
    tion after suitable penance. *Conc. Turonense* 21 (2) (*CCL* 148A, 185)
    quoted directly from Innocent I, *Epistola ad Victricium* (Feb. 15, 404; *PL*
    20, 475–477; JK 286). The idea that a virgin's vow of chastity was a
    marriage pact with Christ was developed by Origen on the basis of the
    Cantica Canticorum and then popularized by Jerome in his *Interpretatio
    Homil. Origenis in Cant. Cant.* 5–6 (*PL* 23, 1180–1182). Waldemar Molin-
    ski traces primary and secondary sources in "Virginity," *Sacramentum
    Mundi,* ed. Karl Rahner S. J., vol. 6 (London, 1970), 333–336. See also
    Jean Gaudemet, "Saint Augustin et le manquement au voeu de virgi-
    nité," *Annales de la Faculté de Droit d'Aix-en-Provence,* Nouv. ser., 43 (1950),
    135–145.

58. *Conc. Turenense* 21 (20) (*CCL* 148A, 187): "Illud vero, quod aliqui dicunt:

'vidua, quae benedicata non fuit, quare non debet maritum accipere?' "
We need further research on the status of widows who had been received into the religious life. André Rosambert's *La veuve en droit canonique* needs to be corrected and brought up to date; see the scathing
criticism of it by G. Le Bras in *Revue des sciences religieuses*, 6 (1926),
281–288. René Metz emphasized that the "ordo viduarum" initially
consisted of elderly widows who had been married only once and
needed material assistance; it was slowly transformed into a group of
women aspiring to lead a life of perfection. "La femme en droit canonique médiéval," p. 93. R. Gryson traced the process of assimilation
between the order of widows and the order of virgins, which began with
the imposition of the same habit by the first Council of Toledo, 9 (Bruns
1, 205). *Le ministère*, pp. 164–169. Despite the assimilation of the juridical status and function of professed virgins and widows, widows were
not eligible for the solemn liturgical rite of consecration; the Council of
Orange in 441 deprived widows of the right to receive benediction at
the time of their profession. It specified that the bishop was to hand a
widow "vestis vidualis," not before the altar, but in the "secretarium,"
the room where bishops received the faithful and arbitrated conflicts.
Conc. Arausicanum 26 (CCL 148, 85). The so-called *Sacramentarium
Gelasianum*, copied at Chelles shortly before 750, made a distinction
between the "Consecratio sacrae virginis" and "Benedictio viduae."
God accepted the former as a bride, but granted only consolation to the
latter (*Liber sacramentorum*, pp. 123–125, 213). On the basis of a twelfth-
century *ordo* for the veiling of widows, which was derived from an eighth
century *ordo*, Ann E. Mather concluded that "the veiling of a virgin was
the marriage of a woman to Christ, whereas a widow, whether or not her
husband was dead, offered herself to religious life in the church within
the contract that bound her to her husband" ("A Twelfth Century Ordo
for the Veiling of Widows," paper read at the Third Berkshire Conference on the History of Women; June, 1976). On the consecration of
virgins, see the articles by René Metz cited in note 31.

59. *Conc. Parisiense* (556–573), 5 (*CCL* 148A, 187); *Conc. Matisconense* (581–
583), 12 (*CCL* 148A, 226).
60. *Chlotharii I regis constitutio* 7 (*MGH Leg.* 1, 2).
61. Baudonivia, *De vita s. Radegundis* 6–7 (*MGH Script. rer. mer.* 2, 382).
62. *Conc. Parisiense* (614): *Edictum Clotarii II*, 18 (*CCL* 148A, 285).
63. Florentius, *Vita s. Rusticulae* 3 (*MGH Script. rer. mer.* 4, 341). On the value
of her biography, see Riché, "Note d'hagiographie mérovingienne: La
Vita s. Rusticulae," pp. 369–377.
64. See note 12, above.
65. *Lex Bai.* 1.11 (*MGH Legum Sectio I*, 5/2, 283–284).
66. *Conc. Clippiacense* (626–627), 26 (*CCL* 148A, 296): "neque per auctoritatem
regiam neque per quacumque potestate suffultus."
67. *Conc. Latunense* (673–675), 12–13 (*CCL* 148A, 316).

68. *Vita Sadalbergae* 8 (*MGH Script. rer. mer.* 5, 54).

69. For a bibliography of secondary sources and for the controversy whether Colomban arrived around 570 or 590, see F. Prinz, *Frühes Mönchtum*, p. 121, nn. 1–3.

70. Ionas, *Vitae sanctorum: Columbani* 1.20 (*MGH Script rer. germ. in usu schol.* 197).

71. For example, Ionas, in his *Vitae sanctorum: Columbani* 1.26 (*MGH Script. rer. germ. in usu schol.* 209), mentioned that the matron Aiga brought her children "ad benedicendum viro Dei." He consecrated them with his benediction, "videns . . . matris fidem." Her oldest son, Ado, and her second son, Iotrus, built Jouarre; her third son, Dado, built Rebais.

72. Ionas, *Vitae sanctorum: Columbani* 1.14 (*MGH Script. rer. germ. in usu schol.* 176).

73. Mary Bateson's *Origin and Early History of Double Monasteries* needs to be revised in view of modern scholarship. In particular, her thesis that there were double monasteries in Ireland must be reexamined. Ferdinand Hilpisch's study, *Die Doppelklöster, Entstehung und Organization,* suffers from the author's reluctance to admit that some of the Frankish double monasteries developed around nunneries, with the female community serving as the spiritually and economically sustaining element. He rejects the possibility of any insular influence and argues that Frankish double monasteries were modeled on Eastern institutions, where nuns lived as parasites upon the monks.

   M. Heinrich summarized the scholarly controversy about double monasteries in Ireland, pointing out that: "The Irish were favorable to it on the continent, but in Ireland only Kildare existed without question." *Canonesses and Education,* p. 62. On double monasteries in seventh-century England, see Joan Nicholson, "Feminae gloriosae: Women in the Age of Bede," in *Medieval Women,* ed. in honor of Rosalind M. T. Hill (Studies in Church History; Subsidia 1; Oxford, 1978), pp. 15–29.

74. Waldebert, *Regula cuiusdam patris ad virgines* 12 (*PL* 88, 1064; Holstenius 1, 400). For a bibliography on Waldebert's authorship, see F. Prinz, *Frühes Mönchtum,* pp. 81, n. 205, 286, n. 97.

75. Ionas, *Vitae sanctorum: Columbani* 1.26; 2.7 (*MGH Script. rer. germ. in usu schol.* 204, 243). Her father, Chagneric, was one of the great officials under Theudebert of Austrasia: "vir sapiens et consiliis regiis gratus." Her mother, Leudegunda, was a noble woman. See F. Prinz, *Frühes Mönchtum,* p. 81. O'Carrol claims Burgundofara was twelve or thirteen when Columban visited her parents ("Sainte Fare et les origines," p. 5). Ionas refers to her as "infra infantiae annis," which means that she had not reached twelve or thirteen, the age of adolescence. The so-called privilege of Saint Faro (Burgundofaro), Burgundofara's brother, is a later forgery, probably drawn up in the twelfth century. See Pardessus 226 (vol. 1, 193). It is contained in two manuscripts: Paris, Bibl. Nat. 928, fols. 56–58; Paris, Bibl. Sainte Geneviève 358, fols. 21–22; see Gougaud,

Les chrétientés celtiques, p. 146. The authenticity of Burgundofara's testament, on the other hand, has been vindicated by its latest editor: Jean Guerout, "Le testament de Sainte-Fare," *Revue d'histoire ecclésiastique,* 60 (1965), 761–821. See Pardessus 257 (vol. 2, pp. 15–17). On the two manuscript collections containing these and other documents, see Jacqueline LeBras-Tremenbert, "Les cartulaires de Faremoutiers," *Sainte Fare et Faremoutiers* (L'Abbaye de Faremoutiers, 1956), pp. 175–213. Faremoutiers became a famous center of learning under Queen Balthild's patronage: *Vita s. Balthildis* 8 (*MGH Script. rer. mer.* 2, 493). It was praised by the Venerable Bede, in *Historia ecclesiastica* 3.8.

76. Hlawitschka, *Studien,* p. 38, and *Liber memorialis von Remiremont* (*MGH Libri mem.* 1, ix).

77. *Vita Filiberti* 22 (*MGH Script. rer. mer.* 5, 595). See also Vacandard, *Vie de Saint Ouen,* p. 209. Hilpisch classified Pavilly-Jumièges as neighboring convents, not as a double monastery (*Die Doppelklöster,* p. 34). A similar type of affiliation existed between Pellemontier-Montiérender and Fécamp-Saint Wandrille, according to Hilpisch (ibid., pp. 33–34). F. Prinz argued that Logium, rather than Fécamp, constituted the female counterpart of Saint Wandrille (*Frühes Mönchtum,* p. 128).

78. "Tantôt et le plus souvent, les moniales sont sujettes à la jurisdiction de l'abbaye des hommes." Schmitz, *Histoire,* vol. 1, p. 322.

79. On the transfer of Dorniaticum to Waldelen, see Pardessus 328 (vol. 2, 105–106). Subsequently, in 666, even Bèze was devastated, perhaps by the same group that threatened Dorniaticum; on this, see Pardessus 348, 356 (vol. 2, 131, 141). For secondary literature, see F. Prinz, *Frühes Mönchtum,* p. 281.

80. *Vita Sadalbergae* 17 (*MGH Script. rer. mer.* 5, 59): "in eodem loco sunt vel monasterio adunatae plus minusve trecentae famulae Christi; illisque dispositis per turmas, ad instar Agaunensium monachorum Habendique normam disposuit; die ac nocte praecepit psallendi canonem omnipotenti." The "laus perennis" was introduced to Remiremont by Amatus, who was a monk at Agaunum before he was invited by Eustachius to join Remiremont. According to Hilpisch, Salaberga was educated at Remiremont (*Die Doppelklöster,* p. 38). Salaberga was in contact with Eustachius, who cured her of blindness, according to *Vita Sadalbergae* 4 (*MGH Script. rer. mer.* 5, 53). The passage was excerpted from Ionas, *Vitae sanctorum: Columbani* 2.8 (*MGH Script. rer. germ. in usu schol.* 244–245). On Laon, see A. Malnory, *Quid Luxovienses monachi, discipuli s. Columbani, ad regulam monasteriorum atque ad communem ecclesiae profectum contulerunt* (Paris, 1894), p. 29.

81. Dom Y. Chaussy et al., eds., *L'Abbaye royale Notre-Dame de Jouarre* (Paris, 1961); Marquise Aliette de Rohan-Chabot Maillé, *Les cryptes de Jouarre* (Paris, 1971).

82. Gregory of Tours, in his *Hist. franc.* 5.39; 6.46; 8.4; 10.19 (*MGH Script. rer. mer.* 1, 231, 286, 293, 433), mentioned the existence of a royal villa at

Cala, with a "coenobiolum virginum" established there by Queen Clotild, wife of Clovis. On its reconstruction by Balthild, see *Vita s. Balthildis*
A 7, 18 (*MGH Script. rer. mer.* 2, 489, 506). On Balthild's monastic
foundations, see Ewig, "Das Privileg," pp. 106–111. As Henri Lévy-
Bruhl, has pointed out, in the Merovingian period the founder chose the
constitution of the monastery and nominated the superior as well. *Étude
sur les élections abbatiales en France jusqu'à la fin du règne de Charles de Chauve*
(Paris, 1913), p. 42. Thus, at Corbie, her other foundation for males,
Balthild installed Theudefrid, a monk from Luxeuil. There are no modern studies on Chelles. Marc Bloch has listed and criticized earlier studies in his "Notes sur les sources d'histoire de l'Ile-de-France au Moyen
Age I: Les archives et cartulaires de l'Abbaye de Chelles," *Bulletin de la
Société de l'Histoire de Paris et de l'Ile-de-France*, 40 (1913), 145–164. The
Vita s. Balthildis 15 (*MGH Script. rer. mer.* 2, 502) mentioned the presence
of "sacerdotes" only at the time of Balthild's death. The *Vita Bertilae*,
composed in the late eighth century, more than once refers to the
presence of monks. For a summary of this issue, see the introduction by
Levison (*MGH Script. rer. mer.* 6, 97–98), and chapter 8, notes 51–55.

83. Hoebanx, *L'Abbaye de Nivelles*, pp. 45–53.

84. The two charters by Aldegund in Pardessus (338–339 [vol. 2, 116–118])
are forgeries; see Paul Bonenfant, "Note critique sur le prétendu testament de sainte Aldegonde," *Académie Royale de Belgique: Bulletin de la
Commission Royale d'Histoire*, 98 (1934), 219–238. On the other hand, the
value of her life, *Vita Aldegundis* (*MGH Script. rer. mer.* 6, 79–90), has been
vindicated by Van der Essen, *Étude critique*, pp. 219–231, and Moreau,
Histoire de l'Église, vol. 1, 121. Moreau suggests that Saint Amand may
have helped with the foundation of Maubeuge (ibid., p. 381). See also
J. Becquet, "Nouveau dépouillement du 'Monasticon Benedictinum,' "
Revue Bénédictine, 73 (1963), 332.

85. According to *Vita s. Rictrudis* 2.16 (*Acta sanctorum Belgii selecta* 4, 496),
written by Hucbald of Saint Amand in 907, Rictrud built Marchiennes
with Amand's help and had Ionas as her coabbot; the latter is not to be
confused with Ionas of Bobbio, according to F. Prinz (*Frühes Mönchtum*,
p. 273, n. 30). See also Hucbald, *Vita s. Jonati* (*AS* 1. Aug.; 1, 75). On
the value of Saint Rictrud's *vita* as a historical source, see Van der Essen,
Étude critique, pp. 260–268; Moreau, *Histoire de l'Église*, vol. 1, 245, and
his *Saint Amand, apôtre de la Belgique et du Nord de la France* (Louvain, 1927),
pp. 224–227; and Hilpisch, *Die Doppelklöster*, p. 40.

86. Jules Dewez, *Histoire de l'Abbaye de St. Pierre d'Hasnon* (Lille, 1890); Becquet,
"Monasticon Benedictinum," p. 331.

87. Pardessus 355 (vol. 2, 138–141), issued by Drausius, Bishop of Soissons,
granted free election of the abbess and referred to "Ebroinus major-
domus, ejusque inlustris matrona Leutrudis, et eorum unicus dilectis-
simus filius Bovo" as the founders and to Etheria as the abbess. A letter
of Bishop Leodegar to Sigrada, written in 688, *Epist. aevi mer.* 17 (*MGH*

Epist. 3, *Mer. kar. aevi* 1, 466), referred to "omnes fratres sanctos, qui cuotidie pro te orant," and "sorores sanctas quarum consortium frueris." See also J. Fischer, *Das Hausmeier Ebroin*, p. 109.

88. Moreau, *Histoire de l'Église*, vol. 1, 177. According to Hucbald, *Vita s. Rictrudis* 9 (*Acta sanctorum Belgii selecta* 4, 492), it was founded by Gertrud, whose grandson Adalbald married Saint Rictrud. It was a double monastery by the ninth century and closely associated with Marchiennes, as the instruction of Charles the Bald, namely, that the monks and nuns of Hamaye were to receive a share of the wine produced by the villa of Vregny belonging to the Abbey of Marchiennes, indicates. Georges Tessier, *Recueil des Actes de Charles II, le Chauve, roi de France* 435, vol. 2, (Chartes et diplomes relatifs à l'histoire de France, 8, no. 2, 9–10; Paris, 1943–45), 473–474.

89. Becquet, "Monasticon Benedictinum," p. 327. It was founded around 660 by Bertha, wife of Gendebert, mayor of the palace and the brother of Nivard of Reims. On the latter, see *Vita Nivardi* (*MGH Script. rer. mer.* 5, 157–171). By the ninth century it had as members forty nuns and twenty clerks; see Flodoard, *Historia ecclesiae Remensis* 3.27 (*MGH Script.* 13, 549). See also Jean Verdon, "Notes sur le rôle économique des monastères féminins en France dans la second moitié du IXᵉ et au dêbut du Xᵉ siècle," *Revue Mabillon*, 58 (1975), 332.

90. F. Prinz, *Frühes Mönchtum*, p. 158.

91. Remiremont and Bèze in the area around Luxeuil; Faremoutiers, Jouarre, Chelles, Soissons, and Laon between the Seine and the Somme; Maubeuge, Marchiennes, Nivelles, Hasnon, and Hamaye between the Somme and the Meuse. Among double monasteries it is possible to include Saint Jean and Saint Mary of Arles, and Holy Cross and Saint Radegonde of Poitiers.

92. Higounet, "Le problème économique," pp. 775–804. Jean Hubert estimated the number of seventh-century monastic foundations in Gaul at about two hundred (see "L'Érémitisme et archéologie," p. 473). In comparison to this figure, the number of double monasteries is very small.

93. Pavilly-Jumièges and Fécamp-St. Wandrille; see note 77, above.

94. Hans-Walter Hermann, "Zum Stande der Erforschung der früh- und hochmittelalterlichen Geschichte des Bistums Metz," *Rheinische Vierteljahrsblätter*, 28 (1963), 164.

95. Eligius, bishop of Noyon, founded one, according to *Vita s. Eligii* 2.5 (*MGH Script. rer. mer.* 4, 697); his goddaughter, Godeberta, built another: *Vita s. Godeberthae* (*AS* 11 Aprilii; 2, 33).

96. *Passio s. Praeiecti episcopi* 15 (*MGH Script. rer. mer.* 5, 235). See also Verdon, "Recherches," p. 125.

97. Berthoara built one under the episcopate of Austregisil; see Ionas, *Vitae sanctorum: Columbani* 2.10 (*MGH Script. rer. mer.* 4/1, 128); *Vita Austrigisili* 10 (*MGH Script. rer. mer.* 4, 197); J. Mellot, "Les fondations colom-

baniennes dans le diocèse de Bourges," *Mélanges Columbaniens: Actes du Congrès International de Luxeuil, 20–23 juillet 1950* (Paris, 1951), pp. 208–211. Later, Saint Eustadiola founded another community of women, according to *Vita s. Eustadiolae* 3 (*AS* 8 Iunii; 2, 132).

98. See Ewig, "Kirche und Civitas in der Merowingerzeit," in *Le Chiese nei regni dell'Europa occidentale* (Centro Italiano di Studi sull'Alto Medioevo; Settimana di Studio, 7, 1; Spoleto, 1960), pp. 45–71.

99. On the number of nuns at Laon, see *Vita Sadalbergae* 17 (*MGH Script. rer. mer.* 5, 59), quoted above note 80. On Remiremont, see note 76. The number of inhabitants at Pavilly is mentioned in *Vita s. Austrebertae* 13 (*AS* 10 Feb.; 2, 422).

100. See, for example, the exemption granted by Bishop Drauscius for Soissons in 666: Pardessus 355 (vol. 2, 138–141). Ewig has pointed out that the same wording appears in the privilege issued for Saint Pierre-le-Vif of Sens ("Das Privileg," p. 93). See Pardessus 335 (vol. 2, 112). Moreover, the Soissons privilege is related to those issued for Saint Denis, Sithiu (Saint Omer), Corbie, and Rebais. For a bibliography of secondary works on proprietary rights exercised over monasteries, see Ph. Schmitz, *Histoire*, vol. 1, p. 89, n. 1.

101. See above, notes 72 and 97.

102. Even the larger houses were aristocratic homes adapted to communal living. Jean Hubert, refers to several studies that demonstrate that the first monasteries constructed for the specific purpose of communal living, with a chapter house, refectory, dormitory, and outbuildings, appeared only in the eighth century. "L'Érémitisme et archéologie," p. 474, in particular, n. 32–34.

103. *Epist. aevi mer. coll.* 17 (*MGH Epist.* 3, *Mer. et kar. aevi* 1, 466).

104. Waldebert, *Regula cuiusdam patris ad virgines* 23 (*PL* 88, 1070).

105. Ibid. 21 (*PL* 88, 1068C).

106. On the rules observed, see H. Mayo, "Three Merovingian Rules for Nuns"; F. Prinz, *Frühes Mönchtum*, pp. 121–151; Ph. Schmitz, *Histoire*, vol. 7, pp. 13–18; L. Gougaud, "Inventaires des règles monastiques irlandaises," *Revue Bénédictine*, 25 (1908), 329–331; T. P. McLaughlin, *Le très ancien droit monastique de l'Occident;* J. Heineken, *Die Anfänge*, p. 103.

107. Waldebert, *Regula cuiusdam patris ad virgines* 17 (*PL* 88, 1065).

108. See chapter 8, notes 20–21, 23, 35–39; Waldebert, *Regula cuiusdam patris ad virgines* 1–4 (*PL* 88, 1054–1057).

109. Waldebert, *Regula cuiusdam patris ad virgines* 24 (*PL* 88, 1070).

110. For example, Gregory of Tours, in *Hist. franc.* 6.29 (*MGH Script. rer. mer.* 1, 268), related that a nun at Holy Cross of Poitiers decided to become a recluse. She was assigned a special cell, which was walled up. Before she entered the cell, she said farewell to all, kissing each one of her sisters.

111. *Vita s. Eustadiolae* 3 (*AS* 8 Iunii; 2, 132).

112. *Vita s. Balthildis* 9 (*MGH Script. rer. mer.* 2, 494).

113. Caesarius, *Regula sanctarum virginum* 61, ed. G. Morin (Florilegium patris-

ticum, 34; Bonn, 1933), p. 20 (*PL* 67, 1105); Aurelian, *Regula ad virgines* 13 (*PL* 68, 401; Holstenius 1, 371). The Benedictine Rule assumed that both nobles and poor people would offer their sons to monastic life; *Regula Benedicti* 59 (Holstenius 1, 132). On Leubovera, see Gregory of Tours, *Hist. franc.* 10.15–17 (*MGH Script. rer. mer.* 1, 423–430).

114. The Council of Herstal, held in 779, ordered that "sanctimoniales" and the men with whom they committed fornication or adultery were to be placed in monasteries and their property used as an entrance fee. If they were paupers and did not have property "qualiter in monasterio vivant," they were to be turned over to the care and supervision of their nearest relative; *Conc. Harist. Capit.* 18 (*MGH Capit.* 1, 46). *Collectio Sangallensis* (ca. 870), 6 (*MGH Form.* 400) is a donation to a monastery for the explicit purpose "ut filius vel filia . . . in congregatione suscipiatur." See also *Cartae Senonicae* 31 (*MGH Form.* 199).

115. Baudonivia, *De vita s. Radegundis* 12 (*MGH Script. rer. mer.* 2, 385–386).

116. *De vita s. Radegundis* 16 (ibid., 388–389). Baudonivia recounted the difficulties Radegund encountered with the local bishop when she adopted Caesarius's Rule, exempting the convent from episcopal jurisdiction.

117. *Conc. Germ.* (742), 6 (*MGH Conc.* 2, 4).

118. On Saint Boniface, see Theodor Schieffer, *Winifrid-Bonifatius und die christliche Grundlegung Europas* (Freiburg i. B., 1954), and *Angelsachsen und Franken* (Akademie der Wissenschaften und der Literatur, Mainz; Abhandlungen der geistes- und sozialwissenschaftlichen Klasse, 20; Wiesbaden, 1950). On the Anglo-Saxon missionaries in general, Wilhelm Levison, *England and the Continent in the Eighth Century*, 2d ed. (Oxford, 1950), and *Aus rheinischer und fränkischer Frühzeit* (Düsseldorf, 1948). See also C. Wampach, *Sankt Willibrord: Sein Leben und Lebenswerk* (Luxembourg, 1953).

119. See Brühl, *Fodrum*, pp. 26–30, 50–52, 102–105 and notes 173 and 185 below.

120. For example, St. Boniface asked Begga to send him works on the lives of martyrs and thanked her for money and vestments. *Die Briefe*, 15 ed. Tangl, p. 27. From Eadburga he requested an illuminated copy of Peter's Epistles and thanked her for some unidentified books. Ibid. 30, 35, pp. 54, 60.

121. For example, in his letter to Begga, Saint Boniface referred to monks and nuns as "omnes milites Christi utriusque sexus." *Die Briefe* 94, ed. Tangl, p. 215.

122. Only Pope Zachary's reply is extant (Nov. 4, 751): "Nam et hoc inquisivit fraternitas tua, si liceat sanctimoniales feminas quemadmodum viri sibi invicem pedes abluere tam in cena Domini quamque in aliis diebus. Hoc dominicum perceptum est. . . . Etenim viri et mulieres unum Dominum habemus." Boniface, *Die Briefe* 87, ed. Tangl, p. 198.

123. Boniface, *Die Briefe* 128, ed. Tangl, pp. 265-266. *Conc. Ver.* (755) 5 (*MGH Cap.* 2, 34).

124. *Conc. Germ.* 7 (*MGH Conc.* 2, 4): "Et ut monachi et ancille Dei monasteriales

iuxta regulam sancti Benedicti ordinare et vivere, vitam propriam guber-
nare, studeant." On Boniface's presence at this council, see de Clercq
La législation, vol. 1, 117. The same provision was made for monks alone
in 743 by the *Conc. Liftinense* 1 (*MGH Conc.* 2, 7); in 744 the Synod of
Soissons required "stability according to the holy rule" on the part of
both monks and nuns: *Conc. Suess.* 3 (*MGH Conc.* 2, 34). The observance
of the Rule was extended to Bavarian monasteries by the *Conc. Asch.*
(756) 8 (*MGH Conc.* 2, 58).

125. *Conc. Vernense* 6 (*MGH Cap.* 1, 34).

126. *Conc. Vernense* 11 (ibid., 35).

127. Eugen Ewig, "Beobachtungen zur Entwicklung der fränkischen Reichskirche unter Chrodegang von Metz," *Frühmittelalterliche Studien,* 2 (1968),
67–77. On the date of the Rule's composition (after 751 and before
766), see de Clercq, *La législation,* vol. 1, 146–155, in particular, 146, n.
3, for editions and bibliography.

128. *Conc. Cabil.* 43–56 (*MGH Conc.* 2, 284–285).

129. *Conc. Franc.* 17 (*MGH Conc.* 2, 171); see also *Conc. Risp. Fris. Salis.* (800),
2 (*MGH Conc.* 2, 207); *Conc. Mog.* 13 (*MGH Conc.* 2, 264); *Capit. missorum
spec.* (ca. 802), 34–35 (*MGH Capit.* 1, 103).

130. See above, notes 67 and 125. Waldron surveyed the external signs of
conversion, concluding that vows, change of habits, and veiling took
many forms and were often privately administered without the presence
of a priest or bishop. But, in the eighth century, the councils began to
regulate these ceremonies, insisting upon veiling as the outward form
of *conversio.* "Expressions of Religious Conversion," pp. 196–207,
218–225, 235–246.

131. *Capit. missorum* (ca. 802) 19 (*MGH Capit.* 1, 103). This did not mean that
parents could not offer their children as oblates; see *Capit. eccl. ad Salz*
(804), 6 (*MGH Capit.* 1, 119).

132. *Conc. Foroiuliense* (796–797), 11 (*MGH Conc.* 2, 193): "ob continentiae
signum nigram vestem quasi religiosam . . . licet non sint a sacerdote
sacratae, in hoc tamen proposito eas perpetim perseverare mandamus."
See also, *Capit. Francicum* (779), 18 (*MGH Capit.* 2, 38). See Catherine
Capelle, *Le voeu d'obéissance des origines au XIIᵉ siècle* (Bibliothèque d'histoire du droit et du droit romaine, 2; Paris, 1959). Capelle discussed the
usage of the term vow in patristic and early medieval sources, arguing
that the promise of chastity by monks, nuns, and consecrated virgins did
not constitute a vow in the strict, juridical sense of the word until the
end of the eighth century. Until that time it resembled the promise of
chastity given by candidates for ordination to the subdiaconate and
higher offices. On the latter, see L. Hertling, "Die Professio der Kleriker
und die Entstehung der drei Gelübde," *Zeitschrift für katholische Theologie,*
56 (1932), 148–174.

133. *Conc. Parisiense* (829), 40–43 (*MGH Conc.* 2, 637–638).

134. *Conc. Parisiense* (829), 45 (ibid. 2, 639). For its precedent, see *Syn. Dioc.*

Autiss. (561–605), 36–37, 42 (*CCL* 148A, 269–270). *Conc. Laodicense* 44 (Mansi 2, 581) and Gelasius, *Epist.* 9, *Decr.* 26 (*PL* 59, 48; JK 636) served as the sources for this misogynist legislation.

135. On new foundations in the Carolingian period, see Heineken, *Die Anfänge.*

136. For a quick summary of this policy, see Karl Siepen, *Vermögensrecht der klösterlichen Verbände* (Paderborn, 1963), pp. 16–21. Dom Schmitz advanced the view that the concept of the "abbatia" was born during the reign of Charlemagne. This meant that the monastery was held as a benefice from the king, with a certain part of the domain set aside for the support of the community and the rest distributed as fiefs. *Histoire,* vol. 1, p. 98.

137. *Duplex legationis edictum* 19 (*MGH Capit.* 1, 69).

138. *Capit. ab episcopis in placito tractanda* (829) 4 (*MHG Capit.* 2, 7).

139. *Epist. Fuldensium fragmenta* 6 (*MGH Epist.* 5, *Kar. aevi* 3, 518).

140. *Conc. Cabil.* 43–56 (*MGH Conc.* 2, 284–285); see in particular article 53, which referred to "sanctimoniales quae se canonicas vocant."

141. *Inst. sanct.* 18 (*MGH Conc.* 2, 449): "quanto enim idem sexus fragilior esse dinoscitur, tanto necesse est maiorem erga eum custodiam adhiberi."

142. *Conc. Aquis.* 115 (*MGH Conc.* 2, 397).

143. *Inst. sanct.* 8 (*MGH Conc.* 2, 444): "committat eas . . . aut propinquo aut alio . . . amico, qui eas iure fori defendat."

144. *Inst. sanct.* 27 (ibid., 455): "Sanctimoniales namque velo ante posito . . . horas canonicas et missarum sollemnia celebrent."

145. Even their contact with priests was to be limited—they could make confession only within sight of their sisters: *Inst. sanct.* 27 (ibid., 455).

146. *Inst. sanct.* 18 (ibid., 451).

147. *Inst. sanct.* 20 (ibid., 451).

148. *Conc. Vernense* (755), 6 (*MGH Capit.* 1, 34).

149. *Duplex legationis edictum* (789), 19 (*MGH Capit.* 1, 63); *Conc. Risp. Fris. Salis.* (800), 27 (*MGH Conc.* 2, 210); *Conc. Cab.* (813), 57, 62 (*MGH Conc.* 2, 284, 285); *Conc. Mog.* (813), 13 (*MGH Conc.* 2, 264); *Conc. Turonense* (813), 30 (*MGH Conc.* 2, 290); *Conc. Mog.* (847), 16 (*MGH Capit.* 2, 180). These documents specified that an abbess could leave her monastery only with her bishop's permission, or if summoned by the king. One of the difficulties in keeping women religious cloistered was the lack of suitable buildings. Recent archaeological excavations have shown that, prior to the mid-eighth century, female communities were housed in structures that did not differ in any way from private homes and therefore lacked enclosed areas. On this, see Hubert, "L'Érémitisme et archéologie," p. 474. Charlemagne, in his *Capit. miss. spec.* (ca 802), 35 (*MGH Capit.* 1, 103), ordered abbesses to house members of their community in "claustra . . . ordinabiliter composita." In a similar vein, *Conc. Mog.* (847), 16 (*MGH Capit.* 2, 180) charged the abbesses with the duty of "aedificando ea, quae ad santimonialium necessitatem pertinent et in restaurando."

150. *Conc. Foroiuliense* 12 (*MGH Conc.* 2, 194).

151. See number 78 in *Die Briefe,* ed. Tangl, p. 169. See also numbers 8, 14, and 27.

152. *Conc. Risp. Fris. Salis.* (800), 28 (*MGH Conc.* 2, 211): "ut sanctae moniales non induantur virilia indumenta . . ." *Conc. Aquis.* (816), 130 (*MGH Conc.* 2, 405): "sicut enim turpe est virum vestem muliebrem et mulierem vestem virilem induere."

153. *Conc. Foroiuliense* (796–797), 12 (*MGH Conc.* 2, 194); *Conc. Cab.* (813), 60 (*MGH Conc.* 2, 285); *Conc. Parisiense* (820), 46 (*MCH Conc.* 2, 640).

154. *Capitula eccl. ad Salz data* (803–804), 7 (*MGH Capit.* 1, 119): "nullus masculum filium aut nepotem vel parentem suum in monasterio puellarum aut nutriendum commendare praesumat, nec quisquam illum suscipere audeat."

155. *Inst. sanct.* 18 (*MGH Conc.* 2, 455): "iuxta ecclesiam . . . sit hospitale pauperum . . ."

156. See the legislation cited in note 149, above.

157. *Admonitio generalis* (789), 76 (*MGH Capit.* 1, 60): "abbatissas contra morem sanctae Dei ecclesiae benedictionis cum manus impositione et signaculo sanctae crucis super capita virorum dare, necnon et velare virgines cum benedictione sacerdotali quod omnino vobis . . . interdicendum esse scitote." Repeated verbatim in *Ansegesi capit.* 1.71 (*MGH Capit.* 1, 404). See also the prohibition against veiling virgins and widows without a bishop's sanction, pronounced by the Council of Paris (829), cited in note 133.

158. *Translatio s. Baltechildis* (*MGH Script.* 15/1, 285), composed in 833, refers to the "clerus tam virorum quam feminarum" at Chelles.

159. *Conc. Risp. Fris. Salis.* 22 (*MGH Conc.* 2, 210): "Ut liceat sanctimonialem signum ecclesiae pulsare et lumen accendere."

160. *Conc. Mog.* (847), 16 (*MGH Capit.* 2, 180): "Sanctimoniales vero in monasterio constitutae habeant studium in legendo et in cantando, in psallmorum caelebratione sive oratione. Et horas canonicas . . . pariter celebrent."

161. *Inst. sanct.* 28 (*MGH Conc.* 2, 455). Although the hospice for the poor had to be located outside the convent (see above n. 155), there was to be a room within the monastery for receiving and feeding widows and poor women.

162. *Inst. sanct.* 22 (ibid., 452): "puellae, quae in monasteriis erudiuntur, cum omni pietatis affectu et vigilantissimae curae studio nutriantur . . ."

163. The best accounts of monastic reforms carried out under Louis the Pious and led by Benedict Aniani are J. Koscheck, *Die Klosterreform Ludwigs des Fr. im Verhältnis zur Regel Benedikts von Nursia* (Greifswald, 1908); J. Semmler, "Reichsidee und kirchliche Gesetzgebung bei Ludwig dem Frommen," *Zeitschrift für Kirchengeschichte,* 71 (1960), 37–65; and idem, "Zur Überlieferung der monastischen Gesetzgebung Ludwigs des Frommen," *Deutsches Archiv,* 16 (1960), 309–388. See also J. Narberhaus,

Benedikt von Aniane, Werk und Persönlichkeit (Münster, 1930); Suzanne Dulcy, *La Règle de Saint Benoît d'Aniane et la réforme monastique à l'époque carolingienne* (Nimes, 1935); and J. Semmler, *Benedikt von Aniane* (Mannheim, 1971).

164. Emile Lesne, "Les ordonnances de Louis de Pieux," *Revue d'histoire de l'Église de France*, 6 (1920), 490–493; Kassius Hallinger, ed., *Corpus consuetudinum monasticarum*, vol. 1 (Siegburg, 1963), pp. 493–499. The five nunneries were Notre-Dame at Soissons, Baume-les-Dames in the diocese of Besançon, Swarzach at Würzburg, Holy Cross at Poitiers, and Notre-Dame at Limoges. This list did not mention Benedictine monasteries that were in the hands of bishops and lay proprietors.

165. E. Hlawitschka, "Zur Klosterverlegung und zur Annahme der Benediktsregel in Remiremont," *Zeitschrift für die Geschichte des Oberrheins*, 109 (1961), 249–269.

166. W. Levison ("Recension: Schäfer," p. 491), demonstrated that "monasterium, coenobium, claustrum, ancillae Dei, Deo sacratae, sanctimoniales, sorores, virgines" were generic terms used to designate both types of houses and their inhabitants. For criticism of Schäfer's thesis with respect to Germany, see Heineken, *Die Anfänge*, p. 113.

167. A. Werminghoff, "Die Beschlüsse des Aachener Conzils im Jahre 816," *Neues Archiv*, 27 (1901), 634, n. 7.

168. *Gesta Alderici* 44 (*MGH Script.* 15, 324).

169. See note 158, above.

170. *Capit. de monasterio s. Crucis Pictavensi* (822–824), 6–7 (*MGH Capit.* 1, 302).

171. Bouquet (*Recueil*, vol. 8, 641–642) lists a donation by Charles the Bald dated 872, that refers to nuns and priests and deacons. See also Tessier, *Recueil* 197, vol. 1, 509; 494, 499, vol. 2, 655, 656. These documents are classified as forgeries from the early eleventh century. Cf. Verdon, "Notes," p. 331.

172. On female saints in ninth-century Saxony, see Stoeckle, *Studien.* pp. 56–87. On Saint Liutberga in particular, see chapter 5, note 13, and note 192, below.

173. For a list of Carolingian princesses and queens holding abbeys, see Emile Lesne, *Histoire de la propriété ecclésiastique en France*, vol. 2, pt. 2 (Fac. Cath. de Lille, Mémoires et travaux, 30; Lille, 1926), 168; and Karl Voigt, *Die karolingische Klosterpolitik und der Niedergang des westfränkischen Königtums, Laienäbte und Klosterinhaber* (Kirchenrechtliche Abhandlungen, 90–91; Stuttgart, 1917), pp. 39–43.

174. Einhard, *Vita Caroli* 19 (*MGH Script.* 2, 454). Nithard, in *Historiarum* 1.2 (*MGH Script.* 2, 651), wrote that Louis the Pious "sorores suas . . . instanter a palatio ad sua monasteria abire praecepit."

175. *Translatio s. Baltechildis* 1 (*MGH Script.* 15/1, 284).

176. On May 12, 889, she was addressed as "famula Christi." See J. F. Böhmer, *Die Regesten des Kaiserreichs unter der Karolingern, 751–918*, new ed. Mühlbacher (Regesta imperii; 1; Innsbruck, 1889), document 1816 (1767).

177. *Vita Hludowici* 44 (*MGH Script.* 2, 633).
178. Flodoard, *Historia ecclesiae Remensis* 3.27 (*MGH Script.* 13, 549).
179. Regino, *Chronicon* (887) (*MGH Script.* 1, 597).
180. *Fragmentum Ann. Chesnii* (*MGH Script.* 1, 33).
181. *Vita Hludowici* 44 (*MGH Script.* 2, 633); *Annales Bertiniani.* (830) (*MGH Script.* 1, 423–424); Agobard, *Libri duo pro filiis et contra Judith uxorem Ludovici Pii* 1.3 (*MGH Script.* 15, 275).
182. *Annales Bertiniani* (862) (*MGH Script.* 1, 456).
183. *Vita Anstrudis* 28, 37 (*MCH Script. rer. mer.* 6, 75–77).
184. *Vita s. Austrebertae* 10 (*AS* 10 Feb.; 2, 421). On the entrance fee, see note 114.
185. Jean Guerout, "Le monastère à l'époque carolingienne," in *L'Abbaye royale Notre-Dame de Jouarre,* ed. Y. Chaussy et al., vol. 1 (Paris, 1961), 75–78. We also know that Thiathilda, the abbess of Remiremont (ca. 818–863), pleaded for the protection of her kinsman, the seneschal Adalard, and asked the proprietress, Empress Judith, not to divert other manors from the nuns' use; see *Indicularius Thiathildis* 3–4 (*MGH Form.* 526–527). As Heineken has noted, the property of both male and female cloisters was theoretically under royal management, but since "die Frauenkloster und ihrer Gutsverwaltung weniger selbständig waren, mussten dadurch die königliche Ansprüche auf die Verfügung gestärkt werden." *Die Anfänge,* p. 73.
186. Bouquet, *Recueil,* vol. 8, 666; Hoebanx, *L'Abbaye de Nivelles,* p. 107. See, also, the grant of immunity Charles issued for Hasnon in Tessier, *Recueil,* vol. 2, 475.
187. Jacques Choux described the transformation of Benedictine houses into chapters of canons by lay proprietors in "Décadence et réforme monastique dans la province de Trèves, 855–959," *Revue Bénédictine,* 70 (1960), 204–233. Despite this tendency and the Viking raids, the author assures us that "quant aux monastères de femmes . . . ils valaient mieux que leur réputation." Ibid., p. 216. He cites from *Vita Iohannis Gorziensis* (*MGH Script.* 4, 349): "Sanctimonialium habitacula . . . etsi non re, fama tamen obscurari . . ."
188. The twenty-second abbess of Remiremont, who lived in the early tenth century, was referred to in a thirteenth-century necrology as "abbatissa atque diachonissa." See Hlawitschka, *Studien,* p. 42. Atto of Vercelli (ca. 924–960) explained in one of his letters that the title deaconess was given to abbesses (*Epist.* 8; *PL* 134, 114–115).
189. Mathilda of Quedlinburg held this title according to the *Annales Quedlinburgenses* (*MGH Script.* 3, 75). See also Karl Hörger, "Die reichsrechtliche Stellung der Fürstäbtissinnen," *Archiv für Urkundenforschung,* 9 (1926), 198; and Heineken, *Die Anfänge,* pp. 125–126.
190. *Conc. Mog.* (888), 26 (Mansi 18, 71–72).
191. See above, chapter 6, note 107.
192. She died between 860 and 865 at Wendhausen; see *Vita s. Liutbirgae* (*MGH*

Script. 4, 158–164). See also Grosse, "Das Kloster Wendhausen, sein Stiftergeschlecht und seine Klausnerin."

193. Agius, *Agii Vita et obitus Hathumodae* 5–6, 9 (*MGH Script.* 4, 168–169). Hathumoda died in 874, at age thirty-four, according to her biographer, who was her brother. On Hathumoda, see note 17, above, and Paul Lehmann, *Corveyer Studien*, (Abh. d. bayerischen Akademie der Wiss., philos.-philol. und hist. Klasse, 33/5; Munich, 1919).

CHAPTER 8

1. Part of this chapter was written in 1976 in honor of the eightieth birthday of Constance M. Winchell, former Reference Librarian of Columbia University Libraries.

2. Moreau, in his *Histoire de l'Église en Belgique*, gave some credit to nuns in the intellectual and artistic movements of Belgian monasteries. Jean Verdon wrote, "Nous avons peu de renseignements sur les activités intellectuelles et artistiques des moniales" ("Recherches," p. 137).

3. Bernhard Bischoff, "Die kölner Nonnenhandschriften und das Skriptorium von Chelles," pp. 395–401.

4. Caesarius, *Regula sanctarum virginum* 7, ed. Morin, p. 7. *Ad sanctimoniales epistola*, 2.3, 7, ed. Morin, 39, 43.

5. Aurelian of Arles, *Regula ad virgines* 26 (*PL* 68, 391); Donatus of Vesuntinus, *Regulae ad virgines* 6 (*PL* 87, 278); Waldabert, *Regula cuiusdam patris ad virgines*, 12; all three are in L. Holstenius's collection (1, 372, 380, 400).

6. Agius, *Agii Vita et obitus Hathumodae*, 2 (*MGH Script.* 4, 167).

7. *Epist. aevi mer. collectae* 11 (*MGH Epist.* 3, *Mer. kar. aevi* 1, 452).

8. Baudonivia, *De vita s. Radegundis* 9 (*MGH Script. rer. mer.* 2, 384). See also note 63, below. Fortunatus, *Opera poetica* 8.1 (*MGH Auct. ant.* 4/1, 1).

9. *Vita s. Geretrudis* A 6 (*MGH Script. rer. mer.* 2, 460). Vulfetrud, her niece, was also characterized as "sanctae regulae normam: sacris litteris imbutam et nutritam."

10. *Vita ss. Herlindis et Renildae* 4–5: (*AS* 22 Martii, 3; 384–385) "divinis dogmatibus sive humanis artibus religiosisque studiis et sacris litteris erudiendas. . . . Quaecumque enim legendo vel audiendo didicerant, memoriter retinebant. . . . In praedicto namque monasterio . . . omni divino dogmate pleniter erant eruditae diversis usibus divini officii et Ecclesiastici ordinis, id est, in legendo, modulatione cantus, psallendo, necnon quod nostris temporibus valde mirum est etiam scribendo atque pingendo. . . . Simili etiam in universis operis arte, quod manibus foeminarum . . . fieri solet, honestissime fuerant instructae, id est nendo et texendo, creando ac suendo in auro quoque ac margaritis in serico componendis."

11. *Ad sanctimoniales epistolae* 2.7 (ed. Morin, 43; *PL* 67, 1124C), excerpted by Amalarius of Metz in *Regula sanctimonialium* 5 (*PL* 105, 953A). The

Regula cuiusdam patris ad virgines 12 (Holstenius 1, 400), attributed to Waldabert, also made it clear that handiwork should not be undertaken to the detriment of the "lectio divina."

12. *Vita s. Geretrudis* A 2 (*MGH Script. rer. mer.* 2, 457): "per suos nuntios . . . sancta volumina de urbe Roma et de transmarinis regionibus gignaros homines ad docendum divini legis carmina, sibi et suis meditandum, Deo inspirante, meruisset habere." The memorization of laws in the form of poetry was an Irish custom, which also became popular in England. A century later, Eadburga, abbess of Thanet, had members of her convent memorize divine laws in the form of poetry, according to a letter from Lioba to Boniface. See number 29 in *Die Briefe*, Tangl, p. 52. See also below, note 46.

13. For a discussion of the Irish tradition of learning, see Eoin MacNeill, "Beginnings of Latin Culture in Ireland," *Studies: An Irish Quarterly Review of Letters, Philosophy and Science,* 20 (1931), 39–48, 449–460.

14. *Vita Bertilae* 6 (*MGH Script. rer. mer.* 6, 106): "electas personas et devotissimos homines."

15. See number 35, in *Die Briefe*, ed. Tangl, p. 60. He asked Begga to send him the passions of martyrs (number 14, in ibid., p. 27). He also thanked Eadburga for some unidentified books she had sent him (number 30, in ibid., p. 54). On nuns as suppliers of books to Boniface and Lull, see, B. Bischoff, "Scriptoria e manoscritti mediatori di civiltà," in *Mittelalterliche Studien,* vol. 2, (Stuttgart, 1967), 324.

16. Boulogne-sur-Mer, Bibl. Mun., MS 74 (82). See E. A. Lowe, *Codices latini antiquiores,* vol. 6 (Oxford, 1936), 738.

17. *Vitae sancti Bonifatii* (*MGH Script. rer. germ. in usu schol.* 95): "unde contigit, ut necessitate compulsus de sua provincia evocaret feminas religiosas, quatinus sui clerici et nobilium filii et eisdem nutrirentur et caelestis praedicationis ministri imbuerentur." On Tecla and Lioba, see also Boniface's letter number 67, in *Die Briefe*, ed Tangl, pp. 139–140. This letter mentions also Lull's aunt Cynehilda and her daughter Berthgyth, who were "valde eruditae in liberali scientia" and were active in Thuringia as teachers. On Kitzingen, see H. Petzolt, "Abtei Kitzingen," *Jahrbuch für fränkische Landesforschung,* 15 (1955), 69–83.

18. Caesarius, *Regula sanctarum virginum* 36 (Morin, 14)

19. *Vita Bertilae* 6 (*MGH Script. rer. mer.* 6, 104): "ut illis de suis discipulis ad eruditionem vel sanctam instructionem . . . dirigeret."

20. According to *Vita Bertilae* 14 (*MGH Script. rer. mer.* 6, 104), the son of Balthild, Clothar III, was educated there. Similarly, Theuderic IV (721–737), the son of Dagobert III, was raised by the nuns of Chelles: *Liber hist. franc.* 53 (*MGH Script. rer. mer.* 2, 328).

21. Paschasius Radbertus dedicated his *Expositio in Psalmum* (*PL* 120, 993–1064) to the nuns of Soissons. See ibid. 994D–995A. He may also have written for them his *De partu Virginis* (*PL* 120, 1365–1386).

22. *Capit. eccl. ad Salz. data* (803/804), 7 (*MGH Capit.* 1, 119): "Omnino

prohibemus, ut nullatenus masculum filium aut nepotem vel parentem suum in monasterio puellarum aut nutriendum commendare praesumat, nec quisquam illum suscipere audeat."

23. Caesarius, *Regula sanctarum virginum* 32 (Morin, 12): "quae . . . codicibus . . . praeponitur, super Evangelium claves accipiant."

24. The books given by two masters of the Cathedral School of Laon, Bernard and Adelelm, to Notre-Dame of Laon bear the notation "Hunc librum dederun[t] Bernardus et Adelemus Deo et Sanctae Mariae Laudunensis ecclesiae. Si quis abstulerit, offensionem Dei et sanctae Marie incurrat." This dedication appears, for example, in Laon, Bibl. Mun., MS 122, fol. 77; on this manuscript, see M. Boutemy, "Chronique: Notes de voyage sur quelques manuscrits de l'ancien archdiocèse de Reims," *Scriptorium,* 2 (1948), 124, and John J. Contreni, *The Cathedral School of Laon: Its Manuscripts and Masters, A.D. 850–930* (Munich, 1978), p. 23, n. 23. For variations of their "ex-dono" in other manuscripts, see Contreni, "The Formation of Laon's Cathedral Library in the Ninth Century," *Studi medievali,* 3 Ser., 13, 2 (1972), 926.

25. *Recueil des chartes de l'Abbaye de Saint-Benoît-sur-Loire* (876), 25.

26. Valenciennes, Bibl. Mun., MS 59. The manuscript is described by Bischoff in "Panorama der Handschriftenüberlieferung aus der Zeit Karls des Grossen," in *Karl der Grosse: Lebenswerk und Nachleben,* vol. 2 (Düsseldorf, 1965), p. 240.

27. Vienna, Österreichische Nationalbibliothek, MS Lat. 2223; B. Bischoff and J. Hofmann, *Libri sancti Kyliani. Die würzburger Schreibschule* (Quellen und Forschungen z. Geschichte d. Bistums u. Hochstifts Würzburg, 6; Würzburg, 1952), p. 53.

28. Autun, Bibl. Mun. MS 3 (S3), fol. 186. For Lowe's reasons for his attribution, see *CLA* 6, p. xv, and for a description of the manuscript, see Number 716 *CLA,* 6, p. 5. Suzanne Martinet, librarian of the Laon Municipal Library, kindly pointed out to me, during my visit there in 1975, that she associates the manuscript with the nunnery of that city, founded by Salaberga in 640. So does Bernard Merlette, "Écoles et bibliothèques à Laon du déclin de l'antiquité au developpement de l'Université," in *Actes du 95e Congrès national des Sociétés savantes (Reims, 1970): Section de philologie et d'histoire jusqu'à 1610,* vol. 2 (Paris, 1975), 26–27. This attribution is based on the argument that Saint Salaberga's father was called Gundoinus and that the convent was also dedicated to Saint John and Saint Mary. According to J. Contreni, the convent was called Notre-Dame-de-la-Profonde and was dedicated to Saint John only at a much later date, after the twelfth century, *The Cathedral School of Laon,* p. 15. See also Jean Porcher, "Les manuscrits à peinture," in Jean Hubert, Jean Porcher, and Wolfgang Fritz Volbach, *L'Empire carolingien* (Paris, 1968), pp. 71–74; and Bonifatius Fischer, "Bibeltext und Bibelreform unter Karl der Grossen," in *Karl der Grosse: Lebenswerk und Nachleben,* vol. 2, ed. B. Bischoff (Düsseldorf, 1965), 169.

29. Laon, Bibl. Mun., MS 113. For a description, see Felix Ravaisson's list of Laon manuscripts in *Catalogue général des manuscripts des bibliothèques publiques des départements de France*, vol. 1 (Paris, 1849), 97–98, and the following note. Bischoff, in the handwritten inventory of Laon MSS, which Madame Martinet kindly showed me, identified the script as one used in the ninth century in a northeastern Frankish scriptorium. J. Contreni, lists this manuscript as being at Laon in the second half of the ninth century. *The Cathedral School of Laon*, p. 53, n. 55.

30. The contents of the manuscript (Laon, Bibl. Mun., MS 113) were described both by Ravaisson in his *Catalogue général* and by Dom. G. Morin, "Un traité priscillianiste inédit sur la Trinité," *Revue Bénédictine*, 26 (1909), 255–257. I have therefore omitted the incipits of those items which have been identified. The codex consists of I + 89 fols., measuring 270 × 209 mm. The writing in Carolingian minuscule is in single lines. The titles and first words of incipits and explicits are usually in red uncials. Fols. Ir–v: Table of contents. Fols. 1–13v: *De Trinitate* (unpublished; Morin attributes it to Priscillian's circle). Fols. 14–24: *Libellus episcoporum catholicorum ad Unericum regem Vandalorum datum* (*PL* 58, 219–234). J. Contreni identifies it as *De persecutione Vandalica* of Victor Vita, *The Cathedral School of Laon*, p. 73. Fols. 24v–33v: *Nomina episcoporum catholicorum diversarum provintiarum qui Carthagine ex precepto regali venerunt pro reddenda ratione fidei* (*PL* 58, 269). Like the previous item, this also bears on the Monothelite controversy, according to Contreni in *The Cathedral School of Laon*, p. 72 and item 363 on p. 185. Fols. 34–36v: *Praefatio orationis Soliloquiorum sancti Augustini episcopi* (*PL* 32, 869). Fols. 36v–38v: *Sermo de fluxu sanguinis.* This has been edited by C. Turner, "A Laon MS in 1906 and 1920," *Journal of Theological Studies*, 22 (1921), 1–5. Dekkers, in *Clavis patrum latinorum* 845, lists this sermon as a spurious sermon by Fulgentius of Ruspe. Fols. 38v–39v: *Sermo de natali sancti Cypriani.* Inc.: Hodierna reddendi non [*sic*] debiti propitio domino. Morin has suggested that it was copied from Augustine's *Serm.* 284 (*PL* 38, 1388). Fols. 39v–40: *Sermo resurrectionis domini.* Inc: Post laborem noctis praeteritae quo. According to Morin, it was paraphrased from Augustine's *Serm.* 228 (*PL*, 38, 1101). Fols. 40–42: *Sermo de nativitate domini.* Inc.: Thalamus Mariae et secreta coniuga quibus Gabrihel. Fols. 42–43v: *De nativitate sancti Iohannis.* Inc.: Ecce amicus sponsi caelestis ponit organa sua in thalamo matris (according to Morin, it was composed in Africa). Fols. 43v–51: *Dogma fidei catholicae* (Gennadius of Marseilles, *Liber eccl. dogm.;* Dekkers, *Clavis patrum latinorum* 958). Fols. 51–58v: *Epistola fidei catholica in defensione trium capitulorum* (Facundus of Hermiane, *Opera omnia* [*CCL* 90A, 419–434]). Fols. 59–59v: *Carmen natalis domini nostri Iesu Christi* (Sedulius, Hymnus II, *Opera omnia* [*CSEL* 10, 163]). Fols. 59v–61v: *Epistola sancti Hieronymi ad Oceanum et Sofronium de vita clericorum* (*PL*, 30, 287; Dekkers, *Clavis patrum latinorum* 145). Fols. 61v–85: *Liber de quattuor virtutibus.* According to Morin, this was paraphrased from Augustine; see also

Contreni, *The Cathedral School of Laon,* Item 382, p. 186. Fol. 85v: four lines of a poem: O crucifer bone . . . Solum mare quam fierent (*Aurelius Prudentii Clementis carmina* [*CSEL* 61, 13]).

31. Alcuin, *Epist.* 15, 84, 88, 154, 195-196, 213-214, 216, 228 (*MGH Epist.* 4; *Kar. aevi* 2, 40–42, 127–133, 249, 322-325, 354-358, 359-360, 371-372).

32. See below, notes 33 and 37.

33. B. Bischoff, "Die kölner Nonnenhandschriften." M. Boutemy attributed these manuscripts to the scriptorium of Saint Amand. "Le scriptorium et la bibliothèque de Saint-Amand," *Scriptorium,* 1 (1946–47), 7.

34. Laon, Bibl. Mun., MS 423, fol. 79v (Lowe, *CLA* 6, 760). The manuscript has 79 numbered folios and two unnumbered ones. It includes: fols. 1–33v: S. Isidorus Hispalensis, *De natura rerum;* fols. 34–45: S. Isidorus Hispalensis, *In libros veteris ac novi testamenti proemia;* fols. 45v–79: S. Isidorus Hispalensis, *De ortu et obitu patrum.* The title, *Liber rotarum,* is on folio one. It is possible to read the last word in the subscription as "rogatum" rather than "rotarum." This is the reading given in a handwritten description of the manuscript in Institut de Recherche et d'Histoire des Textes, Section latine, which Madame Folin has kindly called to my attention. Lowe related to this manuscript: Laon, Bibl. Mun., MS 137 (Lowe *CLA* 6, 765): Orosius, *Historiae;* Cambridge CCC 334 (Lowe *CLA* 2, 128): Origines, *Homiliae in Lucam,* which has on folio 97 the notation: Fortunatus scripsit; London, British Museum Additional MS. 31031 (Lowe *CLA* 2, 174): Gregorius, *Moralia* I–V. 46; Paris, Bibl. Nat. Lat. 2024 (Lowe *CLA* 5, 539): Ambrosius, *De fide;* Paris, Bibl. Nat. Lat. 12168 (Lowe *CLA* 5; 630): Augustinus, *Quaestiones in Hepateuchum;* and also two mutilated volumes, now Colmar 45 + Berne 380 (Lowe *CLA* 6, 752), and Basel NI4A + Freiburg im-Breisgau 483, 12.

35. Contreni identified Martin's notations in the fragment (Paris, Bibl. Nat. Lat. 2024). But he did point out that "nothing concrete is known about the scriptorium at Notre-Dame-de-la-Profonde, if indeed Dulcia did belong to it." *The Cathedral School of Laon,* p. 49.

36. Cambrai, Bibl. Mun., MS 300 (283) fols. 155 (Lowe, *CLA* 6, 739). A. Wilmart, "Le copiste du sacramentaire de Gellone au service du chapitre de Cambrai," *Revue Bénédictine,* 42 (1930), 218–222. Wilmart suggested that she was the illuminator. The other manuscript in question is Paris, Bibl. Nat. Lat. 12048 (Lowe, *CLA* 5, 618). J. Deshusses identified Madalberta with the monk Madalbreto of Rebais. "Le sacramentaire de Gellone dans son contexte historique," *Ephemerides liturgicae,* 75 (1961), 199. For a different view, see Bernhard Bischoff, "Frühkarolingische Handschriften und ihre Heimat," *Scriptorium,* 25 (1968), 307; Carl R. Baldwin, "The Scriptorium of the Sacramentary of Gellone," *Scriptorium,* 25 (1971), 3–17; and idem, "The Scribes of the Sacramentary of Gellone," *Scriptorium,* 27 (1973), 16–20.

37. Würzburg, Univ. Bibl. M. p. th. f. 45: Gregorius, *Homiliae in Evangilia;* fol. 71v, has the name Abirhilt. See Bischoff and Hofmann, *Libri sancti*

Kyliani, pp. 7, 102, 160. The authors suggest that Gunza might have contributed to the copying of Würzburg, Univ. Bibl. M. p. th. f. 13: Defensor, *Liber Scintillarum.*

38. *Liber memorialis von Remiremont* 1 (*MGH Libri mem.* 1, fol. 47r).

39. Paris, Bibl. Nat. Lat. 7560, fol. 54. Colette Jeudy dates the codex to the third quarter of the ninth century. See "L'Institutio de nomine, prono-mine et verbo de Priscien," *Revue d'histoire des textes,* 2 (1972), 123.

40. Paris, Bibl. Nat. Lat. 1 fol. 3.

41. See, for example, Paris, Bibl. Nat. Lat. 13396, fol. 1v, Isidore of Seville presenting his *Contra Judaeos* to his sister Florentina. This manuscript was produced in northeast France around 800, according to Jean Hubert, Jean Porcher, and Wolfgang Fritz Volbach, *L'Europe des invasions* (Paris, 1967), pp. 174, 361. See also the unnumbered manuscript in the basilica of San Paolo fuori le Mura, Rome, fol. 2 verso, produced by the School of Tours in the ninth century. Hubert, Porcher, and Volbach, *The Carolingian Renaissance* (New York, 1970), pp. 142, 350.

42. Pierre Riché, *Education et culture dans l'occident barbare,* 3rd ed. (Paris, 1973).

43. Krusch, the editor of the text, remarked in his introduction (*MGH Script. rer. mer.* 2, 360): "Scribere nesciens, quascumque legeret vitas sanctorum spoliavit." Krusch, of course, treats some male hagiographers similarly.

44. Graus, *Volk, Herrscher und Heiliger,* p. 409.

45. She has identified herself with a cryptograph in the introduction of the "editio princeps" (Munich, MS Clm 1086). B. Bischoff, "Wer ist die Nonne von Heidenheim?" *Studien und Mitteilungen zur Geschichte des Benediktinerordens,* 49 (1931), 387; idem, "Panorama der Handschriften," p. 247; and Eva Gottschaller, *Hugeburc von Heidenheim, philologische Untersuchungen zu den Heiligenbiographien einer Nonne des achten Jahrhunderts* (Münchener Beiträge zur Mediävistik und Renaissance-Forschung, 12; Munich, 1973).

46. In a letter to Saint Boniface, Lioba stated that she had learned poetry from the abbess Eadburga, who had her memorize divine laws in the form of poetry. See number 29, in *Die Briefe,* ed. Tangl, p. 52. Berthgyth, active in Thuringia as a teacher, also wrote poetry. See numbers 143, 147, 148, in ibid., pp. 282, 284–286.

47. H. Hoffmann, *Untersuchungen zur karolingischen Annalistik* (Bonner historische Forschungen, 10; Bonn, 1958), pp. 53–61.

48. J. Nelson has noted that a nun of Chelles wrote the older version of the *Vita.* "Queens as Jezebels," p. 46, n. 33. Krusch, whose introduction to the *Vita* Nelson used as reference, did not identify the hagiographer as a woman, but merely noted that the earlier version was composed at Chelles by a member of the community; see *Vita s. Balthildis* (*MGH Script. rer. mer.* 2, 478).

49. In *Vita s. Balthildis* 19 (*MGH Script. rer. mer.* 2, 506), the author remarked that the events described "nostris peracta sunt temporibus"; *Vita s.*

Balthildis 5 (ibid., 487) listed Chrodobert, bishop of Paris, before Ebroin, the mayor of the palace, in describing the regency after Clovis's death.

50. *Vita s. Balthildis* 1 (ibid., 482).

51. *Vita s. Balthildis* 15 (ibid., 501).

52. Levison has noted this in his introduction to *Vita Bertilae* (*MGH Script. rer. mer.* 6, 97).

53. See Levison's remarks in *Vita Bertilae* (ibid., 99).

54. *Vita Bertilae* 5 (ibid., 106): "plurimi viri ac feminae festinabant, quos ipsa Dei famula Bertila . . . recipiebat . . ."

55. On the date of Bertila's death, see Levison's preface in *Vita Bertilae* (ibid., 96). The emphasis in Bertila's *Vita* on the abbess's fame as an administrator and educator attracting both sexes to the monastery would not have been appropriate if the expansion had occurred while Balthild was still alive.

56. On Theudefrid, see Krusch's preface in *Vita s. Balthildis* (*MGH Script. rer. mer.* 2, 478).

57. *Translatio s. Baltechildis* (*MGH Script.* 15/1, 284).

58. On menial work as a sign of saintly humility, see Graus, *Volk, Herrscher und Heiliger*, pp. 295–296, 409.

59. Baudonivia, *De vita s. Radegundis* 8 (*MGH Script. rer. mer.* 2, 383). *Vita s. Balthildis* 11 (*MGH Script. rer. mer.* 2, 496): "ipsa quoque in quoquina ministraret sororibus et munditias vilissimas, etiam deambulationes stercorum, ipsa mundaret."

60. L. Coudanne, "Baudonivie, moniale de Sainte-Croix et biographe de sainte Radegonde," pp. 45–51.

61. Baudonivia, *De vita s. Radegundis* (*MGH Script. rer. mer.* 2, 378). Radegund's cell was next to the "oratorium." See M. Viellard-Troiekovroff, "Les monuments religieux de Poitiers," in *Études mérovingiennes: Actes des Journées de Poitiers, 1952* (Paris, 1953), p. 287.

62. E. Delaruelle noted that, "Fortunate n'a vu en Radegonde que la moniale . . . soucieuse de tout ce qui s'y déroule et usant de son pouvoir encore royal pour y intervenir." "Sainte Radegonde," p. 69. Graus rejects this and states: "Fortunat in Radegunde vor allem die königliche Asketin sieht, die Nonne Baudinivia hingegen das Vorbild einer Nonne." *Volk, Herrscher und Heiliger*, p. 409.

63. Baudonivia, *De vita s. Radegundis* 9 (*MGH Script. rer. mer.* 2, 383–384): "Cum lectio legebatur, illa sollicitudine pia animarum nostrarum curam gerens, dicebat: 'Si non intellegitis quod legitur, quid est, quod non sollicite requiritis speculum animarum vestrarum?' Quod etsi minus pro reverentia interrogare praesumebatur, illa pia sollicitudine maternoque affectu, quod lectio continebat, ad animae salutem praedicare non cessabat." Pope Gregory the Great attributed motherly feelings to Redempta toward her disciples (*Dialogues* 4.16, trans., O. J. Zimmermann [Fathers of the Church, 39; New York, 1959], p. 209).

64. Baudonivia, *De vita s. Radegundis* 12 (*MGH Script. rer. mer.* 2, 385–386).

65. For example, see Graus, *Volk, Herrscher und Heiliger,* pp. 328, 386–387, 413.

66. *De vita s. Radegundis* 8 (*MGH Script. rer. mer.* 2, 383): "Congregationem ... in tantumque dilexit, ut etiam parentes vel regem coniugem habuisse nec reminisceretur."

67. *De vita s. Radegundis* 10 (ibid., 384): "quia totos diligebat reges, pro omnium vita orabat et nos sine intermissione pro eorum stabilitate orare docebat. Ubi eos inter se amaritudinem moveri audisset, tota tremebat, et quales litteras uni, tales alteri dirigebat ut inter se non bella nec arma tractarent, sed pacem firmarent, et patria ne periret. Similiter et ad eorum proceres dirigebat, ut praecelsis regibus consilia salutifera ministrarent, ut, eis regnantibus, populi et patria salubrior redderetur. Congregationi suae assiduas vigilias inponebat et, ut sine intermissione pro eis orarent, cum lacrimis docebat."

68. *De vita s. Radegundis* 16 (ibid., 388): "ut ei permitteret pro totius patriae salute et eius regni stabilitate lignum crucis Domni ab imperatore expetere."

69. *Vita s. Balthildis* 4 (*MGH Script. rer. mer.* 2, 486). "Nutrix" had a broad connotation; it described teachers, both male and female.

70. *Vita s. Balthildis* 5 (ibid., 488): "Et credimus, Deo gubernante, iuxta domnae Balthildis magnam fidem ipsa tria regna tunc inter se tenebant pacis concordiam."

71. *Vita s. Balthildis* 12 (ibid., 498): "Et conferens sepe cum matre monasterii, ut et regem et reginam et proceres cum digno honore cum eulogias semper visitarent, ut erat consuetudo . . ."

72. *Vita Aldegundis* (*MGH Script. rer. mer.* 6, 79–90). See especially the preface by the editor (ibid., 79–85). Levison omitted chapters 5 to 17; for these I have relied on the edition in *Acta sanctorum Belgii selecta* 4, 315–324. On Aldegund's visions, see Stephanus Axters, O. P., *The Spirituality of the Old Low Countries,* trans. Donald Atwater (London, 1954), p. 11, and Van der Essen, *Étude critique,* pp. 219–260, 282–291.

73. *Vita Aldegundis* 18 (*MGH Script. rer. mer.* 6, 88).

74. *De vita s. Radegundis* 20 (*MGH Script. rer. mer.* 2, 391).

75. *Vita s. Balthildis* 13 (*MGH Script. rer. mer.* 2, 498–499).

76. *Vita Aldegundis* 5 (*Acta sanctorum Belgii selecta* 4, 317).

77. *Vita Aldegundis* 8 (ibid., 318); see Athanasius, *Vita b. Antonii abbatis* 9 (*PL* 73, 132B): "Rugiebat leo, occidere volens . . . luporum impetus ingerebantur."

78. *Vita Aldegundis* 8 (*Acta sanctorum Belgii selecta* 4, 318). The Lord's Angel comforted her by saying, "Pax tibi, confortare, viriliter age . . ." On the "virago" motif in Roman literature and medieval hagiography, see Marie-Louise Portmann, *Die Darstellung der Frau in der Geschichtsschreibung des früheren Mittelalters.*

79. *Vita Aldegundis* 10 (*Acta sanctorum Belgii selecta* 4, 319); cf. Gregory the Great, *Dialogues* 4.18 (Zimmermann 211–212).

80. *Vita Aldegundis* 10 (*Acta sanctorum Belgii selecta* 4, 319): "quid stupes? Ego

sum Petrus Apostolus Jesu-Christi missus ad te, ligandi atque solvendi habens potestatem. In numero Sanctorum es recensita, ô pudica. Illuc egredere, desiderat te Dominus. . . . Noli timere, qui timet, non est perfectus in caritate, sed perfecta caritas foras mittit timorem, quoniam timor poenam habet."

81. Hlawitschka suggests that the *Vitae Amati, Romarici, Adelphii abbatum Habendesium* (*MGH Script. rer. mer.* 4, 211-221), may have been written either by a clerk or nun of Remiremont between 750 and 850. *Studien zur Abtissinnenreihe,* p. 16.

82. *Admonitio generalis* (789), 72 (*MGH Capit.* 1, 60).

83. She referred to herself as "ignara" in the poem introducing her work. *Le Manuel de Dhuoda,* ed. Bondurand, p. 47. *Manuel pour mon fils/Dhuoda,* ed. Pierre Riché, p. 72.

84. Only one complete basic manuscript of her works and two partial copies, one of the twelfth and the other of the fifteenth century, have survived. See Paul de Winterfeld, *Hrotsvithae opera* (Berlin, 1902), pp. iii–v; and K. Strecker, *Hrotsvithae opera* (Leipzig, 1906). The latest edition of her works is by H. Homeyer, *Hrotsvithae opera* (Munich, 1970), and contains a complete bibliography. See, also, the bibliography in Homeyer's translation of her works into German in *Werke* (Paderborn, 1973), and in Ann L. Haight, ed., *Hroswitha of Gandersheim, Her Life, Times and Works, and a Comprehensive Bibliography* (New York, 1965).

CONCLUSION

1. Joan Kelly-Gadol. "Did Women Have a Renaissance?" *Becoming Visible, Women in European History,* ed. Renate Bridenthal and Claudia Koonz (Boston, 1977), p. 139.

BIBLIOGRAPHY

The primary sources include only published works. For a list of the manuscripts consulted for this study, see Index.

Primary Sources

Acta de Theutberga regina emissa, 860–865. MGH Capit. 2, 462–469.

ADO. *Chronicon.* Ed. G. H. Pertz. *MGH Script.* 2, 315–326.

AGIUS. *Agii Vita et obitus Hathumodae.* Ed. G. H. Pertz. *MGH Script.* 4, 165–189.

AGNELLUS (qui et Andreas). *Liber pontificalis ecclesiae Ravennatis.* Ed. O. Holden-Egger. *MGH Script. rer. lang.* 27–391.

AGOBARD OF LYONS. *Epistolae.* Ed. E. Dümmler. *MGH Epist.* 5; *Kar. aevi* 3, 153–239.

———. *Libri duo pro filiis et contra Judith uxorem Ludovici Pii.* Ed. G. Waitz. *MGH Script.* 15, 274–279. *PL* 104, 307–320.

ALCUIN. *Epistolae.* Ed. E. Dümmler. *MGH Epist.* 4; *Kar. aevi* 2, 1–481.

ALDHELM OF SÉEZ. *De sancta Opportuna. AS* 22 Aprilii; 3, 62–27.

AMALARIUS OF MERZ. *Regula sanctimonialium. PL* 105, 935–976.

AMBROSE. *De Abraham.* Ed. Schenkl. *CSEL* 32, 1, 507–638. Vienna, 1897.

———. *Expositio Evangelii secundum Lucan.* Ed. C. Schenkl. *CSEL* 32,4. Prague, Vienna, Leipzig, 1902. *Traité sur l'Évangile de s. Luc.* Ed. and trans. G. Tissot. 2 vols. (Sources chrétiennes, 45, 52). Paris, 1956–58.

———. *De institutione virginis. PL* 16, 315–348.

———. *De virginibus.* Ed. O. Faller (Florilegium patristicum, 31). Bonn, 1933. *PL* 16, 197–244.

AMBROSIASTER. *Commentarius in Epistulas Paulinas.* Ed. H. I. Vogels. 3 vols. *CSEL* 81, 1–3, Vienna, 1966–69.

———. *Quaestiones Veteris et Novi Testamenti.* Ed. A. Souter. *CSEL* 50. Vienna, 1908.

AMMIANUS MARCELLINUS. *History.* Rev. ed. J. C. Rolfe. 3 vols. Cambridge, Mass., 1963–64.

Annales Bertiniani. Ed. G. H. Pertz. *MGH Script.* 1, 419–515.

Annales Fuldenses, sive Annales regni francorum orientalis ab Einhardo, Ruodolfo, Meginhardo . . . conscripti. Ed. G. H. Pertz. *MGH Script.* 1, 337–415.

Annales Quedlinburgenses. Ed. G. H. Pertz. *MGH Script.* 3, 22–69, 72–90.

Annales Regni francorum. Ed. F. Kurze. *MGH Script. rer. germ. in usum schol.* Hanover, 1895; rpt. 1950. Trans. B. W. Scholz, *Carolingian Chronicles.* Ann Arbor, 1972.

Apostolic Constitutions. Ante-Nicene Christian Library. Ed. James Donaldson and
T. T. Clark. Vol. 17. Edinburg, 1870.

ATHANASIUS. *Vita b. Antonii abbatis. PL* 73, 126–194.

ATTO OF VERCELLI. *Epistolae. PL* 134, 95–124.

AUGUSTINE. *De adulterinis coniugiis.* Ed. J. Zycha. *CSEL* 41, 347–410. Vienna,
1900. *PL* 40, 451–486.

———. *De bono conjugali.* Ed. J. Zycha. *CSEL* 41, 187–231. Vienna, 1900.

———. *De haeresibus. PL* 42, 21–50.

———. *De nuptiis et concupiscentia.* Ed. C. F. Urba and J. Zycha. *CSEL* 42, 207–319.
Vienna, 1902. *PL* 44, 413–474.

———. *Epistulae.* Ed. C. Goldbacher. *CSEL* 34, 1–2; 57–58. Vienna, 1895–1923.

———. *Quaestionum in Heptateuchum libri VII.* Ed. J. Zycha. *CSEL* 28, 2. Prague,
Vienna, 1895.

———. *De sancta virginitate.* Ed. J. Zycha. *CSEL* 41, 235–302. Vienna, 1900.

———. *Sermones. PL* 38–39, 23–1638.

AURELIAN OF ARLES. *Regula ad virgines. PL* 68, 399–406.

AVITUS OF VIENNE. *Epistulae ad diversos.* Ed. R. Peiper. *MGH Auct. ant.* 6/2,
35–103. *PL* 59, 219–290, 381–386.

———. *Poematum de Mosaicae historiae gestis. PL* 59, 323–370.

BAUDONIVIA. *De vita s. Radegundis Liber II.* Ed. B. Krusch. *MGH Script. rer. mer.* 2,
377–395.

BEDE, THE VENERABLE. *Historia ecclesiastica gentis Anglorum.* Ed. C. Plummer. 2 vols.
Oxford, 1896. Trans. Leo Shirley-Price, *A History of the English Church and
People.* Baltimore, 1955.

BENEDICTUS LEVITA. *Benedicti Capitularia.* Ed. F. H. Knust. *MGH Leg.* 2, pars
altera, 39–158.

BÖHMER, J. F. *Die Regesten des Kaiserreichs unter den Karolingern, 751–918.* New. ed.
E. Mühlbacher (Regesta imperii, 1). Innsbruck, 1889.

BONIFACE. *Die Briefe des heiligen Bonifatius und Lullus.* Ed. M. Tangl. *MGH Epist.
sel., 1.* Berlin, 1916; 2d ed. 1955. *S. Bonifatii et Lulli espistolae.* Ed.
E. Dümmler. *MGH Epist. 3, Mer. kar. aevi* 1, 215–433.

BOUQUET, MARTIN, ed. *Recueil des historiens des Gaules et de la France.* New ed. 24
vols. Paris, 1869–1904. Rpt. Farnborough, England, 1967–68.

Die Bussordnungen der abendländischen Kirche. Ed. F. W. H. Wasserschleben. Halle,
1851.

CAESAR. *Bellum Gallicum.* Ed. O. Seel (*C. Iulii Caesaris Commentarii,* vol. 1). Leipzig,
1961.

CAESARIUS OF ARLES. *Ad sanctimoniales epistolae.* Ed. Dom G. Morin (Florilegium
patristicum, 34). Bonn, 1933, pp. 33–52. *PL* 67, 1121–1125.

———. *Opera omnia.* Ed. Dom G. Morin. Vol. 2. Maredsous, 1942.

———. *Regula sanctarum virginum aliaque opuscula ad sanctimoniales directa.* Ed. Dom
G. Morin (Florilegium patristicum, 34). Bonn, 1933, pp. 5–27. Trans.
M. C. McCarthy, *The Rule for Nuns* (Catholic Univ. of America, Studies in
Medieval History, n.s. 16). Washington, 1960.

———. *Sermones.* Ed. altera Dom G. Morin. 2 vols. *CCL* 103–104. Turnhout,

1953. Trans. Sister M. M. Mueller, O.S.F., *Saint Caesarius of Arles; Sermons and Admonitions on Various Topics.* 3 vols. New York, 1956–73.

Capitularia regum francorum. Ed. A. Boretius and V. Krause. *MGH Capit.* 2 vols. Hanover, 1883–97.

Cartulaire de Brioude. Ed. H. Doniol. Clermont–Ferrand, 1869.

Cartulaire de l'Abbaye de Redon. Ed. M. Aurélien de Courson (Collections de documents inédits, Ser. 2, 6). Paris, 1863.

Cartulaire de l'Abbaye de Saint-André-le-Bas de Vienne, ordre de Saint Benoît. Ed. U. Chevalier. Vienne, 1869.

Cartulaire de l'Abbaye de Saint-Victor de Marseille. Ed. Benjamin E. C. Guérard. Vol. 2. Reprinted Paris, 1957.

Cartulaire de Saint-Vincent de Mâcon. Ed. M. C. Ragut. Mâcon, 1864.

Cartulaires, de l'Église Cathedrale de Grenoble; dits cartulaires de Saint-Hugues. Ed. Jules Marion (Collection de documents inédits sur l'histoire de France, 8). Paris, 1869.

CASSIODORUS. *Historia ecclesiastica tripartita.* Ed. R. Hanslik. *CSEL* 71, 1–684. Vienna, 1952. *PL* 69, 879–1214.

CHRISTIANUS DRUTHMARUS. *Christiani Druthmari Corbeiensis monachii Expositio in Evangelium Matthaei. PL* 106, 1261–1504.

Codex Carolinus. Ed. W. Gundlach. *MGH Epist. 3, Mer. Kar. aevi* 469–657.

Codex Iustinianus. Ed. P. Krueger (*Corpus iuris civilis.* Vol. 2). Berlin, 1954.

Codex Laureshamensis. Ed. Karl Glöckner. 3 vols. Darmstadt, 1929–63.

COLUMBANUS. *Epistolae.* Ed. W. Gundlach. *MGH Epist. 3, Mer. aevi* 1, 154–190. Ed. G. S. M. Walker (Scriptores latini Hiberniae, 2). Dublin, 1957, pp. 2–59.

Concilia. Vol. 1. Ed. F. Maasen. Vol. 2. Ed. A. Werminghoff. *MGH Conc.* Hanover, 1893–1906.

Concilia Africae. a. 345–a.525. Ed. Charles Munier. *CCL* 259. Turnhout, 1974.

Concilia Galliae, a.314–a.506. Ed. Charles Munier. *CCL* 148. Turnhout, 1963.

Concilia Galliae a.511–a.695. Ed. Carlo de Clercq. *CCL* 148A. Turnhout, 1963.

Concilios Visigothicos e Hispano-Romanos. Ed. José Vivés et al. (España cristiana Textos 1). Barcelona, 1963.

CONSTANTIUS CLERICUS. *Vita s. Germani episcopi Autissiodorensis.* Ed. W. Levison. *MGH Script. rer. mer.* 7, 247–283.

Constitutiones apostolicae. PG 1, 509–1156. See also *Didascalia.*

Corpus iuris canonici. 2d ed. Aemilius Friedberg. Vol. 1. Leipzig, 1879.

CYPRIAN. *De habitu virg.* Ed. G. Hartel. *CSEL* 3, 185–202. Vienna, 1871.

DAMASUS PAPA. *Ad episcopos Galliae. PL* 13, 1181–1196.

Decretales Pseudo-Isidorianae. Ed. P. Hinschius. Leipzig, 1863. Rpt. 1963.

DEFENSOR, LOCOGIACENSIS MONACHUS. *Scintillarum Liber.* Ed. H. M. Rochais. *CCL* 117. Turnhout, 1957.

DESIDERIUS OF CAHORS. *Epistolae.* Ed. W. Arndt. *MGH Epist. 3, Mer. kar. aevi* 1, 191–214.

DHUODA. *Le Manuel de Dhuoda.* Ed. E. Bondurand. Paris, 1887.

———. *Manuel pour mon fils/Dhuoda; introduction, texte critique, notes.* Ed. Pierre Riché (Sources chrétiennes, 225). Paris, 1975.

Didascalia et constitutiones apostolorum. Ed. F. X. Funk. 2 vols. Torino, 1961. Reprint of ed. F. Schoeningh, Paderborn, 1905.

Digesta. Ed. P. Krueger (*Corpus iuris civilis.*, vol. 1). Berlin, 1928.

DONATUS OF VESUNTINUS. *Regula ad virgines.* PL 87, 273–298.

EINHARD. *Vita Caroli.* Ed. G. H. Pertz. *MGH Script.* 2, 443–463.

EKKERHARD IV. *Casuum s. Galli continuatio.* Ed. D. I. von Arx. *MGH Script.* 2, 77–147.

Epistolae ad divortium Lotharii II. regis pertinentes. Ed. E. Dümmler. *MGH Epist 6: Kar. aevi* 4, 207–240.

Epistolae aevi merowingici collectae. Ed. W. Gundlach. *MGH Epist. 3, Mer. kar. aevi* 1, 434–468.

Epistolae Austrasicae. Ed. W. Gundlach. *MGH Epist. 3; Mer. kar. aevi* 1, 110–153.

Epistolae karolini aevi. Ed. E. Dümmler. 2 vols. *MGH Epist.* 5–6, *Kar. aevi* 3–4.

Epistolae selectae Sergii II., Leonis IV., Benedicti III. Ed. A. de Hirsch-Gereuth. *MGH Epist.* 5, *Kar. aevi* 3, 581–614.

Epistolae variorum Carolo Magno regnante scriptae. Ed. E. Dümmler. *MGH Epist.* 4, *Kar. aevi* 2, 494–567.

Epistolarum Fuldensium fragmenta. Ed. E. Dümmler. *MGH Epist.* 5, *Kar. aevi* 3, 517–533.

ERMOLDUS NIGELLUS. *Carmen elegiacum in honorem Hludovici christianissimi Caesaris Augusti.* Ed. E. Dümmler. *MGH Poetarum* 2, 4–79.

EWALD, P., ed. "Die Papstbriefe der 'Brittischen Sammlung'?" *Neues Archiv,* 5 (1880), 276–414, 503–596.

FLODOARD. *Historia ecclesiae Remensis.* Ed. J. Heller and G. Waitz. *MGH Script.* 13, 409–599. PL 135, 23–328.

FLORENTIUS. *Vita s. Rusticulae.* Ed. B. Krusch. *MGH Script. rer. mer.* 4, 339–351.

Formulae merowingici et karolini aevi. Ed. K. Zeumer. *MGH Form.*

FORTUNATUS, VENANTIUS. *Opera poetica.* New ed. F. Leo. *MGH Auct. ant.* 4/1.

———. *Vita s. Amantii.* Ed. B. Krusch. *MGH Auct. Ant.* 4/2, 55–64.

———. *De vita sanctae Radegundis.* Ed. B. Krusch. *MGH Script. rer. mer.* 2, 364–377.

Fragmentum Annalium Chesnii (Annales Laureshamenses). Ed. G. H. Pertz. *MGH Script.* 1, 22–39.

FREDEGAR. *Chronicorum libri IV cum continuationibus.* Ed. B. Krusch. *MGH Script. rer. mer.* 2, 18–193.

FRIEDRICH, J. ed. "Liber die Cenones der Montanisten bei Hieronymus." *Sitzungsberichte der bayerischen Akademie, philosofisch-historische Klasse* (1895), 207–221.

Gallia Christiana. 16 vols. Paris, 1715–1865.

GELASIUS PAPA. *Epistolae et decreta.* PL 59, 13–140.

Gesta Alderici. Ed. G. Waitz. *MGH Script.* 15, 304–327.

Gesta domni Dagoberti I regis Francorum. Ed. B. Krusch. *MGH Script. rer. mer.* 2, 396–425.

Le Grand Cartulaire de Saint-Julien de Brioude, essai de reconstruction. Ed. Anne Marie and Marcel Boudet. Saint Etienne, 1935.

GREGORY I, THE GREAT. *Registrum epistularum.* Nova ed. P. Ewald and L. Hartmann. *MGH Epist.* 1–2.

————. *Saint Gregory the Great; Dialogues.* Trans. O. J. Zimmermann (Fathers of the Church, 39). New York, 1959.

GREGORY OF TOURS. *Historia francorum.* Ed. B. Krusch. *MGH Script. rer. mer.* 1, 1–537. Trans. O. M. Dalton. *The History of the Franks.* Vol.2. Oxford, 1927.

————. *Libri octo miraculorum III–VI: Liber I–IV de virtutibus s. Martini episcopi.* Ed. B. Krusch. *MGH Script. rer. mer.* 1, 584–661.

————. *Libri octo miraculorum VII: Liber vitae patrum.* Ed. B. Krusch. *MGH Script rer. mer.* 1, 661–744.

————. *Libri octo miraculorum VIII: Liber in gloria confessorum.* Ed. B. Krusch. *MGH Script. rer. mer.* 1, 744–820.

HAIMO OF AUXERRE. *In Epist. ad. Col. PL* 117, 753–766.

————. *In Epist. I ad. Tim. PL* 117, 783–798.

HAITO OF BASEL. *Capitulare. PL* 115, 11–16.

HALLINGER, KASSIUS, ed. *Corpus consuetudinum monasticarum.* Vol. 1. Sieburg, 1963.

HATTO. See *Vita s. Verenae*

HERARD OF TOURS. *Capitula.* Mansi 16, 677–686. *PL* 121, 763–774.

HINCMAR OF REIMS. *Capitula in Synodo apud s. Macram. PL* 125, 1069–1086.

————. *De divortio Lotharii et Tetbergae. PL* 125, 619–772.

————. *Epistola 22: De nuptiis Stephani. PL* 126, 132–153.

————. *Epistolae. PL* 126, 9–280.

————. *De ordine palatii. MGH Capit.* 2, 517–530.

————. *Ad proceres. PL* 125, 993–1008.

————. *Ad regem, De coercendo et exstirpando raptu viduarum, puellarum ac sanctimonialium. PL* 125, 1017–1036.

HOLSTENIUS, LUCAS, ed. *Codex Regularum monasticarum et canonicarum.* Vols. 1–2. Augsburg, 1759; rpt. Graz, 1957.

HRABANUS MAURUS. *Epistolae.* Ed. E. Dümmler. *MGH Epist.* 5; *Kar. aevi* 3, 379–516.

HROSWITHA OF GANDERSHEIM. *Hrotsvithae opera.* Ed. Paul de Winterfeld, Berlin, 1902. Ed. K. Strecker. Leipzig, 1930. Ed. H. Homeyer, Munich, Paderborn, Vienna, 1970. German translation, H. Homeyer. *Werke.* Munich, Paderborn, Vienna, 1973.

HUCBALD. *Vita s. Jonati. AS 1* Aug., 1, 70–75.

————. *Vita s. Rictrudis. AS* 12 Maii; 3, 83. *Acta sanctorum Belgii selecta* 4, 488–503. Prologue only, *MGH Script. rer. mer.* 6, 91–94.

INNOCENT I. *Epistulae, PL* 20, 463–642.

IONAS OF BOBBIO. *Vitae sanctorum: Vitae s. Columbani abbatis disciplorumque eius. MGH Script. rer. mer.* 4, 61–112. *Ionae Vitae sanctorum Columbani, Vedasti, Ioannis.* Ed. B. Krusch. *MGH Script. rer. germ. in usu schol.* Hanover, 1905.

ISAAC OF LANGRES. *Canones. PL* 124, 1075–1110.

ISIDORE OF SEVILLE. *De ecclesiasticis officiis. PL* 83, 737–826.

————. *Etymologiarum libri XX.* Ed. W. M. Lindsay. Oxford, 1911. *PL* 82, 73–728.

JEROME. *Adversus Helvidium, de perpetua virginitate b. Mariae. PL* 23, 183–206.

————. *Adversus Jovinianum. PL* 23, 221–352.

————. *Commentaria in Ezechielem prophetam.* PL 25, 15–512.

————. *Commentaria in Zachariam prophetam.* PL 25, 1485–1616.

————. *Contra Vigilantium.* PL 23, 351–368.

————. *Epist. 77: Ad Oceanum.* PL 22, 690–698.

————. *Epistolae.* Ed. I. Hilberg. Vols. 1–3. CSEL 54–56. Vienna, Leipzig, 1910–18.

————. *Interpretatio Homiliarum duarum Origenis in Canticum Canticorum.* PL 23, 1173–1196.

————. *Letters and Select Works.* Trans. W. H. Freemantle (A Select Library of Nicene and Post-Nicene Fathers of the Christian Church, 2d ser., 6). New York, 1893.

JOHN VIII. *Epistolae.* Ed. E. Caspar. *MGH Epist.* 7, *Kar. aevi* 5, 1–272.

JONAS OF ORLÉANS. *De institutione laicali.* PL 106, 121–278.

Leges Burgundionum (Lex Gundobada). Ed. L. R. Salis. *MGH Legum Sectio I,* 2/1, 29–122. Trans. K. F. Drew, *The Burgundian Code.* Philadelphia, 1972.

Leges Visigothorum. Ed. K. Zeumer. *MGH Legum Sectio I,* 1. Berlin, 1902.

LEO I. *Epistolae.* PL 54, 593–1218.

Lex Alamannorum. Editio altera K. A. Eckhardt. *MGH Legum Sectio I,* 5/1 (1969), 35–157.

Lex Baiwariorum. Ed. E. de Schwind. *MGH Legum Sectio I,* 5/2, 197–473.

Lex Ribuaria. Ed. F. Beyerle and R. Buchner. *MGH Legum Sectio I,* 3/2.

Lex Romana Burgundionum. Ed. L. R. de Salis. *MGH Legum Sectio I,* 2/1, 123–163.

Lex Romana Visigothorum. Ed. G. Haenel. Leipzig, 1849.

Lex Salica. Ed. K. A. Eckhardt. *MGH Legum Section I,* 4/2.

Lex Saxonum. Leges Saxonum und Lex Thuringorum. Ed. Cladius Freiherr von Schwerin (*MGH Fontes iuris germanici antiqui in usum scholarum,* 4). Hanover, Leipzig, 1918. *Die Gesetze des Karolingerreiches 714–911; III: Sachsen, Thuringen, Chamaren und Friesen.* Ed. K. A. Eckhardt (Germanenrechte, 2). Weimar, 1934.

Liber historiae francorum. Ed. B. Krusch. *MGH Script. rer. mer.* 2, 238–328. Trans. B. Bachrach. Lawrence, Kansas, 1973.

Liber memorialis von Remiremont. Ed. E. Hlawitschka, K. Schmid, and G. Tellenbach. *MGH Libri mem.* 1.

Liber sacramentorum Romanae aeclesiae ordinis anni circuli. Ed. L. C. Mohlberg et al. (Rerum ecclesiasticarum documenta. Series major, Fontes 4). Rome, 1960.

The Lombard Code. Trans. Katherine Fischer Drew. Philadelphia, 1973.

MAYER, J., ed. *Monumenta de viduis, diaconissis, virginibusque tractantia* (Florilegium patristicum, 42). Bonn, 1938.

Medieval Handbooks of Penance. Ed. and trans. McNeill, J. T., and Gamer, H. M. (Records of Civilization, 29). New York, 1938.

Miracula s. Austrebertae virginis. AS 10 Febr.; 2, 424–427.

THE MONK OF ST. GALL (Notker the Stammerer). *De gestis Karoli Magni.* Ed. G. H. Pertz. *MGH Script.* 2, 731–763. Trans. L. Thorpe, *Two Lives of Charlemagne.* (Penguin Classics). Baltimore, 1969.

Monumenta Novaliciensia vetustiora. Ed. C. Cipolla. Vol. 1 (Fonti per la storia d'Italia, 31). Rome, 1898.

NICHOLAS I. *Epistolae.* Ed. E. Perels. *MGH Epist. 6, Kar. aevi* 4, 257–690.

NITHARD. *Historiarum libri IV.* Ed. G. H. Pertz. *MGH Script.* 2, 649–672. Trans. B. W. Scholz, *Carolingian Chronicles.* Ann Arbor, 1972.

Les ordines Romani. Ed. M. Andricu. Vol. 4 (Spicilegium sacrum Lovaniense. Études et documents, 28). Louvain, 1956.

ORIGEN. *Fragments sur la Première aux Corinthiens.* Ed. Claude Jenkins. *Journal of Theological Studies,* 9 (1907–1908), 231–247, 353–372, 500–514.

Pactus Alamannorum. Editio altera K.A. Eckhardt. *MGH Legum Section I,* 5/1 (1969), 21–34.

Pactus legis Salicae. Ed. K. A. Eckhardt. *MGH Legum Sectio I,* 4/1, 1–267. *Pactus legis Salicae I. Einführung und 80 Titel Text.* Ed. K. A. Eckhardt. Göttingen, 1954.

PARDESSUS, J. M., and DE BREQUIGNY, L. G. O. eds. *Diplomata, chartae, epistolae, leges, aliaque instrumenta ad res Gallo-Francicas spectantia.* Vols. 1–2. Paris, 1843–49.

PASCHASIUS RADBERTUS. *Expositio in Psalmum XLIV. PL* 120, 993–1060.

———. *De partu Virginis. PL* 120, 1365–1386.

———. *Ex vita s. Adalhardi.* Ed. G. H. Pertz. *MGH Script.* 2, 524–532. Trans. A. Cabannis, *Charlemagne's Cousins.* Syracuse, 1967.

———. *Vita Walae.* Ed. G. H. Pertz. *MGH Script.* 2, 533–569. *PL* 120, 1557–1650.

Passio s. Maxellendis. Ed. H. Bevenot. *Acta sanctorum Belgii selecta* 3, 580–589.

Passio s. Praeiecti episcopi Arverni. Ed. B. Krusch. *MGH Script. rer. mer.* 5, 225–248.

Passio s. Sigismundi. Ed. B. Krusch. *MGH Script. rer. mer.* 2, 333–340.

Proverbia Graecorum. In *Sedulius Scottus,* ed. S. Hellmann. Munich, 1960, pp. 121–135.

PRUDENTIUS. *Vita s. Maurae virginis auctore Prudentio episcopo. AS* 21 Sept.; 6, 275–278.

PSEUDO-CHRYSOSTOM. *Opus imperfectum in Matthaeum. PG* 56, 601–946.

PSEUDO-EGBERT. *Poenitentiale. PL* 89, 401–436.

PSEUDO-HIERONYMUS. *De septem ordinibus ecclesiae.* Ed. A. W. Kalff. Würzburg, 1935.

Recueil des chartes de l'Abbaye de Cluny. Ed. A. Bernard and A. Bruell. Vol. 1. Paris, 1876.

Recueil des chartes de l'Abbaye de Saint-Benoît-sur-Loire. Ed. M. Prou and A. Vidier. Vol. 1. Paris. 1900.

Regesta Alsatiae aevi Merovingici et Karolini. Ed. A. Bruckner. Strassbourg, 1949.

Il regesto di Farfa compilato da Gregorio di Catino. Ed. Ugo Balzini and I. Giorgi. Rome, 1892.

REGINO OF PRÜM. *Chronicon.* Ed. G. H. Pertz. *MGH Script.* 1, 544–612.

REMY OF REIMS. *Testamentum. CCL* 117, 473–479. Turnhout, 1957. *PL* 65, 969–976.

RICULF. *Statuta. PL* 131, 15–24.

SCHMITZ, H. J. ed. *Die Bussbücher und das Kanonische Bussverfahren.* 2 vols. Düsseldorf, 1898; reprinted Graz, 1958.

SEDULIUS SCOTTUS. *De rectoribus christianis. PL* 103, 291–332. *Liber de rectoribus,* ed. Siegmund Hellmann (Quellen und Untersuchungen zur lateinischen Philologie des Mittelalters, 1). Munich, 1906.

SIDONIUS APOLLINARIS. *Carmina.* Ed. C. Lütjohann. *MGH Auct. ant.* 8, 173–264.

SIGEBERT OF GEMBLOUX. *Chronica.* Ed. D. L. C. Bethmann. *MGH Script.* 6, 300–374.

SIRICIUS PAPA. *Ad episcopos Africae. PL* 13, 1155–1162.

Les Statuta Ecclesiae antiqua: Edition, études critiques. Ed. Ch. Munier (Bibliothèque de l'Institut de Droit Canonique de l'Université de Strasbourg, 5). Paris, 1960.

SULPICIUS SEVERUS. *Chronicorum.* Ed. C. Halm. *CSEL* 1, 3–105. Vienna, 1866. *PL* 20, 95–160.

———. *Vie de Saint Martin.* Trans. Jacques Fontaine. 2 vols. (Sources chrétiennes 133–134). Paris, 1967–68.

TACITUS. *Germania.* Trans. H. Mattingly. Harmondsworth, 1960.

TERTULLIAN. "The Apparel of Women." *Disciplinary, Moral and Ascetical Works,* trans. R. Arbesmann et al. New York, 1959.

———. *De exhortatione castitatis.* Ed. A. Kroymann. *CSEL* 70. Ed. A. Gerlo. *CCL* 2, 1013–1035. Turnhout, 1954.

THEGAN. *Vita Hludowici imperatoris.* Ed. G. H. Pertz. *MGH Script.* 2, 585–604.

THEODORET OF CYRRHUS. *Historia ecclesiastica libri quinque.* Ed. L. Parmentier (Die griechischen christlichen Schriftsteller, 19). Leipzig, 1911.

Theodosiani libri XVI *cum Constitutionibus Sirmondianis.* Ed. Th. Mommsen and P. M. Meyer. 2 vols., Berlin, 1905.

THEODULF OF ORLÉANS. *Capitula ad presbyteros parochiae suae. PL* 105, 191–208.

———. *Capitulare ad eosdem. PL* 105, 207–224.

Translatio s. Baltechildis. Ed. G. H. Pertz. *MGH Script.* 15/1, 284–285.

Urkundenbuch zur Geschichte der jetzt die preussischen Regierungsbezirke Coblenz und Trier bildenden mittelrheinischen Territorien. Ed. H. Beyer. Vol. 1. Coblenz, 1860.

De virtutibus s. Geretrudis. Ed. B. Krusch. *MGH Script. rer. mer.* 2, 464–471.

Vita Aldegundis, abbatissae Malbodiensis. Ed. W. Levison. *MGH Script. rer. mer.* 6, 79–90. Ed. J. Ghesquière. *Acta sanctorum Belgii selecta* 4, 315–326.

Vita Anstrudis abbatissae Laudunensis. Ed. W. Levison. *MGH Script. rer. mer.* 6, 64–78.

Vita antiquior s. Glodesindis. AS 25 Iulii; 6, 203–210.

Vita s. Austrebertae virginis. AS 10 Feb.; 2, 419–427.

Vita Austrigisili episcopi Biturigi. Ed. B. Krusch. *MGH Script. rer. mer.* 4, 191–200.

Vita s. Balthildis reginae. Ed. B. Krusch. *MGH Script. rer. mer.* 2, 482–508.

Vita Bavonis confessoris Gandavensis 1, Vita prior. Ed. B. Krusch. *MGH Script. rer. mer.* 4, 534–546.

Vita Bertilae, abbatissae Calensis. Ed. W. Levison. *MGH Script. rer. mer.* 6, 95–109.

Vita s. Boniti episcopi Arvernensis. Ed. B. Krusch. *MGH Script. rer. mer.* 6, 119–139.

Vita s. Chrothildis reginae francorum. Ed. B. Krusch. *MGH Script. rer. mer.* 2, 342–348.

Vita s. Deicoli. AS 18 Jan.; 2, 563–574.

Vita s. Desiderii. Ed. B. Krusch. *MGH Script. rer. mer.* 4, 563–602.

Vita Desiderii episcopi Viennensis. Ed. B. Krusch. *MGH Script. rer. mer.* 3, 630–648.

Vita s. Eligii episcopi Noviomensis. Ed. B. Krusch. *MGH Script. rer. mer.* 4, 663–742.

Vita Eugendi. See *Vitae abbatum Iurensium.*

Vita s. Eustadiolae viduae. AS 8 Iunii; 2, 131–133.

Vita Filiberti abbatis Gemeticensis et Heriensis. Ed. W. Levison. *MGH Script. rer. mer.* 5, 583–606.

Vita s. Geretrudis Nivialensis. Ed. B. Krusch. *MGH Script. rer. mer.* 2, 453–464.

Vita s. Godeberthae. AS 11 Aprilii; 2, 32–36.

Vita ss. Herlindis sive Harlindis et Reinulae sive Renildae abbatissarum Masaci in Belgio. AS 22 Martii; 3, 383–392.

Vita Hludowici imperatoris. Ed. G. H. Pertz. *MGH Script.* 2, 604–648. Trans. A. Cabannis, *Son of Charlemagne: A Contemporary Life of Louis the Pious.* Syracuse, 1961.

Vita Iohannis abbatis Gorziensis. Ed. G. H. Pertz. *MGH Script.* 4, 337–377.

Vita s. Lantberti abbatis Fontanellensis et episcopi Lugdunensis. Ed. W. Levison. *MGH Script. rer. mer.* 5, 608–612.

Vita s. Liutbirgae. Ed. G. H. Pertz. *MGH Script.* 4, 158–164. *Vita Liutbirgae virginis (Das Leben der Liutbirg).* Ed. O. Menzel (*MGH* Deutsches Mittelalter; kritische Studientexte des Reichsinstituts für ältere deutsche Geschichtskunde, 3). Leipzig, 1937.

Vita Nivardi episcopi Remensis. Ed. W. Levison. *MGH Script. rer. mer.* 5, 160–171.

Vita Odiliae abbatissae Hohenburgensis. Ed. W. Levison, *MGH Script. rer. mer.* 6, 24–50.

Vita s. Radegundis. See Baudonivia and Fortunatus.

Vita s. Rictrudis. See Hucbald.

Vita Romani. See *Vitae abbatum Iurensium.*

Vita Sadalbergae abbatissae Laudunensis. Ed. B. Krusch. *MGH Script. rer. mer.* 5, 49–66.

Vita s. Sigolenae (vel. Segulinae). AS 24 Iulii; 5, 630–637.

Vita s. Sulpitii Pii episcopi Bituricensis. Ed. B. Krusch. *MGH Script. rer. mer.* 4, 371–380.

Vita s. Verenae virginis. AS 1 Sept.; 1, 164–168.

Vita s. Waldetrudis. Ed. J. Ghesquière. *Acta sanctorum Belgii selecta* 4, 439–448.

Vitae abbatum Iurensium; Romani, Lupicini et Eugendi. Ed. B. Krusch. *MGH Script. rer. mer.* 3, 131–166.

Vitae Amati, Romarici, Adelphii abbatum Habendesium. Ed. B. Krusch. *MGH Script. rer. mer.* 4, 215–228.

Vitae sancti Bonifatii archiepiscopi Moguntini. Ed. W. Levison (*MGH Script. rer. germ. in usum schol.*). Hanover, 1905.

Vitae Caesarii episcopi Arelatensis. Ed. E. Dümmler. *MGH Script. rer. mer.* 3, 457–501.

WALDEBERT. *Regula cuiusdam patris ad virgines. PL* 88, 1053–1070.

WASSERSCHLEBEN, F. W. H., ed. *Die Bussordnungen der abendländischen Kirche.* Halle, 1851.

Secondary Sources

ABEL, S. *Jahrbücher des fränkischen Reiches unter Karl dem Grossen.* 2d ed. B. Simson. Vols. 1–2. Leipzig, 1883–1888.

ACHELIS, HANS. "Diakonissen." *Realencyklopädie für protestantische Theologie und Kirche.* Vol. 4. Leipzig, 1898, pp. 616–620.

AIGRAIN, RENÉ. "Un ancien poème anglais, sur la vie de sainte Radegonde." *Études mérovingiennes: Actes des Journées de Poitiers, 1952.* Paris, 1953, pp. 1–12.

——. "Une abbesse mal connue de Sainte-Croix de Poitiers." *Bulletin philologique et historique* (1946–47), pp. 197–202.

——. *Sainte Radegonde.* Paris, 1918.

——. "Le voyage de sainte Radegonde à Arles." *Bulletin philologique et historique* (1926–27), pp. 119–27.

AMENT, HERMANN. "Zur archäologischen Periodisierung der Merowingerzeit." *Germania,* 55 (1977), 133–140.

AMIRA, KARL VON. *Germanisches Recht.* 4th ed. rev. Karl August Eckhardt. Vols. 1–2 (Grundriss der germanischen Philologie, 5, 1/2). Berlin, 1960–1967.

ARTHUR, MARILYN. " 'Liberated Women': The Classical Era." *Becoming Visible: Women in European History,* ed. Renate Bridenthal and Claudia Koonz. Boston, 1977, pp. 60–89.

AUDET, JEAN PAUL. *Structures of Christian Priesthood: A Study of Home, Marriage, and Celibacy in the Pastoral Service of the Church.* Trans. R. Sheed. New York, 1968.

AUZIAS, L. "Bernard 'Le Veau' et Bernard 'Plantevelue.' " *Annales du Midi,* 44 (1932), 257–295.

AXTERS, STEPHANUS, O. P. *The Spirituality of the Old Low Countries.* Trans. Donald Atwater. London, 1954.

BABUT, E. C. *La plus ancienne décretale.* Paris, 1904.

BALDWIN, CARL R. "The Scribes of the Sacramentary of Gellone." *Scriptorium,* 27 (1973), 16–20.

——. "The Scriptorium of the Sacramentary of Gellone." *Scriptorium,* 25 (1971), 3–17.

BALON, JOSEPH. *Traité de droit Salique.* Vol. 2 (Ius medii aevi, 3). Namur, 1965.

BALSDON, J. P. V. D. *Roman Women: Their History and Habits.* New York, 1963.

BARCHEWITZ, JUTTA. *Von der Wirtschaftstätigkeit der Frau in der vorgeschichtlichen Zeit bis zur Entfaltung der Stadtwirtschaft* (Breslauer historische Forschungen, 3). Breslau, 1937.

BARION, H. *Das fränkisch-deutsche Synodalrecht des Frühmittelalters* (Kanonistische Studien und Texte, ed. A. M. Königen, 5–6). Bonn, Köln, 1931.

BARSTOW, ANNE. "The Defense of Clerical Marriage in the 11th and Early 12th Centuries." Ph.D. dissertation, Columbia University, 1979.

BATESON, MARY. *Origin and Early History of Double Monasteries* (Royal Historical Society, Transactions, n.s. 13). London, 1899.

BECK, HENRY G. *The Pastoral Care of Souls in South East France during the Sixth Century* (Analecta Gregoriana, 51). Rome, 1950.

BECQUET, J. "Nouveau dépouillement du 'Monasticon Benedictinum.'" *Revue Bénédictine*, 73 (1963), 325–339.

BENOÎT, F. "Topographie monastique d'Arles au VIe siècle." *Études mérovingiennes: Actes des Journées de Poitiers, 1952.* Paris, 1953, pp. 13–17.

———. "Le premier baptistère d'Arles et l'Abbaye Saint-Césaire." *Cahiers archéologiques*, 5 (1951), 31–59.

BERNARDS, MATTHÄUS. *Speculum virginum: Geistlichkeit und Seelenleben der Frau im Hochmittelalter* (Forschungen zur Volkskunde, 36/38). Cologne, Graz, 1955.

BERNOULLI, C. A. *Die Heiligen der Merowinger.* Tübingen, 1900.

BEYERLE, FRANZ. "Die beiden süddeutschen Stammesrechte." *ZSSR germ. Abt.* 73 (1956), 84–140.

———. *Gesetze der Burgunden.* Weimar, 1960.

———. "Volksrechtliche Studien I: Die Lex Ribuaria." *ZSSR germ. Abt.*, 48 (1928), 264–378.

———. "Volksrechtliche Studien II: Die süddeutschen Leges und die merowingische Gesetzgebung." *ZSSR germ. Abt.*, 49 (1929), 264–432.

———. "Volksrechtliche Studien III: Das Gesetzbuch Ribuariens." *ZSSR germ. Abt.*, 55 (1935), 1–80.

BICKELL, G. "Der Cölibat, eine apostolische Anordnung." *Zeitschrift für katholische Theologie*, 2 (1878), 26–64; ibid., 3 (1879), 792–799.

BILANIUK, PETRO B. T. "Celibacy and Eastern Tradition." *Celibacy, the Necessary Option*, ed. George H. Frein. New York, 1968, pp. 32–72.

BIONDI, BIONDO. *Il diritto romano cristiano.* Vol. 3. Milan, 1954.

BISCHOFF, BERNHARD. "Frühkarolingische Handschriften und ihre Heimat." *Scriptorium*, 22 (1968), 306–314.

———. "Die kölner Nonnenhandschriften und das Skriptorium von Chelles." *Karolingische und ottonische Kunst.* Ed. Herrmann Aubin. Wiesbaden, 1957, pp. 395–401. Reprinted *Mittelalterliche Studien.* Vol. 1. Stuttgart, 1966, 16–34.

———. "Mediatori di civiltà del sesto secolo alla riforma di Carlo Magno." *Mittelalterliche Studien.* Vol. 1. Stuttgart, 1966, 312–327.

———. "Panorama der Handschriftenüberlieferung aus der Zeit Karls des Grossen." *Karl der Grosse: Lebenswerk und Nachleben.* Vol. 2. Ed. B. Bischoff. Düsseldorf, 1965, 233–254.

———. "Wer ist die Nonne von Heidenheim?" *Studien und Mitteilungen zur Geschichte des Benediktinerordens*, 49 (1931), 387–388.

———. and HOFMANN, J. *Libri sancti Kyliani. Die Würzburger Schreibschule* (Quellen und Forschungen z. Geschichte d. Bistums u. Hochstifts Würzburg, 6). Würzburg, 1952.

BLOCH, MARC. "Notes sur les sources d'histoire de l'Ile-de-France au Moyen Age I: Les archives et cartulaires de l'Abbaye de Chelles." *Bulletin de la Société de l'Histoire de Paris et de l'Ile-de-France*, 40 (1913), 145–164.

BLUM, G. G. "Das Amt der Frau im Neuen Testament." *Novum Testamentum,* 7 (1964), 142–161.

BOELENS, MARTIN. *Die Klerikerehe in der Gesetzgebung der Kirche unter besonderer Berücksichtigung der Strafe. Eine rechtsgeschichtliche Untersuchung von den Anfängen der Kirche bis zum Jahre 1139.* Paderborn, 1968.

BÖHME, HORST W. *Germanische Grabfunde des 4. bis 5. Jahrhunderts zwischen unterer Elbe und Loire: Studien zur Chronologie und Bevölkerungsgeschichte* (Münchner Beiträge zur Vor- und Frühgeschichte, 19). Munich, 1974.

BÖHMER, HEINRICH. "Die Entstehung des Cölibates." *Geschichtliche Studien Albert Hauck zum 70. Geburtstage, dargebracht von Mitarbeiter Kreise der Realencyklopädie für protestantische Theologie und Kirche.* Leipzig, 1916, pp. 6–24.

BONENFANT, PAUL. "Note critique sur le prétendu testament de sainte Aldegonde." *Académie Royale de Belgique: Bulletin de la Commission Royale d'Histoire,* 98 (1934), 219–238.

BONNELL, H. E. *Die Anfänge des karolingischen Hauses* (Jahrbücher der deutschen Geschichte, 1). Berlin, 1866.

BØRRESEN, KARI ELISABETH. *Subordination et équivalence: Nature et role de la femme d'après Augustin et Thomas d'Aquin.* Oslo, Paris, 1968.

BORSINGER, H. *Rechtsstellung der Frau in der katholischen Kirche.* Borna, Leipzig, 1930.

BOSL, KARL. "Der 'Adelsheilige.' Idealtypus und Wirklichkeit: Gesellschaft und Kultur im merowingischen Bayern des 7. und 8. Jahrhunderts." *Speculum Historiale, Festschrift J. Spörl.* Ed. C. Bauer et al. (Travaux du Centre des recherches sur la civilisation de l'Europe moderne, 5). Freiburg, Munich, 1965, pp. 167–187.

———. "Castes, ordres et classes en Allemagne (d'après un choix d'exemples allemands)." *Problèmes de stratification social: Actes du Colloque International (1966).* Ed. Roland Mousnier. Paris, 1968, pp. 13–29.

———. *Franken um 800: Strukturanalyse einer fränkischen Königsprovinz.* 2d ed. rev. Munich, 1969.

BOULDING, ELISE. *The Underside of History.* Boulder, Colo., 1976.

BOUTEMY. M. "Chronique: Notes de voyage sur quelques manuscrits de l'ancien archdiocèse de Reims." *Scriptorium,* 2 (1948), 123–129.

———. "Le scriptorium et la bibliothèque de Saint-Amand." *Scriptorium,* 1 (1946–47), 6–16.

BOUVIER, H. "Histoire de Saint-Pierre-le-Vif à Sens." *Bulletin des sciences hist. et nat. de l'Yonne,* 45 (1892), 1–212.

BRANDENBURG, E. *Die Nachkommen Karls des Grossen* (Genealogie und Landesgeschichte, ed. H. F. Friedrichs, 10; Caroli Magni Progenies, 1). Leipzig, 1935; reprinted Frankfurt, 1964.

BRION, M. *Frédégonde et Brunehaut.* Paris, 1935.

BRISSAUD, JEAN BAPTISTE. *Manuel d'histoire du droit français; sources, droit public, droit privé à l'usage des étudiants en licence et en doctorat.* New ed. Jacques Brissaud. Paris, 1935.

BROWE, PETER. *Beiträge zur Sexualethik des Mittelalters.* (Breslauer Studien zur historischen Theologie, 23). Breslau, 1932.

BROWN, P. R. L. "Aspects of the Christianization of the Roman Aristocracy." *Journal of Roman Studies*, 51 (1961), 1–11.

BRÜHL, CARL, RICHARD. *Fodrum, gistum, servitium regis. Studien zu den wirtschaftlichen Grundlagen des Königtums im Frankenreich und in den fränken Nachfolgestaaten . . . vom 6. bis zur Mitte des 14. Jahrhunderts* (Kölner historische Abhandlungen, 14). Cologne, 1968.

———. "Hinkmariana II: Hinkmar im Widerstreit von kanonischen Recht und Politik in Ehefragen." *Deutsches Archiv*, 20 (1964), 55–77.

BRUNNER, HEINRICH. *Abhandlungen zur Rechtsgeschichte.* Ed. K. Rauch. 2 vols. Weimar, 1931.

BRUNS, HERM. THEOD., ed. *Canones apostolorum et conciliorum saeculorum IV. V. VI. VII.* 2 vols. Berlin, 1839. Rpt. Torino, 1959.

BUGGE, JOHN. *Virginitas: An Essay in the History of a Medieval Ideal* (International Archives of the History of Ideas, Ser. Min., 17). The Hague, 1975.

BULLOGH, VERN, and CAMERON CAMPBELL. "Female Longevity and Diet in the Middle Ages." *Speculum*, 55 (1980), 317–325.

BURN, A. R. "Hic Breve Vivitur: A Study of the Expectation of Life in the Roman Empire." *Past and Present*, 4 (1953), 2–31.

CALMETTE, J. *L'Effondrement d'un empire et la naissance d'une Europe.* Paris, 1941.

CAPELLE, CATHERINE. *Le voeu d'obéissance des origines au XIIe siècle* (Bibliothèque d'histoire du droit et droit romaine, 2). Paris, 1959.

CASEL, ODO. "Die Mönchsweihe." *Jahrbuch für Liturgiewissenschaft*, 5 (1925), 4–5.

CHABOSEAU, A. *Histoire de la Bretagne avant le 13. siècle.* Paris, 1926.

CHADWICK, HENRY. *Priscillian of Avila: The Occult and the Charismatic in the Early Church.* Oxford, 1976.

CHADWICK, NORA. *Poetry and Letters in Early Christian Gaul.* London, 1955.

CHASTAGNOL, ANDRÉ. "Classes et ordres dans le Bas-Empire." *Ordres et classes; Colloque d'histoire sociale, Saint-Cloud, 24–25 mai, 1967.* Ed., D. Roche et C. E. Labrousse. Paris, 1976, pp. 49–57.

CHAUME, M. *Les origines du duché de Bourgogne.* Vol. 1. Dijon, 1925.

CHAUSSY, DOM Y., et al., eds. *L'Abbaye royale Notre-Dame de Jouarre.* Paris, 1961.

CHÉNON, ÉMILE. *Histoire générale du droit français public et privé des origines à 1815.* Vol. 1. Paris, 1926.

CHOUX, JACQUES. "Décadence et réforme monastique dans la province de Trèves, 855–959." *Revue Bénédictine*, 70 (1960), 204–223.

CLERCQ, C. DE. *La législation religieuse franque.* Vol. 1. Paris, 1936. Vol. 2 (Université Louvain, Recueil de travaux publiés par les membres des Conferences d'histoire et de philologie, 2 ser., 38). Anvers, 1958.

COLEMAN, EMILY R. "Medieval Marriage Characteristics: A Neglected Factor in the History of Medieval Serfdom." *Journal of Interdisciplinary History*, 2 (1971), 205–219.

CONRAT, MAX. *Breviarium Alaricianum, römisches Recht im fränkischen Reich in systematischer Darstellung.* Leipzig, 1903; reprinted Aalen, 1963.

CONSTANS, L. A. *Arles antique.* Paris, 1921.

CONTRENI, JOHN J. *The Cathedral School of Laon: Its Manuscripts and Masters, A.D. 850–930.* Munich, 1978.

————. "The Formation of Laon's Cathedral Library in the Ninth Century." *Studi medievali*, 3 Ser., 13,2 (1972), 919–939.

CORBETT, P. E. *The Roman Law of Marriage*. Oxford, 1930.

CORNUEY, LOUIS-MAURICE-ANDRÉ. *Le régime de la "dos" aux époques mérovingienne et carolingienne*. Alger, 1929.

CORSTEN, S. "Rheinische Adelsherrschaft im ersten Jahrtausend." *Rheinische Vierteljahrsblätter*, 28 (1963), 84–129.

COUDANNE, L. "Baudonivie, moniale de Sainte-Croix et biographe de sainte Radegonde." *Études mérovingiennes: Actes des Journées de Poitiers, 1952*. Paris, 1953, pp. 41–51.

COURSON M. AURÉLIEN DE. *Histoire des peuples bretons dans la Gaule et dans les Iles Britanniques*. 2 vols. Paris, 1846.

COURTOIS, CH. "L'Avenement de Clovis II et les règles d'accession au thrône de chez les Mérovingiens." *Mélanges d'histoire du moyen âge, dédiés à la memoire de Louis Halphen*. Paris, 1951, pp. 155–164.

COVILLE, A. "L'Evêque Aunemundus et son testament." *Recherches sur l'histoire de Lyon du Ve au IXe siècle (450–800)*. Paris, 1928, pp. 366–416.

————. "La prétendue charte mérovingienne de Saint-Pierre de Lyon." *Recherches sur l'histoire de Lyon du Ve au IXe siècle (450–800)*. Paris, 1928, pp. 251–266.

————. "Les Syagrii." *Recherches sur l'histoire de Lyon du Ve au IXe siècle (450–800)*. Paris, 1928, pp. 5–29.

DALY, MARY. *The Church and the Second Sex*. New York, 1975.

DANIÉLOU, JEAN. *The Ministry of Women in the Early Church*. Trans. Glyn Simon. London, 1961. 2nd ed. Leighton Buzzard, England, 1974.

DARGUN, L. "Mutterrecht und Raubehe." *Untersuchungen zur deutschen Staats-und Rechtsgeschichte*, 16 (1883), 23–76.

DAUDET, PIERRE. *Études sur l'histoire de la jurisdiction matrimoniale*. Paris, 1941.

DEEN, H. *Le célibat des prètres dans les premiers siècles de l'Église*. Paris, 1969.

DEKKERS, E. *Clavis patrum latinorum* (Sacris erudiri, 3). Steenbrugis, 1961.

DE LA BUSSIÈRE, P. *Le baillage de Mâcon*. Mâcon, 1914.

DELARUELLE, E. "Sainte Radegonde, son type de sainteté et la chrétienté de son temps." *Études mérovingiennes: Actes des Journées de Poitiers, 1952*. Paris, 1953, pp. 65–74.

DELEHAYE, HIPPOLYTE. *Les légendes hagiographiques*. 4th ed. Paul Peeters (Subsidia hagiographica, 18a). Brussels, 1955.

DELUMEAU, JEAN. *Histoire de la Bretagne*. Toulouse, 1969.

DE MAUSE, LLOYD. "The Evolution of Childhood." *The History of Childhood*. Ed. Lloyd De Mause. New York, 1974, pp. 1–73.

DESHUSSES, J. "Le sacramentaire de Gellone dans son contexte historique." *Ephemerides liturgicae*, 75 (1961), 193–210.

DEVISSE, JEAN. *Hincmar, archévêque de Reims. 845–882*. 3 vols. Geneva, 1975–76.

DEWEZ, JULES. *Histoire de l'Abbaye de St. Pierre d'Hasnon*. Lille, 1890.

DHONDTH, J. *Études sur la naissance des principautés territoriales en France*. Brugge, 1948.

DIBELIUS, M. *Die Pastoralbriefe*. 3d ed. H. Conzelmann (Handbuch zum Neuen Testament, 13). Tübingen, 1953.

DIEHL, CHARLES. *Byzantine Empresses*. Trans. H. Bell and Th. de Kerpely. London, 1959.

DOOLEY, W. J. *Marriage According to Saint Ambrose* (Catholic University of America, Studies in Christian Antiquity, 11). Washington, D.C., 1948.

DOPPELFELD, O. "Das fränkische Frauengrab unter dem Chor des kölner Domes." *Germania*, 38 (1960), 89–113.

————, and Pirling, R. *Fränkische Fürsten im Rheinland*. Düsseldorf, 1966.

DRONKE, PETER. *The Medieval Lyric*. 2d ed. New York, 1977.

————. *Women Writers of the Middle Ages*. Cambridge, London, New York, 1984.

DUBY, GEORGES. *Medieval Marriage: Two Models from Twelfth-Century France*. Trans. Elborg Forster (Johns Hopkins Symposia in Comparative History, 11). Baltimore, 1978.

————. *La société aux XIe et XIIe siècles dans la région Mâconnais*. Paris, 1953.

DUCKETT, ELEANOR SHIPLEY. *The Gateway to the Middle Ages: Monasticism*. Ann Arbor, Mich., 1938.

DULCY, SUZANNE. *La Règle de Saint Benoît de'Aniane et la réforme monastique à l'époque carolingienne*. Nimes, 1935.

DUMAS, A. "Eugène II." *Dictionnaire d'histoire et de géographie ecclésiastique*. Ed. A. Baudrillart. Vol. 15, 1963, 1347–1349.

DÜMMLER, E. *Geschichte des ostfränkischen Reichs*. Vol. 1 (Jahrbücher der deutschen Geschichte, 7, 1). Berlin, 1862.

DUPRAZ, L. *Le Royaume des Francs et l'ascension politique des maires du palais au déclin du VII siècle (656–800)*. Fribourg, 1948.

DUQUIT, LÉON. "Étude historique sur le rapt de seduction." *Nouvelle revue historique de droit français et étranger*, 2 (1886), 587–625.

EBNER, A. "Der liber vitae und die Nekrologien von Remiremont in der Bibliotheka Angelica zu Rom." *Neues Archiv*, 19 (1894), 47–88.

ECKENSTEIN, LINA. *Woman under Monasticism: Chapters on Saint-lore and Convent Life between A.D. 500 and A.D. 1500*. Cambridge, 1896.

————. *The Women of Early Christianity*. London, 1935.

ECKHARDT, W. A. "Die Decretio Childeberti und ihre Überlieferung." *ZSSR germ. Abt.*, 84 (1967), 1–71.

EITEN, G. *Das Unterkönigtum im Reiche der Merovinger und Karolinger* (Heidelberger Abhandlungen, 18). Heidelberg, 1907.

ENRIGHT, MICHAEL J. "Charles the Bald and Aethelwulf of Wessex." *Journal of Medieval History*, 5 (1979), 291–302.

ERBE, MICHAEL. *Studien zur Entwicklung des Niederkirchenwesens in Ostsachsen vom 8. bis zum 12. Jahrhundert* (Veröffentlichungen Max-Planck-Instituts für Geschichte, 26; Studien zur Germania sacra, 9). Göttingen, 1969.

ESMEIN, A. *Le mariage en droit canonique*. 2d ed. rev. R. Génestal and J. Dauvillier. Paris, 1935. 2 vols. in 1.

ESSEN, VAN DER, L. *Étude critique et littéraire sur les Vitae des saints mérovingiens de l'ancienne Belgique*. Louvain, Paris, 1907.

EWIG, EUGEN. "Beobachtungen zur Entwicklung der fränkischen Reichskirche unter Chrodegang von Metz." *Frühmittelalterliche Studien*, 2 (1968), 67–77.

———. "Die fränkischen Teilungen und Teilreiche (511–613)." *Akademie der Wissenschaften und Literatur, Abhandl. der geistes- und sozialwissenschaftlichen Klasse*, 9 (1952), 651–715.

———. "Die fränkischen Teilreiche im 7. Jahrhundert (613–714)." *Trierer Zeitschrift*, 22 (1953), 85–144.

———. "Kirche und Civitas in der Merowingerzeit." *Le Chiese nei regni dell'Europa occidentale* (Centro Italiano di Studi sull'Alto Medioevo; Settimana di Studio, 7, 1). Spoleto, 1960, pp. 45–71.

———. "Noch einmal zum 'Staatreich' Grimoalds." *Speculum historiale; Festschrift J. Spörl*. Ed. C. Bauer et al. Freiburg, Munich, 1965, pp. 454–457.

———. "Das Privileg des Bischofs Berthefrid von Amiens für Corbie von 664 und die Klosterpolitik des Königin Balthild." *Francia*, 1 (1973), 62–114.

———. "Studien zur merowingischen Dynastie." *Frühmittelalterliche Studien*, 8 (1974), 1–59.

FAHRNER, IGNAZ. *Geschichte der Ehescheidung im kanonischen Recht*. Freiburg, i.B., 1903.

FICHTENAU, H. *The Carolingian Empire*. Trans. P. Munz. New York, 1964.

FICKER, JULIUS. *Untersuchungen zur Erbenfolge der ostgermanischen Rechte*. Vols. 1–4. Innsbruck, 1891–1899.

FINLEY, M. I. "The Silent Women of Rome." *Horizon*, 7 (1965), 57–64. Reprinted in his *Aspects of Antiquity: Discoveries and Controversies*. London, 1968, pp. 129–142.

———. ed. *Slavery in Classical Antiquity*. Cambridge, 1960.

FISCHER, BONIFATIUS. "Bibeltext und Bibelreform unter Karl dem Grossen." *Karl der Grosse: Lebenswerk und Nachleben*. Vol. 2. Ed. B. Bischoff. Düsseldorf, 1965, 156–216.

FISCHER, JOHANNES. *Der Hausmeier Ebroin*. Bonn, 1954.

FITZER, G. *Das Weib schweige in der Gemeinde: Ueber den unpaulinischen Character der Mulier-taceat-Verse in I Korinther 14* (Theologische Existenz Heute, n.s., 110). Munich, 1963.

FLANDRIN, JEAN-LOUIS. "Contraception, Marriage, and Sexual Relations in the Christian West." *Biology of Man in History: Selections from the Annales*. Ed. Robert Forster and Orest Ranum. Baltimore, 1975, pp. 23–47.

———. *Families in Former Times: Kinship, Household and Sexuality*. Trans. Richard Southern. Cambridge, London, New York, 1978.

FLECKENSTEIN, J. "Fulrad von Saint Denis und der fränkische Ausgriff in den süddeutschen Raum." *Studien und Vorarbeiten zur Geschichte des grossfränkischen und frühdeutschen Adels*, ed. Gerd Tellenbach (Forschungen zur oberrheinischen Landesgeschichte, 4). Freiburg i. B., 1957, pp. 9–39.

———. "Über die Herkunft der Welfen." *Studien und Vorarbeiten zur Geschichte des grossfränkischen und frühdeutschen Adels*, ed. G. Tellenbach. Freiburg i. B., 1957, pp. 7–136.

FLEURY, JEAN. *Recherches historiques sur les empêchements de parenté dans le mariage canonique des origines aux Fausses Décrétales*. Paris, 1933.

FORGET, J. "Diaconesses." *Dictionnaire de théologie catholique*. Vol. 4. Paris, 1911, 685–703.

FORSYTH, ILENE H. *The Throne of Wisdom: Wood Sculptures of the Madonna in Romanesque France*. Princeton, 1972.

FOURNIER, P. and LE BRAS, G. *Histoire des collections canoniques en occident depuis les Fausses Décrétales*. Vol. 1. Paris, 1931. Rpt. Aalen, 1972.

FRANSEN, GERARD. "La rupture du mariage." *Il matrimonio nella società altomedievale* (Settimane di Studio del Centro Italiano di Studi sull'Alto Medioevo, 24). Spoleto, 1974, pp. 604–630.

FÜGEDI, ERIC. "Pour une analyse démographique de la Hongrie médiévale." *Annales-Économies-Sociétés-Civilisations*, 24 (1969), 1299–1312.

FUNK, F. X. "Cölibat und Priesterweihe im christlichen Altertum." *Kirchengeschichtliche Abhandlungen und Untersuchungen*, 1 (1897), 121–155.

GANSHOF, FRANÇOIS L. "L'Étranger dans la monarchie franque." *Société Jean Bodin, Recueils*, 10 (1958), 19–20.

——. "Le statut de la femme dans la monarchie franque." *Société Jean Bodin, Recueils*, 12 (1962), 5–58.

GAUDEMET, JEAN. "Indissolubilité et consommation du mariage, l'apport d'Hincmar de Reims." *Revue de droit canonique*, 30 (1980), 28–40.

——. "Le legs du droit romain en matière matrimoniale." *Il matrimonio nella società altomedievale* (Settimane di Studio del Centro Italiano di Studi sull' Alto Medioevo, 24). Spoleto, 1977, pp. 139–189.

——. "Saint Augustin et le manquement au voeu de virginité." *Annales de la Faculté de Droit d'Aix-en-Provence*, Nouv. ser., 43 (1950), 135–145.

——. "Le statut de la femme dans l'Empire romaine." *Société Jean Bodin, Recueils*, 11 (1959), 191–222.

——. "Les statuts épiscopaux de la première décade du IXᵉ siècle." *Proceedings of the Fourth International Congress of Medieval Canon Law. Toronto, 21–25 August 1972*, ed. Stephan Kuttner. Vatican City, 1976, pp. 303–349.

GÉNICOT, LÉOPOLD. "La noblesse au Moyen Age dans l'ancienne 'Francie.'" *Annales*, 17 (1962), 1–22.

GILLIARD, FRANK D. "The Senators in Sixth Century Gaul." *Speculum*, 54 (1979), 685–697.

GODEFROY, L. "Mariage dans les pères. Le sacrement." *Dictionnaire de théologie catholique*. Vol. 9. Paris, 1927, 2105–2109.

GOODY, J. R., and TAMBIAK, S. J. *Bridewealth and Dowry*. (Cambridge Papers in Social Anthropology, 7). Cambridge, 1973.

GOTTSCHALLER, EVA. *Hugeburc von Heidenheim, philologische Untersuchungen zu den Heiligenbiographien einer Nonne des achten Jahrhunderts* (Münchener Beiträge zur Mediävistik und Renaissance-Forschung, 12). Munich, 1973.

GOUGAUD, L. *Les chrétientés celtiques*. Paris, 1911.

——. "Inventaires des règles monastiques irlandaises." *Revue Bénédictine*, 25 (1908), 329–331.

GRAUS, FRANTIŠEK, *Volk, Herrscher und Heiliger im Reich der Merowinger*. Prague, 1965.

GRIFFE, E. *La Gaule chrétienne à l'époque romaine.* Nouv. éd. 3 vols. Paris, 1964–66.

GRIMM, JACOB. *Deutsche Rechtsalterthümer.* 4th rev. ed. Leipzig, 1899, 2 vols.

GROSSE, W. "Das Kloster Wendhausen, sein Stiftergeschlecht und seine Klausnerin." *Sachsen und Anhalt,* 16 (1940), 45–76.

GRYSON, ROGER. *Le ministère des femmes dans l'Église ancienne* (Recherches et synthèses, Section d'histoire, 4). Gembloux, 1972. Trans. Jean Laporte and Mary Louise Hall, *The Ministry of Women in the Early Church.* Collegeville, Minn., 1975.

———. *Les origines du célibat ecclésiastique du premier au septième siècle* (Recherches et synthèses, Section d'histoire, 2). Gembloux, 1970.

GUERDAN, RENÉ. *Byzantium.* Trans. D. I. B. Hartley. New York, 1962.

GUEROUT, JEAN. "Le monastère à l'époque carolingienne." *L'Abbaye royale Notre-Dame de Jouarre.* Ed. Y. Chaussy et al., Vol. 1. Paris, 1961, 75–78.

———. "Le testament de Sainte-Fare." *Revue d'histoire ecclésiastique,* 60 (1965), 761–821.

GUMMERE, FRANCES B. *Founders of England.* New York, 1930.

HAAG, H., ed. *Bibel-lexikon.* 2d ed. Einsiedeln, 1968.

HAFFLER, CARL. "The Changeling: History and Psychodynamics of Attitudes to Handicapped Children in European Folklore." *Journal of the History of Behavioral Sciences,* 4 (1968), 55–61.

HAIGHT, ANN L. ed. *Hroswitha of Gandersheim; Her Life, Times and Works, and a Comprehensive Bibliography.* New York, 1965.

HAVET, JULIEN P. E. "Questions mérovingiennes VII: Les actes des évêques du Mans." *Bibliothèque de l'École des Chartes,* 55 (1894), 5–60.

HAWKES, SONIA CHADWICK, and WELLS, CALVIN. "Crime and Punishment in an Anglo-Saxon Cemetery." *Antiquity,* 49 (1975), 118–122.

HEINEKEN, JOHANNA. *Die Anfänge der sächsischen Frauenkloster.* Göttingen, 1909.

HEINRICH, MARY PIA. *The Canonesses and Education in the Early Middle Ages.* Washington, D.C., 1924.

HELLMANN, SIEGMUND. "Die Heiraten der Karolinger." *Festgabe K. Th. Heigel.* Munich, 1903, pp. 1–99. Reprinted in his *Ausgewählte Abhandlungen zur Historiographie und Geistesgeschichte des Mittelalters.* Ed. H. Beumann. Darmstadt, 1961, pp. 293–391.

HERLIHY, DAVID. "Land, Family and Women." *Traditio,* 18 (1962), 89–120. Reprinted in *Women in Medieval Society.* Ed. S. Stuard. Philadelphia, 1976, pp. 13–45.

———. "Life Expectancies for Women in Medieval Society." *The Role of Woman in the Middle Ages.* Ed. Rosemarie Thee Morewedge. Albany, 1975, pp. 1–22.

HERMANN, HANS-WALTER. "Zum Stande der Erforschung der früh- und hochmittelalterlichen Geschichte des Bistums Metz." *Rheinische Vierteljahrsblätter,* 28 (1963), 131–199.

HERTLING, L. "Die Professio der Kleriker und die Entstehung der drei Gelübde." *Zeitschrift für katholische Theologie,* 56 (1932), 148–174.

HIGOUNET, CH. "Le problème économique: l'Église et la vie rurale pendant le très haut moyen age." *Le Chiese nei regni dell'Europa occidentale* (Centro

Italiano di Studi sull'Alto Medioevo: Settimana di Studio, 7, 2). Spoleto, 1960, pp. 775–804.

HILPISCH, FERDINAND (P. Stephanus). *Die Doppelklöster, Entstehung und Organization.* Münster, 1928.

———. *Geschichte der Benediktinerinnen.* St. Ottilien, 1951.

HLAWITSCHKA, EDUARD. *Die Anfänge des Hauses Habsburg-Lothringen.* Saarbrücken, 1969.

———. *Franken, Alemannen, Bayern und Burgunder in Oberitalien (774–962)* (Forschungen zur oberrheinischen Landesgeschichte, 8). Freiburg i. B., 1960.

———. "Zur Klosterverlegung und zur Annahme der Benediktsregel in Remiremont." *Zeitschrift für die Geschichte des Oberrheins,* 109 (1961), 249–269.

———. *Lotharingien und das Reich an der Schwelle der deutschen Geschichte* (Schriften der MGH, Deutsches Institut für Erforschung des Mittelalters, 21). Stuttgart, 1968.

———. *Studien zur Äbtissinnenreihe von Remiremont (7.–13. Jh.)* (Veröffentlichungen des Instituts für Landeskunde des Saarlandes, 9). Saarbrücken, 1963.

———. "Die Vorfahren Karls des Grossen." *Karl der Grosse: Lebenswerk und Nachleben.* Vol. 1. Ed. Helmut Beumann. Düsseldorf, 1965, pp. 51–81.

———. "Zur landschaftlichen Herkunft der Karolinger." *Rheinische Vierteljahrsblätter,* 27 (1962), 1–17.

HOEBANX, JEAN JACQUES. *L'Abbaye de Nivelles des origines au XIVᵉ siècle* (Mémoires de l'Académie Royale de Belgique, Classe des Lettres et des Sciences Morales et Politiques, 46). Brussels, 1952.

HOFFMANN, H. *Untersuchungen zur karolingischen Annalistik* (Bonner historische Forschungen, 10). Bonn, 1958.

HOPKINS, M. K. "The Age of Roman Girls at Marriage." *Population Studies,* 18, 3 (1965), 309–327.

HÖRGER, KARL. "Die reichsrechtliche Stellung der Fürstäbtissinnen." *Archiv für Urkundenforschung,* 9 (1926), 195–270.

HUBERT, JEAN. "L'Erémitisme et archéologie." *L'eremetismo in occidente nei secoli XI et XII* (Milan, Univ. Catt. del Sacro Cuore, Contributi, Ser. 3, Var. 4; Studi medioevali: Misc. 4). Milan, 1965, pp. 462–490.

———. PORCHER, JEAN, and VOLBACH, WOLFGANG FRITZ. *L'Empire carolingien.* Paris, 1968. Trans. J. Emmons, S. Gilbert and R. Allen. *The Carolingian Renaissance.* New York 1970.

———. PORCHER, JEAN, and VOLBACH, WOLFGANG FRITZ. *L'Europe des invasions,* 1 (L'Univers des Formes, 12). Paris, 1967.

HUGHES, DIANA OWEN. "From Brideprice to Dowry in Mediterranean Europe." *Journal of Family History,* 3 (1978), 262–296.

IRSIGLER, FRANZ. *Untersuchungen zur Geschichte des frühfränkischen Adels* (Rheinisches Archiv, 70). Bonn. 1969.

JAFFÉ PHILLIP, ed. *Regesta pontificum romanorum.* Ed. secunda curaverunt S. Loewenfeld, K. Kaltenbrunner, P. Ewald. 2 vols. Leipzig, 1885–1888.

JEUDY, COLETTE. "L'Institutio de nomine, pronomine et verbo de Priscien." *Revue d'histoire des textes,* 2 (1972), 73–144.

JOLIOT, P. *La condition juridique du religieux à travers l'histoire.* Bordeaux, 1942.

JOYCE, G. H. *Christian Marriage.* 2d ed. rev. London, 1948.

KÄHLER, ELSE. *Die Frau in den paulinischen Briefen.* Zürich, 1960.

KALIFA, S. "Singularités matrimoniales chez les anciens germains: le rapt et le droit de la femme à disposer d'elle-même." *Revue historique de droit français et étranger,* 48 (1970), 199–225.

KALSBACH, A. *Die altkirchliche Einrichtung der Diakonissen bis zu ihrem Erlöschen* (Römische Quartalschrift für christliche Altertumskunde und für Kirchengeschichte, Supplementheft, 22). Freiburg i. B., 1926.

———. "Diakonissenweihe in Kan. 19 des Konzils von Nicea." *Römische Quartalschrift,* 32 (1924), 166–169.

KANTOROWICZ, ERNST. *Laudes regiae.* Berkeley, 1946.

KELLY, WILLIAM. *Pope Gregory II on Divorce and Remarriage: A Canonical-Historical Investigation of the Letter "Desiderabilem mihi," with Special Reference to the Response "Quod proposuisti"* (Analecta Gregoriana 203; Ser. Fac. Iuris Can. Sectio B, 37). Rome, 1976.

KELLY-GADOL, Joan. "Did Women Have a Renaissance?" *Becoming Visible: Women in European History.* Ed. Renate Bridenthal and Claudia Koonz. Boston, 1977, pp. 137–164.

KING, P. D. *Law and Society in the Visigothic Kingdom.* Cambridge, 1972.

KLEWITZ, H. W. "Germanisches Erbe im fränkischen und deutschen Königtum." *Welt als Geschichte,* 7 (1941), 201–216.

KOSCHECK, J. *Die Klosterreform Ludwigs des Fr. im Verhältnis zur Regel Benedikts von Nursia.* Greifswald, 1908.

KÖSTLER, R. "Raub-, Kauf- und Friedelehe bei den Germanen." *ZSSR germ. Abt.,* 63 (1943), 92–136.

KRULL, P. *Die Salbung und Krönung der deutschen Königinnen und Kaiserinnen im Mittelalter.* Halle, 1911.

KUCHENBUCH, LUDOLF. *Bäuerliche Gesellschaft und Klosterherrschaft im 9. Jahrhundert. Studien zur Sozialstruktur der Familia der Abtei Prüm* (Vierteljahrschrift für Sozial- und Wirtschaftsgeschichte, 66). Wiesbaden, 1978.

KURTH, GODEFROID JOSEPH FRANÇOIS. *Études franques.* 2 vols. Paris, 1919.

LA BORDERIE, ARTHUR DE. *La chronologie du cartulaire de Redon.* Rennes, 1901.

———. *Histoire de Bretagne.* 3 vols. Rennes, 1896–99.

LABRIOLLE, PIERRE DE. *La crise montaniste* (Bibliothèque de la Fondation Thiers, 31). Paris, 1913.

———, trans. *Les sources de l'histoire du montanisme.* Fribourg, 1913.

LADOMERSZKY, NICHOLAS. *Saint Augustin, docteur du mariage chrétien* (Urbaniana, 5). Rome, 1942.

LAEUCHLI, SAMUEL. *Power and Sexuality: The Emergence of Canon Law at the Synod of Elvira.* Philadelphia, 1972.

LALINDE ABADÍA, J. "La sucesión filíal en el derecho visigodo." *Anuario de historia del derecho español,* 32 (1962), 113–129.

LANCASTER, LORRAINE. "Kinship in Anglo-Saxon Society." *Early Medieval Society.* Ed. Sylvia Thrupp. New York, 1967, pp. 17–40.

LASKO, PETER. *The Kingdom of the Franks.* New York, 1971.

LAUER, P. *Nithard: Histoire des fils de Louis le Pieux* (Les classiques de l'histoire de France au moyen âge, 7). Paris, 1926.

Laurissa jubilans: Festschrift zur 1200–Jahrfeier von Lorsch, 1964. Ed. Hans Degen et al. Lorsch, 1964.

LEA, HENRY C. *History of Sacerdotal Celibacy.* 3d ed. rev. New York, 1907.

LE BRAS, GABRIEL. "Pénitentiels." *Dictionnaire de théologie catholique.* Vol. 12. Paris, 1933, 1160–1179.

———. "Compte rendu de André Rosambert, *La veuve en droit canonique.*" *Revue des sciences religieuses,* 6 (1926), 281-288.

LEBRAS-TREMENBERT, JACQUELINE. "Les cartulaires de Faremoutiers." *Sainte Fare et Faremoutiers.* L'Abbaye de Faremoutiers, 1956, pp. 175–213.

LECLERCQ, H. "Diaconesse." *Dictionnaire d'archéologie chrétienne et de liturgie.* Vol. 4. Paris, 1920, pp. 725–733.

LEHMANN, PAUL. *Corveyer Studien* (Abh. d. bayerischen Akademie der Wiss., philos.-philol. und hist. Klasse, 30,5). Munich, 1919.

LEIPOLDT, JOHANNES. *Die Frau in der antiken Welt und im Urchristentum.* 2d ed., rev. Leipzig, 1955.

LEMAIRE, A. "La 'dotatio de l'épouse' de l'époque mérovingienne au XIIIe siècle." *Revue historique de droit français et étranger,* 4th Ser., 8 (1929), 569–580.

———. "Origine de la règle 'Nullum sine dote fiat coniugium.' " *Mélanges Paul Fournier* (Bibliothèque d'Histoire du droit, 1). Paris, 1929, pp. 415–444.

LESNE, EMILE. *Histoire de la propriété ecclésiastique en France.* Vol. 2, pt. 2 (Fac. Cath. de Lille, Mémoires et travaux, 30). Lille, 1926.

———. "Les ordonnances de Louis de Pieux." *Revue d'histoire de l'Église de France,* 6 (1920), 490–493.

LEVILLAIN, L. "De quelques personnages nommés Bernard . . ." *Mélanges dédiés à la mémoir de Félix Grat.* Vol. 1. Paris, 1946, 169–202.

———. "Encore la succession d'Austrasie." *Bibliothèque de l'École des Chartes,* 105 (1945–46), 296–306.

LEVISON, WILHELM. *Aus rheinischer und fränkischer Frühzeit.* Düsseldorf, 1948.

———. *England and the Continent in the Eighth Century.* 2d. ed. Oxford, 1950.

———. "Recension: Schäfer, K. H. 'Die Kanonissenstifter' . . ." *Westdeutsche Zeitschrift für Geschichte und Kunst,* 27 (1908), 491–512.

———. "Sigolena." *Neues Archiv,* 35 (1910), 219–231.

LÉVY-BRUHL, HENRI. *Étude sur les élections abbatiales en France jusqu'à la fin du règne de Charles de Chauve.* Paris, 1913.

LEWIS, ARCHIBALD R. *The Development of Southern French and Catalan Society, 718–1050.* Austin, 1965.

———. "The Dukes in the *Regnum Francorum.*" *Speculum,* 51 (1976), 381–410.

LEYSER, K. J. *Rule and Conflict in an Early Medieval Society: Ottonian Saxony.* London, 1979.

LIEBEN, J. *Histoire économique de l'Abbaye d'Hasnon depuis sa fondation jusqu'à la fin du XIIIe siècle.* Brussels, 1959–60.

LORAIN, P. *Essai historique sur l'Abbaye de Cluny.* Dijon, 1839.

LOT, FERDINAND. "Études carolingiennes. Les comtes d'Auvergne . . . Les comtes d'Autun . . ." *Bibliothèque de l'École des Chartes,* 102 (1941), 282–291.

———. "Note sur le sénéchal Alard." *Le Moyen Age,* 21 (1908), 185–201.

LOUIS, RENÉ. *Autessiodurum christianum: les églises d'Auxerre des origines au XIme siècle.* Paris, 1952.

———. *Girart, comte de Vienne (819–877) et ses fondations monastiques* (De l'histoire à la légende 1). Auxerre, 1946.

———. *Girart, comte de Vienne dans les chansons de geste* (De l'histoire à la légend 2-3). 2 vols. Auxerre, 1947.

LOWE, E. A., ed. *Codices latini antiquiores.* 11 vols. Oxford, 1934–66.

LYMAN, RICHARD B., JR. "Barbarism and Religion: Late Roman and Early Medieval Childhood." *The History of Childhood,* ed. Lloyd De Mause. New York, 1974, pp. 75–100.

LYNCH, J. E. "Marriage and Celibacy of the Clergy: The Discipline of the Western Church; An Historico-Canonical Synopsis." *Jurist,* 32 (1972), 14–38, 189–212.

MAASSEN, I. "Glossen des canonischen Rechts aus dem karolingischen Zeitalter." *Akademie der Wissenschaften Wien, phil.-hist. Classe, Sitzungsberichte,* 84 (1876), 235–298.

MACNEILL, EOIN. "Beginnings of Latin Culture in Ireland." *Studies: An Irish Quarterly Review of Letters, Philosophy and Science,* 20 (1931), 39–48, 449–460.

MAILLÉ, DE ROHAN-CHABOT, ALIETTÉ, MARQUISE. *Les cryptes de Jouarre.* Paris, 1971.

MALNORY, A. *Saint Césaire, évêque d'Arles (503–43)* (Bibl. de l'École des Hautes Études, Sciences Philol. et Hist., 103). Paris, 1894.

———. *Quid Luxovienses monachi, discipuli s. Columbani, ad regulam monasteriorum atque ad communem ecclesiae profectum contulerunt.* Paris, 1894.

MANSELLI, RAOUL. "Il matrimonio nei penitenziali." *Il matrimonio nella società altomedievale* (Settimane di Studio del Centro Italiano di Studi sull'Alto Medioevo, 24). Spoleto, 1977, pp. 287–319.

MARIÉ, GEORGES. "Sainte Radegonde et le milieu monastique contemporain." *Études mérovingiennes: Actes des Journées de Poitiers, 1952.* Paris, 1953, pp. 219–225.

MATHER, ANN E. "A Twelfth Century Ordo for the Veiling of Widows." Paper read at the Third Berkshire Conference on the History of Women. June, 1976.

MAYER-HOMBERG, E. *Die fränkischen Volksrechte im Mittelalter.* Vol. 1. Weimar, 1912.

MAYO, HOPE. "Three Merovingian Rules for Nuns." Ph.D. dissertation, Harvard University, 1974.

MCLAUGHLIN, MARY MARTIN. "Survivors and Surrogates." *The History of Childhood,* ed. Lloyd De Mause. New York, 1974, pp. 101–181.

MCLAUGHLIN, T. P. *Le très ancien droit monastique de l'Occident* (Archives de la France monastique, 38). Ligugé, Paris, 1935.

MCNAMARA, JOANN, and WEMPLE, SUZANNE. "Marriage and Divorce in the Frankish Kingdom." *Women in Medieval Society*, ed. Susan Mosher Stuard. Philadelphia, 1976, pp. 95–124.

———. "The Power of Women through the Family in Medieval Europe: 500–1100." *Feminist Studies*, 2 (1973), 126–141; reprinted in *Clio's Consciousness Raised: New Perspectives on the History of Women*, ed. Mary Hartman and Lois Banner. New York, 1974, pp. 103–118.

———. "Sanctity and Power: The Dual Pursuit of Medieval Women." *Becoming Visible: Women in European History*, ed. Renate Bridenthal and Claudia Koonz. Boston, 1977, pp. 90–118.

MEER, VAN DER, HAYE. *Women Priests in the Catholic Church? A Theological-Historical Investigation*. Trans. Arlene and Leonard Swidler. Philadelphia, 1973.

MELLOT, J. "Les fondations colombaniennes dans le diocèse de Bourges." *Mélanges Colombaniens: Actes du Congrès International de Luxeuil, 20–23 juillet 1950*. Paris, 1951, pp. 208–211.

MERLETTE, BERNARD. "Écoles et bibliothèques à Laon du declin de l'antiquité au developpement de l'Université." *Actes du 95ᵉ Congrès national des Sociétés Savantes (Reims, 1970): Section de philologie et d'histoire jusqu'au 1610*. Vol. 2. Paris, 1975.

MERSCHBERGER, GERDA. *Die Rechtsstellung der germanischen Frau* (Mannus-Bücherei, 57). Leipzig, 1937.

MERZBACHER, F. *Die Hexenprozesse in Franken*. 2d ed. Munich, 1970.

METZ, RENÉ. "La consécration des vièrges dans l'Église franque d'après la plus ancienne vie de Sainte Pusinnne (VIII–IXᵉ siecle)." *Revue des sciences religieuses*, 35 (1961), 32–48.

———. *La consecration des vièrges dans l'Église romaine*. Paris, 1954.

———. "La consecration des vièrges en Gaul des origines à l'apparition des livres liturgiques." *Revue de droit canonique*, 6 (1956), 321–339.

———. "La femme en droit canonique médiéval." *Société Jean Bodin, Recueils*, 12 (1962), 59–113.

———. "La protection de la liberté des mineurs dans le droit matrimoniale de l'Église." *Acta congressus internationalis juris canonici, Romae Pontif. Univ. Gregor., 25–30 Sept. 1950*. Rome, 1953, pp. 170–183.

———. "Les vièrges chrétiennes en Gaul au IVᵉ siècle." *Saint Martin et son temps* (Studia Anselmiana, 46). Rome, 1961, pp. 109–132.

MEYER, BRUNO. "Das Testament der Burgundofara." *MIÖG*, 14 *Ergänzungsband* (1939), 1–12.

MEYER, HERBERT. "Friedelehe und Mutterrecht." *ZSSR. germ. Abt.*, 47 (1927), 198–286.

MITTERAUER, M. *Karolingische Markgrafen im Südosten* (Archiv f. österr. Geschichte, 123). Vienna, 1963.

MOHR, W. "Boso von Vienne und die Nachfolgefrage nach dem Tode Karls d. K. und Ludwigs d. St." *Bulletin Du Cange; Arch. lat. med. aevi*, 26 (1956), 141–165.

MOLINSKI, WALDEMAR. "Virginity." *Sacramentum Mundi*. Ed. Karl Rahner, S.J. Vol. 6. London and New York, 1970, pp. 333–336.

MONSABERT, DOM PIERRE. "Le Testament de Sainte Radegonde." *Bulletin philologique et historique* (1926–27), 129–134.

MOREAU, E. de. *Histoire de l'Église en Belgique.* (Museum Lessianum; Section historique, 1–27). 2 vols. 2d ed. rev. Brussels, 1945.

―――. *Saint-Amand, apôtre de la Belgique et du Nord de la France.* (Museum Lessianum; Section missiologique, 7). Louvain, 1927.

MORHAIN, E. "Origine et histoire de la règle canonique de S. Chrodegang." *Miscellanea Pio Paschini.* Vol. 1 (Lateranum, n.s. 14). Rome, 1948, pp. 173–185.

MORIN, DOM G. "Le destinataire de l'apocryphe hieronymien 'De septem ordinibus Ecclesiae.'" *Revue d'histoire ecclésiastique,* 34 (1938), 238–244.

―――. "Un traité priscillianiste inédit sur la Trinité." *Revue Bénédictine,* 26 (1909), 255–257.

MUSSET, LUCIEN. *The Germanic Invasions.* Trans. E. and C. James. University Park, Pa. 1975.

NARBERHAUS, J. *Benedikt von Aniane, Werk und Persönlichkeit.* Münster in W., 1930.

NELSON, JANET L. "Queens as Jezebels: The Careers of Brunhild and Balthild in Merovingian History." *Medieval Women.* Ed. Derek Baker, in honor of Rosalind M. T. Hill (Studies in Church History, Subsidia 1). Oxford, 1978, pp. 31–77.

NEUNDÖRFER, DANIEL. *Studien zur ältesten Geschichte des Klosters Lorsch* (Arbeiten zur deutschen Rechts- und Verfassungsgeschichte, 3). Berlin, 1920.

NICHOLSON, JOAN. "Feminae gloriosae: Women in the Age of Bede." *Medieval Women.* Ed. Derek Baker, in honor of Rosalind M. T. Hill (Studies in Church History, Subsidia 1). Oxford, 1978, pp. 15–29.

NONN, ULRICH. "Eine fränkische Adelssippe um 600. Zur Familie des Bischofs Berthram von Le Mans." *Frühmittelalterliche Studien,* 9 (1975), 186–201.

NOONAN, JOHN T., JR. "Celibacy and the Fathers of the Church." *Celibacy, the Necessary Option.* Ed. George H. Frein. New York, 1968, pp. 138–151.

―――. *Contraception: A History of Its Treatment by the Catholic Theologians and Canonists.* Cambridge, Mass., 1967.

―――. "Marriage in the Middle Ages 1: Power to Choose." *Viator,* 4 (1973), 419–434.

NUGENT, SISTER M. ROSAMOND. *Portrait of the Consecrated Woman in Greek Christian Literature of the First Four Centuries.* (Catholic University of America. Patristic Studies, 64). Washington, D.C., 1941.

O'CARROL, J. "Sainte Fare et les origines." *Sainte Fare et Faremoutiers.* L'Abbaye de Faremoutiers, 1956, pp. 4–35.

OELSNER, L. *Jahrbücher des fränkischen Reiches unter König Peppin.* Leipzig, 1871.

OPET, O. "Geschlechtsvormundschaft in den fränkischen Volksrechten." *MIÖG,* 3, *Ergänzungsband,* (1890–94), pp. 1–37.

OTIS, LEAH L. "Nisi in Prostibulo: Prostitution in Languedoc from the Twelfth to the Sixteenth Century." Ph.D. dissertation, Columbia University, 1980.

PAGELS, ELAINE. "When Did Man Make God in His Image? A Case Study in Religion and Politics." *The Scholar and the Feminist,* 3 (1976), 31–44.

PARISOT, R. *Le Royaume de Lorraine sous les Carolingiens, 843–923.* Paris, 1889.

PETZOLT, H. "Abtei Kitzingen." *Jahrbuch für fränkische Landesforschung,* 15 (1955), 69–83.

PICASSO, GIORGIO O.S.B. "I fondamenti del matrimonio nelle collezioni canoniche." *Il matrimonio nella società altomedievale* (Settimane di Studio del Centro Italiano di Studi sull'Alto Medioevo, 24). Spoleto, 1977, pp.191–231.

POMEROY, SARAH B. *Goddesses, Whores, Wives and Slaves: Women in Classical Antiquity.* New York, 1975.

——. "Married Women in Rome." *Ancient Society,* 7 (1976), 215–227.

PORTMANN, MARIE LOUISE. *Die Darstellung der Frau in der Geschichtschreibung des früheren Mittelalters* (Basler Beiträge zur Geschichtswissenschaft, 69). Basel, 1958.

POST, J. B. "Ages at Menarche and Menopause, Some Medieval Authorities." *Population Studies,* 25 (1971), 83–87.

POUPARDIN, RENÉ. *Le Royaume de Bourgogne (888–1038)* (Bibliothèque de l'École des Hautes Études; Sciences historiques et philologiques, 163). Paris, 1907.

PREISKER, HERBERT W. C. *Christentum und Ehe in den ersten drei Jahrhunderten* (Neue Studien zur Geschichte der Theologie, ed. R. Seeberg, 23). Berlin, 1927.

PRINZ, FRIEDRICH. "Die bischöfliche Stadtherrschaft." *Historische Zeitschrift,* 217 (1973), 1–35.

——. *Frühes Mönchtum im Frankenreich.* Munich, Vienna, 1965.

PRINZ, JOSEPH. "Ein unbekanntes Aktenstück zum Ehestreit König Lothars II." *Deutsches Archiv,* 21 (1965), 249–263.

PROU, M. *Étude sur les chartes de fondation de l'Abbaye de Saint-Pierre-le-Vif.* Paris, 1894.

RAVAISSON, FELIX. *Catalogue général des manuscripts des bibliothèques publiques des départements de France.* Vol. 1. Paris, 1849.

REINLE, ADOLF. *Die heilige Verena von Zürzach: Legende, Kult, Denkmäler* (Ars docta, 6). Basel, 1948.

REUTER, TIMOTHY, ed. *The Medieval Nobility: Studies on the Ruling Classes of France and Germany from the Sixth to the Twelfth Century* (Europe in the Middle Ages, Selected Studies, 14). Amsterdam, New York, Oxford, 1979.

RICHARDOT, HUBERT. *Les pactes de séparation amiable entre époux.* Paris, 1930.

RICHÉ, PIERRE. *Daily Life in the World of Charlemagne.* Trans. JoAnn McNamara. Philadelphia, 1978.

——. *Education et culture dans l'occident barbare.* 3d ed. Paris, 1973.

——. "La femme dans la société germanique païenne." *Histoire mondiale de la femme.* Paris, 1965, pp. 27-34.

——. "La femme à l'époque barbare." Ibid. pp. 35-46.

——. "La femme à l'époque carolingienne." Ibid., pp. 47-54.

——. "Note d'hagiographie mérovingienne: La Vita s. Rusticulae." *Analecta Bollandiana,* 72 (1954), 369–377.

RITZER, K. *Formen, Riten und religiöses Brauchtum der Eheschliessung in den christlichen Kirchen des ersten Jahrtausends* (Liturgiewissenschaftliche Quellen und Forschungen, 38). Münster i. W. 1962.

ROCHE, D., and LABROUSSE, C. E., eds. *Ordres et classes: Colloque d'histoire sociale, Saint-Cloud, 24–25 mai, 1967* (Congrès et colloques, 12). Paris, 1976.

ROELS, W. *Onderzoek naar het gebruik van de angehaalde bronnen van Romeins recht in de Lex Romana Burgundionum.* Anvers, 1958.

RONDET, H. "Éléments pour une théologie de la femme." *Nouvelle revue théologique,* 79 (1957), 915–940.

ROSAMBERT, ANDRÉ. *La veuve en droit canonique jusqu'au XIVe siècle.* Paris, 1923.

ROSSETTI, GABRIELLA. "Il matrimonio del clero nella società altomedievale." *Il matrimonio nella società altomedievale* (Settimane di Studio del Centro Italiano di Studi sull'Alto Medioevo, 24). Spoleto, 1977, pp. 473–567.

ROTONDI, GIOVANNI. *Leges publicae populi Romani* (Scritti giuridici, 1). Milan, 1912; reprinted in Hildesheim, 1962.

RULLKOETTER, W. *The Legal Protection of Woman among the Ancient Germans.* Chicago, 1900.

SALIN, EDOUARD. *La civilisation mérovingienne; d'après les sépultures, les textes et le laboratoire.* 4 vols. Paris, 1949–59.

——. *Manuel des fouilles archéologiques.* Vol. 1. Paris, 1946.

SCHÄFER, K. HEINRICH. *Die Kanonissenstifter im deutschen Mittelalter. Ihre Entwicklung und innere Einrichtung im Zusammenhang mit dem altchristlichen Sanktimonialentum* (Kirchenrechtliche Abhandlungen, ed. Ulrich Stutz, 43–44). Stuttgart, 1907.

——. "Kanonissen und Diakonissen, Ergänzungen und Erläuterungen." *Römische Quartalschrift,* 24 (1910), 49–90.

SCHANZ, M., et al. eds. *Geschichte der römischen Litteratur.* Vol. 3. 3d ed. Munich, 1922. Vol. 4, pt. 1. 2d ed. Munich, 1914. Vol. 4, pt. 2. Munich, 1920.

SCHERER, RUDOLF VON. *Über das Eherecht bei Benedict Levita und Pseudo-Isidore.* Graz, 1879.

SCHIEFFER, THEODOR. *Angelsachsen und Franken* (Akademie der Wissenschaften und der Literatur, Mainz; Abhandlungen der geistes- und sozialwissenschaftlichen Klasse, 20). Wiesbaden, 1951.

——. *Winfrid-Bonifatius und die christliche Grundlegung Europas.* Freiburg i.B., 1954.

SCHMID, KARL. "Ein karolingische Königseintrag im Gedenkbuch von Remiremont." *Frühmittelalterliche Studien,* 2 (1968), 96–134.

——. "Heirat, Familienfolge, Geschlechterbewusstsein." *Il matrimonio nella società altomedievale* (Settimane di Studio del Centro Italiano sull'Alto Medioevo, 24). Spoleto, 1977, pp. 103–137.

——. "Programmatisches zur Erforschung der mittelalterlichen Personen und Personengruppen." *Frühmittelalterliche Studien,* 8 (1974), 116–130.

——. "Zur Problematik von Familie, Sippe und Geschlecht . . ." *Zeitschrift für Geschichte des Oberrheins,* 105 (1957), 1–62.

SCHMITZ, DOM PHILIBERT. *Histoire de l'Ordre de Saint Benoît.* Vol. 1. 2d ed. Maredsous, 1948. Vol. 7. Maredsous, 1956.

SCHMITZ, H. J. *Die Bussbücher und die Bussdisziplin der Kirche.* 2 vols. Mainz, 1883. Reprinted Graz, 1958.

SCHNEIDER, JOHANNES. "Die Darstellung der Pauperes in den Historiae Gregors von Tours: Ein Beitrag zur sozialökonomischen Struktur Galliens im 6. Jahrhundert." *Jahrbuch für Wirtschaftsgeschichte* (1966, pt. 4), pp. 57–74.

SCHNEIDER, REINHARD. *Königswahl und Königserhebung im Frühmittelalter* (Monographien zur Geschichte des Mittelalters, 3). Stuttgart, 1972.

SCHRAMM, P. E. "Die Krönung bei den Westfranken und Angelsachsen von 878 bis um 1000." *ZSSR kan. Abt.*, 23 (1934), 117–242.

SCHROEDER, R. *Geschichte des ehelichen Güterrechts in Deutschland. Erster Teil: Die Zeit der Volksrechte.* Vol. 1. Stettin, Danzig, Elbing, 1863.

SCHULENBURG, JANE TIBBETTS. "Sexism and Celestial Gynaeceum, 500–1200." *Journal of Medieval History*, 3 (1978), 117–133.

SDRALEK, MAX. *Hinkmar von Rheims kanonistische Gutachten über die Ehescheidung des Königs Lothar II.* Freiburg, i.B., 1881.

SECKEL, E., and JUNCKER, J. "Studien zu Benedictus Levita." *ZSSR kan. Abt.*, 24 (1935), 40–61.

SEMMLER, J. *Benedikt von Aniane.* Mannheim, 1971.

———. "Reichsidee und kirchliche Gesetzgebung bei Ludwig dem Frommen." *Zeitschrift für Kirchengeschichte*, 71 (1960), 37–65.

———. "Zur Überlieferung der monastischen Gesetzgebung Ludwigs des Frommen." *Deutsches Archiv*, 16 (1960), 309–388.

SENN, NOEL. *Le contrat de vente de la femme en droit matrimonial germanique.* Portrentruy, 1946.

SIEPEN, KARL. *Vermögensrecht der klösterlichen Verbände.* Paderborn, 1963.

SIMSON, B. *Jahrbücher des fränkischen Reichs unter Ludwig dem Frommen.* 2 vols. (Jahrbücher der deutschen Geschichte, 6). Leipzig, 1874–76.

SMITH, C. E. *Papal Enforcement of Some Medieval Marriage Laws.* Ph. D. dissertation, Louisiana State University, 1940. Reissued at Port Washington, London, 1972.

SPRANDEL, ROLF. *Der merowingische Adel und die Gebiete östlich des Rheines* (Forschungen zur oberrheinischen Landesgeschichte, 5). Freiburg i. B., 1957.

SPRÖMBERG, H. "Judith, Königin von England, Gräfin von Flandern." *Revue belge d'histoire et de philologie*, 15 (1936), 397–428, 915–950.

STOECKLE, MARIA. *Studien über Ideale in Frauenviten des VII–X. Jahrhunderts.* Munich, 1957.

STÖRMER, W. "Eine Adelsgruppe um die Fuldaer Abte Sturmi und Eigil und die Holzkirchener Klostergründungen Troand." *Gesellschaft und Herrschaft . . . Festgabe für Karl Bosl zum 60. Geburtstag.* Ed. Richard von Dülmen. Munich, 1969, pp. 1–34.

———. *Früher Adel: Studien zur politischen Führungsschichte im fränkisch-deutschen Reich vom 8. bis 11. Jahrhundert.* Vols. 1–2 (Monographien zur Geschichte des Mittelalters, 61–62). Stuttgart, 1973.

STOUFF, L. "Étude sur le principe de la personnalité des lois depuis les invasions barbares jusqu'au XIIe siècle." *Revue bourguignonne de l'enseignement supérieur*, 4, 2 (1894), 1–65 and 273–310.

STROHEKER, KARL FRIEDRICH. *Der senatorische Adel im spätantiken Gallien.* Tübingen, 1948; reprinted Darmstadt, 1970.

TAVARD, GEORGE H. *Woman in Christian Tradition.* Notre Dame, Ind., 1973.

TELLENBACH, GERD. "Der grossfränkische Adel und die Regierung Italiens in der Blütezeit des Karolingerreiches." *Studien und Vorarbeiten zur Geschichte des grossfränkischen und frühdeutschen Adels,* ed. G. Tellenbach (Forschungen zur oberrheinischen Landesgeschichte, 4). Freiburg i.B., 1957, pp. 40–70.

———. *Königtum und Stämme in der Werdezeit des deutschen Reiches* (Quellen und Studien zur Verfassungsgeschichte des deutschen Reiches, 7, 4). Weimar, 1939.

———, ed. *Studien und Vorarbeiten zur Geschichte des grossfränkischen und frühdeutschen Adels* (Forschungen zur oberrheinischen Landesgeschichte, 4). Freiburg i.B., 1957.

———. *Zur Bedeutung der Personenforschung für die Erkenntniss des früheren Mittelalters* (Freiburger Universitätsreden, n.f. 25). Freiburg i.B., 1975.

TESSIER, GEORGES. *Charlemagne.* Paris, 1967.

———. "La conversion de Clovis." *La conversione al christianesimo nell'Europa dell'alto Medioevo* (Centro Italiano di Studi sull'Alto Medioevo, Settimane di Studio, 14) Spoleto, 1967, pp. 149–168.

———. *Recueil des Actes de Charles II, le Chauve, roi de France* (Chartes et diplomes relatifs à l'histoire de France, 8, no. 2, 9–10). 3 vols. in 2. Paris, 1943–55.

TEVENAR, G. VON. "Bretonische Bibliographie." *Zeitschrift für keltische Philologie und Volksforschung,* 22 (1941), 77–92.

THOMPSON, E. A. *The Early Germans.* Oxford, 1965.

———. *The Goths in Spain.* Oxford, 1969.

TODD, MALCOLM. *Everyday Life of the Barbarians.* London, New York, 1972.

TOUBERT, PIERRE. "La théorie du mariage chez les moralistes carolingiens." *Il matrimonio nella società altomedievale* (Settimane di Studio del Centro Italiano di Studi sull'Alto Medioevo, 24). Spoleto, 1977, pp.233–285.

TURNER, C. "A Laon MS in 1906 and 1920." *Journal of Theological Studies,* 22 (1921), 1–5.

TURRIN, H. J. "*Aureo flore* and the Question of Dating the Tradition of Marian Veneration in the Medieval West." *Mittellateinisches Jahrbuch,* 14 (1979), 76–88.

UDDHOLM, ALF. *Formulae Marculfi: Études sur la langue et le style.* (Uppsala Universitets Årsskrift, 1954.2). Uppsala, 1954.

UEDING, L. *Geschichte der Klostergründungen des frühen Merowingerzeit* (Historische Studien, 261). Berlin, 1935. Rpt. 1965.

VACANDARD, E. "Célibat ecclésiastique." *Dictionnaire de théologie catholique.* Vol. 2, pt. 2. Paris, 1905, 2068–2080.

———. "Les origines du célibat ecclésiastique." In his *Études de critique et d'histoire religieuse.* Vol. 1. Paris, 1905, 69–120.

———. *Vie de Saint Ouen, évêque de Rouen (641–84).* Paris, 1902.

VANDENBOSSCHE, A. *La dos ex marito dans la Gaule franque.* Paris, 1953.

VERDON, JEAN. "Notes sur le rôle économique des monastères féminins en France dans la second moitié du IXe et au début du Xe siècle." *Revue Mabillon,* 58 (1975), 329–343.

———. "Recherches sur les monastères féminins dans la France du Sud aux IXe–XIe siècles." *Annales du Midi,* 88 (1976), 117–138.

VERLINDEN, CHARLES. "Le 'mariage' des esclaves." *Il matrimonio nella società altomedievale* (Settimane di Studio del Centro Italiano di Studi sull'Alto Medioevo, 24). Spoleto, 1974, pp. 569–601.

VIELLARD-TROIEKOYROFF, M. "Les monuments religieux de Poitiers." *Études mérovingiennes. Actes des Journées de Poitiers, 1952*. Paris, 1953, pp. 285–292.

VILLIERS, ROBERT. "Le statut de la femme à Rome jusqu'à la fin de la Republique." *Société Jean Bodin, Recueils*, 11 (1959), 177–190.

VOGEL, CYRILLE. *Le pécheur et la pénitence dans l'Église ancienne.* (Chrétiens de tous les temps, 15). Paris, 1966.

——. *Le pécheur et la pénitence au Moyen Age.* Paris, 1969.

——. "Les rites de la célébration du mariage: leur signification dans la formation du lien durant le haut Moyen Age." *Il matrimonio nella società altomedievale* (Settimane di Studio del Centro Italiano di Studi sull'Alto Medioevo, 24). Spoleto, 1977, pp. 399–472.

——. "Le rôle du liturge dans la formation du lien conjugal." *Revue de droit canonique*, 30 (1980), 7–27.

VOGELSANG, THILO. *Die Frau als Herrscherin im hohen Mittelalter.* Frankfurt, Berlin, 1954.

VOIGT, KARL. *Die karolingische Klosterpolitik und der Niedergang des westfränkischen Königtums, Laienäbte und Klosterinhaber* (Kirchenrechtliche Abhandlungen, 90–91). Stuttgart, 1917.

VOLLMER, F. "Die Etichonen." *Studien und Vorarbeiten zur Geschichte des grossfränkischen- und frühdeutschen Adels*, ed. G. Tellenbach (Forschungen zur oberrheinischen Landesgeschichte, 4). Freiburg i. B., 1957, pp. 137–184.

VOLTERRA, EDOARDO. "La conception du mariage à Rome." *Revue internationale des droits de l'antiquité*, 3d ser., 2 (1955), 365–379.

WALDRON, HENRY NEFF. "Expressions of Religious Conversion among Laymen Remaining within Secular Society in Gaul; 400–800 A.D." Ph.D. dissertation, Ohio State University, 1976.

WAMPACH, C. *Sankt Willibrord: sein Leben und Lebenswerk.* Luxembourg, 1953.

WEBER, K. "Kulturgeschichtliche Probleme der Merowingerzeit im Spiegel frühmittelalterlicher Heiligenleben." *Studien und Mitteilungen des Benediktinerordens und seiner Zweige*, 48 (1930), 366–375.

WEHLT, HANS-PETER. *Reichsabtei und König dargestellt am Beispiel der Abtei Lorsch* (Veröffentlichungen des Max-Planck-Instituts für Geschichte, 28). Göttingen, 1970.

WEISWEILER, J. "Die Stellung der Frau bei den Kelten und das Problem des 'keltischen Mutterrechts.'" *Zeitschrift für celtische Philologie*, 21 (1940), 205–279.

WENSKUS, R. *Sächsischer Stammesadel und fränkischer Reichsadel* (Abhandlungen der Akademie der Wissenschaften in Göttingen, philol. - histor. Klasse, 3d. Ser., 93). Göttingen, 1976.

WERMINGHOFF, A. "Die Beschlüsse des Aachener Concils im Jahre 816." *Neues Archiv*, 27 (1901), 605–675.

WERNER, K. F. "Bedeutende Adelsfamilien im Reich Karls des Grossen." *Karl der*

Grosse: Lebenswerk und Nachleben. Vol. 1. Ed. Helmut Beumann. Düsseldorf, 1967, 83–142.

———. "Die Geburtsdatum Karls des Grossen." *Francia,* 1 (1973), 116–157.

———. "Die Nachkommen Karls des Grossen." *Karl der Grosse: Lebenswerk und Nachleben.* Vol. 4. Ed. W. Braunfels. Düsseldorf, 1967, 403–483.

———. "Untersuchungen zur Frühzeit des französischen Fürstentums." *Die Welt als Geschichte,* 18 (1958), 256–289; ibid., 19 (1959), 146–193.

WHITELOCK, DOROTHY. *The Beginnings of English Society.* Hammondsworth, Middlesex, 1959.

———. *English Historical Documents, 500–1042.* London, 1955.

WILMART, A. "Le copiste de sacramentaire de Gellone au service du chapitre de Cambrai." *Revue Bénédictine,* 42 (1930), 218–222.

WINTERER, HERMANN. "Die Stellung des unehelichen Kindes in der langobardischen Gesetzgebung." *ZSSR germ. Abt.,* 87 (1970), 32–56.

WOLLASCH, J. "Das Patrimonium beati Germani in Auxerre." *Studien und Vorarbeiten zur Geschichte des grossfränkischen und frühdeutschen Adels,* ed. G. Tellenbach (Forschungen zur oberrheinischen Landesgeschichte, 4). Freiburg i.B., 1957, pp. 185–224.

YARBROUGH, ANNE. "Christianization in the Fourth Century: The Example of Roman Women." *Church History,* 45 (1976), 149–165.

ZAHN, THEODOR. *Ignatius von Antiochien.* Gotha, 1873.

ZATSCHEK, HEINZ. "Die Benutzung der *Formulae.*" *MÖIG,* 42 (1927), 165–267.

ZOEPF, L. *Lioba, Hathumot, Wiborada: Drei Heilige des deutschen Mittelalters.* Munich, 1915.

INDEX OF PERSONS

INDEX OF SUBJECTS